This book provides the only detailed, systematic philosophical reconsideration of the neglected nineteenth-century positivist Auguste Comte currently available. Apart from offering an accurate account of what Comte actually wrote, it argues for the provocative thesis that Comte's positivism actually has greater contemporary relevance now that no one wants to be a positivist.

Robert Scharff's aim in the first part of the book is to rescue Comte from the common view, urged by later positivists, that his brand of positivism is immature, confused, and deserving of our neglect. Singling out the still widely influential misinterpretations of John Stuart Mill, the author shows that Comte's famous opposition to psychology, to formalizing scientific methods, and to causal theories in science in fact expresses a "historico-critical" outlook that is utterly foreign to Mill and the later positivists. The second part of the book argues that Comte's historically minded concern for the relation between philosophy and its past makes him a natural ally of such well-known post-positivists as Richard Rorty, Charles Taylor, and Hilary Putnam. Like them, but in some ways more successfully, Comte conceives philosophical activity neither as totally separable from tradition (as positivism does) nor as merely a product of tradition (as historicism does). Professor Scharff concludes that even though Comte was the first positivist, he is the one positivist who remains relevant now, "after" positivism as a movement has had its day.

Providing lucid exposition and informed by considerable new scholarship on Comte's work, this book will be valuable to philosophers, especially philosophers of science and those interested in post-positivist developments in Anglo-American philosophy, to a wide range of intellectual historians, and to historians of science and psychology.

COMTE AFTER POSITIVISM

MODERN EUROPEAN PHILOSOPHY

This series comprises a range of high-quality books on philosophers, topics, and schools of thought prominent in the Kantian and post-Kantian European tradition. The series is nonsectarian in approach and methodology and includes both introductory and more specialized treatments of these thinkers and topics. Authors are encouraged to interpret the boundaries of the modern European tradition in a broad way and to engage with it in primarily philosophical rather than historical terms.

Executive editor
ROBERT PIPPIN, UNIVERSITY OF CHICAGO

Editorial board
GARY GUTTING, UNIVERSITY OF NOTRE DAME
ROLF-PETER HORSTMANN, UNIVERSITY OF MUNICH
MARK SACKS, UNIVERSITY OF ESSEX

David Bakhurst, *Consciousness and revolution in Soviet philosophy*
Wolfgang Carl, *Frege's theory of sense and reference*
R. M. Chisholm, *Bretano and intrinsic value*
Maudmarie Clark, *Nietzsche on truth and philosophy*
Raymond Geuss, *The idea of a critical theory: Habermas and the Frankfurt School*
Gary Gutting, *Michel Foucault's archaeology of scientific reason*
Michael O. Hardimon, *Hegel's social philosophy*
David Holdcroft, *Saussure: Signs, system, and arbitrariness*
Karel Lambert, *Meinong and the principle of independence*
Frederick Neuhouser, *Fichte's theory of subjectivity*
Charles Taylor, *Hegel and modern society*
Mary Tiles, *Bachelard: Science and objectivity*
Robert S. Tragesser, *Husserl and realism in logic and mathematics*
Stephen K. White, *Political theory and postmodernism*
Peter Winch, *Simone Weil: The just balance*
Frederick A. Olafson, *What is a human being?*
Stanley Rosen, *The mask of Enlightenment: Nietzche's* Zarathustra

COMTE AFTER POSITIVISM

ROBERT C. SCHARFF
University of New Hampshire

CAMBRIDGE UNIVERSITY PRESS
Cambridge, New York, Melbourne, Madrid, Cape Town,
Singapore, São Paulo, Delhi, Tokyo, Mexico City

Cambridge University Press
The Edinburgh Building, Cambridge CB2 8RU, UK

Published in the United States of America by Cambridge University Press, New York

www.cambridge.org
Information on this title: www.cambridge.org/9780521474887

© Cambridge University Press 1995

This publication is in copyright. Subject to statutory exception
and to the provisions of relevant collective licensing agreements,
no reproduction of any part may take place without the written
permission of Cambridge University Press.

First published 1995
First paperback edition 2002

A catalogue record for this publication is available from the British Library

Library of Congress Cataloguing in Publication Data

Scharff, Robert C.
Comte after positivism / Robert C. Scharff
p.   cm. – (Modern European philosophy)
Includes bibliographical references and index .
ISBN 0 521 47488 4
1. Comte, Auguste, 1798–1857. 2. Positivism. I. Title
II. Series.
B2249.P6S33   1995
194–dc20   94-44551   CIP

ISBN 978-0-521-47488-7 Hardback
ISBN 978-0-521-89303-9 Paperback

Cambridge University Press has no responsibility for the persistence or
accuracy of URLs for external or third-party internet websites referred to in
this publication, and does not guarantee that any content on such websites is,
or will remain, accurate or appropriate. Information regarding prices, travel
timetables, and other factual information given in this work is correct at
the time of first printing but Cambridge University Press does not guarantee
the accuracy of such information thereafter.

CONTENTS

Preface	*page* ix
Acknowledgments	xii
Note on Citations	xiv

Introduction: Comte for a Post-Positivist World		1
1. Today's anti-positivism		2
2. Comte's historico-critical defense of positivism		6
3. Comte (and Mill et al.) on interior observation		11
4. Recovering Comte after Logical Empiricism		13

Part I: Comte Then

1 Mill versus Comte on Interior Observation		19
1. Who are Comte's interior observers?		20
2. Interior observation: Comte's anti-metaphysical critique		24
3. Introspection: Mill's methodological defense		35
4. Mill's mistaken reading of Comte		43
2 Mill versus Comte as Positivist Philosophers of Science		45
1. Philosophy "of" science?		45
2. Mill as philosopher of science		48
3. Comte's "failure" as philosopher of science		52
Science's past		53
Science's future		55
Science's present needs		57

4. The question of an organon of proof	58
5. The question of causal laws	63
6. Philosophy "of" or "about" science?	67

3 Comte's Three-Stage Law — 73
  1. A law about what? — 74
  2. The theological (supernatural) stage — 77
    Fetishism (animism) — 77
    Polytheism — 78
    Monotheism — 79
  3. The metaphysical (abstract) stage — 81
  4. The positive (scientific) stage — 87

Part II: Comte Now

4 Comte's Ambiguous Legacy: Science Defended or Already Justified? — 95
  1. Science defended versus science already justified — 96
  2. Historical versus dogmatical accounts of science — 98
  3. Comte's historico-critical "pragmatism" — 105
  4. The other side of Comte's positivism — 109
  5. Descartes' reflectiveness — 111
  6. Comte's ahistorical reflexivity — 118
  7. Imperious claims and Comte's legacy — 123

5 Cartesian Ahistoricism and Later Epistemic Analysis — 128
  1. Socrates' epistemological silence — 129
  2. Descartes' epistemic imperative and history's irrelevance — 130
    Cartesian epistemology's topic — 132
    Cartesian epistemology's outlook — 134
  3. Logical Empiricism: The turn completed — 135
  4. Epistemic analysis "after" positivism — 137

6 Comte and the Very Idea of Post-Positivist Philosophy — 143
  1. The Positivist Thesis: Hostility to philosophy's past — 144
  2. Revisionist reaction to the Positivist Thesis — 146
  3. Rorty's apparent radicalism — 149
  4. Post-positivist ahistoricism — 156
  5. Comte and philosophy in history — 160
    PIH: Why raise the issue? — 160
      Root questioning — 161
      The case of Taylor — 163
    From what standpoint? — 167
    With what (preliminary) result? — 173

7 Comte for Tomorrow? — 176
  1. Opposing positivism and historicism — 176
  2. Avoiding positivism and historicism (Putnam) — 179
  3. Transforming positivism and historicism — 188
  4. Becoming the "situated" post-positivists . . . — 194
  5. . . . we ("inarticulately") already are — 199

Bibliography — 209
Index — 223

PREFACE

The present work began innocently enough with a small essay correcting Mill's famous and influential misinterpretation of Comte's opposition to "psychology." As I explain in Chapter 1, what Comte rejects and what Mill defends are two different subjects. Comte's arguments are directed against late incarnations of traditional rational psychology, and his prime target is Cousin's pseudoscientific idea of an "interior observation" that supposedly provides metaphysical knowledge of the soul. Mill criticizes Comte for opposing empirical (sc., associationist) psychology and the "introspection" on which it depends. In fact, Comte never considers either of these topics.

Yet Mill's misinterpretation, once identified, seems so obvious that I began to wonder how he could have made it. Indeed, in researching the psychology controversy, I found several other issues on which Mill misinterprets Comte in equally obvious ways (e.g., by criticizing Comte for never getting around to an "organon of proof," when Comte in fact opposes the very idea of one). Eventually I saw the larger problem. Mill takes it for granted that, being both "positivists," he and Comte must be in basic agreement over what this entails. In this, however, Mill – and all of us who have read him rather than Comte – are deeply mistaken. As I explain in Chapter 2, Mill's outlook already resembles our century's Logical Positivism in being both rationally reconstructive and ahistorically oriented. Mill assumes, in other words, that his primary job is to establish science's formal criteria of justification and that, as a scientific philosopher, he need have no further traffic with the prescientific tradition. For such a positivist, a strong antiformalism about scientific method and an extensive campaign against rational psychology *in another positivist* make little sense; hence, when faced with these elements in Comte, Mill tends to assume that Comte must actually be (wrongly but at least intelligibly) arguing against empirical psychology and that he is just neglecting rather than opposing an organon of proof.

In recognizing that, contrary to Mill, Comte sees himself acting *as a positivist* in arguing against both Cousin and epistemic organons, I saw my whole discussion turn into a book. Mill's disagreements with Comte over psychology and scientific epistemology (and several other issues identified in Chapter 2) are only symptoms of a fundamental difference in their positivisms; and I saw that a thorough examination of this difference not only promised to correct Mill's record but lent support to the burgeoning larger interest in a multidisciplinary rethinking of the history of positivism.[1] Beyond issues of cultural and historical scholarship, however, I came to realize that precisely insofar as Comte's positivism differs from Mill's, it also retains a contemporary philosophical relevance that Mill's positivism lacks.

From Comte's perspective, Mill's concept of an epistemic organon, together with his belief that the prescientific tradition is irrelevant to contemporary philosophy of science, betray an essential philosophical weakness. Both ideas are signs of a basically ahistorical attitude – a false confidence that the age of science is here and that philosophy now simply moves to give expression to its structure. The problem with this attitude, Comte argues, is not a minor one. In fact, it threatens to render science itself unintelligible and to foster in us a tendency to carry forward unawares a whole host of theologico-metaphysical assumptions that will actually impede scientific progress. "No idea," says Comte, "can be properly understood apart from its history"; and as I explain in Chapters 3 and 4, this is to him not just a slogan for historians or a useful social-scientific weapon for deflating the positions of one's opponents. Above all, Comte construes it self-referentially. One must recognize not just in general that every orientation in thinking is inescapably shaped by its inheritance, but also that this is true of *one's own orientation specifically*. As a result, in positivism as Comte understands it, a kind of "historico-critical" reflection upon and self-description of this orientation must form an essential and continuous part of one's philosophical practice.

Contemporary philosophers – not only but perhaps especially English-speaking ones – may find Comte's historical-mindedness surprising but not unwelcome. For today, in the long shadow cast not just by Mill but also by more recent positivisms, Comte would find himself in good company. Once again, it seems important to reject formal, scientifically inspired (now also dubbed "internalist") epistemic systems and to criticize ahistorical (and obsessively anti-historicist) attitudes in philosophy. Both are common concerns of a very wide array of thinkers

---

1 To name just four samples (containing extensive references) of work appearing since 1992, see the first volume of Mary Pickering's projected two-volume intellectual biography of Comte (PIC); Oscar Haac's translation of the Comte–Mill correspondence (see under LMC); Rudolf Haller, *Neopositivismus: Eine historische Einführung in die Philosophie des Wiener Kreises* (Darmstadt: Wissenschaftliche Buchgesellschaft, 1993); and David Bell and Wilhelm Vossenkuhl, eds., *Wissenschaft und Subjektivität: Der Wiener Kreis und die Philosophie des 20. Jahrhunderts / Science and Subjectivity: The Vienna Circle and 20th Century Philosophy* (Berlin: Akademie, 1992).

who, whatever else they might aspire to be, would at least want to regard themselves as "post-positivist." That this makes Comte relevant to the present philosophical situation – the situation we want to understand as coming "after positivism" – gave me the title of my book and the topic for its last three chapters.

Where Chapters 1 to 4 speak mainly to readers concerned with Comte, Mill, and the history and comparison of nineteenth- and twentieth-century positivism, Chapters 5 to 7 try to draw out the philosophical implications of those earlier chapters in order to join the current debate over what Giovanna Borradori calls "the epistemological value of *one's own* relationship to tradition."[2] I agree with Borradori that work on this issue may open "a new channel of communication" between contemporary analytic and Continental philosophy – especially, I would add, among adherents of its more overtly post-positivist and hermeneutical strains, respectively. Yet I also think it would be pointless at this time to simply proclaim, from either side of the "wall" that still generally divides the two broad movements, that something in, say, Rorty, Taylor, or Putnam (who figure prominently below) displays a kinship with lines of thinking in, say, Heidegger, Gadamer, or Foucault (which I think may often be true). For the time being, the larger truth would seem to be that such comparisons are premature.

As it happens, however, on the issue of "the epistemological value of one's own relationship to tradition," no crossing of the Continental divide is necessary. Comte is in the direct empiricist–positivist line of contemporary analytic inheritance, and he considered the issue extensively and over several decades. To be sure, the historico-critically sensitive side of Comte's positivism was ultimately overwhelmed – even in his own writings – by the more rigorously and ahistorically "scientific" line of reasoning that we know well from our inheritance of later versions. I shall argue, however, that the presence of this tension in Comte between historical sensitivity and ahistorical objectivity can only make a current effort to rediscover his forgotten side potentially more (self-referentially) illuminating.

---

2 *The American Philosopher: Conversations with Quine, Davidson, Putnam, Nozick, Danto, Rorty, Cavell, MacIntyre, and Kuhn*, trans. Rosanna Crocitto (Chicago: University of Chicago Press, 1994), 2–3, my emphasis. Crucial for me was the appearance in 1984 of the essays in PIH, now in its ninth printing.

ACKNOWLEDGMENTS

My preparation of this book, has passed through three phases of development, and in each one I have received valuable help from many persons. On the Comte–Mill relationship, I gratefully acknowledge the contributions of David Leary, Larry Smith, and Bill Woodward. Concerning the history and philosophy of science, I must thank, above all, Joe Rouse and my colleague Val Dusek for long and informative talks and countless scholarly references. I also received encouragement from Ted Kisiel, Steve Fuller, and Bob Crease at important moments.

As for my work on the larger themes of this book, I could not possibly make a full accounting of my extensive debts. Some idea of my obligations to other scholars can be gathered from a glance at the Bibliography. My colleagues in the University of New Hampshire's Philosophy Department, especially Drew Christie and Bill de Vries, and above all, Ken Westphal, have been consistently supportive and endlessly patient in letting me try out on them embarrassingly unpolished versions of matters now discussed with (hopefully) a bit more clarity here. I am grateful to Terence Moore, humanities editor at Cambridge University Press, for his encouragement and special effort in securing reviews. I thank also my three anonymous readers, who will know this is a better book (if still not quite the one that any of them envisioned) because of their careful readings and perceptive suggestions. Finally, to my friend Gene Gendlin, I offer the inadequate acknowledgment of saying that I know how much our continuing dialogue has affected these pages, even if in unexplicated form.

For institutional support, I express my gratitude to the University of New Hampshire for a Faculty Scholars grant and a sabbatical leave; and to the College of Liberal Arts and to Dean Stuart Palmer for, among other forms of support, a summer research fellowship. During my several summers as a Visiting Scholar, the staffs of the truly marvelous Harvard University Libraries, and especially Julie Blattner, Margaret Bailey, and Melodee Wagen, provided much friendly assistance and ideal working conditions. I thank also the following editors and publisher for allowing me to use material from papers appearing earlier in their journals: "Socrates' Successful Inquiries," *Man and World* 19/3 (1986), 311–27; "Positivism, Philosophy of Science, and Self-Understanding," *American Philosophical Quarterly* 26/4 (1989), 253–68; "Mill's Misreading of Comte on 'Interior Observation,'" *Journal of the History of Philosophy* 27/4 (1989), 559–72; "Comte, Philosophy, and the Question of Its History," *Philosophical Topics* 19/2 (1991), 177–204; and "Monitoring Self-Activity: The Status of Reflection Before and After Comte," *Metaphilosophy* [Blackwell Publishers] 22/4 (1991), 333–48.

My greatest debts are to my family. For their loving patience with my absences, my moods, and my sometime confusions about what matters in life, I am deeply appreciative. I am also especially grateful to Michael for unexpected philosophical companionship; to Adam for his spiritual example; and to Sarah for teaching me the value of listening. To my partner and life's companion, Judith Lutzhoff Scharff, whose love and intellectual kinship I am mysteriously privileged to enjoy, I owe what cannot be repaid.

NOTE ON CITATIONS

Comte's works

CPP   *Cours de philosophie positive*, 6 vols. (Paris: Bachelier, 1830–42). No complete English translation of the *Cours* exists; subsequent French editions all have various paginations for the same 60 "Lessons"; and no edition correlates its pagination with any others. My citations are by volume, lesson, and first-edition pagination. Bracketed references to available English translations (when reliable, sometimes modified) are, in order of preference, Frederick Ferré [F], *Introduction to Positive Philosophy* (Indianapolis, IN: Hackett, 1988); Stanislav Andreski [A], *The Essential Comte* (London: Croom Helm, 1974); or Gertrud Lenzer [L], *Auguste Comte and Positivism: The Essential Writings* (Chicago: University of Chicago Press, 1984). Lenzer's selections from the *Cours*, themselves abridged, are from Harriet Martineau's [M] "authorized" but "freely translated and condensed" version, *The Positive Philosophy of Auguste Comte*, 2 vols. (London: John Chapman, 1853).

DEP   *Discours [préliminaire] sur l'esprit positif*, published separately and as an introduction (same pagination) to *Traité philosophique d'astronomie populaire* (Paris: Carilian-Goeury and Victor Dalmont, 1844) [trans. Edward Spencer Beesly, *A Discourse on the Positive Spirit* (London: William Reeves, 1903)].

SPP   *Système de politique positive, ou traité de sociologie, instituant la religion de l'humanité*, 4 vols. (Paris: L. Mathias, 1851–54) [trans. J. H. Bridges et al., *System of Positive Polity*, 4 vols. (London: Longmans, Green, 1875–77)]. Six "early essays on social philosophy" are reprinted as an "Appendice général" to Volume 4 and are cited here as "SPP4a" to accommodate the separate French pagination (English pagination is continuous).

Mill's works

A *Autobiography, Collected Works*, Vol. 1 (Toronto: University of Toronto Press, 1981)

ACP *Auguste Comte and Positivism, Collected Works*, Vol. 10 (Toronto: University of Toronto Press, 1969) [the second page reference is to the paperback photo reproduction of the third edition (London: Trübner, 1882), University of Michigan Press (Ann Arbor, 1961)].

LMC *Lettres inédites de John Stuart Mill à Auguste Comte avec les responses de Comte*, ed. Lucien Lévy-Bruhl (Paris: Alcan, 1899) [trans. Oscar A. Haac, *The Correspondence of John Stuart Mill and Auguste Comte* (New Brunswick, NJ: Transaction Publishers, 1994)]. References are to the date and Lévy-Bruhl's numbering (both are also in the translation).

SL *A System of Logic, Ratiocinative and Inductive. Being a Connected View of the Principles of Evidence and the Methods of Scientific Investigation, Collected Works*, Vols. 7 and 8 (Toronto: University of Toronto Press, 1973–74). Citations are by book, chapter, paragraph, and sometimes pages.

Other works

PIC Pickering, Mary, *Auguste Comte: An Intellectual Biography*, Vol. 1 (Cambridge: Cambridge University Press, 1993).

RR Putnam, Hilary, *Realism and Reason: Philosophical Papers*, Vol. 3 (Cambridge: Cambridge University Press, 1983).
RHF *Realism with a Human Face*, ed. James Conant (Cambridge, MA: Harvard University Press, 1990).
RTH *Reason, Truth, and History* (Cambridge: Cambridge University Press, 1981).
RP *Renewing Philosophy* (Cambridge MA: Harvard University Press, 1992).

COP Rorty, Richard, *Consequences of Pragmatism: Essays, 1972–1980* (Minneapolis: University of Minnesota Press, 1982).
CIS *Contingency, Irony, and Solidarity* (Cambridge: Cambridge University Press, 1989).
PP1, 2 *Philosophical Papers*, 2 vols. (Cambridge: Cambridge University Press, 1990–91).
PMN *Philosophy and the Mirror of Nature* (Princeton, NJ: Princeton University Press, 1979).

OE Taylor, Charles, "Overcoming Epistemology," in Kenneth Baynes et al., *After Philosophy*, 464–88. [Reprinted in *Philosophical Arguments* (Cambridge, MA: Harvard University Press, 1995), 1–19.]
PH "Philosophy and Its History," in R. Rorty et al., *Philosophy in History*, 17–30.

PIH *Philosophy in History: Essays on the Historiography of Philosophy*, ed. Richard Rorty, J. B. Schneewind, and Quentin Skinner (Cambridge: Cambridge University Press, 1984).

AP *After Philosophy: End or Transformation?* ed. Kenneth Baynes, James Bohman, and Thomas McCarthy (Cambridge, MA: MIT Press, 1987).

IOP *The Institution of Philosophy: A Discipline in Crisis?* ed. Avner Cohen and Marcelo Dascal (La Salle, IL: Open Court, 1989).

COMTE AFTER POSITIVISM

INTRODUCTION: COMTE FOR A POST-POSITIVIST WORLD

As hard as it is nowadays to get agreement on what analytic philosophers could still possibly have in common, at least it seems safe to say that there is something they are universally against, namely, positivism.[1] I start with the fact of this anti-positivism, because it may appear to cast a shadow over the present study. My purpose in what follows is to urge a revival of interest – contemporary and substantive, not just historical and scholarly interest – in the first and most famous of all the positivists, Auguste Comte. I therefore use this Introduction not only to outline my plans but also to counter the suspicion that Comte is not worth the trouble.

---

1 On the elusiveness of acceptable positive characterizations see, e.g., A. J. Mandt, "The Inevitability of Pluralism: Philosophical Practice and Philosophical Excellence," in IOP, 87–98. For a more orthodox account, one that expresses much greater confidence in its view of both the nature and future of analytic pluralism, see Nicholas Rescher, "American Philosophy Today," *Review of Metaphysics* 46 (1993), 717–45. Rescher, who describes his essay as a "descriptive survey" of the current situation (738), asserts that it is "Europe, after all, [that] is the home of ideologies" (727), whereas "much of American philosophy – like much of American politics – is refreshingly free of ideological involvements." In this refreshing atmosphere, Rescher explains, almost any issue can become part of the overall analytic "problem agenda" and receive treatment in a "genuinely collective effort that is best characterized in statistical terms" (728). As for those "pseudo-pragmatists," neo-Marxists, and followers of "writers such as Heidegger, Derrida, and their epigones" who do not participate in this happy collective effort, Rescher calls their refusal to do so an "assault by a disaffected avant-garde against the discipline as normally practiced" (737), and (citing Cohen and Dascal's book as evidence) he concludes that such displays of "postmodern disdain for reason" are not taken seriously by us nonideological Americans who know that "metaphilosophy is part of philosophy" (738). As I shall argue, neither Comte, on the one hand, nor post-positivists as diverse as Rorty, Taylor, and Putnam, on the other, would accept Rescher's forced option between normal (newly pluralized, "metaphilosophically" sensitive) and disdainful (postmodern, reason-disrespecting, probably ideological) thinking as "descriptive."

I

1. Today's anti-positivism

In the English-speaking world, of course, positivism is now inherited through its last and most sophisticated version, namely, Logical Empiricism; and one generalization to be made about Logical Empiricism is that it embodies a sort of ultimate crystallization of two of positivism's core features – namely, the promotion of a rigorously "scientific" epistemology and a supreme self-confidence about its own objective, systematic, ahistorical outlook. Given the current anti-positivist atmosphere, one might suppose that these two features would be especially favored targets of criticism. Certainly this is true of the first feature. Scientific and, by implication, all other single-model accounts of rationality have been under general attack for some time. Regarding the second feature, however, matters are quite different. To be sure, Logical Empiricism's own imperious presumption of objectivity is now rejected with virtual unanimity. A philosophy that dreams of "reconstructing" what "the" conditions of rationality must be is obviously hostage to some inherited dogma.

Yet at the same time, criticisms of this particular logico-reconstructive dream have done little to weaken the ahistorical imperative that lies behind it. The threat of historicism still routinely discourages aspiring post-positivists from questioning whether, as a matter of principle, any philosophy might ever understand itself so well that it could legitimately claim possession of a Completely Objective orientation. Even among those who have long since ceased to regard themselves as scientific thinkers, who have lost the old taste for mathematical rigor and the old hostility toward everything traditional, the ideal of a truly inheritance-free philosophizing often prevails. It continues to seem obvious that in order to protect philosophy against the charge of (vicious) relativism, we presently practicing epistemologists must make it entirely and exclusively *our* job – uninfluenced by the flounderings and partial successes of our forbears – to decide what knowing the true and the reasonable actually involves.

Current anti-positivism, then, tends to be a very unevenly critical and revisionist affair. Everyone wants to leave the scientistic monomania of Logical Analysis and Rational Reconstruction behind; but only a small (and "obviously" historicist) minority are willing to question, *as a model for their own thinking*, positivism's ahistorical conception of philosophy's proper outlook. As one recent writer revealingly puts it, in contemporary analytic philosophy all sorts of topical and methodological pluralisms may be tolerated and quarreled over – so long as the philosophical handling of the whole debate takes place *sub specie aeternitatis*.[2] For the mainstream majority, only Continental thinkers (e.g., Nietzsche, Heidegger, Foucault) and their corrupted American followers (e.g., Feyerabend, Rorty, Taylor) would have the gall to "reduce" philosophical analysis as such to a historically contextualized activity. In life, so goes the objection, there may indeed be

---

[2] See Hector-Neri Castañeda, "Philosophy as a Science and as a Worldview," IOP, 35–60 (specific reference to *sub specie*, 41).

subjectivist and relativist alternatives to the View from Nowhere, but not in philosophy.

Someone might wish to argue that the foregoing description is dated. Perhaps it is true that until about ten years ago the epithet "historicism" could make a tyranny of the majority position; but are circumstances not different now? The answer is, I think, yes, but not tellingly so. Granted, the epithet itself has lost some of its name-calling punch because it is no longer entirely clear just what one is supposed to be against. Granted also that historical studies are less suspect and that the idea of taking Continental sources seriously no longer seems so terrible. A few mainstream radicals even seem to have gone some considerable distance toward embracing historicism.[3] Yet in fact, none of these developments have produced anything like a sea change on the basic issue of proper philosophical orientation. The specter of Analysis Itself being inescapably tainted by historical conditioning continues to haunt the debate over what comes after positivism. In Rorty's provocative image,

> Reichenbach *redivivus* would presumably be appalled by . . . the proliferation of problems and programs in contemporary American philosophy. But he would admire the style, the insistence on argument, the dialectical acuity. He would approve of the widespread distrust among philosophers of those who . . . were "trained in literature and history. . . ."[4]

Under these circumstances, one seems to be driven to the conclusion that there are only three possible philosophical orientations – namely, scientistic objectivity, epistemically pluralistic objectivity, and historicism – and one understands that for "stylistic" reasons, only the second option can legitimately replace the first.

I intend, of course, to describe here an intellectual tendency, not an explicitly affirmed faith; and I take it that, like any such tendency, this one is undoubtedly more influential than many who remain influenced by it are happy about. Hence, it seems clear to me that making serious philosophical trouble for the

---

3 Two of the best known are Alasdair MacIntyre and Charles Taylor. MacIntyre maintains that "although arguments of the kind favored by analytic philosophy do possess an indispensable power, it is only within the context of a particular genre of historical inquiry that such arguments can support the type of claim to truth and rationality which philosophers characteristically aspire to justify" [*After Virtue*, 2nd ed. (Notre Dame, IN: University of Notre Dame Press, 1984), 265; see also "The Relationship of Philosophy to Its Past," PIH, 31–48]. To Taylor, "it is essential to an adequate understanding of certain problems, questions, and issues, that one understand them genetically... and this fact about philosophy, that it is inherently historical, is a manifestation of a more general truth about human life and society" ("Philosophy and Its History," PIH, 17). The most thoroughly historicist transformation of analytic philosophy to date is probably that of Margolis, from whose position one would have to argue that MacIntyre and Taylor are among those postpositivist revisionists who are unwilling to acknowledge the full implications of the very outlook they help create. See Joseph Margolis, *The Flux of History and the Flux of Science* (Berkeley: University of California Press, 1994), esp. Ch. 5, "The Redefinition of Historicism," 110–39, and his "Epilogue," 194–206.

4 Richard Rorty, "Philosophy in America Today," in COP, 223–24. As we shall see later, Rorty's own rejection of this attitude does not make him quite the historicist he thinks he is.

ahistorical imperative under the current partially anti-positivist circumstances will take more than promoting post-Hegelian sources, clarifying what "historicism" means, pluralizing analysis, or embracing the historicist enemy. One must find a way to ask – and really mean it – *What sort of philosophizing could lie beyond both historicism and its (still basically positivist) opposite?* As a start, consider Putnam's observation that

> a certain oscillation between historicism and positivism has been a central feature of late nineteenth-century and twentieth-century thought. Whether it is Nietzsche versus Mill, or Kuhn and Feyerabend versus Carnap and Popper, or Foucault and Rorty versus Quine, the theme has been history versus science. . . . The debate has . . . become boring; yet we seem doomed to repeat it (like a neurotic symptom) unless, perhaps, we can step back and offer a better (and deeper) diagnosis of the situation than the competing diagnoses of historicism and positivism.[5]

Putnam is certainly neither the first nor the only analytic philosopher to make such remarks, though for reasons to be given later, I think his way of posing the issue has (if perhaps only for his readers) an especially radicalizing potential. What would a genuinely post-positivist outlook be? How might our "situation" be reflectively reunderstood so that analysis – if, indeed, philosophical activity would then still be rightly called by this name – no longer appeared to occur somewhere between what is Positivist and what is Historically Relative?

Among those who engage in it, such questioning is not casual. In Putnam's case, it is accompanied by strong appeals for a "moratorium" on all speculation about the Really Real and the Correct Method, and for the production instead of epistemically localized and "internally realistic" accounts of what is reasonable and what is not. The sober and deeply reformist spirit of these appeals tells us that Putnam's characterization of the circumstances that necessitate them is also serious. When he says that the ground rules in current debates over philosophy's aim are "boring," this is no flippant remark. Like a growing number of other aspiring post-positivists, he really does regard the present situation – with its lingering inheritance of an anti-positivist and anti-relativist mood – as tiresome, stuck, and fostering a contentment to replay worn-out variations on two basic orientational themes. And on this score, I think, he is right. It is not scientism and single-model epistemologies but a sort of pervasive, unreflective complacency about the forced option between objective and historicist philosophical orientations that has turned out to be the most durable aspect of the positivist legacy. I take Putnam to be pressing this point in claiming that we need to "step back and offer a *better (and deeper) diagnosis* of the situation" than those now available.

Putnam is correct also, I think, in observing that this diagnostic stepping back must lead us, as he says he was himself led,

> to think about questions which are thought to be more the province of "continental

---

5 Hilary Putnam, "Beyond Historicism," RR, 288.

philosophy" than of "analytical philosophy," for instance, to think about the fact that our notions of rationality evolve in history . . . and about the fact that one's own philosophical tradition has both a past and a future.[6]

Whether Putnam's own internal realism is the right response to these considerations is not my concern here. What interests me is the fact that, as Putnam himself clearly recognizes, *any* response that takes these considerations seriously is very likely to be widely opposed for displaying the wrong philosophical attitude. It is easy to imagine the deflationary critique: If Putnam thinks his inquiries give him kinship with continental philosophers, this simply means that he has joined them in succumbing to historicism. If he says that his position is historically contextualized rather than objective, the burden is on him to show how this differs from thinking of it reductively as historically conditioned. And if he thinks that conducting localized analyses in an internally realistic spirit is better than doing Ontology and Epistemology, what makes him think so in the first place – and must he not treat *that* reason as historically *un*conditioned?

In the present context, the most important fact to note about objections like these is that they come too easily. They simply take up the currently more acceptable side in the very debate whose tiresomeness post-positivists like Putnam would have us reconsider. Hence, rather than immediately responding to these objections, I want to suggest that one might better consider first – as Putnam himself does not – just what a "stepping back to diagnose our situation" that is neither ahistorical nor historicist could be. To give it a label, what sort of *historico-critical reflectiveness* is it that Putnam wants to enact but does not actually speak about? Of what kind of diagnosis might such reflectiveness be capable, such that we could understand our philosophical situation, its past, and its future in non-boring ways?

It is in light of this question that I want to revive interest in Comte. For what is unique to this thinker is that he both aspires to be the kind of positivist who later came to know only Putnam's tiresome options and also inevitably fails, for strikingly Putnam-like reasons, to become one. Like his successors, Comte thinks scientific philosophy is the final stage of intellectual development. At the same time, unlike his successors but very much like someone interested in historico-critically stepping back, Comte's diagnosis of his situation makes philosophy's past essentially relevant to its future practice. Science, he argues, transforms rather than supersedes theology and metaphysics, just as metaphysics did earlier to theology. Hence, unlike later positivists, who assume that real philosophy begins when pre-scientific ways are abandoned, Comte insists that he cannot even be clear about what he is doing without a conscious and critical appropriation of his theologico-metaphysical legacy.

For reasons to be explained later, Comte himself never sees the tension in his

---

6 RR, vii–viii. Cf. RHF, ix–xi.

position. In the end his positivism is left facing Janus-like, both in the familiar direction of dogmatic and ahistorical scientism and yet also toward a never fully appreciated, and now long forgotten, historically minded reflectiveness about scientific practice. But if this double orientation is, for Comte, just an unacknowledged problem, our own recognition of it can, I think, help further the interest of aspiring post-positivists in rethinking the current philosophical situation in less tiresome terms. Reading Comte's writings today, we are witness to our own inheritance in the making – but before it solidified into the position everyone now wants to reject, and while there is still left open, even in the arguments of this science-obsessed thinker, another (yet also nonhistoricist) philosophical option. My thesis, then, is that by recovering Comte's forgotten idea of a historico-critical defense of science, we can place ourselves in the strange position of receiving help from the first positivist in clarifying the possibility of a philosophical stepping back that succeeds in being more thoroughly "after" positivism than anything the current spirit of anti-positivism allows.

2. Comte's historico-critical defense of positivism

For reasons already apparent in Mill's enormously influential *Auguste Comte and Positivism* (1865), Comte's claim that positivism needs a historico-critical defense ceased almost immediately to be taken seriously.

Even during Comte's lifetime, positivism did not remain a unified movement. The two uneven parts of Mill's book convey nicely a sense of the two main positivist factions, of the issues dividing them, and even of the eventual winner. The longer, complimentary part of the book represents the first faction – including most famously Mill himself in England and Littré in France – which embraced the scientific epistemology of Comte's earlier *Cours de philosophie positive* but rejected his later moral and political writings as sentimental and authoritarian regressions.[7] The shorter, strongly critical part of Mill's book represents the other faction, which, citing Comte himself, denounced their rivals as "abortive positivists" and argued that the *Cours* is only an "indispensable preamble" to the grand plan of "social reorganization" set forth in Comte's *Système de politique positive*.[8] It was

---

7 In addition to the two introductory Lessons of CPP1(1–2) and Mill's ACP, 265/4–5, 328–32/125–32, see Émile Littré, *Auguste Comte et la philosophie positive* (Paris: L. Hachette, 1863), i–xi, 518–19, 662–68; and "Comte et Mill," *Revue des Deux Mondes* 36 (1866), 829–66. See also W. M. Simon, *European Positivism in the Nineteenth Century: An Essay in Intellectual History* (Ithaca, NY: Cornell University Press, 1963), 14–24.
8 SPP1, 1–10/ix–xvii; SPP4, 546–49/473–75; and SPP4a, i–ii/i–ii. See also J. H. Bridges, *The Unity of Comte's Life and Doctrine: A Reply to Strictures on Comte's Later Writings Addressed to J. S. Mill* (London: Trübner, 1866); and T. R. Wright, *The Religion of Humanity: The Impact of Comtean Positivism on Victorian Britain* (Cambridge: Cambridge University Press, 1986). As a matter of historical scholarship, the unity view is now generally accepted. See, e.g., Maurice Mandelbaum, *History, Man, and Reason: A Study in Nineteenth-Century Thought* (Baltimore: Johns Hopkins Press, 1971), 10–13. Only very recently, however, has this view been documented in a systematic way. See esp. Pickering, PIC, 3–5, 691–98.

the first faction, of course, whose image of positivism ultimately prevailed; but on one thing, both factions agreed. The success of the sciences demonstrated that a post-metaphysical era was already here; hence, Comte's retrospective defense of positivism appeared to be unnecessary. What comes before science was deemed safely left to the historians; as Mill put it, for philosophers to bother with such matters now would be like trying to relive a battle as if we did not already know who won.

As a representative of the ultimately prevailing faction, however, Mill had further reason to press his criticisms of Comte. In a scientific era, he argued, philosophy's main job must be to analyze the rational conditions of scientific success and produce an "Organon of Proof"; yet this is precisely the task that Comte, in his preoccupation with positivism's intellectual origins and sociopolitical destiny, sadly neglects. Mill's criticism stuck. Later positivists turned to organon production as their real task; and in the end, even as the first advocate of scientific epistemology, Comte is not especially honored. Today, if he is remembered at all, it is for somehow imperfectly anticipating Logical Positivism; and the Logical Positivists themselves preferred the title "Logical Empiricist" precisely so that they could distance themselves from earlier positivism and claim Humean ancestry instead.[9]

In short, even among his own kind, Comte's historico-critical defense of positivism was never much appreciated. From Mill to the Logical Empiricists, the position simply appeared to need no defense. What Carnap wrote in 1928 Mill could have written in 1865. Whenever "our orientation" faces religious and metaphysical opposition, Carnap asks, what gives us

> our confidence that our call for . . . a science that is free from metaphysics will be heard? It stems from the knowledge, or to put it somewhat more carefully, *from the belief that those opposing powers belong to the past*. We feel that there is an inner kinship between the attitude on which our philosophical work is founded and the intellectual attitude which presently manifests itself in entirely different walks of life. . . . We feel all around us the same basic orientation, the same style of thinking and doing. It is an orientation which demands clarity everywhere. . . .[10]

Having such a "belief" and sharing such "feelings" does indeed separate the pos-

---

9 See, e.g., "Editor's Introduction," *Logical Positivism*, ed. A. J. Ayer (New York: Free Press, 1959), 3–28; and Herbert Feigl, "The Origin and Spirit of Logical Positivism," *The Legacy of Logical Positivism*, ed. Peter Achinstein and Stephen F. Barker (Baltimore: Johns Hopkins Press, 1969), 3–24. Logical Empiricists typically show little interest in questions of intellectual inheritance generally or their individual forebears specifically. Feigl and Ayer merely mention Hume a few times, never Comte, and less remote figures like Avenarius, Mach, and Helmholtz a few times more. Historians of the movement have usually followed their subjects' lead and focused primarily on the formation of the Vienna Circle itself. See, e.g., Victor Kraft, *The Vienna Circle: The Origin of Neo-Positivism*, trans. Arthur Pap (New York: Philosophical Library, 1953), 3–11; and Barry Smith, "Austrian Origins of Logical Positivism," in *Logical Positivism in Perspective: Essays on 'Language, Truth, and Logic,'* ed. Barry Gower (London: Croom Helm, 1987), 35–68. But cf. also fn. 11.
10 Rudolf Carnap, *The Logical Structure of the World*, trans. Rolf A. George (Berkeley: University of California Press, 1967), xvii–xviii, my emphasis.

itivists we know from the Comte we barely remember. Certainly there is at least symbolic significance, if not conscious purpose, in the editor's decision to commission a historian, not a philosopher, to write the Comte entry for the 1967 *Encyclopedia of Philosophy*.[11]

In recovering Comte, then, the first feature of his outlook we should note is that, unlike subsequent positivists, he most emphatically does not understand himself to be philosophizing in a "post-"metaphysical world. Rather, he thinks of himself as living in a time of transition, when metaphysics is ending, when the sciences are becoming conscious of themselves as sciences, and thus when their epistemic superiority is still an unsettled issue. All of this he takes with professional seriousness. Positive philosophy is going to be practiced *under these transitional circumstances;* hence, a major part of its job must be to explain both the nature of the transition to a scientific era and the importance of completing it. In the meantime, all the fundamental ideas of positivism – namely, that science is destined to replace theology and metaphysics, that genuine knowledge is of facts discovered by observation, that knowledge of ultimate things is impossible – all these ideas remain controversial, not entirely fixed even in the best of minds, and therefore susceptible to the lingering appeal of prescientific modes of thinking.

Comte's understanding of these transitional circumstances is informed, above all, by his famous law of three stages, according to which human intelligence generally and each of the sciences specifically progress through three successive stages, from a necessarily theological beginning, through a metaphysical transition, to a scientific climax. Just how Comte makes philosophical use of this law without either becoming a historicist or (in Habermas' image) doing public relations for a positivism already dogmatically embraced, we shall have to see. One major misconception, however, should be cleared up here.

Contrary to widespread legend and much sloppy history, Comte does not – indeed, could not – employ his three-stage law to promote the idea that scientific minds should think of the Western tradition's theological and metaphysical periods as times of mere superstition and intellectual nonsense. In his historically minded view, science is simply the last and finally successful expression of humanity's long struggle to explain and control nature; hence, what theology and metaphysics tried to do, and even the ways in which they tried to do it, remain perfectly intelligible. Comte argues, for example, that when primitive peoples spontaneously produced animistic-theological explanations for the awe-inspiring events they experienced in their surroundings, they successfully solved, in the

---

11 Bruce Mazlish, "Comte, Auguste," *Encyclopedia of Philosophy,* ed. Paul Edwards (New York: Macmillan, 1967), II, 173–77. Cf. the recent study by Michael Dummet, *Origins of Analytical Philosophy* (Cambridge, MA: Harvard University Press, 1994), which argues in detail that we ought to see Frege and Husserl (and, by extension, analysis and phenomenology) as philosophical collaborators both intent on coming to grips with the larger modern tradition – but has nothing to say about Comte.

only way possible for human beings, the "vicious circle" of being initially without either informed theories to guide observation or reliable observations to develop theories. Not only is such animistic theorizing therefore still fully understandable; contemporary scientific practice gains clarity about itself by understanding it. For example, in animism's struggle to produce the first explanations of natural events, we find illuminated the epistemic principle of the essential interrelatedness of reason and observation. Moreover, since these primitive explanations are the basis for prayers and rituals designed to move the world's spirits, they also reveal the ultimately praxis-motivated character of all theory and are thus the earliest exemplification of what, in later Baconian form, will be expressed as the principle that "from science comes prevision; from prevision comes action."[12]

The purpose of Comte's historically minded defense of science, then, is to encourage in current philosophers a sense of their kinship with, and not just superiority to, prescientific practice. At every stage, what we have most deeply wanted is "a conceptual system concerning the totality of phenomena" that permits us to know our surroundings well enough to order our lives effectively. At every stage, this goal is pursued by whatever method seems maximally surpassing of earlier ones. What science finally does is to fulfill our deepest aim by transforming the ineffective methods of theology and metaphysics. We humans are thus not fundamentally either theological or metaphysical, but neither are we fundamentally scientific. At bottom, we are practical; hence, for a Comtean positivist, it would be just as misleading to say that a mature mind must be antireligious and antimetaphysical as it once was to say that all philosophy originates either in mystical feeling or in awe. It is true that at specific stages of development, the imaginative response to feelings of mystery and the intellectual response to experiences of wonder are each indispensable stimulants to "speculation" (not a bad word for Comte) – the former response in order to overcome the initial dilemma of being without either theories or data, the latter to effect a subsequent liberation of reason from feeling and imagination. Both responses, however, are driven just as much by the desire for prevision and for satisfaction of natural and interpersonal needs as are the observation-based speculations of science. Thus, science is to modern technology what theology and metaphysics are, respectively, to worship and contemplation – namely, a comprehensive theoretical foundation for a universal form of praxis – only this time, we are really getting our long-desired control over external and social surroundings.

Questions concerning the empirical accuracy of Comte's three-stage law should not be allowed to obscure the philosophical distinctiveness of the approach he marks out in using it. Certainly it is refreshing, if a bit strange, for us to

---

12 CPP1(2), 63 [F, 38]. Comte's epistemology of science is not a primary topic in this study; but I will have occasion in what follows to note some of his remarkably post-positivist positions – as here, e.g., in his idea of the praxis-driven character of all scientific knowledge and in his claim that theory and observation cannot be subjected to separate analyses.

hear a positivist express interest in prescientific history and actually proclaim the technologico-social agenda shared by so many later positivists who are silent about it. My central point, however, is that no later positivist could ever have tolerated Comte's *reflective use* of his law. To everyone from Mill to Reichenbach, the very idea that current decisions about how philosophy should do its job ought to be influenced by historical considerations contradicts in principle the presumption that philosophy must have an objective orientation. Comte, however, not only suggests this idea, he argues for it. In his view no philosophy, not even positivism, will ever succeed in situating itself outside of events; and no analysis of scientific rationality will ever reduce to Logical Reconstruction. The urge to substitute a purely formal and systematic ("*dogmatique*") account for a historical one is, Comte concedes, a constant and even admirable "tendency" of the human mind; but in the end, it remains the case that "an idea cannot be properly understood except through its history."[13]

For Comte, moreover, this is no merely offhand remark; nor is it intended to make work for historians. It is addressed primarily to currently practicing positive philosophers, and even then, not just in general. Above all, Comte means the remark to announce *the dominant theme of his own philosophizing*. His scientism, his sense of social mission, even his specific ideas on logic and methodology – all of these are developed by Comte in what he conceives as a lifelong struggle to transform a still partially prescientific inheritance into a fully "positive" orientation under the stimulus provided to him by the emerging sciences. As in life generally so also in scientific epistemology, "we always labor for our descendants," says Comte, "but under the impetus of our ancestors, from whom we derive both the materials with which and the processes by which we work."[14]

Once recognized, the Comtean strategy of historico-critically defending positivism is fairly easy to describe. More difficult to explain is the fact that Comte advocates this strategy much more consistently than he actually pursues it. The main problem is that he never explores in any detail the question of what kind of philosophical move a historico-critical defense actually is. In fact, I have perhaps already said more about this issue than he does. As a result, one finds in Comte's writings a philosopher who often behaves, we might say, like a historico-critical defender of his orientation but who never considers as such the question of what sort of *reflective self-understanding* is required of one who wishes to mount such a defense. It is clear, moreover, that were we to put this objection to Comte he would rebuke us. He would reply, as twentieth-century positivists often do, that there is something dangerously subjective or "psychological" about this line of questioning – that is, about philosophers trying to understand the way they operate by "looking inward" upon their own case. Yet appearances here are deceiving. The

---

13 CPP1(1), 3 [F, I].
14 SPP4, 34/31, trans. altered.

similarity of his response hides a radically dissimilar sense of why he thinks the response must be made. Comte's reasons for backing away from the reflection/self-understanding issue are in fact very different from those of the later positivists. To understand this difference is to begin to realize why rethinking Comte is worth the trouble.

3. Comte (and Mill et al.) on interior observation

Comte's silence on the question of philosophical reflection is a function of his opposition to what he calls "interior observation." As far as I have been able to determine, however, this crucial point has never been understood – apparently because Comte's treatment of the idea of interior observation is usually discussed in terms of Mill's famous criticism of it, and the fact that Mill fundamentally misinterprets Comte's position has gone unnoticed. According to today's conventional wisdom, backed up by virtually all the intervening reports, Mill's quarrel with Comte prefigures the later debates among structuralists, functionalists, and behaviorists over the value of introspection as a scientific method. Superficially, this interpretation seems plausible. Comte does in fact say that psychology will never be a genuine science because the so-called interior observation on which it is supposedly based is demonstrably impossible. And Mill does in fact reply that Comte's proof is flawed, that we obviously do engage in interior observation, and therefore, that a science relying on this operation is possible. But these facts are misleading, and the conventional interpretation is wrong. Mill and Comte are speaking past each other, not to each other, for the simple reason that they do not mean – and in spite of their extensive correspondence fail to recognize that they do not mean – the same thing by either interior observation or psychology.

On the one hand, what Comte opposes is not Mill's "introspection" – that is, an *empirical* operation yielding first-person reports about inner states or private experiences – but rather a spurious *metaphysical* procedure that Comte traces back to the influence of Descartes and medieval theology. And what Comte means by psychology is not Mill's British-style associationism, but rather a specious enterprise (promoted in Comte's time, above all, by the now nearly forgotten Victor Cousin) that wraps its unscientific speculations about Mind (really, Soul) in the mantle of science by claiming to draw on an "inwardly" focused version of the external observation that grounds the sciences of nature. On the other hand, Mill assumes that Comte is thinking of (associationist) psychology and is rejecting both it and the introspection on which it depends; hence, he thinks Comte's argument is "destroyed" by the "simple fact" that we are all directly aware of our own intellectual activities, and "whatever we are directly aware of, we can directly observe."

Mill's misreading itself, however, is not as important here as what explains it. His mistake lies in assuming that his quarrel with Comte is a methodological one, that is, that Comte is wrong about one of our empirical sources for acquiring data about mental life. In making this assumption, Mill shows himself to already possess the typical orientation of a later positivist who sees the "logic of science" as his main topic. Most later positivists, of course, do not agree with Mill that introspection gives us our "best knowledge" of mental life; but that is not the point here. In fact, it would be just as mistaken for us to praise Comte for anticipating behaviorism as it was for Mill to condemn him for being anti-introspectionist. In both cases, the error lies in assuming that Comte must be, in the same sense befitting everyone from Mill to the Logical Empiricists, just one more philosopher "of" science. For all of them, the issue of introspective versus experimental approaches to Mind is fundamentally a question about method and methodological reliability; and all such questions are to be settled by discussions that take place *within* – that is, on the basis of the assumed legitimacy of – *science*. But Comte's treatment of interior observation is part of his discussion *about science itself*, not just one of its possible methods. His primary target is not an empirically unpromising procedure but an epistemically spurious, unscientific discipline. In his view, interior observation is easily proven impossible because it was never more in the first place than a theologico-metaphysical fiction concocted to lend credibility to an incompetent collection of knowledge claims. Comte's critique of interior observation belongs, in other words, to his historico-critical defense of science itself against a vestige of the prescientific era. He argues that Cousin's kind of psychology, claiming to know all manner of wondrous things about the mind that entirely elude the other sciences, must be shown up for what it is – namely, "the latest transformation of theology," an impediment to progress in knowledge, and thus something to be scrapped rather than reformed.

With this confusion surrounding the Comte–Mill controversy removed, one begins to see why their disagreement is worth rethinking. For behind their radically different views of interior observation lies a radical dissimilarity in basic philosophical orientation – one that gives each thinker, though sharing the title "positivist," completely different reasons for being silent on the question of philosophical self-understanding. Mill, like the later positivists, is simply too confident about the legitimacy of his scientific (that is, objective, neutral) outlook to be reflectively concerned about its defense. Thus for him, the only "turning inward" that remains on the philosophical agenda is introspection; and it is a topic, not because it seems to rival the methods of science but because it purports to be one of them. The subsequent story is well known. After Mill, the empirical reputation of introspection declines, and inwardness of any sort comes to seem philosophically irrelevant. By the time of Logical Empiricism, introspection is as dead a letter as Cartesian meditation, and even the most conscientious scientific philosopher may therefore safely ignore them both.

I argue in the following chapters that it is our good fortune that Comte cannot be made part of this story of what one recent writer aptly calls the "disappearance of introspection."[15] In fact, Comte's opposition to interior observation concerns neither introspection specifically nor scientific methodology generally. Once this is understood, it becomes clear that his silence about philosophical self-understanding is a sign of something very different from the imperious attitude of later positivism. Comte's is a forced rather than a confident silence – that is, a matter of his strong opposition to one idea (interior observation) diverting attention from another idea (historico-critical reflection) that his own philosophical practice otherwise makes pertinent. His writings show him to be so busy debunking pseudoscientific interior consultations with one's soul that he cannot ask if any other, philosophically more legitimate kind of inward turn might be possible. Yet precisely by making the critique of interior observation part of his general defense of science, Comte creates an unacknowledged countertendency in his own thinking – one that suggests that there is a fundamental difference between the spurious operation he opposes and the historico-critical reflection in which he himself engages in order to be its opponent. This kind of reflection, I will argue, differs in principle not only from interior observation and introspection but also from the ahistorical kind of total Cartesian reflexivity that post-positivists now regularly identify as the deeper legacy of Logical Empiricism. Given that Comte could not explicitly consider this, and given (as I will show) that post-positivists have done so with only partial success, I want to further the efforts of the latter by rethinking the struggles of the former.

4. Recovering Comte after Logical Empiricism

Here, then, is the piece of nineteenth-century history I believe can be turned to current philosophical advantage. There is in Comte's works a silently enacted historico-critical kind of reflectiveness that, on the one hand, defines a philosophical attitude unlike any of those left available to us in the wake of Logical Empiricism and, on the other hand, promises to illuminate what Putnam's "stepping back to diagnose one's situation" might involve. Two main difficulties, however, block our recovery of Comte's unusual option. First, decades of positivist prejudice still tend to convert all talk of philosophical self-monitoring into something "merely" psychological, like introspection or interior observation. Second, Comte's own handling of his historico-critical defense is compromised, both by his self-imposed silence about what it is and by his many dogmatic (that is, "later" positivist) enthusiasms – enthusiasms from which historical-minded post-positivists like Rorty, Taylor, and Putnam are now struggling to break free. A separate

---

15 William Lyons, *The Disappearance of Introspection* (Cambridge, MA: MIT Press, 1986). Lyons is one of those who thinks it is "introspection" to which Comte objects (9–16); also, more generally, he assumes that all the medieval (Augustine, Aquinas) and early modern (Descartes, Locke) unclarities about inward turns – whether called introspection, "inner sense," or "reflection" – are at bottom a sign that there had not yet been found a "clear model for *introspection*" (3, my emphasis).

Part of this book is devoted to each of these two main difficulties, and the Conclusion asks what a rethought historico-critical Comte might do for one of Putnam's bored post-positivists.

Part I, containing three chapters, exploits the differences between Comte and Mill on the issue of self-monitoring in order to bring Comte's idea of historico-critical reflection into the open. Chapter 1 analyzes Comte's critique of interior observation and Mill's introspectionist misinterpretation of it. Chapter 2 explains that Mill's misinterpretation is a function of his failure to understand that Comte's critique is part of a defense, not part of a logic of science. Chapter 3 reconstructs Comte's historico-critical defense itself, concentrating on his famous three-stage law, which is the linchpin of this defense. Out of necessity, my treatment of that law is somewhat unconventional. In the usual accounts, it is handled unsympathetically and summarily, either because of its alleged lack of empirical warrant or because it seems to be merely the first principle of an old-fashioned speculative philosophy of history. My own account attends more carefully and less polemically to the law's substantive particulars – not because I care about its scientific value or wish to revive the metaphysics of history but because, without a clear grasp of the *way* Comte's law interprets each stage, it is easy to miss and impossible to understand his reflective use of it.

By the end of Part I, Comte's uniquely defended positivism stands characterized as a provocative presence at the beginning of a philosophical movement that is about to produce a whole line of increasingly imperious practitioners who cannot even imagine that tradition might have contemporary relevance. Yet in spite of the historico-critical sensitivity operating silently throughout Comte's work, there is also much to mark him as just another scientistic know-it-all. I say this, however, not to deflate him but to raise expectations about the benefits of rethinking him. My point in Part II is that these benefits are realized precisely when we play his two sides off against each other. For in this way, something currently worth considering (that is, his idea that philosophy must account for itself historico-critically) can be brought to bear against those boring options of positivism and historicism with which we have since become all too familiar.

In Chapter 4, I analyze the tension in Comte's works between historical-minded and dogmatic/ahistorical treatments of science and the scientific stage. As if in anticipation of things to come, the influence of the latter tends to gain ascendancy over the former, so that Comte often displays a "reflexive" and ahistorical overconfidence in the somehow already justified superiority of scientific rationality that repeatedly undermines his more "reflective" and context-sensitive efforts to present it as an emergent and defensible mode of knowing. In order to explain this tendency, I show that on close inspection, the philosophical attitude displayed by Comte even when he makes his most outrageous claims about science-driven social reorganization is no more imperious than that displayed by Mill when he rejects these claims in the name of common sense. The problem, I argue, is that in each case – and, by implication, in still later versions of positivism as well – this attitude betrays the influence of an earlier and largely unacknowledged Cartesian legacy that ultimately sabotages the historico-critical Comte as much as it satisfies his increasingly ahistorical successors.

Chapters 5 and 6 focus on the fact that this Cartesian legacy, which almost everyone now agrees has skewed the empiricist–positivist strain of the modern tradition toward "reconstructive" epistemology, has also saddled it with a deeply and so far much less effectively opposed antihistorical prejudice. Because of this prejudice, it has been possible to reject almost everything Descartes actually proposed – his meditative style of inquiry, the mathematical ideal, the substantive physics and metaphysics, even the idea that all reasoning must conform to a single set of conditions – and yet to do all this while persisting in the same fundamentally ahistorical attitude Descartes himself embraced. In Chapter 5, the persistence of this side of the Cartesian legacy is briefly retraced, and the suggestion is made (specifically with Rorty in mind) that current and ostensibly post-positivist practices may not be as free from its influence as its advocates appear to think.

Chapter 6 argues this latter suggestion in some detail. Recent efforts to link history with current analytic practice have spawned several increasingly radical varieties of post-positivism; yet all of them continue to display some "Comtean" tension between an expressed demand for contextual sensitivity about methods, topics, and norms and an unexpressed overconfidence that this demand is now at last being met. Hence, on the one hand, methods and inquiry styles are everywhere being pluralized, allegedly objective epistemologies are being recontextualized, and the question is raised regarding what sort of outlook makes all this pluralizing and recontextualizing possible. Yet, on the other hand, even in radicals like Rorty and Taylor, efforts to explicate the general idea of an authentic post-positivist outlook founder, and we are left at best with suggestive hints about what Taylor cryptically calls a "continuation by transformation" of the ancient ideal of critical self-understanding that would somehow enable us to remain untempted by the lure of Descartes' ahistorical dream of "total reflexive clarity."

Finally, my Conclusion shows how reclaiming Comte – or, more precisely, rethinking the silent, historically sensitive Comte *against* the noisy, imperious positivist – sheds light on the current struggle to explain what a genuinely post-positivist orientation would be. Drawing on some of Putnam's recent remarks, I argue as follows. First, Comte's historico-critical kind of philosopher would be equally unmoved by either of the boring alternatives Putnam calls positivism (or, more generally, Cartesianism) and historicism (more generally, relativism). But second, we must understand much more thoroughly than Putnam that *becoming* such a philosopher cannot be accomplished by either *opposing, avoiding,* or *transforming* those alternatives. All three of these options are conceived in ignorance of the fact that even before one might imagine choosing them, we are already, in Putnam's term, "situated" both in our practices and in our reflection on those practices in an insuperable way. Hence, becoming a situated post-positivist – that is, achieving the kind of historico-critical reflectiveness Comte promoted in principle but betrayed in practice – means, above all, realizing that no one can ever *be* the unsituated "God's-eye Viewing" positivist or the uncommitted "Anything Goes" historicist that our Cartesian legacy still urges us to see as the only options. Realizing this can be the fruit of what Putnam only calls, but Comte might actually help us fashion as, a stepping back that effects a "better and deeper" diagnosis of our current philosophical situation.

I

COMTE THEN

I

MILL VERSUS COMTE ON INTERIOR OBSERVATION

Viewed from the present, "introspection" is definitely a phenomenon with an official history. We are given to understand that this procedure has a checkered past and presumably also a questionable future. We remember that it used to be regarded as having scientific credentials, that James and Titchener and Wundt and Brentano all defended versions of it, and that it was once actually regarded as a unique source of information about the human mind. Mill, too, already thought of introspection in this now familiar way; and it is the scientific promise of introspection that he is defending in his famous and influential attack on Comte's alleged refutation of it.

Introspection itself, however, whether in Mill's case or afterward, is not my topic here.[1] Moreover, as I explained in the Introduction, one should initially avoid even using the term when discussing Mill's attack on Comte because Mill fundamentally misunderstands both what Comte wants to refute and why. Comte's villain is something he calls "*observation intérieure*," which he thinks of as a spurious *metaphysical* procedure modeled after Descartes' "meditation"; but what Mill accuses him of attacking is the *empirical-psychological* operation we now call introspection. Ultimately, I want to show that this little episode of misunderstanding points in the direction of much deeper philosophical issues; but first, we must establish what it is that Comte rejects, what his arguments against it are, and how Mill reacts to them.

---

[1] On Mill's own view, see above all the account in Fred Wilson, *Psychological Analysis and the Philosophy of John Stuart Mill* (Toronto: University of Toronto Press, 1990), esp. chs. 3 and 4. For a basically critical account of the fate of introspection after Mill, especially in the English-speaking tradition, see Lyons, *Introspection*, chs. 1–4; but also, more sympathetically, Wilson, 294–342.

1. Who are Comte's interior observers?

In the opening "Lesson" of his *Cours* Comte identifies, as the first of his positive philosophy's four main contributions to intellectual progress, its capacity to furnish the means for replacing an "illusory psychology" allegedly based on "interior observation" with a genuinely scientific account of the laws of mental life.[2] The context is important. Replacement of a non-science, not methodologically reforming a real one, is what Comte intends. He never even considers the possibility that interior observation might somehow be made scientifically useful. For him, interior observation is an illusion; the very idea of such an operation belongs to the spirit of a prescientific past – to rational psychology and its speculative doctrines of the soul. One of positive philosophy's tasks is therefore to hasten the demise of this "last transmutation of theology."[3]

The first point to notice, then, is that Comte's conception of interior observation is not modeled after something like, say, what Wundt's expert introspectors did. Comte's model is a Cartesian one, furnished to him above all by Cousin and the French Eclectics. "Interior observation," he thinks, is what they have shown that Descartes' kind of "meditation" boils down to; and whether there even is such an operation should already seem questionable when one looks at the deplorable metaphysical doctrines allegedly derived from it.

Comte's estimate of Descartes himself is not as negative as his construal of meditation suggests.[4] For two contributions especially, he thinks Descartes deserves high praise, namely, his systematic conception of the sciences and his grasp of the true significance of mathematics.[5] First, as the pioneer of a "vast mechanical hypothesis" for the knowledge of nature, Descartes "render[ed] to the world the glorious service of instituting a complete system of positive philosophy."[6] In

---

2 CPP1(1), 32–34 [F, 19–20]; see also CPP3(45), 769–83.
3 CPP1(1), 34 [F, 20].
4 In general but especially in Part II, I employ the term "Cartesian" as one now typically does, namely, to refer to Descartes' so-called epistemological turn. We should remember, however, that this usage reflects the relatively more recent practice of the last two centuries. Originally, "Cartesianism" was primarily the name for a metaphysical system containing Descartes-like doctrines of self, soul, and God; and "Cartesians" were the defenders of such systems. By the time of the French Enlightenment, however, "most *philosophes* recognized their kinship with Descartes. They accepted...his goals of freedom, mastery, and progress. They adopted his method as the only way to the realization of these goals....They shared Descartes' [epistemic] spirit. They bewailed as tragic the fact that Descartes himself...became a dogmatic metaphysician....Their very recognition of an intimate spiritual kinship made them often vehement and always intolerant with respect to Descartes' failure. They wanted no one to identify them with Descartes the metaphysician" [Peter A. Schouls, *Descartes and the Enlightenment* (Kingston and Montreal: McGill-Queens University Press; Edinburgh: Edinburgh University Press, 1989), 63–76, 173–80, quoted from 176, emphases removed]. Like most later moderns, Comte clearly follows this Enlightenment distinction.
5 As a third compliment, one might add Comte's occasional description of his own account of the scientific method as a present-day equivalent of Descartes' *Discourse on Method*, for example, CPP6(58), 784–85; and LMC XII (June 19, 1842). See Ch. 4, fn. 47.
6 CPP3(45), 761–65 [L, 182–83]; quotation from 761 [182]. Cf. Angèle Kremer-Marietti, *Le Concept de science positive. Ses tenants et ses aboutissants dans les structures anthropologiques du Positivisme* (Paris: Klincksieck, 1983), 10–19.

Comte's view (explained in Chapter 3), the human desire for a comprehensive understanding of our surroundings is evident from the very beginning, not just in the more recent speculations of metaphysics but earlier in the superstitious and imagination-based world pictures of primitive peoples. It is Descartes' hypothesis, however, that shows how it is specifically science, with its greater and methodologically more sophisticated concern for empirical variety and detail, that represents a move from merely speculative toward genuine intellectual "unity."[7] Second, Descartes shares with Newton the honor of having shown that mathematics is less important as a body of knowledge than as "the most powerful instrument the human mind can employ in investigating the laws of natural phenomena."[8] Descartes' distinction between "abstract" and "concrete" mathematics (that is, between arithmetic and algebra, on the one hand, and geometry and mechanics, on the other) is already suggestive of the hierarchical arrangement of the positive sciences; and his attempt to think mathematically about the natural world provides the model for truly scientific conceptions of methodological rigor and of the simplicity and generality of natural laws.

For Comte, the main problem with Descartes is that although his spirit of reform helped him advance the sciences of nature, that spirit failed him when it came to human beings. The failure is evident in his attempt to set up what Comte describes as a "fundamental separation" between our ways of studying humans and everything else. On the one hand, Descartes was ready to extend the idea of scientific study from astronomy to "the principal physical functions of the animal organism." On the other hand, when he came to consider higher-order phenomena, that is,

> affective and cognitive functions, he stopped abruptly and tried to make their study the exclusive prerogative of just the sort of metaphysico-theological philosophy whose scientific pretensions he had already so successfully undermined but into which he now tried to infuse new life.[9]

If one wants telling evidence of Descartes' prescientific motivation here, Comte continues, consider his ingenious but paradoxical conception of animals as automata. For this idea allows him, on the one hand, to embrace the progressive view that animal instinct and intelligence are topics for biological science and yet, on the other, to hang on to the ancient belief that people have souls, even if the success of biology now forces us to say that animals do not.[10]

According to Comte, the fact that Descartes himself thus failed to promote the scientific study of human mental life is understandable, given the limited inroads science had made in his day. At the same time, it remains true that by try-

---

7 CPP1(1), 23, 52–55 [F, 13–14, 30–32]. See also DEP, 21/33.
8 CPP1(2), 112 [F, 66]. See also CPP1(3), 131–32 [A, 70]; and DEP, 100/159, where mathematics is called "the one necessary cradle of rational positivity."
9 CPP3(45), 762–63.
10 CPP3(45), 762–63n.1.

ing to upgrade theologico-metaphysical knowledge of human nature by means of his meditative procedure, Descartes gave countless subsequent thinkers a strategy by which they, too, could chain the study of mental life to the old prescientific model. References to Descartes himself notwithstanding, then, Comte's critique of psychology and interior observation is directed mainly against later versions of Cartesian meditation whose practitioners had much less excuse than Descartes himself for embracing it. Above all, Comte's target is what he takes to be in his day its most influential version, namely, the "spiritualistic" psychology of Eclectics like Royer-Collard, Jouffroy, and especially Cousin.[11] His argument that their discipline is really a pseudoscience appears early and continues unchanged throughout his career.[12]

To appreciate the strength and seriousness of Comte's opposition to Cousin's psychology, one need only look to the philosophy it is associated with and to the role it plays there. Cousin – six years Comte's senior and the dominant philosophical figure in France during precisely the years when Comte was struggling, with little means and no university position, to write his *Cours* – espoused an "Eclecticism" that combines the allegedly "partial truths" of sensationalist, skeptical, idealist, and mystical viewpoints.[13] For Comte it is bad enough that this excessively respectful hodgepodge of dated ideas is so influential; what makes the situation truly intolerable is that Cousin promotes his ideas in the very language of the emerging positive sciences for which he otherwise shows little concern. Thus, in what Comte would regard as a typically deceptive passage, Cousin insists that in the search for knowledge,

> only the method of observation is to be used, but it must be applied to all facts, whatever and whenever they may be. Its accuracy lies in its impartiality, and its im-

---

11 Pierre-Paul Royer-Collard was Cousin's predecessor at the University of Paris; Théodore Jouffroy, was Cousin's student. Mill identifies this trio in ACP, 263/2. J. H. Bridges names the same three in *The Unity of Comte's Life and Doctrine*, 61. As Lucien Lévy-Bruhl indicates, Comte's critique is also indirectly a response to views of Condillac, the French Idéologues (especially Destutt de Tracy), and Reid and the Scottish school. See *The Philosophy of Auguste Comte*, trans. Kathleen de Beaumont-Klein (New York: G. P. Putnam's Sons, 1903), 189–94; and *History of Modern Philosophy in France*, trans. G. Coblence and W. H. Carruth (London: Kegan Paul, Trench, and Trübner, 1899), 373–75. On the linkage between the Scottish school and Cousin, see Fred Wilson, "Mill and Comte on the Method of Introspection," *Journal of the History of the Behavioral Sciences* 27 (1991), 108–12.
12 In addition to CPP, the main sources are SPP and an early article [*Journal de Paris* (1828)], "Examen du traité de Broussais sur l'irritation," reprinted SPP4a, 217–29/645–53. Comte's earliest expression of opposition to interior observation as contradictory seems to be in a letter to Pierre Valat (Sept. 24, 1819), *Lettres d'Auguste Comte à M. Valat* (Paris: Dunod, 1870), 89–90. "Idéologie" is there lumped together with "[systematic] logic and metaphysics" as hopelessly a priori and incapable of being receptive to the observation of facts (90–91). On Comte's evaluations of both Destutt de Tracy's ideology and Broussais, see Pickering, PIC, 153–58 and 406–12, respectively.
13 On Cousin's career, see George Boas, *French Philosophies of the Romantic Period* (Baltimore: Johns Hopkins Press, 1925), 197–253. On Comte's negative perception of Cousin generally, see W. M. Simon, "The 'Two Cultures' in Nineteenth-Century France: Victor Cousin and Auguste Comte," *Journal of the History of Ideas* 26 (1965), 45–58; and Lévy-Bruhl, *History of Modern Philosophy*, 323, 332–41.

partiality is to be found in its extension. Thus, perhaps, may come about the long-sought alliance of metaphysical and physical sciences...[which would] satisfy the conditions of the [experimental and sensationalist] spirit of the 18th Century and yet also the higher needs of human nature which are facts themselves, just as unquestionable and pressing as any others.[14]

In this heady mixture of incompatible ingredients, old-fashioned code words (for example, "metaphysical science," "higher needs") are given renewed legitimacy through their association with the language of experimental research (for example, "observation," "fact," unity of method); and according to Cousin, the foundational discipline for the new system is psychology.

There is no question, says Cousin, that Bacon is right about knowledge depending upon the "experimental method." Bacon, however, misconceives this method by restricting its use to the material world and to external observation. The "world of consciousness," Cousin insists, contains "facts" no less "observable" than natural ones, provided that one properly understands the "psychological method" by which we gain access to them. This method

> consists in entirely withdrawing into and explicitly familiarizing oneself with the world of consciousness, where everything is real but...so diverse and full of subtlety; and a talent for the psychological consists in situating oneself within this inner world, acquainting oneself with the spectacle there displayed, and freely and clearly reproducing all the facts which life's circumstances only bring us fortuitously and in confusion.[15]

Psychologically acquainting oneself with the "spectacle" of all these inner facts, Cousin says somewhere, is the philosophical equivalent of measuring nature with instruments.

In Comte's view, however, once one has detected the unscientific purpose behind all this scientific public relations, there is no hiding the essentially "sophistical" character of Cousin's so-called psychological method. Certainly it is no accident that advocates of this method describe their use of it in very unexperimental-sounding terms as permitting them to take up the viewpoint of "personal existence." Nor is it surprising that they also show no interest in coordinating their findings with those of other legitimate sciences. For after all, as Cousin himself explains, his aim is not to dwell on "sensation and the notions it either furnishes or combines with to constitute an actual order of phenomena in our consciousness" but rather to pass on to those two other "great classes" he identifies as "voluntary and rational facts." Indeed, Cousin's real point of starting with psy-

---

14 *Fragmens* [sic] *philosophiques* (Paris: A. Sautelet, 1826), x–xi.
15 *Fragmens philosophiques*, xii. On the influence of Descartes' idea of rational intuition on Cousin's concept of psychological observation, see Cousin's "Sur le vrai sens du 'cogito, ergo sum,'" *Archives philosophiques, politiques et littéraires* 3 (1818), 316–25 [reprinted in *Fragmens philosophiques*, 312–22]. Cousin renders "cogito" as "personal existence" at 322–23 [320]. On Comte's opposition to Cousin's psychology, see Wilson, "Mill and Comte on the Method....," 110–15.

chology has nothing to do with facilitating experimental natural science; his destination is "ontology." It is a "fact," he assures us, one

> attested to by observation, that in the same consciousness where there is nothing but phenomena, one also finds notions which in their regular course of unfolding pass the limits of consciousness and yet reach real beings (*atteint des existences*). Would you stop the unfolding of these notions? Then you would arbitrarily limit the import of a fact . . . [and] weaken the authority of all other facts. Either one questions the authority of consciousness as such or one follows it unreservedly . . . even through to ontology.[16]

The scientifically regressive character of this sort of talk, argues Comte, must be clearly exposed. For given such license to speculate "beyond consciousness," Cousin and his followers have no trouble imagining that they are able to encounter any number of non-sensual "real beings" – most notably the Ego, or immaterial substance in terms of which the comings and goings of the phenomena of consciousness are explained, and God. At the same time, it is certainly not surprising that they should try to hide what they are doing. For today, Comte asserts, the Baconian imperative has

> acquired so great a hold even over those minds that are least familiar with its immense development that the metaphysicians devoted to the study of the intellect could only hope to arrest the decay of their so-called science by changing their attitude and presenting their doctrines as also founded upon the observation of facts. With great subtlety, they now try to distinguish two equally important kinds of observation, the one exterior, the other interior, the latter being devoted solely to the study of intellectual phenomena.[17].

In short, Eclecticism is a fraud. Its founding science is no science at all; and the job of the positive philosopher is therefore to rid the current scene of this throwback activity by discrediting the supposed method it employs.

2. Interior observation: Comte's anti-metaphysical critique

One can find in Comte's writings three kinds of objection to interior observation, which I will discuss here in ascending order of importance. In objections of the first two sorts, Comte attacks Cousin's "psychological method" the same way he does Descartes' meditation, namely, by moving to discredit its results. In his third and fundamental objection, Comte argues instead against the method's very possibility.

Comte's first and weakest objection is empirical and ad hominem. As a matter of historical fact, he asserts, prescientific thinking about human beings generally and human minds specifically has simply been overtaken by events. With the

16 *Fragmens philosophiques*, xiv.
17 CPP1(1), 34–35 [F, 20].

rapid rise of the positive sciences, "metaphysicians have passed from a state of domination to one of protestation."[18] Nowhere is this more clearly the case than in connection with their promotion of rationalistic doctrines of the soul. Taking advantage of the still incomplete state of genuinely scientific knowledge of human beings, metaphysicians claim to use interior observation to obtain knowledge of those most complex aspects of human life that science has so far cautiously refrained from saying it understands. The bankruptcy of their claims, however, is already demonstrated by their failure to reach agreement on a single internally observed discovery. After 2,000 years, says Comte with characteristic exaggeration,

> they are, even today, still divided into a multitude of schools incessantly disputing the first elements of their doctrines. In fact, interior observation gives rise to almost as many opinions as there are so-called observers.[19]

One might object, of course, that this argument "proves" nothing. Given what has in fact been the case, Comte is permitted to be suspicious; but he cannot conclude that no agreement will ever come. Yet this objection, I think, misses Comte's real point. What is important is whom Cousin et al. are being associated with, namely, two millennia of metaphysics, not the few decades of nascent human science. The crucial phrasing in the passage has these psychologists still disputing "*first* elements." After all this time, *nothing* has been agreed on. What one is supposed to suspect is not that interior observation may never be intersubjectively reliable, but that there is really no method here at all.[20]

Comte's second objection is more substantive. He attacks interior observation by discrediting the Cartesian-inspired idea that this method can pursue its course without reference to any other sciences. Adherence to this idea, says Comte, leads Cousin's psychologists to see the relation between the study of human beings and the study of the rest of the world's phenomena backward. Instead of basing the study of higher-order functions on knowledge of their physical and biological conditions, they claim access to knowledge of the mind (for example, in regard to rational freedom, or selfhood, or immaterial existence) that is independent of and in some cases even overrides the evidence of the physical and biological.

Comte's position here is the familiar and popular one he bequeathed to later positivism. The whole system of the sciences is hierarchically arranged such that the studies of relatively more complex phenomena depend for their most general

18 CPP3(45), 770 [L, 183].
19 CPP1(1), 37 [F, 21–22].
20 In the only two recent papers on the Comte–Mill dispute, both authors miss this point and ask seriously whether Comte really shows that interior observation is too unreliable to be scientifically useful. See Wilson, "Mill and Comte on the Method...," 118–20; and Thomas Heyd, "Mill and Comte on Psychology," *Journal of the History of the Behavioral Sciences* 25 (1989), 129. Both Wilson and Heyd think Comte's topic is introspection, even though both acknowledge at some point that his main target is Cousin.

laws on the studies of the relatively simpler ones.[21] Given that human beings are the most complex phenomena of all, the more species-specific anatomical, physiological, and finally sociological study of them must come (and historically is coming) last. Hence, knowledge of human beings generally and of the "logical laws" of their mental activities specifically must be founded on and developed consistently with prior knowledge in physics, chemistry, and plant and animal biology. Real knowledge of the mind will then come from "static" studies of our organic conditions together with "dynamic" studies of the actions and interactions these conditions permit.[22] Of course, these studies actually include much that passes for psychology today – much that justifies its claim to be both a physiological and a behavioral science. Comte, however, recognizes no such "positive" reference for the term.

> Abandoning as useless the self-inspecting process, [science] subordinates all theories of mind to the positive study of collective human evolution, because it is only here that mental phenomena can display their true character.[23]

Here as elsewhere, Comte may seem for his time much more behaviorist about the scientific study of human beings than almost everyone else. This is, however, a misleading way to put the matter, because it distorts Comte's motivation. He pictures his positive studies of mental phenomena as relying on empirical observation of "external facts" *rather than* on the mind's imagined inspection of its ontological "nature." In his day, this leaves room only for anatomy and physiology (including, for him, phrenology), on the one hand, and "social physics," on the other.[24]

21 CPP1(2), 70–115 [F, 42–67]; DEP, 97–103/153–66; and SPP1, 33–45/26–35. The "social physics" [after 1839, "sociology," CPP4(200–201)] that Comte makes the fifth (or sixth) basic science after the four (or five) already established disciplines of (mathematics,) astronomy, physics, chemistry, and physiology (later, biology) is conceived like our "social sciences," not our sociology proper. See, e.g., Raymond Aron, *Main Currents in Sociological Thought*, Vol. 1, trans. Richard Howard and Helen Weaver (Garden City, NY: Doubleday, 1968), 73–143. An even earlier listing by Comte of the basic sciences (astronomy, physics, mechanics, chemistry, physiology, positive politics) appears in an unpublished paper dating from 1819 (Pickering, PIC, 149, 338).
22 CPP3(43/45), 612–14/769–88; and CPP6(58/59), 692–96/815–17. On the famous static-dynamic distinction, Comte cites Henri Marie Ducrotay de Blainville [*De l'organisation des animaux; ou, principes d'anatomie comparée* (Paris: Levrault, 1822)], CPP1(1), 32–33 [F, 19]. On Comte's scientific debts to but also serious socio-political criticisms of Blainville, see Henri Gouhier, "Blainville et Comte," in *La philosophie d'Auguste Comte: Esquisses* (Paris: J. Vrin, 1987), 165–78.
23 SPP1, 709/573; cf. CPP1(1), 39–40 [F, 23]. See Lévy-Bruhl, *The Philosophy of Auguste Comte*, 189. Heyd ("Mill and Comte on Psychology," 134–35) reduces this to a merely "pragmatic" consideration involving the avoidance of a misleading word; but this interpretation would make sense only if Comte actually understood (as he did not) that there was something else to which the label might be, yet on balance should not be, applied.
24 George Henry Lewes is typical of Comte's early followers in failing to face squarely Comte's refusal to acknowledge any legitimate "psychology." In his influential *Comte's Philosophy of Science: Being an Exposition of the Principles of the 'Cours de philosophie positive' of Auguste Comte* (London: Henry G. Bohn, 1853), Lewes, appealing to Comte's *Système* rather than to the *Cours*, argues that there can indeed be a Comtean psychology, viz., a creative transformation of Franz Josef Gall's brain physiology (213–32). But Comte in fact refuses to call Gall's work "psychology" precisely because its

On Comte's view, however, Cousin and his school have good reason to ignore the scientific arrangement of study. Comte observes that before the rise of science, all the warring theological and metaphysical schools,

> in spite of the innumerable profound [doctrinal] differences by which they cancel each other out, at least agreed on the one basic point of conceiving the study of man as primary and the study of the external world as secondary – mostly neglecting the latter almost entirely.[25]

This tendency is still present even, for example, in the structure of so late a work as Descartes' *Meditations*, where knowledge of mind and God are secured first and become the foundation for the study of nature. According to Comte, this arrangement of topics is symptomatic of deeper commitments. Behind the three Cartesian doctrines of thinking ego, nondeceiving God, and extended substance there lies the all too obviously theological conception of their relationship, according to which human beings are God's special creatures, possessing immortal souls, and the rest of nature (including our own bodies) constitutes our material and merely temporary surroundings.

For Comte, then, the fundamental trouble with Cartesian-inspired psychology is not that it is bad science but rather that it is not and cannot ever be science at all. No method that bases its claim to legitimacy on the presumed specialness of human beings is ever going to furnish any positive knowledge. In fact, says Comte, scientific advances have already placed the transparently nonscientific motivation behind such claims beyond question.

> The case of animals is the reef on which all psychological theories have foundered, because the naturalists have forced metaphysicians to abandon the strange expedient imagined by Descartes [that animals are soulless machines] and to admit that animals, at least in the upper parts of the zoological scale, display most of our affective and even intellectual faculties, with mere differences of degree – a fact which no one today dares to deny and which, quite apart from any other consideration, is enough to demonstrate the absurdity of [psychological] theories.[26]

---

object is physiological, not "psychic." Moreover, Lewes' defense distorts in this way the fact that Comte's mental science is at least as much behavioral and sociological as it is physiological (for example, CPP1(1), 33 [F, 19–20]; and SPP1, 708–709/572–73). In a later piece Lewes, now under the influence of Mill and Littré, concludes that "internal observation" is a legitimate scientific method after all. At the same time, he retracts his earlier opinion and agrees, with Comte and against Mill and Littré, that the study of the mind must be thought of as a branch of biology rather than as a separate basic science because psychic phenomena are "neural processes," i.e., one feature of "living" things; and if they were afforded special independent status, that would encourage the old "unscientific farrago about le Moi" ["Comte and Mill," *Fortnightly Review* 6 (1866), 389–91]. But again, if psychic phenomena are simply one class of biological facts, then their manner of observation must in principle be the same as for all biological phenomena, and there is still no justification for anything like Lewes' special "inner" kind.

25 CPP3(40), 271–72 [A, 110–11]. Since, as is discussed later in this chapter, Comte's conception of "*l'homme*" is in fact anything but gender neutral, when I quote him directly I leave the implied sexism unmodified.

26 CPP3(45), 774 [M1, 461]; cf. CPP6(60), 846–47 [A, 213–14].

In desperation, latter-day Cartesians like Cousin cling to doctrines that have already been scientifically discredited. Preoccupied with the "higher" powers of mature, healthy human adults, they ignore the advancing studies of abnormal, pathological, and less developed states; they continue to insist that intellect is more important in life than affect when the truth is clearly the reverse; and they explain the unity of human experiences by means of metaphysical theories of the ego or substantial self when the facts show that this unity is actually grounded in a sense of bodily "equilibrium" already possessed by lower species.[27]

In the old days, of course, these thinkers were called "rational psychologists," and they could appeal openly to religious faith and promote their dogmas about the soul with minimal interference from empirical challenge. But times have changed, and they know that their claims must now at least sound scientific. Fearing that their traditional, self-gratifying beliefs about our unique possession of intelligence and free will are being undermined, they lay claim to a special observational "method" of their own and at the same time encourage adoption of the most crudely mechanistic theories about "mere" animal instinct, hoping thereby to legitimate their rejection of the relevance of animal studies to their own work on the grounds that facts about brutes can tell us little about humans.[28] But that strategy, says Comte, is mere pretense. Psychology's prescientific bias is fixed, and it has a "method" only in the sense that it promotes its theologico-metaphysical doctrines any way it can.

In retrospect, however, there might seem to be this obvious rejoinder. Granted that no "observation" can be taken seriously if, as Comte asserts of Cousinian psychology, it claims to "know" a thing in ways that empirical research can neither confirm nor be permitted to contradict. But what if this bias were removed? Might it still not be possible to transform Cartesian meditation into pure, unadulterated self-observation? After all, discrediting the alleged results of meditation can at most make us suspicious of the procedure; it does not establish that nothing can come from its future use. Why does Comte not even consider this?

Comte's third and most important criticism covers this objection and goes to the heart of his opposition. The very suggestion that there are two equally legitimate kinds of observation – the one involving external objects, the other, one's own intellectual life – contains, he thinks, a "fundamental sophism." In Comte's

---

27 As Wilson explains, one finds here Comte's motivation for turning to the phrenologists after rejecting Cousin. Where Cousin promotes a metaphysical basis for conscious phenomena, researchers like Gall insist upon a physiological one ("Mill and Comte on Method...," 112–15). See also Pickering, PIC, 597–601.
28 CPP3(45), 778–85 [M1, 462–66]; cf. CPP3(43), 618–19. Comte traces the "gratuitous" opposition to theories of human instincts to Descartes, and it is hard to ignore the irony here. Within 15 years of Descartes' death, his works were all on his church's index of forbidden books – for, among other things, daring to extend the mechanistic hypothesis to *human* bodies. By Comte's time, however, the fact that Descartes was willing to extend the latest scientific conceptions only to human *bodies* is read as the last vestige of a religious agenda.

view, so-called interior observation is not just hard to accomplish or prone to bias; it is impossible. Belief in such an operation involves a refusal to face the fact that, "by inevitable necessity, the human mind can observe all phenomena directly, except its own."[29]

That Comte thought the battle against psychology must make this impossibility its "primary consideration" is already clear in his 1828 essay on Broussais. Calling him the "founder of positive pathology," Comte lauds Broussais for having produced antipsychological arguments essentially like the two just discussed. He concludes, however, that Broussais did not draw out sufficiently the radical contrast between physiology and psychology – that is, as a contrast between what is and what is not science – that his own arguments imply. Above all, Broussais should have dealt with the issue "still more directly" and "proved that interior observation is necessarily impossible."[30] Comte's clearest account of his proof appears in the first Lesson of his *Cours*. To see the impossibility of interior observation, he argues, all one has to do is consider carefully what it would actually have to involve to "observe" one's own thinking process while it is going on. Then it becomes obvious that

> The thinking individual cannot cut himself in two – one of the parts reasoning, while the other is looking on. Since in this case the organ observed and the observing organ are identical, how could any observation be made?
>
> The principle of this so-called psychological method is therefore entirely worthless. Besides, consider to what thoroughly contradictory proceedings it immediately leads! On the one hand, you are recommended to isolate yourself as far as possible from the outer world, and you must especially give up all intellectual work; for if you were engaged in making only the simplest calculation, what would become of *interior* observation? On the other hand, after having, by means of due precautions, at last attained this perfect state of intellectual slumber, you must then occupy yourself in contemplating the operations that will be taking place in a mind supposed to

---

29 CPP1(1), 35 [F, 20–21]. It appears that Comte's impossibility claim is not taken very seriously by either Heyd or Wilson because both follow Mill in assuming that the topic must be introspection and that this operation at least exists, even if there are problems about its reliability. Heyd is actually disappointed that Mill bothers to make the impossibility claim Comte's primary one ("Mill and Comte on Psychology," 129).

30 SPP4a, 219/647. Comte is discussing François Joseph Victor Broussais, *De l'irritation et de la folie, ouvrage dans lequel les rapports du physique et du moral sont établis sur les bases de la médecine physiologique* (Paris: Delaunay, 1828), xi–xx; and Ch. 5 (133–35 is loosely quoted, ibid.). See also LMC, VII (June 19, 1842), 75. Pierre Macherey has recently claimed that Comte's September 1819 letter to Valat (see fn. 12) suggests the influence of Louis de Bonald's *Recherches philosophiques, sur les premiers objets des connaissances morales* [2 vols. (Paris: Adrien Le Clere, 1818), esp. I, Ch. 1] on Comte's critique of psychology [*Comte. La philosophie et les sciences* (Paris: Presses Universitaires de France, 1989), 50–55]. Comte may have been familiar with this work (see Pickering, PIC, 157), but the possibility of influence seems unlikely, given that de Bonald opposes the Idéologues' psychology on religious grounds, not out of any specific misgivings about interior observation. Their psychology is sensationalistic, de Bonald argues, and sensationalism, by giving our ideas a material origin, violates the fundamental principle that reason is a function of the immaterial soul rather than our bodily organs (*Recherches*, I, 296–315).

be blank! Our descendants will no doubt see such pretensions ridiculed on the stage some day.[31]

When "self-observation" is defined in this way, it is, of course, logically contradictory. Yet Comte's argument clearly turns on a conception of observation whose problematic character he does not consider. I will return to this matter shortly. First, however, we must see how Comte does try to meet another sort of objection, namely, that even if we limit ourselves to the sort of evidence that Comte himself would consider scientific, we do not in fact seem to be entirely without access to our inner lives. This objection, Comte replies, rests on a confusion between physiological and psychological knowledge. Admittedly,

> a man can observe the passions which animate him, for the anatomical reason that the organs which are their seat are distinct from those whose functions are devoted to observation. . . . [B]ut such observations would clearly never have much scientific value. The best way of knowing the passions will always be to observe them from the outside; for a person in any state of extreme passion – that is, in precisely the state it is most essential to examine – would necessarily be incapacitated for observing himself.[32]

In other words, the fact that I can have knowledge of my feelings and desires is no evidence of *self*-knowledge – that is, of knowledge of one of Cousin's "rational facts" – at all. It is evidence only of the possibility of my observing, among other objects in the world, my own body and at least some of its actions. Yet even this possibility is not empirically very significant, since such observing tends to be least objective at precisely the moments when there is the most to see.

Comte's idea here of the "best way of knowing" has, of course, its own serious problems; and one may be tempted at this point to settle his case by simply using the work of the intervening 150 years against him. As I have already suggested in the Introduction, however, I am no friend of the forced option between "Was he right by current standards?" and "Is he historically interesting?" I propose, therefore, to delay the question of how we should now respond to Comte's idea. Instead, I want to identify one central problem connected with it – in order, on the one hand, to prepare for the discussion of Mill's critique of Comte and, on the other, to show that Comte's idea, even by today's standards, is at least no mere muddle.

The most obvious problem with Comte's idea of the best way of knowing is that it rests on a somewhat loose and untechnical notion of observation and its "objects." In Comte's view, there are in science "four modes of the art of obser-

---

31 CPP(1), 36–37 [F, 21], Comte's emphasis; see also CPP3(45), 774–76 [M1, 461–62].
32 CPP1(1), 35 [F, 21]. Comte's language, both here and in the last cited passage, closely follows SPP4a, 219/647. I agree with Wilson that trying to make Comte a materialist, or any other kind of consistent ontologist, on the basis of passages like this one is "doing him a favor" ("Mill and Comte on Introspection," 109). In fact, and for historico-critical reasons that we will see later are perhaps not bad ones, Comte never engages in the kind of ontological investigations that might settle what "reality" is.

vation," namely, observation proper, experimentation, comparison, and the "historical method."³³ Each method, though present to some degree in all the sciences, predominates in that science or group of sciences for whose objects it is most suited. As for these objects themselves, Comte's position is also not a highly technical one. Mass and molecular structure are called objects of observation, but so are the familiar phenomena of our everyday surroundings. In astronomy, for example, observation proper (instrument-aided, of course, and also dominated by one of our senses) is the most suitable procedure, and stars and planets are its objects. Similarly, Comte expects sociological observation to be typically "comparative," that is, to range across cultures and historical periods, juxtaposing and contrasting such "social facts" as customs, languages, and monuments. Comte is not completely consistent about the number of modes of observation. In earlier volumes of the *Cours*, he says there are three (namely, observation proper, experimentation, and comparison); but in his discussion of sociology, he characterizes the historical method (that is, the "comparison of the various consecutive states of humanity") both as the "last part of the comparative method" and as a separate "fourth mode" that forms the "very basis" of sociology as a science.³⁴ In any case, the historical method is what Comte employs to establish his own famous three-stage law, and among the objects it studies are thus the theological, metaphysical, and scientific stages themselves, along with their distinctive "methods of philosophizing."

This seemingly untechnical conception of observation is not merely a function of its nineteenth-century origins or Comte's naiveté. Comte has definite epistemic views that make him an opponent of later, more sophisticated kinds of analysis. For one thing, as we shall see in Chapter 2, Comte opposes any formalization of the logic of inquiry, in part because the determination of what constitutes genuine observation depends crucially for him on which science one is talking about, what it studies, and even the degree to which that science has developed toward a positive state. From this viewpoint, any foundationalist/reconstructivist move to fix either ontologically What Science Studies or epistemologically How It Does So appears regressive – and perhaps even, with its totalizing aspirations, suspiciously metaphysical.

Moreover, as famous as Comte is for the slogan that "there can be no real knowledge except that which rests upon observed facts," his positivism is not straightforwardly empiricist.³⁵ It is, to be sure, an antispeculative position – one

---

33 Cf. CPP1(1/2), 8–9/108 [F, 4–5/63–64]; CPP2(19/28), 7–8, 19–21/403–407 [A, 74, 78–79/88–89]; CPP3(40), 313–58 [M1, 366–78]; CPP4(48), 412–69 [A, 178–98].
34 CPP4(48), 449–68 [A, 192–98]. Comte's fourth mode is Mill's model for the "inverse deductive" method in social science. See Mill's *Logic*, VI, x, pars. 4–8. On January 28, 1843, Mill wrote Comte to say that he was holding up publication of his *Logic* until he could revise Book VI in accordance with his reading of Volume VI of Comte's *Cours*, which had just come out (LMC, XXII, 153–54). See also Mill's *Autobiography*, 217–19.
35 For the Comtean slogan, see, e.g., CPP1(1), 8, 34 [F, 8, 20]. As M. J. Hawkins rightly insists, Comte neither reduces observation to "the recording and organization of sensory impressions"

that labels all of reason's efforts to transcend sense "mysticism." Contrary to long-standing opinion, however, Comte is just as unsympathetic to the "[mere] empiricism" of eighteenth-century thinkers like Condillac, according to which thought is simply transformed sensation.[36] Though it would be misleading to press the comparison very far, Comte is, on this issue, like Kant – that is, he thinks the trouble with both mysticism and empiricism is that they do not appreciate the inseparability of sense and reason. Even in prescientific times, according to one of Comte's favorite images, sense and reason work together in human affairs to solve what would otherwise amount to a vicious circle of our being either without facts to guide theory or without theory to inform facts.

I will have more to say later about the surprising deviance of Comte's epistemic views from what one expects in a positivist. For now, however, I note only that his inseparability thesis clearly affects his concept of observation, namely, by prompting Comte to construe all four methods of scientific observation as simply "perfections and extensions" of ordinary practices.[37] Scientific knowledge is not more but differently dependent on sense and is not less but differently "speculative." On the one hand, all of us encounter sensually our natural and social surroundings; scientists, however, are guided in their encounters not by feelings or imaginings of what *must* be there, but rather by the idea of directly examining what is "phenomenally" present (as in observation proper), or what results from circumstances artificially modified by us (in experimentation), or what forms part of a series of analogous or consecutive cases (in comparison or with the historical method), and so on. On the other hand, all of us produce explanations of what we encounter; but scientific explanations are better ones because, instead of let-

---

nor subordinates reason to sensation ["Reason and Sense Perception in Comte's Theory of Mind," *History of European Ideas* 5 (1984), 149–51, 153–55, 159–60]. Unhappily, Hawkins himself reduces observation to "having sensations" and is thus forced to conclude that for Comte, sensations are always "contaminated by the psychic [sc., intellectual] predispositions of the perceiving subject" (154). In fact, Comte's epistemology is common sense, French Enlightenment realist to the core. See Heyd, "Mill and Comte on Psychology," 130–31; Craig Dilworth, "Empiricism vs. Realism: High Points in the Debate during the Past 150 Years," *Studies in the History and Philosophy of Science* 21 (1990), 431–34; and H. B. Acton, "Comte's Positivism and the Science of Society," *Philosophy* 26 (1951), 293–97. Acton suspects, as I do, that a sensationalist/phenomenalist picture of Comte derives from too much reading of him secondhand through Mill.

36 CPP3(43), 626–27. For samples of this influential but mistaken opinion, cf. Carnap, "Testability and Meaning," *Philosophy of Science* 3 (1936), 420; and Roy Wood Sellars, "Positivism in Contemporary Philosophic Thought," *American Sociological Review* 4 (1939), 26–27. See also C. S. Peirce, ["Critique of Positivism"], reprinted in *Writings of Charles Sanders Peirce: A Chronological Edition*, Vol. 2 (Bloomington: Indiana University Press, 1984), 126–29, which may have influenced Jürgen Habermas in *Knowledge and Human Interests*, trans. Jeremy J. Shapiro (Boston: Beacon Press, 1971), 74–75.

37 On this point, though not on the nature of observation itself, cf. Dewey, for whom "the rudimentary prototype of experimental doing for the sake of knowing is found in ordinary procedures" that are "reinforced," not rejected or suppressed, by science [*The Quest for Certainty: A Study of the Relation of Knowledge and Action, Later Works, 1925–1953*, Vol. 4: *1929* (Carbondale: Southern Illinois University Press, 1984), 70]. Comte, however, would reject Dewey's further claim that when life starts to be construed as filled with "problems," this utterly transforms the spirit, even if it reinforces the type, of practices that occur before science.

ting their encounters be informed by common prejudice and superstition, scientists

> only employ observations that are attached, at least hypothetically, to some law; it is *this connection* that constitutes the principal difference between the observations of scientists and those of the common man.[38]

Finally, since this "connection" between direct examination and hypothesis varies across the special sciences according to the method employed, phenomenal findings, and laws deemed fitting, "observation" and "object" are not univocal epistemic terms. They must always be understood in relation to some specific scientific context and circumstances – or as we might say, pragmatically.

Yet whatever epistemic revisions may, happily or unhappily, have been made since Comte – for example, whatever may have been done to make observation a more rigorously scientific notion – two closely related assumptions about it have passed through to us like unchanged themes to be varied. Observation is always directed *away from itself* and toward something else; and that something (object, phenomenon) is best (or perhaps even only) known in terms of its *presentation* to an observer. These ideas are, of course, part of the familiar modern tale of subjects and objects: To be an observer is to be occupied elsewhere, with what is over against and external to us. To observe, one says, is to be "attentive," stimulated by and receptive to whatever is there. To be an object is to be what is there for the attentive observer. These are the twin themes – quite straightforward assumptions about the third-person point of view – on which Comte's argument centrally depends; and this is so, moreover, not only because Comte himself accepts these assumptions but also because Cousin and his associates, in describing the operation of the supposedly inner-directed version of the already acceptable outwardly oriented procedure, accept them, too. Thus if, as Comte puts it, one performs even the "simplest calculation" and tries to consider it, then it is not oneself but the calculated thing that is in view, and "What becomes of interior [that is, not externally directed] observation?" is already a rhetorical question. This, of course, is also the point of Comte's remark about potential self-observers having to have "blank [that is, attentive and receptive] minds." In both cases "interiority" is exactly what an observer, by definition, cannot be caring about. Though Comte does not do so, it is useful to consider his arguments in light of Kant's Paralogisms. "Observing the Observer" is fatally equivocal.

A final note of caution: Close reading of the passages quoted earlier may seem

---

38 CPP4(48), 418–19 [A, 181], et seqq.; my emphasis. Cf. SPP1, 711–13/575–76, where Comte, having noted that "all the positive studies show the radical vacuity of the traditional separation of observation and reason," says that because science is "only a prolongation for special purposes" of spontaneous common sense, it "offers a clearer and logically developed illustration of ordinary rational processes" in action. On the inseparability of theory and observation in Comtean science generally, see CPP2(28), 433–52 [L, 146–51]; and Larry Laudan, "Towards a Reassessment of Comte's 'Méthode Positive,'" in *Science and Hypothesis: Historical Essays on Scientific Methodology* (Dordrecht: D. Reidel, 1981), 145–56.

to imply that Comte's critique also rests on two ancillary principles, namely, (a) that observation is passive and (b) that objects must be in some way active to be observed. After all, Comte does say that the observer must "give up all intellectual work" and that the mind that is supposed to be observed must be engaging in "operations." In fact, however, neither (a) nor (b) is a characteristically Comtean assumption; moreover, even if Comte is inconsistent about them, this makes no difference to the fundamental issue of what it takes for interior observation to be impossible.

As regards (a), it is clearly not Comte's considered view that observers are inactive, let alone (and even allowing for metaphorical license) in a "perfect state of intellectual slumber." "Experimenting" and "comparing," for example, are kinds of observings, but it makes no sense to think of these as slumbering conditions. Moreover, Comtean physiology calls the observation of objects and events, respectively, the two modes of "contemplation," which, Comte says, is no merely passive registration of sensations but involves recognition of objects ("not mere phenomena") in terms of "real, though particular notions" and "general, but more or less artificial, concepts."[39]

As regards (b), it seems clear that Comte does not generally hold this to be true, either. After all, historical periods, monuments, and various anatomical, physiological, and social structures are all observable objects for him, but they hardly qualify as in any straightforward sense active. Moreover, the idea that all observed objects must somehow be "in operation" is incompatible with Comte's claim that there are *static* as well as dynamic scientific studies.

On this issue, therefore, my own suggestion is that one think of Comte's occasional use (or misuse) of the old metaphors of passivity and activity as responsive mainly to their prior employment in the writings of his enemies, and thus as incidental to his explicit and unwavering view of observation as directed away from itself and toward something else. Read this way, whatever one assumes about his various characterizations of the mechanics of this operation, his case against interior observation as such does not suffer. For once it is settled that observation is always occupied elsewhere, observing the observer is by definition impossible.

Here, then, we have Comte's central argument. Interior observation, the last variation on the theme of Cartesian meditation, is not just difficult, disappointing, or biased. It is an illusion. All it has ever produced are theologico-metaphysical doctrines of the soul and bad epistemology; and now it merely impedes the development of the kinds of study that will complete the scientific hierarchy by furnishing us with knowledge of human beings that is as reliable as the knowledge of nature we are already beginning to obtain. For someone like Comte, whose fundamental aim is to advance these human sciences for the sake of the sociopolitical reorganization they will make possible, interior observation is

---

39 SPP1, 718–19/580–81. When reading phrases like "contemplating the operations . . . taking place in a mind supposed to be blank" (CPP1(1), 36–37 [F, 21]), it is useful to know also that, as in English, "contempler" means to gaze at, behold, even look at thoughtfully, not just contemplate.

therefore a most important enemy. Indeed, Gouhier exaggerates only slightly in calling Comte's refusal not just to make use of "the facts given in interior experience" but to accord any meaning to the very idea of such experience "the point of departure" for his entire position.[40] Comte believes that with interior observation discredited, the pseudoscience of psychology can be eliminated, and we will then be left, on the one hand, with logic, mathematics, and the natural and social sciences and, on the other hand, with the task of analyzing and defending the historical development, nature, and use of these sciences. Straddling traditional and contemporary terminologies, Comte calls both sets of activities together positive "philosophy."

3. Introspection: Mill's methodological defense

Comte's efforts to prove the impossibility of interior observation, though widely known, appear to have convinced almost no one. Few joined, or even appear to have understood, his crusade against old-fashioned rational psychology, and those who played key roles in interpreting the Comte–Mill controversy clearly had more sympathy for Mill. In Germany, no one of any stature spoke flatly against interior observation (however defined), let alone argued for its impossibility; and after Brentano, who took the position that Comte had simply conflated the very real "inner perception" with an impossible "inner observation," even those who were unsympathetic to Mill's kind of psychology gave the operation some credit.[41] In France, the widely influential Ribot simply began by announcing that interior observation (sc., Jouffroy) is just as important as external observation (sc., Broussais) – indeed, is in a way "more necessary, because without it we would not even know what we are talking about."[42] In the United States,

---

40 *La philosophie d'Auguste Comte*, 9. See also Lévy-Bruhl, *The Philosophy of Auguste Comte*, 350–52.
41 See Franz Brentano, *Psychology from an Empirical Standpoint* [1874], trans. Antos C. Rancurello et al. (New York: Humanities Press, 1973), 28ff., 405ff. As Simon notes, even Mach (who, with Vaihinger, is the only direct link between Comtean and logical positivism in Germany) accepts introspective data about "psychical sensations" (*European Positivism*, 257–58). Cf. Hermann Ebbinghaus' famous defense, against Dilthey, of psychology as an explanatory natural science. Rejecting Dilthey's claim that we introspectively discover (rather than theoretically construct) the "coherence" of discrete experiences, Ebbinghaus nevertheless concedes that we do introspect these experiences themselves ["Über erklärende und beschreibende Psychologie," *Zeitschrift für Psychologie und Physiologie* 9 (1895), 192–94]. In an unpublished draft for Volume 2 of his *Einleitung in die Geisteswissenschaften* [*Selected Works*, Vol. 1: *Introduction to the Human Sciences*, trans. Rudolf A. Makkreel and Frithjof Rodi (Princeton, NJ: Princeton University Press, 1989)], Dilthey agrees with Mill that the mere fact that introspection (*Selbstbeobachtung*) exists refutes Comte's alleged claim that it is impossible (377–78); but without referring to Comte, he adds that the moral self-observation (*Selbstbetrachtung*) advocated by Stoics and Christians for rooting out character defects "is not feasible and leads only to illusions" (376). In general, his analysis of a whole family of ideas about inward turns (376–81) is much more subtle than is typical in English-speaking accounts.
42 Théodule [Armand] Ribot, *La psychologie anglaise contemporaine* (Paris: Ladrange, 1870), 30–31, and his sympathetic summary of Mill, 87ff. See also D.G. Charlton, *Positivist Thought in France during the Second Empire, 1852–70* (Oxford: Oxford University Press, 1959), 82ff.

William James spoke for the majority in simply declaring against Comte that for psychology, "introspective observation is what we have to rely on first and foremost and always."[43] Most important, however, everyone appears to have assumed with Mill that the issue Comte raises concerns the viability of an empirical method, not the unmasking of a metaphysical sham.[44]

If there is anything different about Mill's reaction to Comte, then, it lies only in its being perhaps more pointedly dismissive: "There is little need for an elaborate refutation of a fallacy respecting which the only wonder is that it should impose on anyone."[45] But Mill is concerned with more than just the silliness of Comte's proof. He insists that Comte is rejecting something scientifically important and defensible, namely, "psychological observation properly so called." As I explained in the Introduction, my ultimate purpose is to establish that this "psychological observation" is in fact something very different from Comte's interior observation, and that Mill's misinterpretation of Comte's critique shows that he understands neither its prescientific object nor its historico-polemical purpose. First, however, we must see both what it is that Mill actually defends and also why, when he is defending it, he regards himself as an opponent most particularly of Comte.

According to Mill, "psychological observation" is a quite ordinary and unmysterious operation. It is simply our capacity to be self-conscious, to attend introspectively to our own mental lives, and to give first-person reports of what we find there. "Whatever we are directly aware of," asserts Mill, "we can directly ob-

---

43 *The Principles of Psychology*, 3 vols. (Cambridge, MA: Harvard University Press, 1981), I, 185. First Brentano and then James seem to have been stimulated in their treatment of this issue by the same passages from Comte [CPP1(1), 32–40] and Mill [ACP, 296–98/62–67]. Both follow Mill in holding that direct, simultaneous "observation" ("inner perception" for Brentano, "immediate inner apprehension" for James) of mental life forms the basis of psychology as a science. Both reject Mill's associationism, but both agree with him that memory (especially shared memory leading to "consensus") plays the crucial role in making what is directly apprehended the object of disciplined study. Cf. Brentano's *Psychology*, 32–43, and James' *Principles*, I, 186–91, 194–96.

44 That this is still assumed is evidenced by the concluding sections of the two most recent – and in other respects atypically detailed – analyses of the controversy by Heyd ("Mill and Comte on Psychology," 135) and Wilson ("Mill and Comte on the Method of Introspection," 123).

45 ACP, 296/63. ACP reflects Mill's mature position: Comte's earlier, no-nonsense, epistemologically oriented *Cours* makes pioneering contributions to the philosophy of science, but his later sociopolitical writings – inspired by adoration of Clotilde de Vaux – are marked by "almost as much improvement in his feelings, as deterioration in his speculations" (332/132). Through Mill, this view became the received wisdom about Comte for English-speaking philosophers. Yet the Comte–Mill correspondence, initiated by Mill, shows him to have been at one time much more admiring of Comte's work [e.g., his first letter (November 8, 1841), LMC, 1–4]; further, although rejecting its political contents, Mill always shared Comte's idea of the possibility of a posttheological "religion" whose "psychic power and . . . social efficacy" could make civilized societies more altruistic [*Utilitarianism* (1861), *Collected Works*, Vol. 10, 232; also ACP, 334–35/137–38]. Cf. Roger N. Hancock, "A Note on J. S. Mill and the Religion of Humanity," *Mill Newsletter* 18 (1983), 11–14; John M. Robson, *The Improvement of Mankind: The Social and Political Thought of John Stuart Mill* (Toronto: Toronto University Press, 1968), 95–109; and T. R. Wright, *The Religion of Humanity*, 44–50. This point is insufficiently stressed in Simon's otherwise more thorough study of Mill's central role in promoting Comte's views, *European Positivism*, 172–95.

serve"; and this is as true of what lies within as it is of what lies without. Granted, reliance on introspective data, especially for scientific purposes, poses some "difficulties." (Mill mentions as a case in point the tendency for attention to be weakened by having to inspect several impressions at once.) Yet such difficulties do not change the fact that it is commonplace for us to perceive our own impressions, both while having them and as immediately remembered. In fact, these are the only two ways we could have "acquired the knowledge, which nobody denies us to have, of what passes in our minds."[46]

Although Mill does not mention it here, his argument relies on the considerably more detailed analysis of Bailey, who stressed above all that Comte's critique involves

> an utter misconception of the way in which the knowledge of our own mind arises, and prove[s], at the same time, the danger of indiscriminately applying to purely mental phenomena the language which originates in our perception of what is external....[47]

In Mill's discussion, it is never made entirely clear what he thinks could prompt such a misconception; but Bailey's linguistic explanation is probably Mill's own – given, of course, that both of them are already making the more general assumption that the mistake itself is a methodological one.

Mill is quite serious in claiming that all of this should be obvious. With pointed reference to Comte's remark that "intellectual slumber" would be necessary for a self to observe itself, Mill insists that despite such remarks, even

> Comte would scarcely have affirmed that we are not aware of our own intellectual operations. We know of our observings and our reasonings, either at the very time, or by memory the moment after; in either case, by direct knowledge, and not (like things done by us in a state of somnambulism) merely by their results. This simple fact destroys the whole of Comte's argument.[48]

---

46 ACP, 296–97/64. Cf. LMC, III (December 18, 1841), 43–44. For the view that introspection is possible but hard, Mill appeals to Jean-Jacques Séverin de Cardaillac [*Études élémentaires de philosophie*, 2 vols. (Paris: Firmin Didot, 1830), I, 3–11] and to William Hamilton [*Lectures on Metaphysics and Logic*, 4 vols., ed. H. L. Mansel and J. Veitch (Edinburgh: Blackwood, 1859–60), I, 254]. Cf. his *An Examination of Sir William Hamilton's Philosophy, Collected Works*, Vol. 9 (1974), esp. 138ff. Mill distinguishes here a narrowly "introspective" method from his own broader "psychological" one – marking off the former from the latter in terms of its assumption that if mental phenomena appear intuitively unanalyzable, they are considered unlearned and not the product of any associations. I ignore this technical distinction in what follows. For discussion, see Wilson, *Psychological Analysis*, 141–42, 157–60.
47 Samuel Bailey, "M. Comte on Psychology," *Letters on the Philosophy of the Human Mind*, 3rd Series (London: Longman, Green, Longman, Roberts, and Green, 1863), 1–13 (citation, 2). In a note to Bailey (January 21, 1863), Mill praises and expresses agreement with his analysis. Mill's general regard for Bailey, however, was not high; and we might surmise that this has something to do with his not being cited. Five years later (December 6, 1867), Mill complains to his friend Alexander Bain "how very, very shallow he [Bailey] is!". See *The Later Letters of John Stuart Mill, 1849–1873, Collected Works*, Vols. 14–17 (1972), v. 15, 824 (to Bailey) and v. 16, 1333–34 (to Bain).
48 ACP, 297/64. It is here, Mill notes with derision, that Comte relies on what he believes are the

But Mill's assertion here of what Comte cannot possibly deny is not telling; rather, it should put us on notice of Mill's very different agenda. According to Mill, Comte's critique of interior observation is undermined because he fails to acknowledge that we have "awareness" of our intellectual operations. But this objection is a red herring. Comte rarely even mentions and never makes a problem out of whether we can *be aware that we have* mental states.[49] The issue is whether Comte says anything about obtaining *knowledge of the laws* of these states that we should take to be directed against Mill's position. Recall what Comte opposes – namely, "so-called observations [that is, that contradictory operation described above] made on the mind, considered in itself [that is, with no reference to any "positive" science] and a priori [that is, with theologico-metaphysical ideas about Mind kept free from "naturalistic" evaluation]."[50] As we will see, the more one understands Mill's project, the clearer it becomes that none of the three topics Comte identifies in this phrase has anything to do with "introspection" or with Mill's science of "associative mental laws."

At the outset, let us remember that if Mill himself feels comfortable starting with the "simple fact" of immediate self-awareness, it is for everyone thereafter an endless source of controversy. Are "[immediate] awareness" and "direct knowledge" of our intellectual operations the same thing? Is direct knowledge of our mental activity ever simultaneous with that activity, or is it always retrospective? To the extent that it is simultaneous, and given that coexisting impressions "weaken" one's "attention," when does attention become too weak to trust? To the extent that it is retrospective, how can we be sure that memory serves us reliably here?[51] These issues themselves lie beyond the scope of the present study.

"admirably scientific" phrenologies of Gall and Johann Gaspar Spurzheim (297/65). See also the inconclusive exchange in LMC, XI (June 11, 1842), XII (June 19, 1842), and XIII (July 11, 1842) – 65–69 (Mill to Comte), 72–75 (Comte to Mill), and 79–81 (Comte to Mill), respectively.

49 Comte does say in two places that during his mental breakdown in 1826, he personally "experienced" the three stages of intellectual development, first "inversely" and then "directly" – thus "decisively confirming" the correctness of his three-stage law (CPP6, xxx; SPP3, 75–76/62–63). In both places, however, the context makes it clear that Comte is not considering the epistemic value of introspection; rather, he is doing autobiography, recounting anecdotally how he "personally" acquired a sympathetic feel for a scientific law already discovered in the usual (externally) observational manner. He calls this event a "terrible episode which enabled me thereafter to identify myself more completely with any one of the human phases in accordance with my own experience"; and he hopes that readers who are already "suitably prepared will...be able to utilize this brief account of a memorable anomaly" (75/63). For discussion and references concerning the episode itself, see Pickering, PIC, 400–403.

50 Previously cited letter of September 24, 1819, *Lettres d'Auguste Comte à M. Valat*, 90.

51 These questions reflect Henry Maudsley's views in "Recent Metaphysics," *Journal of Mental Science* 11 (1866), 542–50. In his long review of Mill's *Examination of Sir William Hamilton*, Maudsley berates him for ignoring the new "physiological method" in mental science; for "trying to do by the old method, what Plato, Descartes, Locke, Berkeley, and a host of others have not done" (548); and for thus having not only "failed in his arguments against Comte" but also "where he has deviated from that philosopher's track he has gone astray into psychological mazes, in which he wanders round and round as others have before him, making much motion but little or no progress" (550).

What is important is that we recognize that they become issues in the first place only when one has already, like Mill, construed "interior observation" as "introspection" – that is, assumed, contra Comte, that one is analyzing an actual operation for its scientific worth as a source of empirical data.

For Mill, introspection is the primary source of our knowledge of those associative mental laws that constitute the subject matter of psychology – a discipline that he conceives, analogously to Newtonian mechanics in relation to the physical sciences, as forming a basis for the sciences of human nature (that is, the "moral sciences").[52] Mill's psychology is supposed, therefore, to be scientific but not physiological. On the one hand, it is not a rational psychology but an empirical "science of mind," concerned with the study of uniformities in the succession of our inner states. Confident that he can draw and maintain this distinction without further ado, Mill simply announces that his study of the mind will

> keep clear of all speculations respecting the mind's own nature, and ... understand by the laws of mind, those of mental phenomena; of the various feelings or states of consciousness of sentient beings ... [which] consist of thoughts, emotions, volitions, and sensations; the last being as truly states of mind as the former.[53]

On the other hand, precisely because psychology (like the rest of the moral, or human, sciences) is just as interested in thoughts and feelings as in overt behavior, it cannot be a physical science. More specifically, says Mill with pointed reference to Comte, it is not part of physiology. Mill grants that some states of mind (e.g., sensations) are directly produced by bodily states and that causal explanation in such cases is, of course, in terms of physical laws. He grants also that physiological influence on all mental successions is "one of the most important departments of psychological study." He stresses, however, that we do not possess a physiology powerful enough to establish that the uniformities of successions of mental states are always merely derivative uniformities. In fact, he adds, at the present time physiology is actually a less advanced science than psychology and in certain ways is even dependent on it. For in regard to neurological states,

> our only mode of studying their successions or co-existences must be by observing the successions and co-existences of the mental states of which they are supposed to be the ... causes. The successions, therefore, which obtain among mental phenomena do not admit of being deduced from the physiological laws of our nervous sys-

---

52 SL, VI, iii. See generally Oskar Alfred Kubitz, *The Development of John Stuart Mill's System of Logic* (Urbana: University of Illinois Press, 1932), esp. 242–54; and in connection with more recent issues, Alan Ryan, *The Philosophy of John Stuart Mill*, 2nd ed. (Atlantic Highlands, NJ: Humanities Press, 1990), 149–67.
53 SL, VI, iv, 1. Mill holds that sensations themselves must be classed as mental, even though their "mechanisms of production" – viz., the body itself and external nature – are both certainly physical. Whatever opinion one forms regarding the "identity or diversity of matter and mind ... the distinction between mental and physical facts, between the internal and the external world, will always remain" (ibid.).

tem; and all real knowledge of them must continue, for a long time at least, if not always, to be sought in the direct study . . . of the mental successions themselves.[54]

It is not clear how the presence of a more successful brain science would have affected Mill's argument. Though he condemns Comte's efforts to extend physiology in the way contemplated by Gall and the phrenologists, though he also opposes those who are ready to claim a priori that psychology is reducible to physiology, and though he appears to have some doubts about the future possibility of any such reduction in fact, he nevertheless refuses to rule it out in principle. In the passage just cited, he even ventures that it is "extremely probable" that "every mental state has a nervous state for its immediate and proximate cause" – qualifying this only by adding that it remains unproved and that we are for the moment still "wholly ignorant of the characteristics of these nervous states." What does seem clear, however, is that in the actual pursuit of his inquiries, Mill treats the presence or absence of a competent physiology as irrelevant in principle to the epistemic issue of whether there can or should be "direct study . . . of the mental successions themselves."[55] And this kind of study is, of course, "introspective analysis," as already practiced by Mill's father and by Spencer and Bain.[56]

Even if, however, we now understand what Mill means by interior observation and why he values it, that still does not explain why, in the process of defending it, he is especially intent on singling out Comte from among all his potential opponents. His Comte commentary gives us part of the answer; the *Logic* and some of Mill's letters provide the rest.

In general terms, Mill appears to see in Comte the worst possible kind of antipsychologist, and for three reasons. First, Mill thinks Comte's critique is a sin of commission rather than just of omission. Instead of at least leaving open a matter he apparently knew little about, Comte

---

[54] SL, VI, iv, 2 (851).

[55] For detailed, and I think persuasive, unraveling of Mill's views on this question, see Wilson, *Psychological Analysis*, 294–311. In its three most essential features, Mill's position seems to be that even if what is now only hypothesis – viz., that there really is a thoroughgoing parallelism between mental and bodily states – turns out to be true, and even if all laws of the succession of mental states turn out to be translatable into laws about bodily states, this would not mean that introspective study of mental phenomena would be eliminated. Wilson connects his exposition of Mill with an interesting defense of the need for renewed interest in introspective analysis, especially in regard to economics and moral philosophy (344–49).

[56] SL, VI, iv, 3 (853). Mill cites the second edition (which he and Bain edited) of James Mill, *Analysis of the Phenomena of the Human Mind*, 2 vols. (London: Baldwin and Cradock, 1869); also the "striking applications of the laws of association" apparently in the first edition of Herbert Spencer, *The Principles of Psychology* (London: Longman, Green, and Longmans, 1855); and, "incomparably," Bain's *The Senses and the Intellect* (London: Parker, 1855) and *The Emotions and the Will* (London: Parker, 1859). In ACP, Mill also praises the work of David Hartley and Thomas Brown (298/66).

not only denies to psychology, or mental philosophy properly so-called, the character of a science, but places it, in the chimerical nature of its objects and pretensions, almost on a par with astrology.[57]

Second, Comte's sin is for Mill all the greater because it comes from a professed positivist. In spite of allegedly having respect for science, by refusing to avail himself of the latest associationist findings Comte manages to remain one of those who, as Mill puts it, continues to "speculate on human nature [and] prefer dogmatically to assume that the mental differences which . . . they think they perceive among human beings are ultimate facts." In Mill's eyes, Comte's particular brand of dogmatism (to which I will return in a minute) shows itself especially in his promotion of theories of individual human differences that grossly exaggerate the influence of anatomical and physiological conditions at the expense of the effect of sociocultural circumstances and education on particular individuals.[58]

Even sympathetic readers of the *Logic* might well be puzzled by Mill's intemperance here. Concerning Comte's allegedly metaphysical dogmatism, Mill asserts flatly that "no writer, either of early or of recent date, is chargeable in a higher degree with this aberration from the true scientific spirit."[59] Is it really the case that no one has ever been as "unscientific" about human nature as Comte? Suppose it is true that, regarding the study of human life, Comte fails to achieve a proper balance between biology and sociology. Is it really a greater sin to be imperfectly scientific than to be no scientist at all? To understand why Mill resorts to such hyperbolic language, one must see that he has here a third and more specific grievance against Comte that the *Logic* does not mention.

Early in their correspondence, Mill discovered that one consequence of Comte's excessive praise for physiological studies of human nature is that it allows him to indulge his prejudices concerning women. Above all, there is Comte's obvious misuse of "scientific" findings to legitimate the dominant social and political status of men. As imperfect as biology still is, writes Comte to Mill, we already have enough evidence to establish that

---

57 SL, VI, iv, 2 (850–51). Cf. Mill's letter, near the end of their period of correspondence, in which he tells Comte that his lack of familiarity with (associationist) psychology makes him unsuited to judge its worth for social science. LMC, LXXXIII (March 26, 1846), 523.

58 SL, VI, iv, 4 (858–59). Here, as typically elsewhere, Mill is silent about the social behaviorist side of Comte's view of mental phenomena. In his introduction to the *Cours*, for example, Comte sets the tone for the rest of his work in arguing for the "dynamical" study of "the actual march of the human intellect, in practice" as it has advanced toward science. "We must look upon all scientific theories as so many great logical facts," he says, because only by observing them can we obtain knowledge of the mind's "logical laws." CPP1(1), 33, 38–39 [F, 19–20, 23].

59 SL, VI, iv, 4 (859). This passage (and the other part, cited in fn. 58) appears only in later editions of Mill's *Logic* and reflects a larger practice. Many complimentary comments about Comte in the first 1842 edition were removed or watered down by the eighth edition as Mill grew more familiar with Comte's work and corresponded with him. For details, see Simon, *European Positivism*, 180–83; cf. Mill's *Autobiography*, 615–16.

both anatomically and physiologically, in virtually the entire animal kingdom and especially in our own species, the female sex is constituted in the condition of a sort of radical infancy, making it essentially inferior as regards the corresponding organic type.[60]

Against this crude simplification Mill protests, in what might seem to us the obvious vein, that to use differences in brain size and physical strength to deduce that women deserve their traditionally subordinate position is to deflect attention entirely from the powerful influence of the lessened educational and social opportunities that go with this position. Comte, however, is adamant. One does not, he says, give persons opportunities to engage in activities they could never do well and would therefore feel unhappy in undertaking. Your problem, he explains to Mill, is that you have failed to

> give sufficient weight to the real implications of a natural inferiority. [Women's] characteristic lack of aptitude for abstract thought and argumentation, the virtually complete inability to set emotion aside in rational discourse . . . must make them forever unsuited to assuming any high level organizational positions, not only in science and philosophy . . . but in the arts and even practical affairs, both industrial and military. . . .[61]

Such "facts," concludes Comte, show clearly that it is right for women to be – and to continue to be – wives, mothers, and moral persuaders rather than scientists, rulers, and captains of industry.[62]

It is well known, of course, that Mill found such opinions distasteful in the extreme – and that he was encouraged in this regard by Harriet Taylor.[63] What is

---

60 LMC, XXXIII (July 16, 1843), 231. Here Comte puts anatomy in service to sexist prejudice, but elsewhere he repudiates physiologists who give "an exaggerated importance to characteristics of race as explaining political phenomena" (SPP4a, 126/582). Yet if this means that Comte is no "genetic" racist, he may be an "environmental" one. On this distinction, see Peter T. Manicas, *A History and Philosophy of the Social Sciences* (Oxford: Basil Blackwell, 1987), 54n.1.
61 LMC, XXXVI (October 5, 1843), 246–47.
62 Much has been written about Comte's change of attitude toward women following his passionate (if also platonic) association with Clotilde de Vaux. See, for example, Wolf Lepenies' recent summary in *Between Literature and Science: The Rise of Sociology*, trans. R. J. Hollingdale (Cambridge: Cambridge University Press, 1988), 25–34. But this way of putting things is, I think, quite misleading. If the later Comte is less the hard critic of what women should not do and more the sentimental advocate of what they should, he is – as both his patronizing attitude toward de Vaux's career aspirations and his own *Système* show – always the believer in a "natural hierarchy" of man over woman. See, e.g., his reaffirmation (in one short paragraph) of how women, with their "eminently affective nature" and "passive circumstances," are "peculiarly suited" to be the moral educators of children, counsels and moderating influences on their husbands, and molders of right opinion for society – all the better if men provide for their material needs and women themselves "remain strangers to wealth and power" (SPP1, 327–28/260–61). Cf. SPP1, 204–73/164–219.
63 See *John Stuart Mill and Harriet Taylor: Their Correspondence and Subsequent Marriage*, ed. F. A. Hayek (Chicago: University of Chicago Press, 1951). According to Hayek, it was after Taylor wrote to Mill (1844) of her "surprise and disappointment" at Mill's "half-apologetic" presentation of his opinions on women against one such as Comte, who is "scarcely a worthy opponent," that Mill began to feel "dissatisfied with the concessions he had made to Comte" [114fn.8; cf. JSM to HTM (January 17, 1854), 189]. But Bain, whom Hayek cites, recalls only that Mill said that his

most important to note here, however, is that in his correspondence with Comte, Mill attacks not so much Comte's prejudices themselves as the way he tries to support them. He argues that there is a direct connection between Comte's sexist misuse of anatomy and physiology and his rejection of psychology. Without psychology, Mill argues, one remains ignorant of the basic laws of the mind; and without knowledge of these laws, one cannot have "ethology" (i.e., the derived science of character formation), which provides more "exact" knowledge of how basic psychic dispositions develop and are modified by external conditions in actual individual persons. It is from these two "sciences of the individual" that one learns to appreciate both how differences in character and social circumstances contribute significantly to differences in people's behavior, and also how much "education" (i.e., an alteration of external circumstances) might bring about changes in that behavior. Hence, it is precisely because he rejects these sciences that Comte can remain free to cultivate a perspective on human action that exaggerates the importance of anatomical and physiological conditions, so that presently perceived differences between the behavior of women and the behavior of men are made to appear "naturally" fixed and unalterable.[64]

In short, Mill has reason both as a philosopher of science and as a social theorist to single out Comte for criticism. Not only does Comte, a supposed positivist, deny – against "obvious" evidence – that there can be a genuine mental science; but his antipsychological outlook is connected in a particularly obnoxious way with the promotion of unscientific theories about human, especially allegedly masculine and feminine, behavior. Given Mill's own methodological concerns and personal beliefs, then, his treatment of Comte's critique of interior observation is certainly understandable. It is also, however, inaccurate.

4. Mill's mistaken reading of Comte

Almost from the moment it appeared as two articles in the *Westminster and Foreign Quarterly Review*, Mill's commentary has been the major secondary source on Comte. Indeed, it is probably fair to say that in the English-speaking world *Auguste Comte and Positivism* been consulted more than Comte himself.[65] Of course, much of what Mill reports is true. Comte in fact inserts no basic science between

---

dissatisfaction came "some years later," when he reread his correspondence [*John Stuart Mill: A Criticism, with Personal Recollections* (London: Longmans, Green, 1882), 74].

64 See LMC, XXXV (August 30, 1843), 237–40; XL (October 30, 1843), 259–68; and LXXXIII (March 26, 1846), 523. At one point Mill, replying to Comte's boast that his opinions on "the female organism" rest on extensive personal observation [XXXVI (October 5, 1843), 247], tauntingly suggests that in France the situation of women is so bad that it is impossible for Comte to have seen anything there but behavior reflecting [sexist] social pressures (XL, 263–64). Comte does not get it. Cf. Mill's *The Subjection of Women, Collected Works*, Vol. 21 (1984), 304–20, passim.

65 In the recent past, there was even a whole decade (1961–71) when ACP, but no English editions of Comte's own works, was in print.

biology and sociology; and he appeals to Broussais and Gall but never to Hartley, Brown, or James Mill. He does indeed have some strangely unscientific ideas about human nature, and he certainly does play fast and loose with anatomy and physiology to suit his sexist prejudices.[66] Yet none of this supports Mill's specific contention that Comte rejects "psychological observation properly so called" and the associationist laws derived from it. The basic problem clearly seems to be that when Comte writes his critique and when Mill reads it, they are thinking of two very different topics.

Comte's critique is, as we have seen, entirely retrospective and antimetaphysical. *"Observation intérieure"* is a specious operation promoted by incurably prescientific thinkers to legitimate prescientific doctrines; and the *"psychologie,"* or *"idéologie,"* this operation allegedly supports is merely another version of old-fashioned rational psychology – the "last transmutation of theology," Comte calls it, whose so-called laws of the mind are as "illusory" as the science itself. As for Mill's topic of introspection, or psychological observation, however, and regarding the empirical psychology it is supposed to support, Comte is simply silent.

Had Comte occasionally given signs that one of his targets was associationist psychology, had he at least sometimes appeared to be ridiculing Millian introspection, then we might credit Mill with defending one – even if not the most important – of Comte's targets. And, of course, anyone is free to argue that Comte *should* have asked whether internal experiences are facts and whether introspection is a valid form of observation from which to acquire knowledge of the laws explaining the relations among these facts. It is, however, a radical misunderstanding and a clear case of presentism for Mill to assume that Comte cared about *any* such questions. The passages Mill cites have nothing to do with associationist psychology or introspection; and even in their six-year correspondence, Comte never considers either one.

Mill's attack of Comte's critique constitutes, therefore, a serious misinterpretation. The obvious question, then, is, what makes such a misconstrual possible?

---

66 The consensus is that Mill's discovery of Comte's view of women probably played a major role in the cooling of his attitude toward Comte's position generally, but that other factors (sc., differences in personal philosophical style) must also be mentioned. Bain notes that Mill's way of learning from others typically involved great initial enthusiasm and displays of deference (*John Stuart Mill*, 144) – an approach that seems to have misled Comte when he received Mill's first few letters. Mill surely never wanted to be Comte's pupil; in fact, his initial reaction to Comte, on reading his 1824 "Plan des travaux scientifiques nécessaires pour réorganisation la société," was apparently quite unfavorable (see the thorough discussion by Pickering, PIC, 509–27). We know also that Mill grew increasingly uncomfortable with Comte's tendency to look for disciples instead of colleagues. See, e.g., Simon, *European Positivism*, 183–85, 194–95; and Iris W. Mueller, *John Stuart Mill and French Thought* (Urbana: University of Illinois Press, 1956), 128–31.

2

MILL VERSUS COMTE AS POSITIVIST PHILOSOPHERS OF SCIENCE

Now that it is clear how Mill's account of Comte's critique of interior observation is mistaken, the next step is to note that this is not an isolated mistake. It is, as we are about to see, one of at least three similar misinterpretations of Comte by Mill; and in each case, the explanation for it is the same. Mill misses Comte's point not, say, out of his enthusiasm for some particular idea that Comte is against or due to unfamiliarity with certain texts or sources,[1] but because he wrongly assumes that Comte is speaking from a philosophical perspective that is essentially like his own. Comte's idea of what it means to be a positivist, however, is fundamentally different from Mill's. Before beginning my diagnosis of Mill's misinterpretations, then, I want to say a few words about the difference in their positivisms.

1. Philosophy "of" science?

The key factor here is that Comte's view of philosophy's relation to science is not what one expects from a nineteenth-century positivist. According to received wisdom, nineteenth-century positivists are of two types. All reject metaphysics and embrace the scientific ideal for knowledge, but the original ("systematic") proponents use what they take to be the ultimate implications of this ideal to develop totalizing conceptual schemes and programs of utopian sociopolitical reform. Yet gradually, both of these grander ambitions get discredited by the efforts of a more methodologically rigorous ("critical") breed of positivist that

---

[1] Both, of course, are reasons Mill gives to explain Comte's failure to appreciate him.

subjects science itself to searching criticism in order to eliminate any traces of metaphysics which might be sheltering themselves beneath the cloak of experimental theories...[and thus] approximates less closely in its methods to the older system of positivism than it does to the empiricism of David Hume and Stuart Mill, of which it is the logical conclusion.[2]

In general, this story does seem accurate enough. During the nineteenth century, positivists do tend increasingly to wield their antimetaphysical imperative against anything – past or present, in or out of science – that even hints of speculation and do at the same time increasingly make the analysis and purification of scientific rationality philosophy's primary task. Certainly also, it is in this movement from systematic to critical positivism that we see a foreshadowing of our own century's Logical Empiricism. Finally, the distinction between systematic and critical positivism is helpful for locating transitional figures like Mill who, although still openly espousing the earlier progressive and social regenerationist view that the world will be a better place when the "positive mode of thought" triumphs, is already in fundamental spirit a critical positivist who makes the "organon of proof" philosophy's primary topic.

There is, however, this problem with the usual story. In a very important respect, it starts too late to include Comte – or perhaps better, Comte's position does not yet belong in it. As I warned in the Introduction, one should not assume that Comte is straightforwardly antimetaphysical. Unlike either systematic or critical positivists, his view of the relation between scientific and prescientific thought is not essentially disjunctive; nor would he approve of the idea that positive philosophy is primarily post-traditional metamethodolgy of science. To line up against the past in either of these two ways would be, in Comte's eyes, to display a completely unjustified confidence in the epistemic hegemony of science. Empirical observation and scientific rationality may indeed be "destined" to replace theology and metaphysics, but this destiny is only partially realized and poorly understood. To set philosophy immediately to work establishing criteria for rationality and truth on the model of science would be to assume the preeminence of that model. Yet for Comte, precisely this assumption is still controversial; hence, to simply begin with the aim of cleansing science of its lingering metaphysical influence – let alone to take scientism for granted – is philosophically naive. The first order of philosophical business is to determine whether and to what extent such efforts are rightly directed.

In the present context, this difference between Comtean and either systematic

---

2 Antonio Aliotta, *The Idealistic Reaction Against Science*, trans. Agnes McCaskill (London: Macmillan, 1914), 53; cited in part by Mandelbaum, *History, Man, and Reason*, 376fn.23. I cite the original at greater length here to make clearer that there is historical continuity of interpretation concerning the existence of a basic division that I follow Mandelbaum in calling "systematic [earlier, classical]" versus "critical [at least proto-Logical Empiricist]" positivisms (ibid., 11–20). Cf. Leszek Kolakowski, *The Alienation of Reason: A History of Positivist Thought,* trans. Norbert Guterman (Garden City, NY: Doubleday, 1968), Ch. 1.

or critical positivism is crucial. If we follow the conventional practice of reading works like Comte's *Cours* as imperfect anticipations of later positivism, the very thing we need to know in order to understand the point of Comte's critique of interior observation will remain as lost to us as it already is on Mill. Granted, if one compares Comte's *Cours* and Mill's *Logic* primarily in terms of their epistemic commitments, their positions appear more similar than different. In both works, "knowledge" means scientific knowledge; science explains "experienceable" phenomena only; and the special sciences are united by their use of the explanatory methods that it is philosophy's job to explicate. From the similarity of their commitments *in* methodology, however, we cannot deduce similarity with respect to Mill's and Comte's treatment *of* methodology. Mill thinks the age of science is an accomplished fact; he sees nothing left that needs defending; and he therefore asks, "What do scientists do when they are doing it right?" His philosophy "of" science answers this question. Comte, however, sees himself as a witness to the emergence of science; he feels obliged to smooth its developmental path; and he therefore asks, "Is what scientists do the right thing?" His philosophy "of" science gives this question priority over Mill's.

At the same time, however, if Comte's sense of historico-critical obligation thus necessitates a philosophical outlook that is in some sense external to science in a way that a critical outlook such as Mill's is not, *this* does not make Comte a systematic positivist – not even if in *other* respects (sc., in what he says about future social reorganization) he might be so classified. According to the usual picture, the systematic positivist rejects metaphysics, embraces scientism, and then goes on to the questionable practice of thinking in grand terms about what the growing influence of scientific ideas and findings Really Means. Yet when Comte starts by asking about the right of science to supplant metaphysics, he has already *stopped short* of assuming an either antimetaphysical or extrascientific stance. As we will see, his inquiry is in this way not so much external to as *reflective about* science – which is something Mill neither understands in Comte nor attempts himself. It is because of this historically obligated reflectiveness that Comte is led not only to oppose psychology but also, as we will see, to refuse to produce a formalized "logic of proof" and to reject the very idea of "causal" natural laws. In all three instances, Mill fails to get Comte's point.

The diagnosis of Mill's three misunderstandings of Comte – misunderstandings not only of Comte's critique of psychology but also of his opposition to organons of proof and to a genuinely scientific concept of causality – is, then, the central topic of this chapter. After preliminary treatment of Mill's view of what the philosophy of science is and of how he thinks Comte fails to live up to it, I devote a section each to the two still undiscussed misunderstandings and then conclude by explaining how Mill – and by implication, of course, any other essentially critical positivist – is bound to misread all three of Comte's reflectively motivated moves.

2. Mill as philosopher of science

What, then, does Mill think positivist philosophers of science should do? His answer flows directly from his general conception of the nature of philosophy as such. "The proper meaning of philosophy," he asserts, is "what, in the main, the ancients understood by it – the scientific [sic] knowledge of Man, as an intellectual, moral, and social being." The "knowing faculty" itself, he continues, is, of course, part of our intellectual being; hence, everything we can know, viewed in terms of our "mode of knowing it," is a possible topic for science. It therefore follows that

> the philosophy of a science thus comes to mean the science itself, considered not as to its results, the truths which it ascertains, but as to the processes by which the mind attains them, the marks by which it recognizes them, and the coordinating and methodizing of them with a view to the greatest clearness of conception and readiest availability for use: in one word, [it is] the logic of the science.[3]

Two aspects of Mill's reasoning here tell us something we need to know about his general philosophical orientation. First, his cursory reference to the ancients – with its questionable use of the same word, "science," for both classical and modern thought – gives a preliminary measure of how Mill's self-assurance as a positivist can frequently make him a poor judge of others' purposes. He does not seem to have noticed, for example, how very modern is his characteristic practice of reading the classical philosophers in terms of their methods of inquiry – as if Plato, for example, would have been just as eager as Mill is to suspend interest in substantive claims in order to produce a treatise on logic.[4] Moreover, Mill does not notice that his appeal to Greek "science," taken together with his affirmation elsewhere of Comte's three-stage law, is in fact contradictory. As we will see, Comte's law says that the pre-Socratics, Plato, and Aristotle all belong to a time when philosophy is struggling to make a transition from theological to metaphysical thinking, and their views are very much more attuned to theological concerns than to the spirit of positive science. Indeed, in summarizing and expressing his agreement with this part of Comte's law, Mill himself observes that

> no one, unless entirely ignorant of the history of thought, will deny that the mistaking of abstractions for realities pervaded speculation all through antiquity and the middle ages. The mistake was generalized and systematized in the famous Ideas of Plato. The Aristotelians carried it on.[5]

But if the ancients are in this and in other respects (e.g., in using their abstrac-

---

3 ACP, 291/53. Cf. SL, Intro., pars. 5 [Logic is "the science of science"] and 16 (10 and 12–16); and SL, III, i.
4 See, e.g., Mill's review of George Grote's *Plato* in *Collected Works*, Vol. 11 (1978), 375–441; and Geraint L. Williams, "J. S. Mill on the Greeks: History Put to Use," *Mill News Letter* 17/1 (1982), 1–11.
5 ACP, 271/16.

tions to explain the apparent by the hidden) incurably metaphysical, their conception of philosophy cannot serve Mill as a model for philosophy as science.

Second, in describing the philosophy of science as immanent to science rather than as a distinct activity or the result of such activity, Mill is promoting something like an official, pristinely empiricist picture of his position that is in fact quite misleading. Here and frequently elsewhere, he assures us that his philosophy of science does not "speculate" about (e.g., add rational abstractions to) the scientific activity it considers. In his *Logic* as in his philosophy generally, he often describes himself as aspiring to what has come to be called "global empiricism."[6] By making the philosophy of science just science itself considered from a certain angle, he is attempting to put the same rigorously anti–a priorist face on the "logic of science" in general that he does on scientific theory construction in particular. Mill's usual claim about theorizing – derived primarily from a combination of Locke's epistemology and the psychology of his father – is that experience, plus the operation of associationist psychological laws, accounts for all our knowledge.[7] So, for example, against Whewell's claim that Kepler unified the available facts about the motion of Mars by imposing on them the concept of an ellipse, Mill argues that Kepler "did not *put* what he had conceived into the facts, but *saw* it in them."[8] In the same way, Mill's description of the philosophy/logic of science as really "of" – that is, intrinsic to – scientific activity has the effect of placing the philosopher of science in the same position vis-à-vis scientific activity that Mill thinks Kepler was in relation to the data about Mars. So placed, Millian philosophers of science would be obliged to read off the laws of good reasoning from the facts of scientific activity. Otherwise, they would be guilty of assuming a priori powers in metascience that they deny to science itself.

Such, at least, is the approach that Mill – the anti-intuitionist, radically empiricist "philosopher of experience" – might be expected to take; and sometimes, as here, he does indeed appear to do so. He declares repeatedly that no a priori method can be imposed on science. He describes science as just an "improved form of that which was primitively pursued by the human understanding while undirected." He even says that his *Logic* depends on the existence of some scientific successes because it is never possible "to frame any scientific method of in-

---

6 See Geoffrey Scarre, *Logic and Reality in the Philosophy of John Stuart Mill* (Dordrecht: Kluwer, 1989), 126–53. The contrast I am developing here between Mill's official empiricism and his commitment to certain "metaphysical enthusiasms" that seem incompatible with it is not the same as the distinction Scarre finds in Mill between two incompatible varieties of global empiricism itself – one closer to scientific realism, the other to reductivist sensationalism (214–16).
7 On the epistemological side, see especially Scarre's thorough analysis of Mill's account of the possibility of inductive inference (*Logic and Reality*, 15–37, 80–103). On the psychological side see, e.g., Wilson's analysis of Mill's view that "associationist learning theory is a generic theory that has been confirmed by, and explains, a variety of specific laws and generates a research program for the discovery of specific laws in further areas" (*Psychological Analysis*, 84–90; quote, 90).
8 SL, III, ii, 4 (295), Mill's emphasis.

duction, or test of the correctness of inductions, unless on the hypothesis that some inductions deserving of reliance have already been made."[9]

Yet in the end, Mill's *Logic* is much more prescriptive than this respectful nod at scientific practice might lead one to expect. Indeed, there is little evidence that the work was actually shaped along austerely empiricist and inductivist lines.[10]

That Mill's philosophy of science involves extra-empiricist elements is clearly evident, to return to the previous example, in his quarrel with Whewell over the nature of induction. According to Whewell, Kepler's conceiving of the motion of Mars in terms of an ellipse involved a hypothesis (an "invention"), the mind's introduction of which makes possible an "inference by induction" that, when confirmed by the data, produces a scientific "discovery" that "explains" those data.[11] At first, Mill's response appears unexceptionably empiricist. He begins by arguing that what Whewell talks about is still just a form of "description" (that is, what the classical empiricists called "abstraction") and not yet induction. Induction involves going from individual instances – no matter how well described – to a generalization, not just to the sort of "guesswork" Whewell calls invention.[12] As for the generalization itself, Mill insists that although it does involve going beyond some instances to many or all instances, this inferential process has merit only

---

9 SL, III, iv, 2 (318, 319); also Preface; III, iii, 1 (308–309n.); and VI, Intro., par. 1. Mill's familiarity with both the history of science and the science of his day was limited. He says he owes his "comprehensive and . . . accurate[!] view of the whole circle of physical science" primarily to two works. The one, by John F. W. Herschel, is more systematic than historical, and the level of sophistication in its estimation of the prescientific past can be gathered from Herschel's remark, in his only retrospective chapter, that "previous to the publication of the Novum Organum of Bacon, natural philosophy, in any legitimate and extensive sense of the word, could hardly be said to exist" [*A Preliminary Discourse on the Study of Natural Philosophy* (London: Longman, Rees, Orme, Brown, and Green, 1830), 105]. The other work, by William Whewell, although ostensibly more historical, has a strong presentist streak that Mill finds appealing. In Whewell's opinion, for example, the ancients' "ideas" concerning force, motion, and matter "were very poor, and the stunted and deformed growth of their physical science was the result of this penury" [*History of the Inductive Sciences, from the Earliest to the Present Times*, 3 vols. (London: John W. Parker, 1837), I, 83]. On current science, Mill acknowledges heavy debts to Bain (A, 255n.), who not only added illustrative material to Mill's first draft but also corrected a number of serious errors in Mill's own examples. See Bain, *John Stuart Mill*, 66–67.

10 Scarre, e.g., shows that neither Mill's conviction that there is no such thing as genuinely "deductive" inference nor his confidence in the soundness of induction are ever directly made secure against, say, the skeptical implications of a Hume or a Sextus (*Logic and Reality*, 100–103). Moreover, analysis of the alterations Mill made to later editions of the *Logic* suggests that this radical inductivism may not in fact have been his mature view at all. Struan Jacobs argues that Mill's study of Comte and Whewell persuaded him that hypothesis is the principal instrument of discovery, and induction, of justification ["John Stuart Mill on Induction and Hypotheses," *Journal of the History of Philosophy* 29 (1991), 79–80]. Jacobs is right, I think, in finding the distinction in Mill's text but too generous in putting it also in Mill's mind (see fn. 34).

11 See, e.g., *Novum Organon Renovatum: Being the Second Part of the Philosophy of the Inductive Sciences*, 3rd ed. (London: John W. Parker and Son, 1858), 70–83. The publication history here is complicated. See editor's notes, SL, 1238–39.

12 SL, III, ii, 4. In this section, Mill ignores Whewell's additional claim that one also necessarily makes use of certain preexistent "fundamental ideas" – a claim Mill clearly repudiates elsewhere [SL, IV, ii, 2 (651)].

when it can withstand the appropriate "test of proof."[13] Yet at this point, Mill's official empiricism leaves him. Every such inferential process, he asserts, depends additionally upon "the proposition that the course of nature is uniform, [which] is the fundamental principle, or general axiom, of induction."[14] I will return to this "general axiom" and the subsequently well-traveled terrain of a supposed justification for induction itself later in this chapter, in my discussion of Mill and Comte on causality. In the meantime, however, it is already obvious that such an axiom cannot be a straightfowardly empirical generalization like other generalizations. Given that it is, as Mill says, "the ultimate premise in all cases of induction," any "test of proof" for it in the usual sense would be too little and come too late. Moreover, Mill insists that inductions have always depended on this axiom, even though "it has scarcely entered into the minds of any but philosophers" and even then has been treated inadequately. Here, in other words, Mill extends to himself a perspective on science quite different from the one he describes as analogous to Kepler's when thinking of the data about Mars. A good philosopher of science, he is claiming, knows something about what scientists must "really" be doing, whether they are aware of it or not. In contrast to Whewell, who justifies his own conception of scientific induction by appeals to the history of scientific practice, Mill explicitly denies that practice should have the last word.

In short, there is between the lines in Mill's *Logic* a "metaphysical enthusiasm" about its perspective and its purpose that may in fact be characteristic of his empiricism but that is not, by his own standards, very empirical. For Mill possesses a firm idea – one he never claims to have first "seen" in any practice – both of what the sciences must do and of how he is going to help them do it. On the one hand, the *Logic* is not just a systematic account of any logical reasoning whatever; it confidently takes itself to be the logic *of science* and as such, a "larger logic of truth" concerned with the acquisition of knowledge, not merely a "smaller logic of consistency" concerned only with forms of argument. On the other hand, in spite of Mill's official empiricism, the *Logic* is simply not the "[empirical] science of science [as actually practiced]." It is, by design, *the* logic of science – a study of knowledge under ideal conditions, a conceptual analysis of the "validity" of thought, not a factual study of "thought as thought."[15] Somehow, Mill intends his normative logic to be both "the common ground on which the partisans of Hartley and of Reid, of Locke and of Kant, may meet and join hands" and also "the science of the operations of the understanding which are subservient to the

---

13 *Logic*, III, ii, 5; III, ix, 6; and Whewell's reply, in *Of Induction, with Especial Reference to Mr. J. Stuart Mill's System of Logic* (London: John W. Parker, 1849), 18–26.
14 SL, III, iii, 1 (307); III, v, 2; III, ix, 6; and ACP, 294/58–59.
15 See *William Hamilton's Philosophy*, 359. Also SL, Intro., 1–6; and II, iii, 1. The phrase about Mill's "metaphysical enthusiasm" occurs in Ryan, *The Philosophy of John Stuart Mill*, 72, in his defense of Mill against the charge by R. P. Anschutz that assertions about the uniformity of nature commit Mill to a species of Platonism (59–72).

estimation of evidence" – as if "evidence" were not precisely the sort of phenomenon whose treatment produced contending "partisans" in the first place.[16]

To sum up this section, then, the two features of Mill's reasoning that we have been discussing here – his preemption of the Greek idea of science, and the tension between his empiricist credo and his actual philosophy of science – reveal him to be a philosophically "interested" thinker with commitments and enthusiasms that antedate and even conflict with the *Logic*'s official characterization.[17] In my view, as in Comte's, there is nothing scandalous about possessing such interests. What is objectionable is not reflecting on them because one is under the impression that one does not have any interests. Yet that is precisely how Mill behaves. It is as if, as a positivist philosopher of science, he understands himself to be simply looking out with attentive but completely neutral and historically unburdened eyes, just concerned to "see" the logic of science there in scientific activity itself. But Mill is neither neutral nor historically unburdened; he is a philosopher of science with an agenda – one that in many respects anticipates the agenda of Logical Empiricism – and it is this philosopher of science who criticizes Comte for failing to be sufficiently positivistic and who thereby succeeds in missing the point of Comte's opposition to psychology, methodological reconstruction, and causal laws.

3. Comte's "failure" as philosopher of science

Let me introduce here an image I will exploit further in the next chapter, when I contrast Comte's own philosophical outlook with Mill's. I suggest that we think of Mill's evaluation of Comte as developed from a standpoint that is temporally structured in such a way that the three moments of time are ranked in just the order one would expect from a clear-eyed, historically unburdened philosopher of science. From this perspective, it becomes clear why, above all, Mill reproaches Comte for being neglectful of science's greatest *present* need, namely, an organon of proof. For as a dedicated epistemologist of science, Mill has little use for what

---

16 SL, Intro., 7 (12, 14).
17 Besides commitments to the previously mentioned axiom of universal causality and that ideal of methodological formalization that I will be emphasizing later, Mill also has, of course, other substantive metaphysical convictions. Ryan, e.g., finds an underlying atomistic phenomenalism with respect to both physical nature (87ff.) and human actions (157ff.) – a view Heyd accepts ("Mill and Comte on Psychology," 130) and Wilson rejects ("Mill and Comte on the Method . . . ," 109). R. P. Anschutz, *The Philosophy of John Stuart Mill* (Oxford: Clarendon Press, 1953), argues (165–66, 170–82) in favor of a realist construal of Mill's bald assertion that "Nature in the abstract is the . . . sum of all phenomena, together with the causes that produce them; *including not only all that happens, but all that is capable of happening;* the unused capabilities of causes being as much a part of the idea of Nature, as those which take effect" (*Three Essays on Religion, Collected Works*, Vol. 10, 374, emphasis added). Most careful on these issues is Scarre, who finds a realist strain in the *Logic* (*Logic and Reality*, 105–10) that is probably incompatible with Mill's general "leaning towards idealism, and his enthusiasm for Berkeley" (4; but cf. 193–95) – a leaning that does not, however, make him a phenomenalist in Ryan's sense (176–88).

can only seem to him to be Comte's indulgent preoccupation, on the one hand, with the historical rise and *past* triumphs of science and, on the other hand, with utopian projections of its *future* glories. Mill's own self-confidence does not, of course, make it true that he is in fact any less committed than Comte to substantive views about science's past and future; nevertheless, a presumption of neutrality operates decisively in his criticisms.

Science's past

Regarding the rise of science, Mill agrees wholeheartedly with the basic teaching of Comte's three-stage law that science must necessarily supersede – and has in fact been superseding – theology and metaphysics. He also shares Comte's conviction that the intellectual triumph of science makes radical social regeneration possible. Concerning this latter possibility, Mill is not at all as certain that a "fully positive condition" is imminent; indeed, he often criticizes Comte for failing to appreciate the political and religious forces that impede its development. Yet if Comte is more optimistic about social *progress,* Mill is the more self-confident positivist about the triumph of scientific *knowledge.* Epistemologically speaking, Mill thinks that the point of Comte's three-stage law has been sufficiently made. The historical revolution is largely over; the principles of positivism are already "the general property of the age"; and as anyone familiar with the rise of science knows,

> the positive explanation of facts has substituted itself, step by step, for the theological and metaphysical, as the progress of inquiry brought to light an increasing number of the invariable laws of phenomena. In . . . [noting this] . . . Comte has not originated anything, but has taken his place in a fight long since engaged, and on the side already in the main victorious.[18]

We may note in passing how different the options look to us than they did to Mill. By later (i.e., Logical Empiricist) standards, Mill's own positivism hardly qualifies as a fully scientific philosophy; and by still later standards (viz., our own), one can no longer speak proudly of positivism being "victorious" at all. I will argue later

---

8 ACP, 267, 269/8–9, 12. Because Mill does not always carefully distinguish his less sanguine attitude toward social progress from his epistemological optimism, his writings can make him appear inconsistently disposed toward Comte's law. In the self-confident remarks just cited, e.g., Mill's topic is epistemology. In the Comte–Mill correspondence, where the concern is often social progress, Mill displays much less optimism and remains more cautious and historically minded about what it would take to change prescientific minds (Lévy-Bruhl's "Introduction," LMC, xxii). In still other places, however, Mill uses precisely Comte's phrasing to characterize the belief that prescientific dogmatism and absolutism must be rejected *both* in politics *and* in science as a "conviction" that is common to "all thinkers who are on a level with the [present] age," and he says it "comes . . . naturally to any intelligent reader of history" (ACP, 323/115). Cf. Lewes' equally undiscriminating claim that, thanks to Comte, (prescientific) philosophy has already come in general to have "merely historical" interest [*The Biographical History of Philosophy: From Its Origins in Greece down to the Present Day*, rev. ed. (New York: D. Appleton, 1875), esp. xx–xxiii, xxxi, 769, 776–89].

that these changes in perspective that come after Mill make Comte the more interesting positivist for us; for now, I note only that Mill (wrongly) thinks of Comte's use of the three-stage law as a mainly retrospective affair.

Comte's genius, argues Mill, lies in his having formulated a law (i.e., a "generalization") that not only accounts for a historical process that is "in the main" already over but also, much more importantly, that can now serve as the ordering principle for a "wonderful systematization" of the sciences. Comte himself may have failed to appreciate the greater significance of the latter; but it is precisely the working out of this systematization that, "if he had done nothing else, would have stamped him . . . as one of the principal thinkers of the age."[19]

The systematization to which Mill refers is Comte's famous hierarchical arrangement of the sciences, ordered from mathematics and astronomy (the "least complex") through physics, chemistry, and biology to sociology (the "most complex").[20] True to form, Mill heaps his praise upon what Comte calls the "analytical" (or "dogmatical") classification – that is, the kind of classification, let us say, that is of greatest concern to a mind wholly engaged in a current, formal-methodological task. According to Comte himself, however, there is another "historical" classification, which, although admittedly coinciding in substance with the analytical one, has an important philosophical as well as empirical priority. Empirically, Comte argues, no analytical ("purely rational") study of the arrangement of the sciences "could have made any real progress . . . until there had been a considerable development of the earlier [i.e., less complex] sciences." When science tries to extend its investigations from planets and rocks to animals and people, however, its progress can no longer be expected to occur "spontaneously." Powerful reactionary forces, as we have seen, stand ready to resist the scientific study especially of human beings; hence, at this point, the whole idea of the development of a truly positive body of knowledge must be made explicit and articulated within the context of a "history of the human mind."[21] In other words,

---

19 ACP, 290–91/53; also 269, 279/13, 32–33.
20 ACP, 279–83/32–40; CPP1(1–2), 18–23, 85–98, 112–15 [F, 10–14, 51–58, 65–67]; and DEP, 101/160–61. Comte's labels undergo some alteration. In the introductory lectures of the *Cours*, biology is "organic physics" or "physiology properly so called," and sociology is "social physics." In the *Système*, anthropology, or morals *(morale)*, is added as the seventh, "true science of man" that combines the biological and sociological perspectives in order to obtain "special knowledge of man's individual nature" (SPP2, 437–38/356–57). See also Ch. 1, fn. 21.
21 CPP2(2), 100–101 [F, 59]; also DEP, 97–98/153–54. As I will explain in Chapter 4, Comte thinks a crucial factor missed by any merely analytical classification is the teleological aspect of both the three-stage law and the system of the sciences. In his view, the law and the system together codify a purposiveness that was in the first instance displayed in "spontaneous" intellectual developments expressive of "a long-experienced feeling of the mind's true needs" (CPP2(2), 99 [F, 58]). It is important to remember here that, thanks to the efforts of his friend Gustave d'Eichthal, by late 1824 Comte was thoroughly familiar with Kant's *Idea of a Universal History from a Cosmopolitan Point of View* [trans. Lewis White Beck in *Kant on History* (Indianapolis, IN: Bobbs-Merrill, 1963), 11–26] – to which he reacted at the time by saying that if he had known of this work six or seven years earlier, he would not have needed to write the very "Plan des travaux scientifiques nécessaires pour réorganiser la société" that so impressed Mill (SPP4a, 47–136/527–89; see also Pickering, PIC, 290–91).

Comte sees his "historical" classification of the sciences as forming the basis of a needed philosophical argument in favor of scientific progress that a purely "dogmatical" classification cannot provide.

Science's future

As for the question about the ultimate promise of science, Mill agrees in general with Comte that science facilitates both technological and social progress; and he seconds Comte's Baconian slogan that from science comes prevision, and from prevision comes action.[22] Yet once again, as a critical positivist Mill objects to Comte's misuse of his three-stage law for allegedly utopian speculations. I cannot, declares Mill,

> see any scientific connection between [Comte's] theoretical explanation of the past progress of society, and his proposals for future improvement. The proposals are not . . . recommended as that towards which human society has been tending and working through the whole of history. . . . They rest as completely, each on its separate reasons of supposed utility, as with philosophers who, like Bentham, theorize on politics without any historical basis at all.[23]

We have here, complains Mill, the "singular anomaly" of someone who, after carefully marshaling ample evidence for his historical account of the growth of science, turns around and makes wholly speculative forecasts about future science. As Mill argues elsewhere, this anomaly arises from the fact that although Comte knows that his social and historical generalizations must ultimately be linked to more basic "laws of human nature," he fails to recognize that these more basic laws are the psychological and characterological "laws of *individual* human nature."[24]

According to Mill, historical generalizations such as Comte's three-stage law are merely "empirical laws" describing "derivative uniformities." Yet if, strictly speaking, they are not truly scientific laws, when appropriately circumscribed they are extremely important in science. Suppose, for example, that we want to consider some set of social regularities at a fairly abstract level. Provided that sufficient factual detail is available, we may still obtain positive knowledge both of the regularities and of their causes. Thus in the case of the three-stage law, says Mill, given the way Comte restricts himself to "the main stream of human

---

22 ACP, 265, 288/6–7, 48. In his first letter to Comte (1841), Mill stresses his indebtedness to Comte's *Système de politique positive* (the 1824 "Plan" essay, not the *Système* of 1851–54), which he says helped free his social thinking from the shackles of Benthamism (LMC, I, 2; also XIX, 149ff., and an early draft of his *Autobiography*, 615–16). But by 1865, Mill is more anxious to argue that Comte's view of the usefulness of science is ultimately shortsighted – especially in his later work, where he shows that he "gradually acquired a real hatred for scientific and all purely intellectual pursuits" (ACP, 355/176).
23 ACP, 325/118–119; cf. 333–34, 353–54/135–37, 172–73.
24 SL, VI, x, 3 (915) and VI, vii, 1 ("The laws of the phenomena of society are, and can be, nothing but the laws of the actions and passions of human beings . . . obedient to the laws of individual human nature" [879]).

progress" and seeks "to characterize truly, though generally, the successive states of society through which the [intellectual] advanced guard of our species has passed," and given also the "vast mass of historical observations which he has grouped and coordinated" in the service of this aim, we may rightly conclude that "the chain of causation by which he connects the spiritual and temporal life of each era with one another and with the entire series . . . [is] in all its essentials, irrefragable."[25] The point we must never forget, Mill argues, is that no high-level regularities of this sort represent laws of nature; and that is just what Comte appears to assume when he uses his three-stage law to predict future conditions. The deficiencies of Comte's predictions themselves, however, are ample evidence of their unscientific nature. For example, he appears to believe that "the mere institution of a positive science of sociology" – from which, supposedly, will come the knowledge necessary for social harmony" – is "tantamount to its completion." "As if," Mill continues mockingly, "all the diversities of opinion on the subject, which set mankind at variance, were solely owing to its having been studied in the theological or the metaphysical manner."[26]

As we shall see in later chapters, little illumination can come from such attempts as these to squeeze Comte's *philosophical* use of his three-stage law between the demands of Mill's official empiricist epistemology of science and the familiar black hole of mere speculation. I have, however, let Mill loose here at some length to illustrate something more about his frame of mind as Comte's critic. Quite apart from whether Mill's characterization of Comte's alleged penchant for utopian projection is accurate, there is in this instance the question of his condemning in Comte what he considers virtuous in himself. In fact, Mill promotes his *Logic* (and specifically, its methods of induction) in just the same way Comte does his *Cours* (and specifically, its case for a social physics), namely, as being an agent of intellectual and social change. Mill argues that the currently dominant Kantian ("intuitionist") epistemology, by defending the idea that there are eternal truths knowable a priori, constitutes "the great intellectual support of false doctrines and bad institutions"; and he explains that he has designed his *Logic* to combat such "mischief" by providing what is "much wanted," namely, "a textbook of the opposite [that is, experiential] doctrine."[27] Is this sort of forecasting

---

25 ACP, 318–19/106–108. Indeed, says Mill, "whoever disbelieves that the philosophy of history can be made a science, should suspend his judgment until he has read [CPP4-5] of Comte" (318/106). See also SL, VI, x, 3 (915–16), where the tribute to Comte is followed by Mill's division of empirical social laws into those involving uniformities of coexistence and of succession, and of sociology itself into social statics and social dynamics (917–25).

26 ACP, 325/119–20; also SL, VI, x, 3 (914–15). There is, of course, a now familiar controversy in the philosophy of social science brewing here, with Mill clearly playing methodological individualist to Comte's methodological holist. See Ryan, *The Philosophy of John Stuart Mill*, 149–66, 178–85.

27 A, 233, 269–70. In the year before its publication, Mill wrote Comte of the *Logic*'s polemical purpose [LMC, XIII (July 11, 1842), 77–79]. Scarre is certainly correct that Mill's aim is not primarily or essentially political (*Logic and Reality*, 12–14); but this should not blind us to the fact that Mill is just as willing as Comte to regard his work as socially efficacious. See also Michael St. John Packe, *The Life of John Stuart Mill* (New York: Macmillan, 1954), 251–55, 266–71.

about the intellectual and social efficacy of a systematic logic of proof any less of an "unscientific projection" than the sort Mill alleges in the case of Comte's promotion of sociology?

Science's present needs

Yet for Mill, the heart of the problem is that even if Comte's forecastings were empirically better grounded, they would still be peripheral to what must be made the main philosophical issue, namely, the current need for *A System of Logic*. Mill's three main criticisms of Comte's position are in some way related to this present-centered assumption. The formalization of method, the defense of a scientific notion of causality, and the clarification of the relation between logic and psychology are all, in Mill's eyes, essential topics for the *Logic;* and Comte fails to appreciate any of them.

It is not, however, Mill's criticisms themselves but rather their philosophical grounds to which I want to draw special attention. Not surprisingly, Mill finds many other issues to disagree about in Comte's extensive writings – for example, his theory of chemical composition, certain illiberal political ideas, his anti-Protestantism, and an excessively altruistic interpretation of ethical action, as well as his belief in the natural inferiority of women, as we have already seen.[28] In these other cases, Mill's opposition follows a perfectly ordinary and straightforward pattern. An offending Comtean claim or theory is singled out, Mill's own alternative is compared with it, and the latter is argued to be superior on empirical, or conceptual, or ethical-political grounds.[29] In the case of Mill's three criticisms of Comte's philosophy of science, however, the pattern is very different. As we will see, in these three instances it is not a matter of challenging this or that belief and simply arguing that it is contrary to the facts, or conceptually unclear, or ethically objectionable. Instead, Mill's objection (often tainted with a personal aside) is that in some general way, Comte's position is unbecoming for a positivist philosopher. The basis for such criticism is nothing less than Mill's own rival but largely unstated sense of what such a philosopher must hold. Hence, these are the important criticisms in the present context because they are the ones that account for Mill's deepest misunderstandings of Comte.

---

28 See ACP, 289, 294–95/49–50, 59–61 (on chemical composition); 301–06, 326–27/73–83, 121–23 (illiberal politics); 321–22, 338–40/111–13, 144–47 (anti-Protestantism); 334–36/137–40 (altruism); and 344–45/156–58, together with LMC, XXXV and XL, 237–40 and 259–71 (sexism). See also Mill's 1848 letter to John Pringle Nichol (professor of astronomy at the University of Glasgow), *Collected Works*, Vol. 13 (1963), 738–39.

29 In his *Autobiography*, Mill reports that he lost his initial enthusiasm for corresponding with Comte when he discovered that their differences were not mere matters of "simple doctrine" but involved "those points of opinion which blended in both of us with our strongest feelings, and determined the entire direction of our aspirations." He goes on to characterize Comte's political theories as "the completest system of spiritual and temporal despotism, which ever emanated from a human brain" (A, 219–21).

4. The question of an organon of proof

According to Mill, one fundamental flaw in Comte's philosophy of science is his failure to see that there are two "parts" to science and thus also to its logic. There are, to be sure, "methods of investigation," or discovery; but there must also be tests, or "requisites of proof."

> The one points out the roads by which the human intellect arrives at conclusions, the other the mode of testing their evidence. The former if complete would be an Organon of Discovery, the latter of Proof. It is to the first of these that Comte principally confines himself, and he treats it with a degree of perfection hitherto unrivaled. [With Comte] we are taught the right way of searching for results, but when a result has been reached, how shall we know that it is true? . . . On this question Comte throws no light. He supplies no test of proof.[30]

Mill does not, as we have noted, find this state of affairs surprising. Given Comte's historical preoccupation with the mind's struggle to become scientific, it stands to reason that he would be most illuminating about the "right way of searching for results." Yet even in his inadequate account of proof, Mill argues, Comte points in the right direction; for although he did not himself supply any tests of proof, Comte did say that scientific hypotheses must still be directly "verified" even if they do seem to "account for the [original set of] facts." In this, claims Mill, he already shows that such tests are "needed." Comte's specific failure, then, lies in his not seeing that the *systematization of those tests* is "the main problem of Logic properly so called."[31]

If we are to understand Mill's objection to and misconstrual of Comte here, it is important that we not read back into this controversy the more familiar logical empiricist distinction between the so-called contexts of discovery and justification. Especially the concept of a context of discovery – whether intended to identify a topic of relative disinterest for Logical Empiricists or an issue of renewed concern for post-positivists – is self-consciously worked out on very differently defined terrain from the idea of scientific discovery that is taken for granted by both Comte and Mill.[32] Comte certainly does not understand "discovery" as an activity to be clearly distinguished from justification or confirmation, let alone reduce it to a philosophically uninteresting subjective operation. He typically employs the term unspecifically, so that in phrases like "science 'discovers' the actual laws of phenomena," it refers in various contexts to everything from fact gathering and theory constructing to empirical testing and proof. Mill's terminology in the *Logic* makes him more easily misread today as falling squarely on the justification

---

30 ACP, 291–92/54–55; cf. A, 217. Mill gets his discovery–proof distinction from Herschel's *Preliminary Discourse*, Ch. VII, esp. 208–209. But see also fn. 33.
31 ACP, 292/56.
32 For a recent survey, see Thomas Nickles, "Discovery," in *Companion to the History of Modern Science*, ed. R. C. Olby, G. N. Cantor, J. R. R. Christie, and M. J. S. Hodge (London: Routledge and Kegan Paul, 1990), 148–65; and also his "Discovery Logics," *Philosophica* 45 (1990), 7–32.

side of a discovery–justification split; but Mill was not in fact so unambiguously aligned. In the book's subtitle, he declares interest in both "methods of investigation" and "principles of evidence"; and he insists, for example, in his replies to Whewell, that his methods are as much methods of "discovery" as of "proof."[33] Thus, even if he does tend to emphasize proof over discovery, he is not as careful with this distinction as would be the case with a thinker for whom justification is explicitly recognized to be the only genuine question.[34] Finally, neither Comte nor Mill construes "justification" as "confirmation" in anything like the rigorous Logical Empiricist sense.[35]

In the present context, then, our question cannot (yet) be whether discovery is one thing and justification another. In fact, Mill's criticism is not about discovery versus justification at all. His real concern is the formalization of scientific procedure, whatever its function; and on this issue, Mill is appalled by Comte's refusal to "speak of a doctrine of Method apart from particular applications" and by his insistence that method "is learnt only by seeing it in operation, and the logic of a science can only usefully be taught through science itself." Indeed, Mill complains, Comte seems to grow progressively – even willfully – more mistaken on this issue. At least in Volume One of his *Cours*, a doctrine of method is thought to be "conceivable, but not needful"; but in later volumes, Comte

> assumes a more decidedly negative tone, and treats the very conception of studying Logic otherwise than in its applications as chimerical. He got on, in his subsequent writings, to considering it as wrong. This indispensable part of Positive Philosophy he not only left to be supplied by others, but did all that depended on him to discourage them from attempting it.[36]

---

33 The *Logic*'s full title is *A System of Logic, Ratiocinative and Inductive: Being a Connected View of the Principles of Evidence and the Methods of Scientific Investigation*. On Whewell, see SL, III, ix, 6; and III, ii, 5. Bain recalls being "struck with the seeming incompatibility between the definition of Logic in the Introduction – the Science of Proof or Evidence – and the double designation in the title"; but, he says, "the title, although larger than the definition, is not larger than the work; [Mill treated] the methods of Investigation, as aids to Discovery, as well as means of Proof; only, he never explained the mutual bearings of the two. Anyone who tries, will find this not an easy matter[!]" (*Mill*, 68).

34 Larry Laudan argues that before "confirmation" (in the Logical Empiricist sense of checking consistency and testing consequences) could become the question, the epistemic infallibilism of the seventeenth and eighteenth centuries and a related confidence in purely generative evaluation of theories had to go out of favor. See "Why Was the Logic of Discovery Abandoned?" in *Science and Hypothesis*, 188–91. If Laudan is right that such a change occurs during 1820–50, it comes too late for Mill to have simply begun with the confirmation question self-evidently in focus.

35 On Mill, cf. Ryan, *The Philosophy of John Stuart Mill*, 30–43; and Georg Henrik von Wright, *The Logical Problem of Induction*, 2nd ed. (Oxford: Basil Blackwell, 1957), 60–75. For Comte on verification (and brief comparisons with Mill and other nineteenth-century thinkers), see Laudan, "Towards a Reassessment," in *Science and Hypothesis*, 144ff. Occasionally, when the issue is whether Comte had clear views on matters we now treat with great sophistication (e.g., the justification of induction, the status of hypotheses), Laudan tends to be too generous, with the result that Comte is defended against a vagueness and lack of system that (as I think) he himself might have insisted on.

36 ACP, 292/56.

The two features of Mill's complaint we should note here are its display of epistemological self-confidence and its unphilosophical handling of Comte. Mill is convinced that philosophers of science must produce what Logical Empiricists later call a rational reconstruction, or explication, of the scientific method. Thus, he assumes his "main problem" is that of developing a "systematic" (i.e., idealized) substitute for the actual (i.e., sloppier) thing. Yet nowhere does Mill present a case for this view; and when he encounters Comte's obviously different orientation, he refuses even to treat him as a genuine opponent. Instead, he explains him away. When he is thinking of Comte's earlier *Cours,* he still characterizes him in somewhat more generous terms as "not so solicitous about completeness of proof as becomes a positive philosopher," and he argues that because Comte did not develop a formalized "doctrine" of method,

> the unimpeachable objectivity ... of a conception – its exact correspondence to the realities of outward fact – was not, with him, an indispensable condition of adopting it, if it was subjectively useful, by affording facilities to the mind for grouping phenomena.[37]

When, however, Mill is thinking of Comte's later *Système,* his attacks become less measured and more personal. There he finds evidence of Comte's "inordinate demand for 'unity' and 'systematization' "; his humorlessness; his excessive admiration for "submission and obedience"; and a "frenzy for regulation" that, Mill informs us, is typically French.[38]

In short, as we have already seen with psychology and will soon see again with causality, when the ostensible topic is the logic of proof, Mill speaks of Comte in the same dismissive way that Logical Empiricists later treated their predecessors. The reason is not hard to find. In all three cases, careful reading reveals that Mill is not speaking as one engaged in an intramural disagreement with another positivist over how to handle a given topic. In each case, Mill is concerned with the defense against an unbeliever of a basic tenet of positivism – respectively, the epistemic legitimacy of psychology, the centrality of an organon of proof, and the scientific value of the concept of causality. And in each case, his tactic is the same, namely, to contrast the older thinker – who, alas, still suffers from prescientific afflictions – with one's own more successfully post-traditional self.[39] Un-

---

37 ACP, 294/59. Mill's own very loose adherence to so pure an empiricism gives this criticism a disingenuous appearance.
38 ACP, 336/141; 343/153–54; 352/171; 366/196; and 343/153.
39 See, e.g., Neurath's promise to "solemnly cut the strings which connect us with the positivism of the past," in "The Orchestration of the Sciences by the Encyclopedism of Logical Empiricism," *Philosophy and Phenomenological Research* 6 (1945), 500–501; Carnap's suggestion that the label "logical positivism" implies "too close a dependence upon the older positivists, especially Comte and Mach," in "Testability and Meaning," *Philosophy of Science* 3 (1936), 422n.2; and Moritz Schlick's observation, which he applies without considerations of modesty to his own associates, that "it is the ablest thinkers who most rarely have believed that the results of earlier philosophizing ... remain unshakable," in "The Turning Point in Philosophy," in Ayer, *Logical Positivism,* 53. I shall have more to say about Schlick's sort of easy association of philosophical talent and historical disbelief, for it has not disappeared with the demise of Logical Empiricism.

surprisingly, in the process of so dismissing Comte's claims, Mill misconstrues them.

The truth is, Comte does not simply fail to produce a logic of proof or in cranky old age discourage others from trying; he actively and explicitly opposes the very idea of such a logic, and for what he takes to be sound positivist reasons. In his view, to identify the philosophy of science with the logic of science, as Mill does, will lead inevitably to one of two opposite errors. On the one hand, there is the old danger of "mysticism" (i.e., theological and metaphysical speculation). Given that we are just emerging from an era in which everything important is explained in terms of unobservable abstractions, Comte explains, for all those who still think of logic on the traditional (disputational) model of an abstract system of deduction, any separate formalizing treatment of logic today is bound to encourage an overestimation of reason's role in knowledge. Comte remarks pointedly that the sort of mind that is proficient in following idealized formulations of the rules of thought is the dogmatic metaphysical mind.[40]

On the other hand, there is the new danger of "empiricism" (i.e., "the barren accumulation of unrelated facts"). To all those emerging positive thinkers, freshly imbued with the modern scientific spirit of inductive research, any idealization at this time of "the" alleged logic of their practice will likely encourage them to underestimate reason's role in knowledge. Unquestionably, says Comte, reason should be subordinated to observation; but there is no absolute set of rules for doing this. Actual scientific research in various fields must discover for itself the specific ways to accomplish this subordination; and anyway, it is always a matter of placing reason in the service of experience, not of making it experience's slave.[41] A "purely empirical spirit," asserts Comte, using one of his favorite adjectives, produces "mischievous results" – for example, he might have added, the demotion of hypothesizing in science to a mere "operation subsidiary to induction" (Mill's phrase). Excessive inductivism, like unbridled speculation, can be avoided only

> by the positivist plan of never separating logic from science. Studying each part of the inductive method in combination with the doctrines [that is, phenomenal laws developed in the various sciences] which have called it into existence . . . enables

---

40 DEP, 46–47/74; cf. CPP3(40), 427–28.
41 "Every science consists in the coordination of the facts; if there were only a collection of separate observations, there would be no science. Indeed . . . science is essentially destined to *dispense with direct observation, as much as the phenomena will permit,* by warranting the deduction of the greatest possible number of results from the smallest possible number of immediately given data." CPP1(3), 131, my emphasis; cf. CPP1(2), 77–82 [F, 46–49], and CPP4(48), 418–19. By the time Whewell wrote "Comte and Positivism" [*Macmillan's Magazine* 13 (1866)], the myth was well on its way to creation that Comte (and, under his influence, probably Mill) "reject[s] all abstract conceptions, causes, theories, and the like; and . . . assert[s] that phenomena alone are the proper subject of science" (353–54). In fact, however, Comte's attitude toward empiricism is much more like that of, e.g., Alan Chalmers in *Science and Its Fabrication* (Minneapolis: University of Minnesota Press, 1990), 41–60, 66–67.

the student to steer between the two opposite dangers of mysticism and empiricism, to which all investigations are liable. . . . [42]

Even then, however, the understanding one obtains about induction will always remain for Comte "incompetent . . . to furnish actual solutions" for scientific reason's problems and will be able only to "supply general indications" and to "mark out a direction to follow."

Clearly, then, Comte must oppose the very intention of works like Mill's *Logic*,[43] because it is wrong both (a) conceptually, for implying that a single set of rules structures every science, and (b) practically, because it threatens to straitjacket scientific activity itself. Comte's holding on (a), of course, puts him squarely at odds with everyone from Mill to Reichenbach; but the point is obvious this late in the twentieth century. I therefore close this section with a brief further consideration of Mill versus Comte on (b), on the relation of methodology to practice, from a somewhat pedestrian angle.

In his introduction, Mill addresses potential critics of his *Logic* who might argue that just as we cannot learn to how to use our muscles by studying anatomy, we cannot learn to think by studying logic. Mill replies that, up to a point at least, the analogy is in both cases quite wrong. For in thinking as in exercising, we must learn to distinguish those moves we ought to make from those we ought not to make.[44] This reply is, of course, perfectly sensible, but I believe it would strike Comte as missing the main point. It may be true that, for example, joggers can save themselves a lot of grief by exploiting the knowledge of physical therapists. Other things being equal, it might also seem that learning "the" logic of scientific reasoning would lead to better science. But in Comte's view, other things are not equal. Scientists cannot be expected to act like Millian joggers. The sociocultural atmosphere is never rich with Mill's sort of naive sensibleness, and people will not become less unreasonable by studying Mill's methods. For Comte, a more appropriate analogy to use against Mill would be that of a budding scientist to, say, a tennis novice who imagines that expert play can come from knowing and applying all the game's rules. At a time when, as Comte understands it, humanity is finally learning that the power of reason must be neither over- nor underestimated but rather always coordinated with observations, what a maturing mind least needs to hear is that scientific activity is a matter of following "rules." It is this contextualized image of the emergent positive mind that Comte is think-

---

42 SPP1, 518/419. Cf. CPP1(1–2), 39–40, 107–108 [F, 23, 63]; CPP6(58), 702–703; and DEP, 16–17/24–26, and 46–47/73–74. For Comte on hypotheses in science, see esp. CPP2(28), 433–54.
43 In 1844, Comte cites Mill's *Logic* (III, vii–xiii) for its "admirable systematic [*dogmatique*] exposition . . . of inductive logic" (DEP, 17n.1/26n.), but even though he appears to have read the work in the spring of 1843 [LMC, XXVIII (June 16, 1843), 189–92] there is no evidence that Comte either studied it in detail or understood its reconstructivist intentions. Mill himself, in derisive tones, describes Comte as giving the *Logic* "high approval" without becoming "indebted to it for a single idea" (ACP, 293/58n.).
44 SL, Intro., 7. Mill's editors trace the analogy to Thomas Carlyle.

ing of when he gives lengthy historical accounts of actual episodes of scientific observation, experimentation, and theory construction but refuses to offer organons of either discovery or proof.[45]

5. The question of causal laws

According to Mill, Comte's failure to recognize the need for a logic of proof is connected with his failure to understand how the concept of causality figures in scientific explanation. In science, asserts Mill, there are three kinds of inductive laws: (a) empirical laws, (b) genuinely causal ("ultimate") laws, and (c) the "law of universal causation." Mercilessly summarized,[46] Mill's view is that (a) empirical laws concern uniformities of "coexistence and succession" that are "conditionally" or "locally" invariable and of relatively limited scope; (b) causal laws concern "unconditional" sequences of much less restricted scope; and science's ultimate aim is to account for (a) by means of (b) in a deductively arranged system of inductively generated "laws of nature." This whole system of explanations, moreover, depends on (c) a fundamental "premise," namely, the "principle of the uniformity of nature," where uniformity is understood as nothing other than "the universality, throughout nature, of the law of cause and effect."[47] For Mill, this principle of [causal] uniformity

> stand[s] to all inductions in the relation in which . . . the major proposition of a syllogism always stands to its conclusion; not contributing at all to prove it, but being a necessary condition of its being proved; since no conclusion is proved, for which there cannot be found a true major premise.[48]

We cannot discuss here the whole nest of problems spawned by Mill's claims for the "necessity" of this ultimate inductive premise.[49] What is important in the pre-

---

45 In the year after the appearance of *Auguste Comte*, Lewes replied on Comte's behalf that even if Comte failed to make explicit how formal logic fits into scientific hierarchy, and even if logic might indeed be thought of as the "grammar" of science, neither concession justifies the reduction of the philosophy of science to its logic, let alone any search for general tests of truth "more valid than experience" itself. See "Comte and Mill," *Fortnightly Review* 6 (1866), 394. Lewes relies heavily on Littré, "M. August Comte et M. J. Stuart Mill," *Revue des Deux Mondes* 64 (1866), 829–66. Cf. Lévy-Bruhi, *The Philosophy of Auguste Comte*, 103–14.
46 For the details, see SL, III, iv, 1 (laws of nature generally); III, xvi (empirical vs. causal laws); and III, v, 1–3 (law of universal causation). See also, Scarre, *Logic and Reality*, 89–90; and Ryan, *The Philosophy of John Stuart Mill*, 60, 68–72.
47 SL, III, xxi, 1 (567). As Scarre notes, Mill typically speaks of the "principle of uniformity" and the "universal law of causation" interchangeably (*Logic and Reality*, 85ff.).
48 SL, III, iii, 1 (308). Cf. SL, III, v, 1–2; III, xxi, 4; and the text of III, v, 9, from the first two editions, 1118–19.
49 Among the most prominent, of course, are (a) what it can mean for Mill to call this principle the supreme "premise" in a "deductively" arranged system when he holds that all "real" inferences are from particulars to particulars (SL, II, iii, 3) and that deduction is simply a way of handling the results of inductions (II, iii, 4–7); (b) what a general "justification" of induction can thus be for him; and consequently (c) how he can defeat Hume's skepticism about induction. On (a), see Ryan, *The Philosophy of John Stuart Mill*, Ch. 2; and Scarre, *Logic and Reality*, Ch. 3. On (b) and (c), I

sent context is simply that we see the central epistemic role it plays in his overall conception of scientific explanation.

As Mill pictures the matter, science would reach its final ideal were it to answer the question "What are the fewest general propositions from which all the uniformities which exist in the universe might be deductively inferred?"[50] To explain nature fully, in other words, would be to rehearse, as if in one vast syllogism, a total system of laws already inductively established that accounts for every instance of successive phenomena. Yet to explain nature even in part, the laws involved must do more than empirically identify "invariable sequences." Life, says Mill, is full of examples of invariable phenomenal sequences that are nevertheless conditional upon other phenomena. His favorite example is that of day and night, which constitutes an invariable sequence and is also conditional upon the earth's rotation. Truly scientific laws explain events in terms of antecedents upon which phenomena are "unconditionally" as well as invariably consequent. They are, in a word, causal laws; and it is this sort of law with which all induction is concerned. Hence, behind Mill's picture of the scientific ideal – that is, the dream of a perfect theoretical system "exactly corresponding to . . . outward fact" – lies his fundamental legitimating concept of the one, ultimate, realistic, fundamental Causal Law; and "it is on the universality of this law that the possibility rests of establishing a canon of induction."[51]

Mill's view here is, of course, certainly respectable, but not even in his day was it uncontroversial. Yet when faced with Comte's explicit rejection of any such creature as the Causal Law, Mill not only fails to offer reasons for taking a philosophical perspective from which he can defend such a law, he also dismisses Comte's own outlook as merely a function of his "mental dispositions." Specifically, he says Comte has a quirky hostility to the very *word* (Mill's emphasis) "cause," and he suggests that this costly psychological infirmity may be traced to Comte's antimetaphysical preoccupations. Thus on the one hand, Mill asserts, Comte is right to object to the metaphysical ideas of "ultimate" and "efficient" (i.e., nonphenomenal) causality, and he is correct in asserting that science must stick to the study of "physical" (i.e., phenomenal) succession. We can all agree with Comte that, in Mill's words, science must avoid

---

find Scarre convincing that Mill neither knows nor cares about Hume's problem, that for him the so-called problem of induction is important "for its bearing on the practical task" of distinguishing sound from unsound inductions, and that this approach is a "natural corollary" to his general theory of inference (ibid., 82–100).
50 SL, III, iv, 1 (317). Cf. III, v, 1; and Ryan, *The Philosophy of John Stuart Mill*, 3–10.
51 ACP, 293/58; also, SL, III, v, 6. In the *Logic*, Mill explains that the causal law, though fundamental, has only lately become evident via induction. Some few philosophers now see its importance, but for generations of scientists, "it scarcely entered their minds" [III, iii, 1 (307)]. How warranted inductions can made without explicit awareness of the causal law is thus one of the "problems of induction" for Mill (Scarre, *Logic and Reality*, 95–96).

the notion of causation... deemed, by the schools of metaphysics most in vogue at the present moment, to imply a mysterious and most powerful tie, such as cannot, or at least does not, exist between any physical fact and that other physical fact on which it is invariably consequent.[52]

On the other hand, Comte's opposition to the "study of causes" in this metaphysical sense is so overzealous that he fails to recognize another, entirely different idea of cause that "can be gained from experience" directly. Lacking this experiential notion, Mill argues, Comte's conception of the "subject matter of scientific investigation" – and thus also of its inductive procedures – is fundamentally defective. Blind to the difference between empirical and genuinely causal laws [in Mill's sense of (a) vs. (b) earlier], and blind also to the legitimacy of an entirely phenomenal yet also universal causal principle, Comte is forced into assuming that the study of phenomenal coexistence and succession itself is the end of science. He even, states Mill flatly, "sees no difference between such generalizations as Kepler's laws, and such [causal laws] as the [Galilean] theory of gravitation."[53] Comte's "determined abstinence from the word and the idea of Cause," concludes Mill, has two direct consequences. It leads to his excessively loose characterizations of scientific theorizing; and it leads to "his inability to conceive of an Inductive Logic, by diverting his attention from the only basis [i.e., the experienced as opposed to the metaphysical notion of cause] on which it could be founded."[54]

Again, however, as with the question of an organon of proof, Mill's criticism distorts Comte's view and misses his point. Contrary to the accusation, Comte does have a distinction similar to Mill's between empirical and causal laws. What he calls "concrete" laws deal, like Mill's empirical ones, with special, local, and more straightforwardly observed phenomenal sequences; what he calls "abstract" laws identify the fundamental invariabilities regulating all phenomena. The fit is not exact – among other reasons because Comte's concrete relations are not always even invariable; because his distinction is not formulated, like Mill's, with virtually exclusive focus on phenomenal *succession;* and because his distinction serves to classify sciences as well as scientific laws. Nevertheless, like Mill's causal laws, Comte's abstract ones are the "laws of nature" that "ultimately" account for merely observed or concrete regularities.[55] Given this distinction between concrete and abstract laws, plus his hierarchical conception of the sciences (which recognizes that, e.g., physical explanations are more "complex" than astronomical ones), together with his idea that the "real aim" of science is to

---

52 SL, III, v, 2 (326). Mill's confident summary dismissal of the "metaphysical" notion of causality indicates how far he is from taking Hume's doubts about "necessary" connection seriously.
53 ACP, 293/57. In general, *Auguste Comte,* the later work, takes a more critical (and personally derogatory) tone toward Comte than the *Logic.* See also, Ch. 1, fn.59.
54 ACP, 292–94/56–59, quote on 94/58–59; cf. SL, III, v, 6 (341–42).
55 See, e.g., CPP1(2), 70–74 [F, 42–45]; SPP1, 39–41/30–32, 425–26/345. On "laws of nature," see CPP3(40), 269–71 [A, 110–11].

substitute predictive laws as much as possible for mere observations, Comte certainly has no trouble understanding the epistemic difference between Kepler's and Galileo's theories, as Mill believed. Finally, Comte even agrees, in one place specifically citing Mill as an ally, that positive philosophy has a "fundamental principle," namely, that "all phenomena whatever ... are subjected to rigorously invariable laws"; and he, too, holds that although this principle cannot be demonstrated a priori, every additional discovery of natural invariability adds to that "immense induction" that gives it the greatest possible certainty any scientific principle can have.[56]

In Comte's view, however, none of this justifies the conclusion that either abstract laws or the fundamental positivist principle should be construed in terms of causality. On the contrary, taking his cue from Hume, Comte argues that for historico-critical as well as epistemological reasons, they should not be so construed.[57] It is true, says Comte, that phenomenal relations are often "rigorously invariable"; and where this is so, the laws of nature should be formulated accordingly. Traditionally, however, when invariability was conceived in terms of "causes," this led not to the clarification of phenomenal relations themselves but instead to speculation about their hidden efficient or final causes. Traditionally also, talk of an ultimate, specifically causal law sprang from prior metaphysical convictions, not from any urge to justify research, inductive or otherwise.[58]

Whether Comte's conception of scientific explanation is better than Mill's is not the issue here. What is important is to see once again, from the kind of arguments Comte gives, that his philosophical perspective on scientific activities is historical-minded in a way Mill neither shares nor appears to understand. Far from being – as Mill would have it – regrettably preoccupied with a past that is over and done with, Comte is trying to show how current thinking still in fact inherits and tends to be affected by that past. For my purpose, then, perhaps the best way to capture quickly the radical difference between Mill's and Comte's positions here is to see why Comte could never share Mill's characterization of "cause" as just a scientifically useful word. When Mill introduces the term, he just stipulates that he will mean phenomenal, not metaphysical cause; and when

---

56 See CPP6(58), 710. The reference to Mill is in DEP, 17/26; see also the reply to Mill on Comte's behalf in Bridges, *The Unity of Comte's Life and Thought*, 64–66. Laudan thinks that it may be Mill's influence that got Comte to take both the general question about induction and the principle of the invariability of natural laws seriously ("Comte's Méthode Positive," *Science and Hypothesis*, 149–50). At least with respect to induction, however, it seems more likely that Comte worked out his view in the 1820s in connection with his critique of excessively "mathematical," or Cartesian, interpretations of science that encourage too much respect for pure reasoning and too little enthusiasm for experimentation (see Pickering, PIC, 576–77, 578–79).

57 On Comte's early familiarity with Hume specifically and the Scottish Enlightenment generally, see Pickering, PIC, 305–14.

58 All attempts to systematize either scientific laws or scientific activity in terms of "substantive" principles must therefore be avoided; and science must conceive its "unity" and "destination" in terms of its method alone. See, e.g., CPP1(1), 53–56 [F, 30–32]; SPP1, 361, 521–23/289–90, 422–23; and Lévy-Bruhl, *The Philosophy of Comte*, 85–94.

he wants to stress the distinction between merely invariable and unconditionally invariable (i.e., "genuinely causal") succession, he asks that we simply

> adopt the convenient modification of the meaning of the word cause, which [usually, traditionally] confines it to the assemblage of positive conditions without the negative . . . [so that, henceforth] instead of "unconditionally," we must say, "subject to no other than negative conditions."[59]

Mill psychologizes away Comte's refusal to accept such stipulations, calling it an obsession over a word; but this is a distortion. For Comte, the word itself is not the issue; or better, "cause" is not for him a mere label, to have its meaning "conveniently modified" to suit a chosen epistemic purpose. Words, or at least a few of them, carry philosophical histories; and it is unrealistic to assume that even resolutely positive minds might just "decide" to stop thinking of causation metaphysically. Indeed, with respect to "cause" in particular, there is even something a bit disingenuous in Mill's criticism, given that he himself argues elsewhere that we should abandon the word "necessity" in favor of "unconditionedness" for historico-critical reasons quite similar to those Comte uses in connection with "causality."[60]

6. Philosophy "of" or "about" science?

Recalling Chapter 1, we can see now that Mill's criticism of Comte on psychology follows the same pattern as the two criticisms just discussed. His differences with Comte are not, as he appears to assume, those of one logician of science quarreling with another – here over the best method for studying mental phenomena, there over the need for an organon of proof or the usefulness of a term. Nor is Mill right to measure Comte by his own conception of a rigidly separated pair of tasks, history of science and logic of science, supposedly revealing that Comte does too much of the former and too little of the latter. What Mill does not appear to understand is that there is between himself and Comte a fundamental disagreement about *philosophy's relation to science*, mental or otherwise, methodologically formalized or not. And nowhere is this more evident than in their treatments of the possibility of psychology.

For Mill, an empirical and introspective psychology is already here; the only philosophical task left is to facilitate this wider factual study of "thought as thought" by adding a narrower normative analysis of "valid thought." For Comte, however, old-fashioned "rational" psychology is not over; even the best of the positive minds are not operating in pure, post-traditional space; and philoso-

---

59 SL, III, v, 6 (340).
60 SL, VI, ii, 2–3. Especially interesting is that here, Mill argues, the term has a pernicious *sociopolitical* effect, especially when used to characterize human actions. In doing so, Mill no longer speaks as metamethodological philosopher but instead, like Comte in a very similar vein concerning "cause," e.g., in his *Discours* (DEP, 40/64), as one who is historically sensitive about a scientific era still conceived as emergent.

phy therefore cannot reduce, in Mandelbaum's phrase, to the "self-criticism of science." Here and in general, Comte does not think positivism can be, as the title of this section designates it, a philosophy only "of" science, that is, one that originates within and is always immanent to it. He insists, rather, that positivism must remain "about" science, that is, be reflectively, historico-critically concerned with it.

Let us be cautious, however, not to read too much social-historical constructivism back into Comte here. Comte's reflective purpose is not one of "*re*contextualization" – that is, deflating the objectivist pretensions of Logical Empiricists, cutting science itself down to size after a heyday of epistemic imperiousness. As we are about to see, his purpose is to make nascent scientific reasoning – above all, his own – self-conscious enough to continue the job of transforming a theologico-metaphysical inheritance. Thus, for example, in Comte's eyes the very possibility of a "scientific" study of mental phenomena is still in jeopardy from the lingering influence of traditional inheritance and thus requires philosophy's assistance even to be taken seriously. Indeed, says Comte, it is one of the four "principal general advantages" of positive philosophy that by fighting off appeals to interior observation and urging instead the consideration of

> the activity of our intellectual faculties in terms of their [observable] results, [it] furnishes us with the only really rational means of exhibiting the logical laws of the human mind, which have hitherto been sought by methods so ill calculated to reveal them.[61]

In Comte's view, as we have seen, mental science especially needs this kind of help. The natural sciences made their way to the methods of observation and experiment in the absence of any positive philosophy, but this cannot happen with the study of human beings as such. To be sure, anatomy and physiology are already succeeding in linking us up with the rest of nature; but for scientists to go on to illuminate our distinctively human complexity, they must first overcome long-held theologico-metaphysical beliefs about our being God's special creatures. These beliefs, which depict us as having immortal souls, reason, and (unfortunately though temporarily) bodies, find expression in the current unscientific tendency to stress intellect at the expense of affect, promote theories of substantial selfhood, ignore the empirical study of abnormal states, and attribute instincts to animals but not to human beings. Here is an instance, Comte argues, when philosophy must help a science become a science. Those flattering old be-

---

[61] CPP1(1), 32 [F, 19]. Comte offers the political counterpart of this argument by making the fourth principal advantage of positive philosophy its capacity for being the "only solid basis of the social reorganization," something that is needed to overcome the current "crisis" of the civilized world. This crisis is the lack of any stable social order, at bottom due to a state of "intellectual anarchy" brought on by "the simultaneous employment of three radically incompatible philosophies – the theological, the metaphysical, and the positive." The solution, of course, is the third type's gaining "complete and universal preponderance" (CPP1(1), 47–50 [F, 28–29]).

liefs about our special status must be unmasked as pure inventions; otherwise, the study of human beings cannot emerge from its prescientific condition.[62]

Yet one should not be misled here – as Mill seems to have been – by the fact that Comte shares Mill's desire to have knowledge claims about human beings judged according to "scientific" standards. The point is to see that *this very epistemic commitment* is one of Comte's, but not Mill's, express philosophical topics. As a philosopher "of" science, Mill simply begins by separating his logical study of "valid thought" from the larger psychological study of "thought as thought," drawing confidently on what seem to him the obvious distinctions between the "form" and the "matter" of thought, its "necessary" and "contingent" properties, and its "process" over against its "product," and then combining the second members of each set to designate the subject matter of logic.[63] As a philosopher "about" science, however, Comte begins by searching self-consciously for a satisfactory way of marking off positive from metaphysical mental science, using his own previously defended conception of what constitutes the "mature" state of knowing.

If both thinkers may therefore be equally said to *act* on their epistemological convictions, only Comte appears to be *reflectively concerned* about his doing so. Mill separates logic from psychology, deems the latter introspective, idealizes the former, and concludes that Comte is insufficiently positivistic in not seeing all this; but nowhere does he defend either these pronouncements or the standpoint from which they are made. Comte, however, although just as interested as Mill in furthering the scientific study of mental activity, begins with a critique of rational psychology which is only secondarily an expression of that interest. First of all, it is part of his general project of distancing the positive philosophy of the *Cours* itself from prescientific modes of thinking; and traditional doctrines of the self are offered as especially unfortunate examples of the results of such thinking.

---

62 Like Comte, the Logical Empiricists reject metaphysical talk about self or soul and tend to favor some species of behaviorism. However, their views on psychology seem to be shaped not by Comte or Mill directly but by their own favorite metaphysical or epistemological assumptions about how empirical verification is possible. Thus, e.g., Carnap's plan to reduce all psychological terms to thing-language derives from his general thesis of physicalism. See "Psychology in Physical Language" in Ayer, *Logical Positivism*, 165–98. Neurath follows Carnap in advocating this reduction, but does so more in the name of his antimetaphysical polemic than out of any commitment to physicalism or any preconceptions about scientific method. See "Unified Science and Psychology" in *Unified Science: The Vienna Circle Monograph Series*, ed. by Brian McGuinness and trans. by Hans Kaal (Dordrecht: D. Reidel, 1987), 1–23. Reichenbach, although citing Carnap's reduction with approval, is motivated primarily by his methodological concern to show how inferential processes in psychology are no different from those of physics. See *Experience and Prediction: An Analysis of the Foundations and Structure of Knowledge* (Chicago: University of Chicago Press, 1938), 225–47.

63 These distinctions, presupposed but not even mentioned in the *Logic*, are discussed in *William Hamilton's Philosophy*, 359–61. Logic, Mill argues there, is a "branch of psychology," which later studies the form, the necessary properties, and the process of thought generally. For recent discussion (with numerous references) of the probably insoluble problem of whether Mill thus psychologizes logic, see, e.g., Scarre, *Logic and Reality*, 110–25.

Here, I think, lies the real explanation for Mill's somewhat surprising and otherwise uncharacteristic displays of intolerance toward Comte's position, as well as the deeper significance of the fact that this intolerance emerges specifically in connection with the three aspects of Comte's position on which I have focused. For when the issue is the status of psychology, the need for a logic of proof, or the idea of causality in science, Mill does not offer a different opinion. Nor does he only, though he certainly manages at least to, misinterpret his opponent. What he does, in addition and more fundamentally, is to reject the very legitimacy of Comte's opinion – and this he does on the basis of a rival but always simply assumed understanding of what it is to be a positivist. One can find, to be sure, numerous lower-level disagreements between Mill and Comte on specific ethical and political issues. There is also undoubtedly a difference of intellectual temperament in something like the Jamesian sense, with Mill displaying a more tentative and open-minded attitude than Comte on these same issues. In the often-cited image of Lévy-Bruhl, Mill at first sought to correspond with Comte on their different "opinions" on various matters, only to find that Comte had nothing but nonnegotiable "doctrines" instead.[64]

We now see, however, that it is very misleading to compare these two thinkers only on the level of doctrine and opinion. Both of them appear in a very different and philosophically more revealing light when the focus is on their general epistemological orientations rather than on their specific scientific or sociopolitical disagreements. Comte's conception of the scientific value of logic, causality, and psychology is at least as reasonable as, say, Whewell's; yet Mill treats Whewell with infinite patience and dismisses Comte for his "mental inclinations." The basic trouble is, from his confidently postmetaphysical vantage point Mill appears unable to appreciate the sorts of battles that, in Comte's eyes, one becomes a positivist by fighting.[65] He complains, for example, that Comte's "lax use" of the term "metaphysics" permits him to exaggerate both its historical importance and its present danger; and on those infrequent occasions when Mill himself considers contrasts between scientific and prescientific thinking, it is not to any lingering metaphysical controversies in his own era but to the folklore of remote theological speculations that he typically refers. In Mill's eyes, metaphysical issues that may once have been central to the emergence of science – for example, overreliance on deductive logic, speculation about hidden causes, theories of substantive selfhood – have all been resolved. Mill therefore condemns the way Comte rhapsodizes about science in such prescientifically charged phrasings as that it is "destined" to satisfy our "predilection for order and harmony" or that it is responsive to our intellectual "need for idealizations *(besoin d'idéalité)*." Such needs

---

[64] LMC, XIII, 76–91. ACP, 270/14–15. In the same year that he finished the *Cours*, Comte wrote Valat that the time for "discussion" was over for him; henceforth, it would be a matter of exposition and application of his "principles" [*Lettres d'Auguste Comte à M. Valat* (September 17, 1842), 304–305].

[65] ACP, 277–78, 289/29, 49.

and predilections, says Mill, may have figured necessarily in earlier efforts to explain nature; but they are now of merely "personal" and historical interest. Thus Comte's persistence in taking this sort of thing seriously is "a complete dereliction of . . . the positive conception of science."[66] From Mill's post-metaphysical vantage point, then, uneven treatment of Whewell and Comte actually makes sense. Whewell, not being a positivist, cannot be expected to get these matters right; however, Comte, in refusing to forge ahead with the obvious methodological task when the epistemological war is clearly won, puts himself "willfully" at odds with his own professed positivism.

Mill is in this regard already like the Logical Empiricists, insofar as he pictures the authentic positive philosopher as one who holds everything that led up to scientific cognition at arm's length and gets on with the job of laying down the conceptual and methodological requirements for good science. Here is the picture that informs Mill's treatment of all three epistemic issues treated in this chapter: *Given* that discoveries of what there is are always made by observation and experiment, he seeks only to codify the rules of confirmation for alleged discoveries. *Given* that extraphenomenal explanation is passé, he simply stipulates that "causality" means "unconditionally invariable" phenomenal sequence. And *given* that "interior observation" is always an encounter with associated mental events and never with a mental substance, he knows psychology is a science. From this angle, Comte's positivism does indeed appear historically preoccupied and incomplete. Why should it matter to us what "logic" or "cause" or "psychology" was traditionally and wrongly taken to mean? For Mill, ensconced in a scientific present, it is enough that we should state clearly what they are supposed to mean and get on with the *Logic*.

Yet it is precisely this self-possessed, present-minded attitude that Comte opposes. He does not share Mill's confident picture of current philosophical thinking. In his view, not even committed positivists are safe in assuming that they have thoroughly gotten over theology and metaphysics. In contrast to Mill, he therefore displays much greater concern for recent rather than remote examples. "Metaphysical abstractions," he warns, "far more than theological fictions, present a semblance of rationality capable of *seducing the understanding.*"[67] And that is why Mill's easy separation of mere *words* from the *activities* named by them simply will not do. The very attempt to work out "a canon of proof," or to search for "causes," and to "look within" arrives for us as a tainted possibility. Just engaging in such activities tends to carry the mind back toward prescientific modes of thinking. In short, for Comte but not for Mill, a *reflective recognition of precisely this historical state of affairs* is fundamental to an authentic positivist outlook.[68]

---

66 ACP, 296/61–62. Mill quotes here mostly from CPP6(58), 676–85. Cf. CPP1(2), 63–64 [F, 38–39].
67 CPP6(58), 722–23, my emphasis.
68 Laudan describes this shift toward a more uncritical positivism from another angle in "Peirce and the Trivialization of the Self-Corrective Thesis," *Science and Hypothesis*, 226–51. He observes that

As I suggested in the Introduction, on the issue of the relevance of history to current practice, Comte gives what for the past several decades has seemed precisely the wrong answer. Yet for that very reason, he now begins to look more interesting than Mill. The post-metaphysical posture characteristic of Logical Empiricism as well as Mill has fallen out of favor. Two of its basic features – namely, its resolutely ahistorical outlook and its lack of self-criticism – have come to be suspected of naiveté. By contrast, neither of these features figures prominently in Comte's "older" positivism. "An idea," says Comte at the very beginning of the *Cours*, "cannot be properly understood except through its history." For him, this means that before one can become a philosopher of science in Mill's sense, the question of the emergent status of science itself must be raised. As we will see next, Comte takes up this historico-critical question by recourse to his three-stage law.

---

when early modern philosophers argue that scientific methods are self-correcting, they are defending science itself, not just their methods; but from Peirce on, yet under the mistaken assumption that earlier thinkers had done the same, the focus turns toward the more specific issue of the self-correcting nature of inductive inference. Thus "in an unnoticed sleight of hand . . . the problem of *the justification of science* has been displaced by the problem of *justifying induction*" (244, my emphasis). Comparing Comte with Mill suggests that a suppression of reflection facilitates this displacement.

3

COMTE'S THREE-STAGE LAW

Regarding Comte's "great fundamental law of the development of human intelligence," the primary source material is vast. Substantial portions of his six-volume *Cours*, two massive volumes of the four-volume *Système*, and a number of lesser works are all concerned with the nature and applications of this three-stage law.[1] Yet according to the received view in English-speaking circles over the past several decades, there is at bottom nothing philosophically very exciting about this law. Above all, it is said to lack empirical warrant. Even if Comte himself often calls it a "hypothesis" subject to both "historical testing" (especially in light of the actual course of maturation in the sciences) and "reasoned demonstration" (on the basis of what is "generally known about human intelligence"), and even if Mill still speaks of its "striking and instructive" general accuracy, eventually the law came to be assumed incapable of passing any rigorous efforts at confirmation – and therefore as probably never having been more in the first place than the first principle of a merely "speculative" philosophy of history. We recognize, of course, that these are the forced options of Logical Empiricism; and today, that is perhaps already enough to purchase my reconsideration of Comte's substantive idea of the law without interference from the familiar obsessions about its epistemic status. As I will argue in Part II, turning too quickly to the question of its empirical warrant obscures Comte's critically reflective use of the law; and it is this latter use that has contemporary relevance.

---

1 In addition to the *Cours, Discours,* and *Système,* there is also the "Plan des travaux scientifiques nécessaires pour réorganiser la société," first published in 1822 and reprinted in SPP4a, 47–136/527–89. Another relevant work, *Discours sur l'ensemble du positivisme* (Paris: L. Mathias, 1848), became the first part of the *Système* and will be so cited. On Comte and his predecessors regarding the law, see Pickering, PIC, 187–88, 199–203; and Gouhier, *La jeunesse* 3, 395–403.

1. A law about what?

According to Comte's first formulation of the law, written when he was still in his early 20s,

> by the very nature of human intelligence, each branch of our knowledge must of necessity pass successively through three different theoretical stages: the theological or fictive, the metaphysical or abstract, and the scientific or positive stage.[2]

"Stage" is my attempt to convey in English Comte's sense that each *"état"* is not a static state but instead a developing "condition," both in itself and with respect to earlier and later conditions. To take a biological example of which Comte would approve, the "fetal stage" is no permanent "state [of affairs]." As the passage just cited says, the three-stage law is, first and foremost, about human thought; but the title of the essay in which the passage appears should warn us that it is not about thought exclusively. Comte announces here what he continually reaffirmed as being his primary aim, namely, to develop a "Plan of the Scientific Operations Necessary for Reorganizing Society." In this manifesto, he outlines his argument that current social arrangements are still mostly structured by theological and metaphysical ideas; that reorganizing these arrangements into something more satisfying will have to involve displacement of theologico-metaphysical ideas by scientific knowledge; and that, above all, this displacement will require scientific knowledge of the laws of human interaction.[3] However, a science of these laws [here, "social physics," later, "sociology"] does not yet exist. To establish this science, it must be conceived as the final member of an ensemble of hierarchically arranged sciences on which it depends and of which it is the completion. From astronomy to biology, all the other sciences in this hierarchy have already reached or are now reaching the positive stage. The phenomenal laws established by these sciences give us "prevision"; the practical application of their findings has already begun to improve our relations with nature.[4] Hence it is the story of these natural and life sciences, the possibility of a genuine social science, and the implications of their combined application for the improvement of human as well as natural relations with which the "Plan" is concerned; and it is within the context of this larger story that the question of the nature of knowledge is considered.

The three-stage law, then, is not about human thought considered abstractly or structurally or as such. It is about how strictly intellectual (sometimes, "spiritual") developments ultimately influence practical and social (sometimes, "temporal") activity – and, most particularly, how this is so in the third, or positive, stage.

---

2 SPP4a, 77/547; cf. SPP4a, 111–13/572–73 and 137–47/590–98.
3 SPP4a, 93–100/558–64. Cf. CPP4(48), 324–99.
4 SPP4a, 118–36/576–89. Comte's mature conception of the scientific hierarchy and its sociopolitical significance emerges in the *Cours* (CPP1(1), 21–26, 47–51 [F, 12–15, 28–30]), with some later modifications that need not concern us here (see, e.g., DEP, 98–104/154–66; and SPP2, 432–39/352–57).

"From science comes [at last!] prevision; from prevision comes [genuinely productive and satisfying] action," Comte says in the *Cours*, explaining that the positivist slogan ("Order and Progress") expresses this principle insofar as science gives us genuine knowledge of the natural and social "order," and that knowledge facilitates "progress" in practical and social life.⁵ In the *Système* he goes even further, adding a third idea to the slogan and explaining that with the improvement of our natural and interpersonal circumstances, there will eventually come a similar improvement in our affective life, and self-centeredness will begin to give way to universal "love," or benevolence.⁶

Yet if it would thus be wrong to say the three-stage law is exclusively about thought, it would also be misleading to say it is about our "thoughts." Comte's law is about intellectual approaches to things, about global ways or "methods" of thinking, not about the particular ideas, opinions, and beliefs to which one is led in using these methods. At the start of the *Cours*, having repeated the "Plan's" description of the three-stage law almost verbatim, Comte adds:

> In other words, in all of its investigations, human intelligence – by its very nature – successively makes use of three methods of philosophizing whose characters are essentially different and even radically opposed to each other.⁷

Seeing just how Comte's position here agrees with and differs from that of later positivism is vital. Most especially has his insistence on studying "methods" of cognition rather than actual cognitions been misunderstood; for if this makes him sound like an early logician of science, it does not turn him into one. We noted earlier that Comte opposes formalizing treatments of rationality for practical reasons; here we discover that he also has reasons of principle. It is not just that the production of an organon might have the effect of discouraging flexibility in conducting research; in addition, whether one views intellectual life diachronically or synchronically, our "ways" are irreducibly plural. For Comte, "philosophy" is something that can be done theologically, metaphysically, or scientifically. In his terminology, all philosophizing involves "speculation"; and each of the three kinds of speculation is guided by its own sort of method. This emphasis on the variety of methods of thought has important implications for any Comtean epis-

---

5 Since he understands progress to be first intellectual and then social, Comte can correctly say that in working out the three-stage law he recognizes Condorcet as his "true philosophic father" (SPP3, 1/11) – though Pickering may be right that in part Comte stresses this lineage to avoid the impression of having been influenced by Saint-Simon (PIC, 240–42).
6 CPP1(2), 63 [F, 38]; SPP1, 1–7, 321, 701–705/1–5, 257, 566–70. In the *Système*, Comte not only explicitly adds "Love" to his earlier "Order and Progress" as Positivism's motto but also lists it first. "We tire of thinking and even of acting; we never tire of loving," says the *Système*'s dedication. Let this stand as a symbol for the question – not addressed here – of the relation between Comte's earlier and later works. What is no longer open to question, however, is that the underlying sociopolitical purpose expressed in 1822 runs throughout all of Comte's works and figures prominently even in his unpublished writings at least as early as 1819–20 (see Pickering, PIC, 147–58, 691–710).
7 CPP1(1), 1 [F, 1–2].

temology of science. In contrast to the Logical Positivists, Comte does not think of philosophy as something only we moderns know how to do properly; nor, conversely, does he evaluate theology and metaphysics only in terms of their having failed to use our scientific method. In fact, as we shall see, it is Comte's view that so negative an attitude toward prescientific thinking threatens to obscure the very character of science itself.

With these qualifications, then, we may start by saying that the three-stage law is indeed concerned primarily with intellectual development. It is, moreover, informative about this development in several ways. Epistemologically, it explains how each species of "natural philosophy" comes to be a true science by passing first through the theological and metaphysical stages.[8] Sociopolitically, it depicts the development of the types of human societies that follow, but with a time lag, the passage within the society from one dominant intellectual stage to the next.[9] Biographically, the law characterizes the stages of intellectual maturation for individuals.[10] And historically in the most general sense, it describes the stages of intellectual growth for the whole of humanity. Behind all of these explanations, there lies an idea of human progress that Comte may be happy about but that he believes is in any case inevitable. Arguments for alternative directions or against the prevailing pattern of change would therefore be both regressive and ultimately futile.[11]

In discussing each stage, I shall be guided especially by Comte's general historical articulation of them, which is how Comte himself proceeds in both the introductory lessons of his *Cours* and in the *Discours*. From this angle, human progress is analyzed by focusing primarily upon the history of the race rather than on specific individuals or sciences; and concern for sociopolitical developments is present but muted.

---

8 Viewed from this angle, the three-stage law is a law of "filiation" for the theories in each science. As Comte explains, one uses this law in connection with the "law of classification [of the sciences]" in order to understand why, given the different degrees of generality and complexity of their respective phenomena, the various sciences develop at such different rates (SPP3, 40ff./33ff.). The law of classification explains the systematic, or "dogmatical," arrangement of the sciences in a hierarchy, the three-stage law, their historical development from theological into scientific kinds of inquiry [CPP1(2), 77–78 [F, 46–47]; DEP, 97– 98, 104–105/153–54, 166–67].

9 Lest this make Comte seem old-fashioned, it is worth recalling the now frequently forgotten fact that Vienna Circle Positivists regularly pursued their ostensibly formal analyses with serious sociopolitical hopes. See, e.g., Warner Wick, "The 'Political' Philosophy of Logical Empiricism," *Philosophical Studies* 2 (1951), 49–57.

10 As the famous passage has it, "Does not each of us in contemplating his own history recollect that he has been successively – as regards the most important ideas – a *theologian* in childhood, a *metaphysician* in youth, and a [positive, or] *natural philosopher* [*physicien*] in maturity? This verification is easily made today by all men who are on a level with their age" (CPP1(1), 7 [F, 4], author's emphasis).

11 SPP4a, 93–95/558–59; cf. SPP1, 24–31/19–24. Pickering (PIC, 209n.62) cites the happy remark of Gérard Buis that the only liberty Comte recognizes is our power to "regularize a spontaneous evolution" ["Le Projet de réorganisation sociale dans les oeuvres de jeunesse d'Auguste Comte" in *Régénération et reconstruction sociale entre 1780 et 1848*, ed. A. Amiot et al. (Paris: J. Vrin, 1978), 145].

2. The theological (supernatural) stage

According to Comte, in humanity's first, or theological era, one can discern three substages, namely, fetishism, polytheism, and monotheism.[12] Like the three master stages themselves, these three come in roughly chronological order. In all three substages, (a) feelings or instincts predominate over the capacity for thought; but in each one, they predominate differently.[13] The result is that fetishistic, polytheistic, and monotheistic beliefs about both (b) what is real and (c) how the real behaves are not the same.

Fetishism (animism)

Although Comte does not actually say so, behind his explicit pronouncements about intellectual and social development is the implicit understanding both that the relations between human beings and their surroundings are most properly conceived as harmonious ones and also that practical-mindedness is the attitude most suitable to maintaining such relations. This twofold understanding quite obviously informs Comte's defense of the "maturity" of the scientific stage, as we will see in a moment; but perhaps not so obviously, it also informs his interpretation even of the religious ideas and activities of our most remote ancestors. In primitive human life, according to Comte, experiences of mysterious and disturbing ruptures in what are otherwise expected to be predictable and peaceful interactions with the world give rise to (a) spontaneous reactions of the feelings or instincts. Afraid or awe-struck in the presence of some apparently uncontrollable natural force (e.g., an eclipse, earthquake, or epidemic), people are excited by these feelings into thinking about (b) the actually experienced thing itself precisely in terms of its frightful or awesome countenance. And since at this point the human race possesses no theoretical repertoire, all of the resulting conceptions tend to depict the frightful or awesome thing as (c) alive with power or energy

---

12 Comte is not the only one considering such a classification of stages of religious development at this time. Cf. the writings of Benjamin Constant, who also sees theology developing through three progressively more sophisticated forms; distinguishes between humanity's enduring "religious sentiment" and its changing historical manifestations; thinks polytheism is a more "genuine" kind of theology than monotheism; and judges all forms of theology finally in terms of their effects on social organization. See, e.g., his *De la religion, considérée dans sa source, ses formes, et ses développements*, 5 vols. (Brussels: P. J. De Mat, 1824–34), esp. Vol. 1, Bk. 1, 30–48, and Vol. 2, passim. Constant's work was known to Comte at the time he was preparing the first lectures of his *Cours;* he owned Volumes 1 and 2 of *De la religion* and may very well have picked up the term "fetishism" directly from Constant [see Pickering, PIC, 273–74 and (for background on Comte's three substages of theology generally) 633–48].

13 Comte adopts the threefold Kantian division of the basic human capacities into thinking (*spéculation*), willing (*activité*), and feeling (*sentiment*, or what in the *Système* is designated the "heart" as opposed to the intellect); but he typically treats them in what we would now call behavioral rather than subjective terms. Comte's view here is inspired by nineteenth-century biology – not, for reasons already discussed, psychology. Thought, will, and feeling are thus emphatically not regarded by Comte as mental "faculties" but are instead conceived as abilities or powers we understand largely by observing their "results" – e.g., their manifestations in theological or scientific theorizing, technical or social practices, and displays of affection.

analogous to but (given the nature of the present encounter) greater than the human will.

The formation of such analogies is, according to Comte, the first sign of speculative activity, the purpose of which is to explain the mystery of some unexpected course of events. Primitive speculation utilizes the image of the human will because what is sought is the "cause" of the occurrence, and the only causally effective power with which the primitive mind is directly familiar is that of its own acts of choosing. Yet once these spontaneously produced, animistic "theories" appear, their unsatisfactory character gradually becomes evident. As explanations of disruptions in relations taken to be "normally" harmonious, they come at too high a price. For if these disruptions were indeed simply displays of the superior power of nonhuman things, then fetishistic theories carry the intolerable implication that our true condition is one of total subordination to arbitrary external powers. While the long reign of fetishism lasted, says Comte, "humanity learned to submit to the world but without hope of modifying it."[14]

Polytheism

Stimulated now not only by feelings of awe or fear but also (a) by a sense of dissatisfaction with fetishistic responses to such feelings, early humanity begins to employ the imagination in speculation and attempts to explain events by picturing (b) the "hidden causes" of things, systematized eventually into a pantheon of invisible gods, who together preside over the natural world as (c) the controllers not just of this or that event but of classes of events (e.g., the sun god is responsible for the behavior of the sun generally, not just the occurrence of one particular eclipse). To understand why Comte thinks polytheism is the "truest" of the three theological stages, one must compare it both to the fetishism it surpasses and to the monotheism into which it ultimately gets transformed.

In contrast to fetishism, polytheism focuses on general "phenomenal" manifestations of things (e.g., the awe- or fear-inspiring actions or motions) and not on "existent" things themselves – thereby intimating for the first time the possibility of systematic intellectual abstraction. Polytheism is thus the "true theologism" insofar as it stimulates the development of genuine theorizing "by supplying all intellects with images extremely well adapted for fixing the attention habitually upon general phenomena apart from particular bodies."[15] Moreover, by making the control of these phenomenal generalities a function of divine wills instead of material forces, polytheism draws the world closer to us both theoretically and practically than fetishism could. Theoretically, the world (i.e., the "external order") seems more accessible because the course of things is now thought to be determined by beings analogous to ourselves (we know, after all, what it is to purposefully will something). Practically, the world is thus also made to seem more accessible, for unlike fetishism's mysteriously operating arbitrary powers, events

14 SPP3, 160/133; see also CPP5(52), 1–114 [M2, 181– 207].
15 SPP3, 171/142; also 149–50/123–24.

controlled by the wills of gods seem in principle understandable, hence potentially predictable, and perhaps even modifiable – especially given that the gods are usually interpreted as caring about us.[16]

In relation to monotheism, polytheism may be viewed as instituting "the great theoretic dualism of humanity and the world" that will ultimately make genuine knowledge possible; but it does so only in a rudimentary and intellectually inadequate form.[17] On the positive side, when polytheism makes satisfying relations between ourselves and the world depend on our understanding the wills of the gods, it makes spontaneous use of what we recognize to be the prototype of the now familiar epistemological model of thinking subjects seeking the right theoretical system of the world regarded as external object. In twentieth-century terms, the polytheistic mind begins to learn what it is to think representatively. On the negative side, however, polytheistic speculations remain fundamentally creations of the imagination. This may keep them close to our daily affairs and make them infinitely responsive to immediately felt encounters. (There is, e.g., always room for another god if the circumstances prove uncanny enough.) What they gain in practical appeal, however, they lose in speculative clarity and consistency. (There are, e.g., too many gods with too many competing purposes.) When *this* dissatisfaction grows strong enough, rational concepts begin to displace mere "images," and the transition is made to monotheism.

Monotheism

In the final analysis, Comte asserts, even monotheism (a) arises out of the feelings or instincts, but now reason struggles to gain the upper hand in responding to them by restricting the use of imagination in order to produce (b) a more logically organized and coherent account of divine causality – one that depicts the whole surrounding natural world as a cosmos (c) created by and subject to the will of a single god who acts not capriciously but in accordance with a set of universal and invariable laws. For Comte, the resulting picture of things is not very satisfying either intellectually or practically, and far from being a kind of completion of this first intellectual stage, it actually signals the beginnings of "decay" in the theological era. Monotheism's accounts of how the laws work remain incurably vague and abstract, since for monotheists the real point is always simply that they are God's laws; and the god who applies these laws seems increasingly remote from human affairs.[18] Indeed, according to Comte's unflattering image, the very point the monotheistic mind comes most to insist on – namely, the essential disjunction between divine and human natures – guarantees that its theories undermine the sense of (sometimes disrupted) intimacy that lies at the heart of our

---

16 SPP3, 160, 165–66/132–33, 136–38; also SPP2, 86–87, 90–91/76–77, 81–82. See also CPP5(53), 115ff. [M2, 208ff.].
17 SPP3, 159/132; cf. SPP1, 439–53/357–68.
18 CPP5(54), 297ff. [M2, 256ff.]. The "social usefulness" of monotheism lasted until the late Middle Ages (DEP, 12/18–19), says Comte, but its intellectual unsatisfactoriness was already realized in ancient Greece.

most primitive experiences of world and also gets restored when science at last provides us with genuinely efficacious theories. Yet it remains true that once the polytheistic imagination awakens reason, monotheistic speculation is forced on us by our sense that, for all its mystery and variety, the world around us is somehow one "connected" whole.

In general, then, the three stages of theology form the necessary "childhood" of the human race. Primitive humanity had neither theories to explain natural events nor observations from which to build such theories. Since reliable theory must be based on observation and fruitful observation must be guided by previously established theory, we would have been caught forever in a "vicious circle" had it not been for those spontaneously produced fetishistic conceptions of a world full of spirits through which primitive peoples expressed their fears and aspirations.[19] This "solution" made intellectual "progress" possible. It involved the initial self-display of all our human capacities – that is, our instincts and feelings, will, and imagination, as well as reason – and through the coordinated employment of these capacities, we learned for the first time that we have them and, more important, that they all play some role in our acquiring knowledge of our surroundings.

Of course, the capacity destined to be the foundation for all genuine theorizing is still little in evidence. The stimulus of instincts and feelings still holds the place of honor later to be given to "observation." But this is as it has to be. Initially, "mere" knowledge of resemblance and succession, which the scientist realizes is the real key to the knowledge and control of nature, simply cannot seem important enough to prescientific minds to attract any effort. The "overstimulation" of the mind by feelings and imagination conquers this initial mental innocence by appearing to promise an understanding of life's great mysteries. Although no such ultimate answers are ever found, the effort to find them marks our first attempt to subdue the unknown by means of thought. Theological speculation shows the mind that theorizing is possible. Moreover, insofar as these early efforts assume that understanding the ways of the gods is also the source of our conception of moral do's and don'ts, everyday life for the first time comes to be ordered comprehensively and communally instead of simply in terms of momentary individual whims. In fact, at the risk of a little exaggeration, I suggest that we translate Comte's teaching here as follows. Insofar as "worship" (or any other form of religious activity) necessarily involves the application of fetishistic, polytheistic, or monotheistic theory, it constitutes our first form of "universal praxis" – that is, the theological anticipation of modern technology considered as applied science.

19 CPP1(1), 9 [F,5]; DEP, 5–6/8–9. The 1822 "Plan" already stresses the necessity of fetishism but does not mentioned its solving of any vicious circle (SPP4a, 77/548). According to Comte, the sort of spontaneous theorizing manifested in fetishism is still appropriate even for modern scientists when they find that they possess neither reliable data nor plausible explanations (SPP3, 82–83/68–69). A case in point, says Comte, is the present condition of sociology (CPP4(48), 412–21 [A, 180–82]).

In the end, however, no theological conception of our surroundings can be intellectually satisfying, since it is inevitably more dependent on feeling and imagination than on reason. Moreover, if there is indeed to be a comprehensive representation of universal cosmic necessity mapped out in a system of laws explaining why everything hangs together, it is these "natural" laws themselves that are the important topic, not the gods' or God's employment (let alone miraculous circumvention) of them. The mind therefore grows increasingly unhappy with even the most ambitious and consistent supernaturalism, and it turns in critical reaction toward metaphysics.

3. The metaphysical (abstract) stage

According to Comte, the metaphysical stage – unlike the theological – has no separate, conceptually distinctive substages. Sometimes, in fact, he suggests that it is not a full-fledged stage at all but a merely transitional period between theology and science, "in reality just a general modification" of the theological – or even, in one place, a period of "gradually devitalized theology."[20] Starting during Comte's lifetime, however, the point of these deflationary remarks has been widely misunderstood, with the result that Comte's conceptions of the nature of metaphysics and the importance of the metaphysical era have been obscured and his position is now usually – and wrongly – taken to be pretty much like that of the later positivists. The case of Mill is, again, instructive – both in itself and for its anticipation of what we inherit more directly through others.

In his comments on the three-stage law, Mill complains that Comte "considerably exaggerates" the contribution made by metaphysics to the rise of science because he fails to distinguish rigorously between the mode of thought Mill calls "dialectics and negative criticism" and "the metaphysical spirit strictly so called," which Mill defines as a propensity to explain divine actions in terms of "impersonal entities, interposed between the governing deity and the phenomena." Granted that before there was science, the same minds might in fact have practiced both criticism and metaphysics (Mill mentions Plato); but the former is clearly capable of operating independently, and we now know that it is this critical mode of thought and not the metaphysical spirit that did more to facilitate the development of science.[21] Here we recognize, of course, Mill's agreement with the standard view of later positivism, according to which metaphysics is basically speculation about unobservables and critical thinking is the scientifically minded philosopher's superior response to such nonsense. The distinction is thus a familiar one. Unfortunately, it is not Comte's.

We should suspect that something is wrong when Mill declares that if he does not share Comte's estimation of the importance of the metaphysical spirit, at least he can agree that it "did…contribute largely to the advent of monothe-

20 See, respectively, CPP1(1), 4 [F, 2] and DEP, 10/16. See also CPP5(55), passim.
21 ACP, 277–78/29.

ism."²² In fact, Mill has it backward. According to Comte, metaphysics is a response to monotheism, not its catalyst. The problem is that Mill confuses his own conception of the metaphysical spirit with Comte's. Unlike Mill, who defines this spirit in positivistic retrospect as a sort of urge toward unscientific results, Comte treats it as a historically contextualized activity.

Strictly speaking, says Comte, "the metaphysical spirit properly so called…can never be anything but critical."²³ In other words, metaphysics is for Comte precisely the logical operation of "dialectics and negative criticism" that Mill wants to separate from what he calls metaphysics. What has gone wrong here? Were Comte to reply to Mill's objections, he would complain that Mill's attempt to separate criticism from unscientific theorizing both distorts the historical record and obscures what actually makes critical reasoning beneficial. Historically speaking, Mill fails to see that the metaphysical spirit's so often expressing itself "ontologically" (i.e., producing theories of abstract "entities") is a function of its origin, not of its nature. If one places metaphysical theories in context rather than obsessing over their illegitimacy, they will be recognized as constituting a critically inspired revolt against theology. And philosophically speaking, it is only when ontology is thus positioned between theology and science that the activity that animates the metaphysical revolt – what Mill calls "dialectics and negative criticism" – can be properly appreciated. "When the mind first enters this transitional stage," Comte explains, "critical reasoning [*raisonnement*] plays an excessive role" in our speculations about nature; and in its "obstinate proneness to argue rather than observe," the metaphysical mind is more interested in the dissolution of theological ideas than in "truly scientific work."²⁴

For Comte, in other words, the crucial fact about metaphysics is not that it produces ontological theories or that it has an essentially critical (he sometimes says "destructive") character; it is rather that, when taken together, its theories and the spirit in which they are produced demonstrate how, unlike either the theology it rejects or the science for which it paves the way, metaphysics is entirely driven by intellectual dissatisfaction with existing ideas and not by direct experiential encounter with our surroundings. Theology has three substages, because theological speculation is stimulated by feelings and instincts in three different ways. Feelings and instincts hardly qualify nowadays, of course, as a genuinely "observational" basis for theorizing; but at least they guarantee that all theology is grounded in some concrete, experiential relation with the world. And that, asserts Comte, is precisely what is not the case with metaphysics. No metaphysical system expresses any kind of experientially distinctive relationship to the world that would make it representative of a really separate post-theological stage;

---

22 ACP, 278/29. "The whole of the prevalent metaphysics of the present century is one tissue of suborned evidence in favor of religion" [*Three Essays on Religion* (1874), *Collected Works*, Vol. 10, 404].
23 DEP, 42/68.
24 DEP, 8–10/12–15. The aim of metaphysical technique, says Comte in his very unpositivistic assessment of critical reasoning, is "barren asceticism" (SPP1, 427/346).

hence, in spite of its often irreverently naturalistic tone, metaphysics remains at bottom simply a conceptual variation on theological themes. It is precisely this combination of intellectual irreverence and emotional-experiential dependence that makes metaphysics interesting to Comte – and that is because these are the two characteristics one must stress if the significance of the metaphysical era as a "transitional period" is to be understood.

The uniqueness, among positivists, of Comte's interpretation of metaphysics is now evident. Unlike both Mill and the later positivists, Comte neither writes it off as mere speculation nor assures us, with mock generosity, that the great metaphysicians were really scientists or logicians of science in the making. Instead, he insists upon the distinctiveness of metaphysical thinking and argues that the clarification and understanding of science itself depend on recognizing this distinctiveness. As he sees it, metaphysics is, above all, a critical response to theology – one that helps pave the way for positive knowledge by radically altering inherited theological conceptions of both the proper function of reason and the nature of explanation.

With respect to reason, the metaphysical period marks the time when humanity learns to free its thinking from superstition and authority. The metaphysical mind begins to appreciate the power of abstraction, discovers the value of logical argument, and develops mathematics. Reason, one finds, is capable of gaining the upper hand over feeling. In other words, as we would say now, the exercise of this capacity anticipates what will later become scientific objectivity.

With respect to explanation, metaphysical thinking helps wean the mind from its original tendency to invest all speculation about natural phenomena with the felt sense that something extra-natural controls them. To understand how this weaning happens, one must see that although the metaphysical era has no sub-stages, it does have an earlier and a later phase. In the earlier phase, intellectual dissatisfaction with theology centers on the vagueness and inconsistency of its accounts of all those hidden forces that allegedly control things. In this phase, metaphysics produces detailed, logically coherent naturalistic theories of these forces, but also continues to presume that these forces are themselves moved by God's agency. In a later phase, "nature" replaces "God" as the name for that ultimate power that, considered epistemically, provides a "vague, universal bond of connection for all phenomena." With this substitution, Comte tells us, the revolt against supernaturalism is complete.[25] Whereas, for example, an Aristotelian "physics" can still be treated as an auxiliary to theology, a Kantian "metaphysics of nature" cannot.

To be sure, according to Comte, even late metaphysical concepts are still, at best, only naturalized versions of theology's "hidden causes" of phenomena – that is, "equivocal" or, better, hybrid concepts that explain what is observable in

---

25 See, e.g., DEP, 9–10/14–15. The discussion in CPP5(55), a rambling and repetitious Lesson of nearly 300 pages written in less than six weeks, is summarized (with references to sources of influence) in Pickering, PIC, 649–55, and Lévy-Bruhl, *The Philosophy of Auguste Comte*, 286–94.

terms of what is not. Yet at the same time, it is precisely the production of such concepts that gives the metaphysical spirit its special significance.

> In its radical inconsistency, this equivocal [metaphysical] spirit retains all the basic precepts of any theological system, but in a way that increasingly deprives them of the power and stability which is indispensable for their effective authority. Bringing this about is, in fact, the chief transient utility of metaphysics; for although the old [theological] regimen had long been a progressive force in human evolution,...it inevitably reached a point of wholly inappropriate prolongation and threatened to perpetuate the stage of infancy which at one time it so happily guided.[26]

To understand the "transient utility" of metaphysics is to see how its hybrid concepts, by at once pointing back toward the old supernaturalist explanations and moving forward toward purely natural ones, gradually prepare the mind to concentrate exclusively on the phenomena themselves.

In short, for Comte the most important thing about metaphysical thinking is that it is Janus-faced. It is at once too independent to be theological and too theological to be scientific. On the one hand, metaphysical concepts differ profoundly from theological ones in their subordination of feelings and imagination to purely rational considerations. For precisely this reason, however, they are bound eventually to reveal their unsatisfactory character and ultimately force the mind to look to science. The problem is, once metaphysical theories are proposed and provided only that they are "reasonable," there is no satisfactory means for deciding among them. With nothing analogous to theology's feelings and instincts to hold them back, liberated metaphysical minds are able to produce an endless stream of complete, coherent, but also incompatible conceptual systems. In the first phase of metaphysics, during its time of ascendancy, the advocates of competing systems tried to meet this difficulty with realist construals of their own favored notions of the purposes, forces, and causes. In the late Middle Ages, however, when the intellectual ties with theology had grown "feeble," the nominalistic character of all these metaphysical notions became inescapably clear. By the end of the second phase of metaphysics, "the concepts of metaphysical agents [had become] so empty through oversubtle qualification that all right-minded persons considered them to be only the abstract names of the phenomena in question."[27]

Let me emphasize, however, that Comte makes this point not, as one might expect of a positivist, in order to advertise the superiority of scientific concepts, but rather to stress the degree to which scientific thinking benefits from having lived through a period of metaphysical abstractionism. By interposing a hypothetical world of "real" entities between God and phenomenal experience, metaphysics redirects attention away from the supposed ruler of that world and toward the agencies through which the ruler allegedly works; and as it becomes clear that these are *hypothesized* agencies and that their presumed operation is on

26 DEP, 15/10 (translation revised).
27 CPP1(1), 13–14 [F, 8]; see also SPP3, 38–39/31–32.

the phenomena we actually observe, the mind can gradually cleanse from its thoughts about our surroundings all hypotheses, not only about a supernatural agent but eventually about extraphenomenal agency in general. Indeed, says Comte, "it is impossible to imagine by what other method our understanding could have passed from frankly supernatural to purely natural considerations, or, in other words, from the theological to the positive intellectual regimen."[28] Viewed from this angle, metaphysics thus appears to make science possible by *naturalizing* theology.

On the other hand, metaphysics always remains at bottom naturalized *theology*. Parasitic from the start on the feelings and instincts that grounded speculation in the theological stage, the metaphysical mind is to the end still unable to let go of, as Comte says, the old precepts. It remains just as committed to its detheologized "inner essences" and "things in themselves" that supposedly lie hidden behind phenomena; its concepts of how such hidden powers and inaccessible things work are just as dependent on the root metaphor of "will"; and its explanations are therefore presumed to be just as absolute, that is, just as final and total an accounting of "why" things are and act as they do, as any theological explanation. Acorns become oak trees because that is their end or "purpose." Sleeping powder works because of its "dormative virtue." The behavior of beasts is caused by "animal instincts." Like theological accounts, such "explanations," once given, leave nothing further to say.

Finally, that metaphysics wears this Janus face is, Comte claims, an important fact for contemporary philosophers to understand. His argument for this claim takes us back to one of the fundamental differences between Comtean and later positivism. As we have already seen, in contrast to everyone from Mill to Reichenbach, who all tend to assume that the age (if not all the influence) of metaphysics has already passed, Comte holds that humanity is still in the process of making the transition from the second to the third stage. For him, this means that an essential part of positive philosophy's job is to explain both the transition itself and the intellectual as well as the social importance of completing it. In other words, one must begin with a historically informed defense of science and scientific thinking itself rather than plunge directly into questions of method.[29] Viewed from this angle, the important thing about the metaphysical stage is what the mind learns by passing through it. To understand this process is to comprehend the inspiration for and character of scientific thought itself – and thus to be consciously prepared to carry out positive philosophy's "educational" task.[30]

28 CPP1(1), 14 [F, 8]. Cf. DEP, 35–40/53–64.
29 The idea that theology and metaphysics have a cumulative effect on science was, in Comte's day, a fairly popular notion. What Comte adds to the mix is the conclusion that the understanding of this effect is therefore an essential part of any philosophical reflection on science. Cf. Frank Manuel, *The Prophets of Paris* (Cambridge, MA: Harvard University Press, 1962), 282.
30 At least one writer has even argued that this task ought to be regarded as central to Comte's purposes generally. See Paul Arbousse-Bastide, *La doctrine de l'éducation universelle dans la philosophie d'Auguste Comte: Principe d'unité systématique et fondement de l'organisation spirituelle du monde*, 2 vols. (Paris: Presses Universitaires de France, 1957).

What, then, does the human mind learn by passing through a metaphysical stage? Above all, says Comte, metaphysical thinking leaves the mind in a promising but also unstable condition – a condition he characterizes in what amounts to a universalized and socialized version of that sorry theoretical state described by Kant in his critique of the antinomies.

In general, as Comte sees it, it is good that one should have learned to speculate without reliance on feelings, imagination, or dogma. A mind that is merely liberated, however, has no resources of its own for deciding among equally "reasonable" theories. Even theoretically, this ultimately leaves us with serious problems. It is true that concerning our external relations, the realization that reason is unfit to be its own authority seems to drive the mind spontaneously toward science. This is understandable because even during the theological stage, one is aware that in some of our experiences of nature, there are "perceivable" regularities that require no special explanation in terms of hidden causes. Hence the "mature," or postmetaphysical mind's move toward reliance on observation is no mere leap toward an entirely new approach but a conscious and systematic return to "instinctively" employed "good sense."[31] Yet Comte notes that this spontaneous move toward science is largely confined to the study of objects other than ourselves; and, as we have seen in our discussion of Comte's views on psychology, he does not think this is accidental. Metaphysics, lacking an experiential base of its own, carries forward theology's flattering sense of our species as special, superior, and centrally important. Metaphysical speculation about humanity is therefore much harder to give up than metaphysical speculation about nature because accepting the scientific alternative means considering ourselves as just one more (albeit very complex) kind of natural entity. Part of positive philosophy's job, then, is to provide the needed incentive for the extension of observational study to humanity by exposing the bankruptcy of metaphysical concepts in the one area where we are most reluctant to give them up.

Metaphysical concepts are thus ultimately something of a theoretical roadblock; they threaten, however, to become a political nightmare. The metaphysical mind, motivated in the first place by conceptual, not practical, concerns, easily turns into a free-floating promoter of intellectual and social "anarchy." Comte's descriptions of metaphysics are therefore kinder in his epistemologically oriented works like the *Cours*, where speculative independence can be praised for opening the door to science. In the *Système*, however, where the central issue is social reorganization, metaphysics is seen primarily in terms of what it is always threatening to become, namely, a prideful "insurrection of the intellect against the heart."[32] Another part of positive philosophy's educational task, then, is to

31 DEP, 44–45/71–72. Thus, "in principle . . . science is simply a methodological extension of universal sensibleness [*sagesse universelle*]" (ibid.) or even a radicalization of fetishism (SPP4, 204/180).
32 SPP2, 130/113. In earlier works, this danger is more typically described simply as intellectually or socially destructive. Cf. SPP4a, 77/548; CPP5(55), 492–775 [M, 304–62]; and DEP, 8–12/11–19. That in contrast to the *Cours*, the *Système*'s more sociopolitical critique stresses heart over intellect is judiciously treated by Pickering in "Comte and the Saint-Simonians," *French Historical Studies* 18 (1993), 229–35.

explain the practical danger in metaphysics. "The absolute in theory," the young Comte had already remarked, "leads necessarily to the arbitrary in practice."[33] Just as this is true of theological and metaphysical systems of nature, it is true of such systems of social organization. "Divine right" is acceptable to kings, and "the rights of man" are pleasing to those (men) to whom the rights are already fully accorded; but in societies founded on religious dogma or abstract principle, there is ultimately no way, short of war or revolution, to resolve disagreements over the dogma or principle itself.

To sum up: In a colorful phrase that perhaps comes close to capturing Comte's overall evaluation of stage two, he suggests that the metaphysical spirit is best regarded "as a kind of chronic distemper [*maladie chronique*] naturally inhering in our individual and collective mental evolution between infancy and manhood."[34] And, to continue the parallel I began at the conclusion of my discussion of theology, I suggest that, for metaphysics, the ideal of universal praxis is at best and in its earlier period, the "contemplative" life and at worst and toward the end, the love of argument and criticism for its own sake – which means, as Comte would be eager to point out, there is no genuinely "metaphysical" form of praxis at all, for its ideal is in fact neither materially practical nor social.

4. The positive (scientific) stage

For Comte, the positive stage begins when the nominalistic and anarchic implications of metaphysics push the mind toward subordinating itself to observation. For this to happen, however, the whole tenor of intellectual expectation that characterizes both theology and metaphysics must change. Speculation can no longer be regarded as providing absolute knowledge of what lies above, behind, or within the things we encounter. All theorizing must come to be construed not as concerned with anything absolute but as "relative" to the amount and quality of our observations of phenomenal events and properties that are actually present in our encounters with the world. "Relativity" is one of six qualities that, Comte argues, are characteristic of a truly "positive" philosophy – the other five being "real [in the sense of eschewing any interest in the merely imaginary]," "useful," "certain [as opposed to indecisive]," "precise," and "organic [i.e., concerned to organize and unify rather than dissolve and destroy]."[35] In his *Système*, he adds a seventh meaning, namely, "sympathetic," for which he admits he cannot make much of an empirical or lexicographic case but which he argues should be included anyway in order to indicate that positive philosophy – precisely as "philosophy," and especially in light of its concern for the ultimately sociopolitical ends of knowledge – "recaptures the lofty original direction of which its etymology reminds us."[36] How far removed Comte's philosophy "about" science is

---

33 SPP4a, 102/565.
34 DEP, 11/17. Cf. SPP1. 49/38.
35 DEP, 41–44/66–71.
36 SPP1, 58/45; also SPP4, 547/473.

from those philosophies "of" science in Mill and later positivism is sharply represented here.

Comte singles out three pivotal modern figures as symbols for what the positive, or scientific, intellectual revolution entails. He cites Bacon for directing philosophy toward observation; Descartes for encouraging explicit concern for method; and Galileo for pioneering a scientific way of actually "discovering nature's invariable laws." He warns, however, that only the "combined influence" of their teachings leads from metaphysics to positive thought.[37] I stress this warning here so as to counter another misconception. Contrary the usual story, Comte's positivism neither traces all observation back to sense impressions nor subordinates reason to observation. On the one hand, as we saw in Chapter 1, in his view, everything from stars and planets to languages and historical epochs is "observable." On the other hand, although Comte certainly holds that there can be no positive era until reason is willing to put itself initially in the service of observation, he also insists that even a scientific mind is always rightly struggling to

> dispense with direct [empirical] exploration, as much as the phenomena will permit, in order to warrant deduction of the greatest possible number of results from the smallest possible amount of immediately given data.[38]

Indeed, he says, this continual intellectual tendency to comprehensively make something of the phenomenal data is a fundamental sign of a mind's "maturity." Thus, let us recall here from Chapter 2 that Comte conceives positivism as steering a middle course between the extremes of what he calls "mysticism" and "empiricism." Descartes and Bacon need each other. On the one hand, although it is surely true that, left to itself, Cartesian meditation – given its extra-observational orientation – can seduce reason into believing it has the power to discover nature's fundamental laws all by itself and so fall back into metaphysics or even theology, on the other hand it is equally true that Baconian induction by itself is little more than a "barren accumulation of unconnected facts" – a "mere" empiricism and not yet science. Here lies Galileo's importance. His principles of nature constitute a mediation between mysticism and empiricism and thus exemplify for us the kind of science a synthesis (recall that positive means "organic") of Bacon and Descartes makes possible. Finally, too, the resultant phenomenal knowledge provides for really successful prevision unavailable at earlier stages; and this prevision, construed in light of Bacon's other memorable precept that knowledge is power, effects a genuine coordination of theory with practice.

This is not the place for extensive treatment of Comte's epistemology of science.[39] Certainly his belittling of "bare observation," his eagerness to "dispense" with observation as soon as possible, his opposition to any formalization of scientific procedure, and his heaping praise on "rational prevision" without sharing

37 CPP1(1), 19–20 [F, 11]; also, 52 [F, 30].
38 CPP1(3), 131. Cf., DEP, 16/25; SPP1, 518/419; and SPP3, 24/21.
39 But see Laudan, "Comte's Méthode Positive," *Science and Hypothesis*, 141–62, and references cited, 157n.5. I shall have a bit more to say on this topic in Chapter 6.

the subsequent preoccupation with the issue of verification – such features alone are surprising enough in a positivist to justify his reconsideration in these postpositivist times. What I want to emphasize here, however, is not Comte's deviant views on specific issues but his insistence that such issues cannot even be understood as issues without recourse to current philosophy's past. It is as if Comte had already heard the complaint now made by aspiring post-positivists that positivism fosters a historically naive and uncritical outlook, and he wants to assure them that his positivism is different. I conclude this chapter with a summary of what Comte thinks one needs to understand about philosophy's past in order to see why one's own philosophical practice should be "scientific."

Stated in general terms, Comte's view is exactly what his fundamental law would lead us to expect: The scientific stage constitutes the fulfillment of the *aims* through a surpassing of the *methods* of the first two stages. In every phase of intellectual development, what is wanted is "a conceptual system concerning the totality of phenomena" that permits us to understand our surroundings well enough to order our lives effectively; in each phase, this goal is pursued by the only means possible at the time. For a Comtean positivist, then, it is wrong to think of a prescientific mind as essentially either theological or metaphysical. As much as any scientific mind, its operations are at bottom just as much a response to experience and just as concerned with *la vie active* and with normalizing relations to our surroundings so as to meet our human needs.[40] From Comte's viewpoint, therefore, the traditional stories about philosophy's origin are quite misleading. Theologians and metaphysicians tell us that philosophy originates in feelings of mystery or intellectual wonder, respectively; and it is a fact that both are, for a time, indispensable stimulants to speculation – the former to overcome the vicious circle of being initially without either theories or data, the latter to free reason from feeling and imagination. In the final analysis, however, both theology and metaphysics are intended just as much as means to prevision and to the satisfaction of practical and social needs as is science. To complete the parallel I suggested in connection with the first two stages, Comtean science is for modern technology what theology and metaphysics are for worship and contemplation, respectively, namely, the comprehensive theoretical basis for a universal form of praxis – only this time, it is one that really does give us control over our external and social surroundings.

Unlike later positivists, then, Comte does not regard scientific thinking as a leap beyond tradition. Science does not leave theology and metaphysics behind,

---

40 As we have seen, however, this is true of metaphysical thinking only indirectly or parasitically. Cf. CPP2(2), 61–64 [F, 37–39]; and SPP1, 8–15/6–11. There is an interesting tension between the accounts of the relation between reason and experience in Comte's two major works. Both agree that scientific speculation must be at once sufficiently ambitious in scope and yet forbearing in relation to research; but the more epistemologically oriented *Cours* finds room for a separate "profound craving of our minds to know the laws of phenomena" (39 [63]), whereas the sociopolitically concerned *Système* insists that "the only position to which the mind is permanently adapted is to serve our social needs [*servir la sociabilité*]" (14/11).

any more than metaphysics leaves theology behind; science is what develops from them. Hence, understanding the superiority of the positive stage is inseparable from understanding its continuing indebtedness to the previous two stages. Rather than see virtue in past procedures only when they approximate current practices, Comte reconstructs current practices in terms of what they owe to theologico-metaphysical ones. Traditional theories may indeed be called unscientific, but only if "scientific" is understood, to begin with, as characterizing an orientation formulated as a response to the foundering of traditional speculation. Genuine knowledge must indeed be limited entirely to phenomena; but an informed claim asserting this limitation depends on understanding it in the first place against the background of earlier ambitious but failed attempts to know more.

Thus, if Comte eschews questions about hidden causes, for example, it is because he thinks traditional theological and metaphysical struggles with such questions have shown us that they are unanswerable. It emphatically does not mean that he thinks that either the questions or the attempted answers are meaningless, or that they reduce to expressions of emotion or cultural idols. Comte's alternative – that they are meaningful but ultimately futile – is, of course, hardly more likely to please committed theologians or metaphysicians; nevertheless, it is a profoundly different attitude from the one for which positivists are famous. Because he thinks history is necessary for rather than irrelevant to the understanding of current philosophy, Comte would have regarded their dismissive, present-minded smugness about theology and ontology as not just ignorant but destructive. Regardless of how right they may be in seeing scientific rationality as the superior means to knowledge, they entirely misuse this rationality when they turn it back upon traditional speculation, so that nothing is left of it but pseudo-problems and unverifiable propositions. There is perhaps some irony in Comte's calling such "purely critical" treatment of previous speculation an expression of the *metaphysical* spirit run wild. But he does, and he is serious. A truly positive kind of reasoning involves taking up the materials provided us by past thinkers in order to go them one better; indeed, that is what makes positive philosophy "useful" instead of idle ("the necessary aim of all sound speculation is the continual improvement of our true condition") and "organic" instead of subversive ("the dissolutive effects of real science are purely indirect and secondary," and its very advance "tends to render criticism superfluous"). The point is, transition from prescientific to positive thought cannot be made by acts of "pure [intellectual] negation."[41]

Finally, let me stress that Comte does not just have, de facto, a different opinion about the relevance of philosophy's past than do later positivists. His conception of the third stage as a cumulative transformation of the first two is neither

---

41 DEP, 41, 42/66, 68; and SPP1, 46–49/36–39, where the example of metaphysical excess is atheism.

unconscious nor merely dogmatic; and it is not something one must hunt for between his lines and in occasional remarks. It is openly espoused, consciously defended, and specifically identified as informative of Comte's own orientation. This historico-critical use of his three-stage law, the promise and weaknesses of which will be considered in Part II, marks the deepest difference between his positivism, on the one hand, and that of both Mill and the Logical Empiricists, on the other.

II

COMTE NOW

4

COMTE'S AMBIGUOUS LEGACY: SCIENCE DEFENDED OR ALREADY JUSTIFIED?

In light of Part I, the unusual character of Comte's positivism should now be clear. Whereas later positivists tend to simply begin – without further ado, ahistorically, as if in complete intellectual self-possession – by inquiring how a good scientist thinks, Comte stops to give historico-critical consideration to the current philosophical appropriateness of conducting such an inquiry in the first place. In other words, in contrast with advocates of the positivism we more directly – and now, unhappily – inherit, Comte tries to (as we say now) "contextualize" current inquiry. More specifically and quite unlike a sociologist speaking of the current thought of others, however, Comte is above all concerned with understanding that contextualization in the case of his own philosophizing.

Yet it is time to acknowledge that Comte does not always – in fact, does not mostly – display such historico-critical sensitivity. Indeed, it is no accident that the side of Comte I am trying to retrieve has gone relatively unappreciated. There are plenty of passages in which he appears to speak from a vantage point just as far beyond the need for further reflection as that of any later positivist. Hence, in Part II, my focus is on the fundamental tension in Comte's writings between *two* conceptions of third-stage philosophizing – namely, the one I have so far emphasized, which pictures its orientation as historically contextualized and *defensible*, and another, more akin to that of later positivism, which represents this orientation as context-free and somehow *already justified*. I want to show that, far from weakening my case for Comte's contemporary relevance, it is the presence of this tension in Comte's writings – or, more precisely, this tension *as something he does not acknowledge* – that makes him a valuable progenitor for today's aspiring post-positivists to rethink. I begin in this chapter with an analysis of the tension itself, first briefly summarized and then in light of Comte's own distinction between historical and dogmatical methods. Finally, I review the results of my analysis with some comparative help from Descartes – from whom, it appears, Comte inherits an ahistorical imperative in spite of himself.

1. Science defended versus science already justified

So far, we have seen that from 1822 on, Comte consistently speaks of the third stage as already emerging without assistance from any positivists; and in all his major writings, positive philosophy is made to take its bearings from this display of "spontaneous superiority" by the scientific mode of reasoning.[1] Under the auspices of the motto "No idea can be properly understood except through its history," Comte explains this superiority in terms of its success in responding to the human needs with which theology and metaphysics have already struggled less successfully. We human beings, it seems, have always expected satisfactory relations with our surroundings; and whenever this expectation is frustrated, we seek explanations that make reorganization of those relations possible. For various reasons, our initial efforts at explanation must first be theological and then turn metaphysical; hence, elucidation of the partial successes and ultimate failure of these prescientific efforts is an inseparable aspect of any inquiry concerning scientific rationality itself.

Yet because, in Comte's view, the "mental revolution" from theological and metaphysical to positive reasoning remains incomplete, acknowledging the superiority of positive rationality is not as important as defending it – and this, again, historico-critically. Spontaneous development has left science stalled, so to speak, between biology and sociology; hence, an account is currently needed of both how and why positive rationality deserves our favor. Comte addresses the "how" question primarily by arguing that scientific reasoning must be extended into areas still treated theologico-metaphysically. He answers the "why" question by explaining that science fulfills the underlying aims of prescientific speculation; and he stresses that if those aims appear in the short term to be primarily intellectual, they are also ultimately political and social.

This, then, is what Comte is committed to in principle. A positive philosophy subordinates the logical analysis of scientific procedures to the historico-critical defense of science itself; and this makes Comte, as I put it in Chapter 2, less a philosopher "of" science than a philosopher "about" science. One implication of this commitment is that in Comtean positivism, epistemological matters can never be formally separated from either actual scientific practice, on the one hand, or the issues of prevision and social reorganization, on the other. Even when he thinks of the philosophy of the future, practiced after all the sciences have become thoroughly positive, Comte never dreams that so "purely" epistemological a project as an organon of proof, or rational reconstruction, or "study of evi-

1 DEP, 76/120–21.

dence" might some day dominate the field.² One reason is that ontogeny recapitulates phylogeny; and for Comte, this means that each new generation of scientists will again need the same historico-critical elucidation of what science is.³ Also, as noted in Chapter 2, Comte thinks methodological formalism threatens innovation by practicing scientists, who alone are in a position to understand what their present research conditions (and for the time being, also the existing degree of positivity in their disciplines) makes procedurally appropriate. But in the end, the main reason Comte's positivism can never be defined in terms of purely epistemic projects is that "it is principally distinguished through a continual preponderance...of the historical point of view" – which it acquires, of course, through the good offices of the three-stage law.⁴

So is Comte committed in principle. In fact, however, he often speaks as if he has forgotten this commitment. At times, he links the very idea of taking the historical viewpoint to the aim of a "complete emancipation from the past," that is, to the establishment of "a first philosophy such as Bacon sought...[which] is destined henceforth to serve as the permanent basis for all human speculations," as well as being the "spiritual foundation" of all social order "so long as the human race shall endure."⁵

How does it happen that Comte sometimes appears to understand science as defensible and sometimes as already justified? It has been common practice to explain rather than try to understand this conflict; but in addition to their often unkind intentions, such explanations have also usually been flawed. Thus it will not do, for example, to follow Mill and Littré in making the conflict a fundamentally chronological one, so that Comte is said to get more opinionated and authoritarian as he turns from his earlier concern with science itself to his later promotion of it for establishing the Religion of Humanity. Even if it is true that Comte does seem to grow increasingly doctrinaire, the fact is that this supposedly later attitude is also clearly displayed even in his earliest and in his least socially concerned writings. Nor will it do to interpret all of Comte's displays of dogmatism, early or late, as signs of his "divergence from positivism" due to other motives.⁶ The trouble with explanations of this sort is that Comte winds up being

---

2 Writing in 1982, Ayer still believes that if he had to choose "a single phrase to capture the stage to which philosophy has progressed," he would pick "the study of evidence" [*Philosophy in the Twentieth Century* (New York: Random House, 1982), 18].
3 CPP1(1), 6–9, 41–43 [F, 3–5, 24–25]. Positivist education is not confined to those directly concerned with the sciences; it includes "all classes of society" (DEP, 82/129–30) – including (for Comte conceives them as a separate class of non-laboring, man-supported, entirely domestic moral educators) women (SPP1 250–51/201–202). Equality of the sexes, Comte remarks confidently, is nothing but "subversive fancy" (SPP1, 248/199); and, of course, positive philosophers are therefore all men.
4 DEP, 1–2/2.
5 See, e.g., SPP2, 85/68; CPP1(2), 75 [F, 45]; and SPP4a, 607/161, respectively.
6 See especially D.G. Charlton, *Positivist Thought in France during the Second Empire, 1852–1870* (Oxford: Oxford University Press, 1959). Charlton argues that Comte's "starting point is consistently positivist" (34) but that he "abuses the scientific method" (44) both in dealing with his own empirical hypotheses about future science and in pressing his social agenda. See also Warren Schmaus, who

measured instead of understood. For even if we imagine that there is a standard conception of "consistent positivist" – indeed, one which is not merely ours, or today's, but one we can extract from Comte's own writings – we would seriously distort his position by reading that conception back into him *as* an explicit idea and then criticizing him for inconsistently adhering to it. Precisely what I want to draw attention to is the fact that Comte does not have any such explicit conception, let alone does he use one to mediate his conflicting impulses. My question, therefore, shall be this: How could Comte, in philosophizing about the sciences, consider the same cluster of epistemic and social concerns in two such different ways – that is, sometimes historico-critically, more often imperiously – *and not even notice, let alone try to resolve, the conflict between them*? A good place to start is with Comte's own distinction between two "methods of exposition" – methods he himself suggestively designates as "historical" and "dogmatical."

2. Historical versus dogmatical accounts of science

Mature minds, Comte is fond of saying, "see for the sake of foreseeing" – that is, they "dispense as much as possible" with a mere gathering of the empirical materials of science and "substitute" instead a consideration of the invariable natural laws these materials permit one to develop.[7] The world, however, is not (yet) dominated by mature minds; and if this famous "fundamental principle of the whole positive philosophy" is ever to be fully appreciated, it must be philosophically explicated using the "historical method." The reason for this is that

> over the last three centuries, the principle itself has become familiar *in such a way* [*tellement*] that *until now* [*jusqu'ici*] its true source has nearly always gone unrecognized, *in consequence of* [*par suite*] the deeply rooted habit of thinking in terms of absolutes. . . .[8]

The three italicized phrases control Comte's argument. (a) "Until now" the sciences have developed spontaneously, that is, without epistemic self-consciousness. (b) Positive speculation has so far been displacing theologico-metaphysical speculation "in such a way" that, however obvious the new demand for *observation* may have become, the fundamental *intellectual* sea change that goes with this demand

---

thinks Comte "strays from his positivism" when he "attributes a kind of causal efficacy [sic] to scientific progress which leads him to look for laws of...the social progress which 'results' from the scientific" ["A Reappraisal of Comte's Three-State Law," *History and Theory* 21 (1982), 266]. For Lenzer (among many others), all of Comte's historical talk is from the beginning consciously aimed at producing a "grand scheme" for sketching the role of social science "in directing the course of history in the service of the governing classes" because Comte "is, in fact, the theoretical exponent par excellence of modern capitalism" (L, xlii–xliii).

7 DEP, 16/25. Cf. CPP1(2), 63–64 [F, 38–39], where Comte says there is evidence for the urgency and depth of our "craving" for knowledge of nature's laws in the "physiological effects" of our experience of wonder, as well as in the fact that "the most terrible sensation we can experience occurs whenever something happens which seems to violate those laws."

8 DEP, 17 (my emphases and translation; Beesly's obscures precisely these points).

is still underappreciated. Hence (c), "in consequence of" the lingering influence of prescientific modes of thought, it follows "naturally" that even honest efforts to properly describe scientific thinking tend not just to miss but to actually distort its true character. For Comte, of course, the third point is the philosophically crucial one, and he develops it here by analyzing in detail a typical distortion, namely, of the positive reinterpretation of the "invariability" of natural events.

Comte's strategy recalls his similar treatment of the concept of causality, discussed in Chapter 2. The basic problem is that "invariability" already has common currency as an idea whose meaning is established "from a metaphysical point of view." So long as this "deeply rooted habit of mind" continues to provide the context for the idea's discussion – so long, that is, as natural knowledge continues to be understood in terms of a priori reasoning about what "necessarily" lies above or behind phenomena – any new interpretation of invariability will tend to be turned into just another effort to reconceive the "rational grounds" we have for thinking that everything we experience hangs together. According to Comte, however, the scientific idea of invariability is not the result of any such process of rational reconception or redefinition. We should not be misled by his calling this scientific idea a "principle," or "law," as though it were replacing a theologico-metaphysical first principle. In Comte's often undisciplined prose, almost anything worth remembering is given these labels at some time. What he is really arguing is that "invariability" is being recontextualized. A whole new "way of thinking" is emerging, and the idea no longer expresses the metaphysician's overblown faith in reason but rather the positivist's "convictions" about observation, "considered in relation to our speculations about external objects."[9] The key to understanding scientific invariability thus lies in recognizing how radically its general background of intelligibility has changed from the one constituted by metaphysics; and this, in turn, requires recognition that the metaphysical idea of invariability, like metaphysics itself, is at bottom only a variation on a still older theological theme, namely, that even the most obvious, "spontaneously observed" natural regularity must be given a supernatural (instead of an a priori rational) explanation.[10]

What Comte says here about the dangers of misconstruing "invariable natur-

9 DEP, 19/30.
10 DEP, 17–18/27. On the scientific search for invariable natural laws, Comte cites "the last seven chapters of the first volume" of Mill's *Logic* [i.e., on the four methods, plus a brief preliminary on the nature of observation (SL, III, vii–xiii)] as a perhaps unsurpassable "dogmatic exposition of induction" (17n./26n.); but it is very misleading here for Beesly to cite (DEP, 27n.1) and for Laudan, probably following him, to allude ("Comte's 'Méthode Positive,'" 148) to Book III, iii, 1 (on the uniformity of nature axiom) when Comte does not. For here Comte is trying to understand positive-phenomenal vs. theologico-metaphysical ideas of invariability, employing the method of historical exposition; but there, Mill is logically analyzing only the former idea as the justified ultimate "premise" of all inductions. The same contrast appears in Book VI, x, 3–8, when Mill treats the historical method almost entirely in terms of its value for "prediction of future events" (915) and ignores what should be made instead of his own passing remark that with Comte himself, the three-stage law seems to have issued in "predictions with respect to the future...greatly inferior...to his *appreciation of the past*" (928; my emphasis).

al law" is true in general about the treatment of any aspect of scientific knowledge. Those who fail to take his historico-critical approach will continue to misunderstand such knowledge in one of two familiar directions. Either they will tend to give it an inflated, theologico-metaphysical construal, so that scientific theories will be regarded as legitimated by reason itself and as permitting the "absolute" comprehension of extraphenomenal realities. Or in overreaction to such "mysticism," others will become mere "empiricists" who radically undervalue all scientific speculation by reducing knowledge to the accumulation of observations and thus confuse "real science" with "vain erudition."

For Comte, then, the historical method must be employed to ward off further misinterpretation of what scientific knowledge is. Yet he is equally insistent that actual scientific practice must also be conceptualized in such a way that, ultimately,

> all the particular labors [that contributed to its progress] have been *recast into a general system*, in order that they may be presented in a more natural, logical order . . . [and] from a more direct point of view.[11]

Such a systematic "recasting" of scientific activity is accomplished by the second, or "dogmatical," mode of exposition.

In Comte's writings, there are passages in which the dogmatical method is explicitly contrasted to the historical with what I would call (à la Part I of the present study) the proper acknowledgment of its subordinate status. Even its name – *méthode dogmatique* – seems well chosen. Just as religious dogma looks back for its authority to, say, a sacred text or divine revelation, so a point made dogmatically about science ultimately stands or falls on the basis of a historico-critical account that for the moment is being taken on faith. Both because Comte does sometimes evaluate the dogmatical method in this respectfully derivative way and because in plenty of other passages he clearly does not, I prefer a literal translation of *dogmatique* to (the otherwise not incorrect) "theoretical," or "systematic." Often, in other words, he treats dogmatical expositions like a dogmatist; but in the respectfully derivative treatments, he prefaces some particular dogmatical recasting with remarks about its "inescapable" limitation. "We must recognize," he asserts in a typical passage, their "genuine imperfectness." No matter how "natural" a scheme may be, it necessarily involves a kind of intellectual "impounding" *(renfermer)* of actual phenomena – that is, it always presents them, "if not arbitrarily, then at least artificially."[12] It is to those passages in which dogmatical accounts are subordinated in this way that I want to draw special attention.

I start by considering a possible objection. Might someone not argue that historical schemes seem just as deserving as dogmatical ones of being called "artificial," given the obviously abstractive character of any conceptual scheme? Comte does not (and, with his aversion to "purely logical" treatments of epis-

---

11 CPP1(2), 78 [F, 47], my emphasis; also DEP, 97/153.
12 CPP1(2), 76 [F, 46]. Cf. CPP1(2), 84 [F, 50]; DEP, 23, 101/36, 160; and SPP4, 187/165–66.

temic matters, might even refuse to) deal with this question; but the contours of a Comtean reply are, I think, fairly clear. Stated simply, the answer lies in distinguishing what he calls here "artificiality" from mere abstractness.

On the latter notion, Comte himself provides some direct testimony. Of course, he says, both historical and dogmatical methods involve abstraction – that is, they "tend toward generalization" at the expense of whatever is not selected for conceptualization. Sometimes he explicitly contrasts both methods with "empirical" accounts, which in this context he characterizes not so much as the unfortunate source of "vain erudition" but simply as displaying the tendency opposite to that of the historical and dogmatical methods by pursuing ever fuller descriptions of some "concrete circumstance in all its details." Comte's point in these comparisons is to emphasize the fact that both historical and dogmatical methods are concerned with prevision, and achieving prevision always involves generalizing from cases. Yet none of this means that Comte conceives historical and dogmatical accounts as lying, so to speak, at the opposite pole from empirical description. On the contrary, all positive theorizing falls between the extremes of "total generality" and "perfect reality." In this, it models itself after

> that happy combination in our ordinary affairs of dogmatism and empiricism, which in isolation are each equally incompetent, the former from its liability to illusion, the latter from its lack of foresight.[13]

In other contexts, we know, Comte portrays theology and metaphysics as actually encouraging an "incompetent" form of dogmatism called mysticism and an equally incompetent overreaction called "mere" empiricism; but here his focus is prospective, not retrospective, and he envisions a potentially "happy combination" of dogmatism and empiricism in science. To see what he means by this phrase, one must notice that he conceives dogmatism and empiricism here not as methods but as prephilosophical tendencies that theology and metaphysics tend to cripple and science, to enhance. In our "ordinary affairs," he explains, these tendencies appear to be something like instinctive "natural processes" *(marches)* for making sense, respectively, of future possibilities and present realities. In theologico-metaphysical philosophy, the dogmatic tendency is rendered incompetent and the empirical tendency worthless by the assumption, first, that all good generalizations yield absolute knowledge of extraphenomenal "causes" and second, that it is thus God or Nature and not anything in the experienced world that is always the ultimate object of these generalizations. But when positive reasoning emerges out of disenchantment with these assumptions, an informed exploitation of a happy everyday condition is possible. To achieve it, dogmatism and empiri-

---

13 SPP1, 427/346. I pass over here the question of what Comte is ontologically committed to in arguing that "generalization always presupposes prior analysis of particular existences into universal phenomena which alone permit of being conceived in terms of invariability" (428/347). In the other direction Laudan argues, correctly I think, that Comte has a generous rather than a narrow conception of legitimate abstraction, allowing for hypotheses that contain nonphenomenal predicates and are therefore only indirectly confirmable (Comte's 'Méthode Positive,'" 150–55).

cism must both be reconceived, not only to undo the damage of theologico-metaphysical distortion but also to improve upon their prephilosophical form. The spirit of dogmatism must be "relativized," so that all theorizing is seen to depend on forever incomplete research results; and empiricism must be "elevated," so that its interest in the immediate facts and its concern for practical affairs are praised for being integral to the positive idea of prevision, rather than condemned for being impediments to theologico-metaphysical speculation.

One is tempted, in Peircean spirit, to call the relativized dogmatism that accompanies elevated empiricism "dogmaticism," but whatever its title, its epistemic character is depicted the same way in both the *Système* and the *Cours*.

> No matter how prominent the positive spirit may have become, one must never forget that in every case it emanated from practical activity by a gradual substitution of the study of laws for a study of causes. Even the universal principle of invariable natural relations . . . is itself an essentially empirical acquisition. *So far from originating in the dogmatism of earlier times, it was directly opposed to it;* and this accounts for its slow and gradual formation, which has only just been completed by the founding of sociology.[14]

So far, however, I have deliberately omitted the line that immediately precedes this passage, in which Comte jointly sums up the scientific significance of our two natural tendencies by saying, "All induction is empirical in its origin and *dogmatical in its completion*." The statement is no mistake. In works like the *Système* where social reorganization is Comte's primary concern, scientific theories are typically viewed as "dogmatically completed" (so that the issue becomes what course of action they make possible) rather than as "relative" to inductive research (where the question is their epistemic character). There are, to be sure, historico-critical reminders made in passing – for example, the one just cited, which stresses what we should "never forget" about positive as opposed to theologico-metaphysical speculation. This whole way of treating knowledge, however, is more characteristic of the *Cours*, where Comte's primary concern is understanding positive speculation rather than using its results.

In short, the contrasting treatments of the scientific appropriation of our ordinary dogmatical tendency in the *Système*, on the one hand, and in the *Cours*, on the other, are themselves examples of dogmatical and historical expositions, respectively. Only in this case, they are expositions of the character and worth of science itself, not just of its specific findings and procedures. There is obviously an ambiguity, then, in Comte's conception of historical and dogmatical "methods." Evidently, they can be used *on* science as well as *by* science. I will return to this later; but first, let it at least be clear that as he moves from the *Cours* to the *Système*, a shift occurs in Comte's primary focus on science, namely, a shift from historical to dogmatical presentations of it. In the *Système*, he is interested in how science can be the basis for effective action. His tendency, therefore, is to recast

---

14 SPP1, 428–29/347, my emphasis. In my analysis here, I make explicit what Comte does not, viz., that the "gradual substitution" is at the successive expense of both theology and metaphysics.

all of science's theoretical results – sometimes even merely anticipated results – as finished products. Put another way, the *Système* takes as its point of departure the second half of the Baconian motto, " . . . from prevision comes action." It thereby recasts the current scientific enterprise in an idealized projection of the condition it must be in if social reorganization is to become as viable a possibility as the manipulation of nature already partially is. In the *Cours*, on the other hand, the point of departure is the first half of the motto, "From science comes prevision." It thereby produces a retrospective account of science in its "emerging" condition as that very "study of laws, not causes" that can give the *Système* what it wants.

From all of this, at least one essential difference between Comte's historical and dogmatical generalizations can be made out. Both are necessarily abstract in the obvious sense that they focus on what is general and central in a given set of circumstances rather than on the concrete circumstances themselves. Dogmatical accounts, however, are abstractive in a second and less obvious way. For they tend, in addition, to conceptually freeze some reality *in its present condition, idealized*, and to treat this frozen picture as if it were no longer "relative" to past or future research. In other words, a dogmatical account tends to suppress the conditions of its own formation; and that makes it "artificially" selective in a way historical accounts are not. No doubt there are plenty of occasions when artificiality of this sort is theoretically harmless (e.g., in the development of "static" structural or classificatory laws) or practically unavoidable (e.g., in the moment when a theory is being practically employed). Suppose, however, that what is being conceived in so dogmatically "completed" a fashion is not this or that theory about this or that phenomenon but the *whole body* of scientific laws about phenomenal reality (as is characteristically the case in the *Système*, when the Religion of Humanity is depicted making use of "them"). Or suppose that what is dogmatically completed is the *whole system* of scientific disciplines conceived as functioning with full positivity (as is the case much of the time in the *Cours* when Comte is busy classifying them). In these instances, there is the real danger – especially if some of what is completed conceptually is not yet well formed actually, as in the case of social scientific laws and sociology itself – that one will forget that this is supposed to be the era of a newly "relativized" dogmatism in which no theoretical account is ever sacrosanct. Comte's decision, after completing the *Cours*, to stop discussing his theories in order to facilitate applying them, or his use of "recent findings" in physiology to argue that smaller brains make women less intelligent, would seem to be glaring examples of this danger.

Comte's principle here, however, is better than his practice. For it is precisely in order to avoid this danger that he insists on the "respectful subordination" of dogmatical accounts. The artificiality of a dogmatic scheme, as one might put Comte's point, can only be forgiven by not being forgotten. In part, this means that in order to avoid an unwanted excess of artificiality, dogmatical generalizations must always continue to be employed jointly with historical ones. The three-stage law, for example, formulated as it usually is in the *Cours* as the (dynamical) "law of filiation" depicting the serial dependencies of metaphysics on theology and of science on both of the others, must be "combined" with the (statical) "encyclopedic formula" of the basic sciences if the emergence of hierarchically organized science as a distinct intellectual stage is to be adequately depicted.[15] Comte's reasoning here is interestingly ontological and realist. Our surroundings, he argues, offer us a variety of phenomena to think about, and we must therefore think of scientific theorizing as emerging not only in general from theology and metaphysics but also specifically at different rates in different disciplines, depending on the kind of objects studied.

It is on the basis of this combination of historical with conceptual considerations that Comte claims legitimation for his hierarchical ordering of the sciences. One may think of my hierarchical scheme as "objective," he argues, but only so long as one understands that

> an essential feature of my proposed encyclopedic scale is its general conformity with the whole history of science – by which I mean that, in spite of the real and continuous simultaneity of development of the different sciences, those to be classed as anterior did, as a matter of fact, start earlier and always continued to be more advanced than those to be classed as posterior to them.[16]

Philosophically speaking, Comte regards the "real and continuous simultaneity" of actual scientific development as an honesty factor for his encyclopedic scheme; and in this passage, the point has at least four implications. (a) Empirically scrutinized, all the sciences will be seen to have their actual beginnings and "innumerable reciprocal influences" already in theological times. (Think, e.g., of astronomy and its relation to mathematics.) (b) From mathematics at least to biology, the sciences have made substantial progress without any positivist understanding of them. Until now, in other words, they have developed without conscious help from anything like Comte's analytical distinctions either among the basic sciences or between these and concrete, descriptive sciences like mineralogy or botany. Not surprisingly (c), this means that scientific advances were often made gropingly, through a process of trial and error involving countless intermediate steps (e.g., between astrology and astronomy) and contingent events having no "rational link" to what is "logically" required for a science (e.g., the development of the telescope or global exploration). Finally from (a) to (c), it becomes clear to Comte (d) what is important about his encyclopedic scheme and how it should be

---

15 See, e.g., CPP1(2), 101 [F, 59–60]; and SPP3, 40–41/33–34. Due again to Comte's often imprecise use of terms, one might get the impression that in "combining" the "general law" of the three stages and the "encyclopedic formula" of the sciences, one is handling two schemes that are epistemologically on equal footing. In fact, however, Comte sees the latter formula (increasingly called the "law of classification") as "complementing" the former, sc., by "coordinating the basic sciences according to subject matter" (SPP3, 17/15).

16 CPP1(2), 84 [F, 50]; also CPP1(2), 81 [F, 49]. Criticism of Comte's classification on the grounds that a purely sequential ordering ignores the interdependency of the sciences is as old as it is misinformed. See, e.g., Mill's telling criticism of Herbert Spencer on this issue (ACP, 284–87/41–46) and Whewell (SL, VI, x, 8, 928–29n.).

COMTE'S HISTORICO-CRITICAL "PRAGMATISM"   105

treated. A science's logical requirements are often hard to discern within the workings of its actual process; hence, our knowledge of the "true history" of each science (as opposed to mere possession of the details of that process in "historical order") depends on our consciously relating the encyclopedic scheme to the law of filiation and making

> a direct study of the general history of humanity. That is the reason why all the documents hitherto collected on the history of mathematics, astronomy, medicine, etc., however valuable they may be, can only be regarded as raw material for that study.[17]

In other words, both the emergence of the sciences from theology and metaphysics and their unfolding from mathematics to biology can now be rendered "intelligible" through a dogmatical exposition that identifies what, at some point, became (or, in the case of sociology, will become) "epistemologically necessary" for each area of study to leave theology and metaphysics firmly behind. From the standpoint of this dogmatical exposition, the scientific past is nine parts messy empirical detail and one part significant intellectual progress. Historico-critically understood, however, any dogmatic exposition must know itself to be an "artificial" compromise both with past and with anticipated events.[18]

3. Comte's historico-critical "pragmatism"

With the dogmatical method thus understood, it is not surprising that Comte often defends its employment in explicitly pragmatic terms. In one of the more admiring passages of his commentary, Mill captures this spirit exactly.

> It is always easy to find fault with a classification. There are a hundred possible ways of arranging any set of objects, and something may almost always be said against the best and in favor of the worst of them. But the merits of a classification depend on the purposes to which it is instrumental.[19]

And there are, Comte explains, numerous occasions on which dogmatical exposi-

---

17 CPP1(2), 81–82 [F, 49]. On the interplay between Comte's historical and dogmatic treatments of the scientific hierarchy see, e.g., G. H. Lewes, *Comte's Philosophy of the Sciences: Being an Exposition of the Principles of the 'Cours de philosophy positive' of Auguste Comte* (London: Henry G. Bohn, 1853), 40–50; and Pickering, PIC, 571–74.
18 Comte's classification of the sciences is much more complex than I need to explain here. In general, epistemically oriented works like the *Cours* emphasize (a) the objective (i.e., observation-based) character and unity of the hierarchy; (b) the logical relations among the sciences (i.e., from astronomy to sociology, a decreasing generality of explanation and independence from other sciences and an increasing complexity of phenomena explained); and (c) the dynamics of future progress, especially in the younger disciplines. See, e.g., CPP1(2), 86ff. [F, 51ff.]. Reformist-oriented works like the *Système* emphasize (a) the "subjective" (i.e., human-practical) unity and static totality of the hierarchy (i.e., as fully developed and ready for social use); and (b) the social value of the individual sciences (i.e., sociology and ethics ranked as the most important existentially rather than as the last to develop logically). See, e.g., SPP3, 40ff./33ff.
19 ACP, 284/41. The remark is made in defense of Comte against Spencer, whom Mill perceives as having criticized Comte's encyclopedic system out of a failure to understand its purpose.

tions of science are in this way more meritorious than historical ones. The more developed a science is, for example, the more its historical exposition becomes "impracticable," given all the material one would have to go through to trace its actual progress.[20] Then, too, in positive philosophizing about science, one always faces the "general pedagogical problem"

> of enabling individuals with often no more than average ability to reach the same stage of intellectual development in a few years that has taken centuries of effort by a great many superior minds. . . . Clearly, this aim would be impossible if every student were compelled to rehearse the same series of intermediate steps . . . followed by the collective genius of the race; hence, the indispensable need for the dogmatical method. . . .[21]

It is, in fact, with this pedagogical problem in mind that Comte draws up the outline for his entire *Cours*, dogmatically arranging its 60 "lessons" in accordance with the "objective order" of the basic sciences but switching to historical exposition when he gets to sociology. As he explains, the mathematical, natural, and life sciences have all advanced sufficiently to be accessible to newcomers through the static, logical presentation of their current epistemic conditions; but because sociology is still in a prescientific condition, an exposition of the "true history" of the other basic sciences is initially required in order to demonstrate the need for such a discipline.[22]

Let us be clear, however, that the pragmatism Comte displays here is a very special sort. In the first place, it is a strangely mitigated pragmatism. As we have just seen, given the way Comte describes the usefulness of his dogmatical schemes, it is just as important to keep in mind why these schemes need not be any more historically sensitive than they are as it is to see what outcomes they facilitate. Second and more important, however, Comte's is not a pragmatism concerning the handling of methods or theories *within* science at all. Rather, it is one that concerns his efforts to contextualize his philosophizing *about* science. It is therefore a very different pragmatism from the sort often embraced by later positivists.

To clarify this point, consider for contrast Reichenbach's calling his theory of meaning a "further development" of the "important and healthy tendency . . . to combine meaning and action" that he finds in both pragmatist and Vienna Cir-

20 CPP1(2), 78 [F, 47].
21 CPP1(2), 79 [F, 47–48]; cf. DEP, 80–90/126–41, where the discipline concerned with this education is called "First Philosophy," and its aims are said to be applicable to the general population through the exploitation of that "universal good sense" already praised by Bacon and Descartes (86/135). Comte's concept of good sense is discussed later.
22 CPP1(2), 82 [F, 49]; CPP5(52), 1–40 (summarized in M2, 181–91; 1–24 in A, 199–209). I ignore again, of course, numerous complications – e.g., (a) that basically similar epistemic conditions are nevertheless both ontologically (Comte says, "doctrinally") and (so also) methodologically unique to each science (CPP1(2), 108 [F, 63–64]); (b) that epistemological accounts themselves must be more extensive for sciences of "greater complexity and imperfection" (CPP4(48), 287–89 [L, 137–38]); and (c) that no logic of any science is ever to be taught without considerable use of empirical information about its present and past activities (CPP1(2), 79–80 [F, 48]).

cle positivist epistemologies. To say that the meaning of a proposition is its "method of its verification," he explains, is "the same idea" that pragmatists express "by calling observation propositions the 'cash value' of indirect propositions."[23] Reichenbach does not agree that cash value or true–false are completely adequate tests in a really scientific theory of meaning, and he goes on argue for the importance of the concepts of weight and probability; nevertheless, he concludes that his modified verificationist theory actually furthers the same basically "antimetaphysical" intent of his pragmatist progenitors' theory because it holds that

> *there is as much meaning in a proposition as can be utilized for action.* With this formulation, the close relation . . . to pragmatism becomes still more obvious; we think, though, that our theory . . . may furnish a better justification of the relation between meaning and action than pragmatism is able to give. This outcome . . . seems to me the best guaranty of its correspondence to empirical science and to the intention of language in actual life.[24]

A pragmatism of sorts this undoubtedly is, but it is not Comte's. The "theory" Reichenbach praises in this passage is, of course, his theory of meaning; and the question of its pragmatism thus arises at the level of reconstructive analysis of research practice. In contrast, Comte's pragmatism is displayed on the level of historico-critical reflection, where one would ask such questions as whether reconstruction is the proper philosophical approach to science in the first place. Or to put the contrast the other way around, Reichenbach's pragmatism implies that the Comtean variety is worthless. For as he sees it, the whole story of how scientists came to think as they do, of the beliefs they have embraced, and of the hopes they have entertained is the tale of a "mystical mist lying *above* the research methods of science" – a mere "superstructure of images and wishes" through which the real philosopher looks to discover "the solid foundation . . . of inductive operations" that is evident "below."[25]

In Reichenbach's presumptive distinction regarding where the real philosopher does and does not look, it is easy to spot another display of that same sort of ahistorically self-possessed philosophizing already found in Mill. Using the material from the last few pages, we might recapitulate a Comtean response to it as follows. Reichenbach's exposition of the task and topic of philosophy is not just dogmatical but also dogmatic. It forgets what Comte insists we remember that all dogmatical expositions take on faith, namely, that they are responses to some aspect of an intellectual and sociopolitical inheritance that provides them with

---

23 *Experience and Prediction*, 49; also, 53.
24 *Experience and Prediction*, 80, author's emphasis; cf. 30, 69, 73. I note in passing that Reichenbach's writing is almost as full of loosely so-called principles as Comte's.
25 *Experience and Prediction*, 403–404, my emphasis. For Carnap, too, "above" the level of scientist practicing as scientist, there is only the domain of "the philosopher," where one finds no hypotheses but just "theses" that make no cognitive difference ("Pseudoproblems in Philosophy," in *Logical Structure*, 306, 333–34). See also Ayer, *Language, Truth, and Logic*, 2nd ed. (New York: Dover, 1952), 46–57.

their context of "intelligibility" and that is ultimately to be explicated in accordance with the three-stage law.

Both Mill and the Logical Empiricists would argue, of course, that this allegedly *philosophical* appeal to the three-stage law is at best expressive of a merely "external," sociological interest in science or at worst the sign of metaphysical speculation arising out of the "mystical mists" that "does not itself meet the standards of the positive spirit."[26] By definition, they would say, scientific laws are empirical propositions, something open to discussion *within* science; hence, they cannot provide grounds for judgments *about* either science or the scientific character of one's own thinking. To a Comtean, however, it is not just this conclusion that is wrong; it is only the now long-familiar forced option between mere historical accounts and reconstructive analysis that make it seem necessary. For the fact is, when Mill banishes all "outlying" historical and metaphysical questions from his "correct analysis of reasoning," when Reichenbach "looks through" the superstructural mists above ongoing research in order to reconstruct the latter's "supporting structure," or when Carnap ignores the "subjective origins" of knowledge in order to offer a "constructional system . . . identical for all observers" instead[27] – when all these later positivists confine themselves to analyzing scientific rationality, it is by acting on a fundamentally similar but unspoken *understanding of how to philosophize about science*. Viewed from this angle, the basic difference Comte would see between himself and the later positivists boils down to this: He accepts the responsibility to defend his understanding, and they assume that no defense of theirs is required. In Chapter 6, I will return to this point and ask whether reconsidering the historico-critical explanation Comte actually gives might not further Putnam's remark about philosophers needing to "step back to diagnose their situation." In the meantime, we can at least conclude that Comte's "pragmatism" on this issue amounts to a commitment to the idea that, given the contextualizing purpose of all such steppings back, none of them can ever settle the matter so thoroughly that the issue itself may at some point be properly forgotten.

Having said all of this, however, I must now turn to the important respect in which it is too generous. Granted that Comte often *behaves* in accordance with the kind of historico-critical positivism I have been analyzing – for example, in stressing the emergence of science over its structure, in describing dogmatical accounts as subordinate to historical ones, and in characterizing both of these moves in

---

26 The external–sociological vs. internal–epistemological distinction is appealed to by Reichenbach in the opening pages of *Experience and Prediction* (4–5), with the remark that it is the one "usually" made to delimit philosophy of science proper. The crack about mystical mists is by Habermas, citing Popper (*Knowledge and Human Interests*, 71), though what Popper actually says is that Comte's (and Mill's!) three-stage law is "little better than a collection of misapplied metaphors" [*The Poverty of Historicism* (Boston: Beacon, 1957), 119].

27 For Carnap's phrasing, see *Logical Structure*, 7. In an unpublished letter to Carnap dated May 9, 1936, Neurath remarks that Comte should be defended for having promoted the idea of the unity of the sciences, but that his "metaphysics" makes the very term "positivism" one to be avoided [cited in Haller, "Was Wittgenstein a Positivist?" in *Questions on Wittgenstein* (Lincoln: University of Nebraska Press, 1988), 34–35].

pragmatic terms. Yet nowhere does he give anything like the explicit account of this position that I have been providing for him. Earlier, we saw why this is so – namely, because he is too deeply involved in opposing everything resembling Cartesian meditation to *reflectively acknowledge* his fundamental commitments. Now, however, let us look at what this overreaction costs him.

4. The other side of Comte's positivism

Quickly summarized, Comte's belief that there can be no "inward turns" in positive philosophizing prevents him not only from acknowledging his fundamental commitments explicitly but also from recognizing the countless occasions when he speaks as if he has abandoned them. He does not notice, for example, the lack of fit between his calling the third stage a successful transformation of the previous two and his claiming that it is necessarily the "final" one. Nor does he explain how, as a supposedly historical-minded positivist, he can openly wonder whether "in the future" the whole system of positive knowledge might not be "[re]constructed entirely by a priori reasoning." In a word, Comte does not question his frequent tendency to act like Mill – and thus also to anticipate still later positivists – in making dogmatical philosophical pronouncements . . . with a dogmatic, ahistorical air.

The presence of a dogmatic, even "tyrannical" side of Comte is too obvious to require much documentation, though as I noted earlier, one should take care not to link it too exclusively with his interest in social reform.[28] What deserves attention, however, is not its presence but the extent of it. A reader of course expects to find inconsistencies, even fairly serious ones, in any ambitious philosophical project. What one does not expect to find is an author's continual tendency to say things in a way that is at odds with the fundamental orientation of the project. Yet this is precisely the case with Comte. We have seen *that* he fails to work out the distinction between historico-critical reflection and interior observation that is actually called for by his own activity. We have also seen *what* are some of the consequences of that failure. But why, of all things, *these* consequences? Why, of all things, should Comte so often speak as if his pronouncements were being made from a context-free and fully justified position when he himself repeatedly describes his position as contextualized and needing (pragmatic) defense? A telling clue lies between the lines in another of his descriptions of the dogmatical method that I have not yet cited. When a system of ideas – for example, about a particular science – is formulated in dogmatical fashion, he says, that system

> is presented as it could be conceived today by a single mind which, positioned at the proper point of view and possessing sufficient knowledge, engages in the task of reconstructing that science as a whole.[29]

---

28 In addition to Mill, ACP, 328–68/125–200, this is the tendency of Popper, *The Poverty of Historicism*, Ch. 4; Kolakowski, *The Alienation of Reason*, Ch. 3; and Isaiah Berlin, "Historical Inevitability," in *Four Essays on Liberty* (Oxford: Oxford University Press, 1969), 109ff.
29 CPP1(2), 77 [F, 47].

What sort of "mind" is this that, though "single," is clearly meant to speak for everyone and appears to have earned that right by already being in possession of the "proper" viewpoint and "sufficient"[30] knowledge? We are familiar with this mind. It is Descartes' methodologically purified "I" – the objective thinker that has left its origins behind and is now prepared, without further worry about uncertainty, to get matters right.

What we have here, it seems, is a second case where the critique of an opposing position is conducted with such self-assurance that the critic fails to recognize how its influence nevertheless continues in him. Our first example was that of Mill on Comte. Mill never tries to analyze closely Comte's attempt to prove that interior observation is impossible because he is already certain that a good positivist cannot believe it is. Yet in his polemical preoccupation with Comte's conclusion, he lets the anti-reflective implications of the proof itself shape his own philosophical outlook. In the rest of this chapter, I want to show that there is a similar structure of continuing influence working in Comte's critique of Descartes. As a "scientific" opponent of any metaphysics of the soul, Comte sees no need to retrace the operation he supposes produced one. Yet in his preoccupation with such Cartesian results, he fails to recognize the imperious tone in which he himself tends to speak not only of the pseudopsychology he opposes but of the scientific activity he defends. And in precisely such imperious moments, he allows Descartes' ahistorical ideal of the Objective Thinker to pass through to him, silently and unrecognized, so that it haunts his own efforts to develop a historico-critical alternative to this ideal.

I am not interested, however, in dwelling on familiar criticisms. Everyone knows that Descartes' impossible metaphysics is finally inseparable from his promising epistemology; and no one consults Comte for scholarly commentary. Moreover, I will suggest in Chapter 6 that we contemporaries still have so much at stake where both Descartes and positivism are concerned that it is probably dangerous for us to assume that we can even be just their detached critics. My question, then, is not whether Comte got Descartes right; rather, it is what he managed to inherit from him by opposing Cartesian metaphysics in lieu of analyzing Descartes' meditation. Comte is certainly not the last philosopher whose sense of the contextualized character of his own thinking is continually sabotaged by a more powerful demand for objectivity. Nor, more importantly, was he the first; and here some additional discussion of Descartes can further my purposes. For what is famously present in his *Meditations* is not only the objective ideal itself but a display of *its deliberate employment against habitual and traditional cognitive tendencies*. I want to say that Comte himself, not having followed Descartes' account of this struggle, is condemned, against his own best instincts, to be influenced by its ahistorically characterized purpose. We, on the other hand, are free to reconsider Cartesian "ahistoricity in the making" – and that means, first, dis-

---

30 The other meaning of *suffisant* is "conceited."

tinguishing within Descartes' meditative process between the objective ideal itself and the only partially successful reformation of his own resistant thinking; and second, transposing this pattern of reform and resistance from Descartes to Comte in order to see how its inherited presence in the latter subverts his historico-critical intentions.

5. Descartes' reflectiveness

What Descartes actually practiced is, of course, not captured by Comte's description of interior observation. Whatever it is, meditation is at least possible. Yet if few followed Comte in explaining such reflection away, many have joined Mill in regarding it primarily as an empirical (or more loosely, a positive knowledge-seeking) operation. Though Mill did not invent this unfortunate practice, his famous quarrel with Comte and his obviously scientific purpose in opposing him certainly encouraged it. Today, it is still widely assumed that Mill and Comte and Descartes, together with Locke, Hume, Kant, and a host of others, are all participants in a story of the rise and demise of *introspection,* where the issue is whether this process can give us *self-knowledge* to match the natural knowledge available by other means.[31]

My objection is not to Descartes being made a part of this story. He does indeed claim "knowledge" of the cogito; worry about what nature teaches me through the "internal senses"; and purchase endless trouble by writing materialistically about human bodies and dualistically about human nature. From an entirely contemporary perspective, then, one well understands why Descartes could be said to

> deserve the greatest intellectual respect for setting a sincere and profound challenge ... [i] to the scientist ... of generating a theory of human nature which does not deny the purposeful, cognitive, deliberative, willful, and free aspects of human cognition and human action ... and [ii] to the philosopher of ... explaining whether and how ... our sense of ourselves and our sense of scientific explanation can be meshed without doing radical violence to either.[32]

Yet even if Descartes' writings do offer such "challenges" for today's "scientists and philosophers of the mind," to picture Descartes himself as actually setting this particular agenda would be anachronistic in the extreme. Descartes does not begin as a Cartesian dualist intent on issuing and defending controversial claims about minds and bodies; and if he does not closely analyze the differences between introspection, inner sense, and reflection, this by no means justifies the common Anglo-American penchant for collapsing all three in the direction of

---

31 See, e.g., the recent collection edited by Quassim Cassam, *Self-Knowledge* (Oxford: Oxford University Press, 1994); also Lyons, *Introspection,* Ch. 1; Owen J. Flanagan, Jr., *The Science of the Mind,* 2nd ed. (Cambridge, MA: MIT Press, 1991), 1–22, 66–67, 193–200; and Gerald E. Myers, "Introspection and Self-Knowledge," *American Philosophical Quarterly* 23 (1986), 199–207.
32 Flanagan, *Science,* 22.

"introspection, or one of [those] more or less indistinguishable cognate processes" by which we gain a first-person "sense of ourselves."[33] For my purposes, however, what is of still greater importance than the sheer presentism of this image of the challenging Descartes is its power to deflect attention from that feature of meditation that Descartes himself makes primary, namely, its being a form of *critical reflection* – a philosophical monitoring of how one's own course of reasoning should go, under the guidance of the standards of clarity and distinctness borrowed from mathematics. Meditation, so understood, may correctly be said to involve a kind of "self-discovery"; but this is emphatically not (a) self-knowing in the substantive, science-of-the-mind sense, nor is it subjective in any (b) straightforwardly psychological or (c) first-person, autobiographical sense. In discussing each of these three points, I shall have in mind the question of what the historico-critical Comte might have found congenial in Descartes' meditation had he not remained a stranger to it in reaction to its apparent results.[34]

(a) To see the difference between Descartes' concern for reflective self-discovery and the science/philosophy of mind's interest in self-knowledge, consider the recent analysis by Flanagan of how to develop a "credible . . . constructive-naturalistic theory of consciousness." Calling his approach the "natural method," he argues first that we must learn to "listen" impartially to each of three separate "lines of analysis" – namely, phenomenology ("what individuals have to say about how things seem"), psychology and cognitive science ("descriptions about how mental life works and what jobs consciousness has . . . in its overall economy"), and neuroscience ("how mental events of different sorts are realized"). The object of his pluralistic approach

---

33 Flanagan's phrasing leaves it unclear whether his own view is anachronistic in the way I describe. The tendency to collapse Descartes' entire orientation in the direction of introspection is nicely illustrated in Flanagan, *Science*, 66; Cassam's "Introduction" to *Self-Knowledge*; and Lyons, *Introspection*, 3. To substantiate the claim that there was a general lack of clarity about introspection and reflection in the seventeenth century, Lyons cites J. Douglas Rabb, apparently not realizing that Rabb opposes precisely the standard interpretation of reflection in terms of introspection that Lyons adopts. See Rabb's *John Locke on Reflection: A Phenomenology Lost* (Lanham, MD: University Press of America, 1985), 11–20.

34 In thus reading backward from the historico-critical Comte to the meditative Descartes, I mean to express solidarity with recent efforts to reverse the tendency of several decades in Anglo-American circles to treat Descartes as if his six Meditations were an unsuccessful attempt to do analytic epistemology. A prime example of this tendency is Bernard Williams' *Descartes: The Project of Pure Inquiry* (Atlantic Highlands, NJ: Humanities Press, 1978), self-described as a "rational reconstruction of Descartes' thought...in contemporary style" (10); also, Peter J. Markie, *Descartes' Gambit* (Ithaca, NY: Cornell University Press, 1986). The pioneering opposition is L. J. Beck, *The Metaphysics of Descartes: A Study of the 'Meditations'* (Oxford: Clarendon Press, 1965). Cf. Marjorie Grene, "Idea and Judgment in the Third Meditation: An Approach to the Reading of Cartesian Texts," in her *Descartes* (Minneapolis: University of Minnesota Press, 1985), 3–22; also esp. Amélie Oksenberg Rorty, "The Structure of Descartes' *Meditations*," L. Aryeh Kosman, "The Naive Narrator: Meditation in Descartes' *Meditations*," and Gary Hatfield, "The Senses and the Fleshless Eye: The *Meditations* as Cognitive Exercises," all in *Essays on Descartes' 'Meditations'*, ed. A. O. Rorty (Berkeley: University of California Press, 1986), 1–20, 21–43, and 45–79; and Emmet T. Flood, "Descartes' Comedy of Error," *MLN* 102/4 (1987), 847–66.

is to see whether and to what extent the three stories can be rendered coherent, meshed, brought into reflective equilibrium. The only rule is to treat all three . . . with respect. Any a priori decision about which line of analysis "gets it right" prejudges the question of whether different analyses might be legitimate for different explanatory purposes and thus . . . at least capable of peaceful coexistence. . . .

One might think that the natural method must be either the preferred method or at least have been tried . . . and shown to be deficient. This is a plausible but false thought. The natural method is certainly not the canonical method at the present time.[35]

This passage, condensed from several successive paragraphs, illustrates how and (more significantly) in what sequence Flanagan makes what amount to four general claims. First, he reports the existence of three possible sources of information – one of which, the "phenomenological," is intended to be an updated and more generous-spirited construal of introspective, or folk, psychology. Second, he asserts that no one source ought a priori to be made the measure of the others. Third, he describes the standpoint from which the second claim's advice can be taken as a "synthetic" (and faintly Rawlsian) kind of "reflective equilibrium." Finally, he admits that this threefold claim defines a method that is not but ought to be our preferred one.

Now let us note that the claim Flanagan makes last is on precisely the question that occupies Descartes (and Comte!) first and most fundamentally, namely, what kind of philosophical outlook is now best able to determine how to understand X, and how does one defend that outlook against the unsatisfactory but still dominant inherited approaches? On this question, however, Flanagan merely makes a few quick remarks to the effect that the methods of phenomenology, cognitive psychology, and neuroscience have been "tried and tested" and "when taken alone, do not work." Beyond this, and concerning the merits of his own natural method of "seeking reflective equilibrium among the phenomenological, psychological, and neuroscientific levels" of analysis, he simply leaves it "for others to judge."[36]

What is it, however, to say that the three other methods taken alone "do not work"? How was it determined that they are even expressive of the same or sufficiently related human interests that they can or should work together on anything? If phenomenology, cognitive psychology, and neuroscience cannot offer

---

35 Flanagan, *Consciousness Reconsidered* (Cambridge, MA: MIT Press, 1992), 11. A similarly pluralistic methodology is advocated by Lyons, *Introspection*, 154–56.
36 Flanagan, *Consciousness*, 12, 20; also 220–22. My remarks here are not intended as criticisms of the book Flanagan chose to write – as if he should have doubled its size to increase the treatment of claims three and four. I do in fact confess to having ontological misgivings about the sort of "theory" we can expect from Flanagan's "reflective synthesis"; but at present, I single out Flanagan's work for being, as he rightly says, more generously pluralistic in approach than most. For precisely by thereby short-circuiting much of the current methodological infighting in current cognitive philosophy, it brings into sharper relief the general absence of interest among Anglo-Americans of any methodological stripe in the sort of reflectiveness Flanagan's fourth claim would quickly have stimulated in both Descartes and Comte.

adequate orientations from which to "construct a naturalistic theory of consciousness," what may we expect from such a theory that we cannot obtain from phenomenological, psychological, and neuroscientific theories taken separately? And if the method of reflective equilibrium is not beholden to any of these lesser methods, from what source does it obtain its own "naturalistic" inspiration and the authority to adjudicate for "peaceful coexistence" among them? Such questions go to the roots of the tree of knowledge, said Descartes – which means they call for a kind of philosophical self-discovery never attempted by those who already understand themselves as constructors [?] of comprehensive naturalistic [?] theories of consciousness [?] and are therefore content to simply begin with the currently conceived trunk of knowledge and look toward its branches.

(b) To twentieth-century ears, however, and even if we ignore our feelings about the fact that Descartes linked his meditation specifically to a quest for "certainty," his personalized account of that quest itself can sound indulgent, that is, insensitive to the seemingly obvious need for keeping matters of general epistemic substance separate from those of individual psychic detail. In the *Rules for the Direction of the Mind*, for example, he tells us that "the greatest pleasure I have taken in my studies has always come not from accepting arguments of others but from discovering arguments by my own efforts."[37] But, we hear the objection, what does epistemic analysis have to do with pleasure? And why bother even mentioning the self-evident fact that this sort of analysis is not sociology? Or again, in the *Discourse on Method*, Descartes says, "My plan is to reform my own thoughts and construct them upon a foundation that is all my own."[38] But does it not seem obvious now that epistemic analysis is not about the reformation of any particular person's thoughts, let alone about learning to accept "the" foundations of thinking as "my own"?

From Descartes' standpoint in the *Meditations*, however, there is a false dichotomy at work in these objections. To "meditate" is precisely not to drive a wedge between The Structure of Thought and my thinking. Hence, to avoid the common twentieth-century psychologistic interpretation of Descartes' first-person language, we must always read that language precisely in terms of his reformist proclamations. Consider, for example, his famous assertion of radical methodological resolve near the end of Meditation I. Having realized that he must withhold assent not only from obviously false beliefs but also from all beliefs that are to any degree uncertain, Descartes asserts that

> it is not enough merely to have noticed this; I must make an effort to remember it. My habitual opinions keep coming back, and, despite my wishes, they recapture my belief, which is as it were bound over to them as a result of long occupation and the

---

37 *Oeuvres de Descartes*, ed. by Ch[arles] Adam and P[aul] Tannery, new rev. ed., 11 vols. (Paris: J. Vrin, 1964–76), X, 403; also 367. [Translations (sometimes with minor alterations) are from John Cottingham et al., *The Philosophical Works of Descartes*, 3 vols. (Cambridge: Cambridge University Press, 1984–91), which carries the AT pagination in its margins.]
38 AT, VI, 15.

law of custom.... In view of this, I think it will be a good plan to turn my will in completely the opposite direction and deceive myself, by pretending for a time that these former opinions are [not "what in fact they are, namely, highly probable" but] utterly false and imaginary.[39]

To actually make this special effort, to confess to being repeatedly sabotaged by old mental habits, to resolutely plan a strategy of self-correction – these are not, for Descartes, mere matters of individual psychological detail, out of place in an epistemological work. The trick is to stop accusing Descartes of failing to make the proper distinction and ponder for a moment whether our having learned to make it is a blessing.

If we ourselves are especially likely to remember from the *Rules* and the *Discourse* all the abstract and general pronouncements about the unreliability of common opinion, the universal applicability of the rules of method, the criteria for certainty, and so on, we should now "make an effort" to do so in conjunction with the recognition that in the *Meditations*, pronouncements about procedure are inseparable from and continually fleshed out by accompanying reports of *what it takes to set aside* common opinion, *adopt* the method, *actually search* for certainty, and so on. Descartes is in this respect perhaps still more ancient, even Socratic, than he is modern. For according to his picture of the philosophical terrain, *knowing* and *knowing that I know* have not yet been split off into an anonymous, formal system of rules, on the one hand, and the merely psychological fact of my struggle to use these rules, on the other. Genuinely Cartesian teachers would never sneer at a beginning geometry student, "Your conclusion may be new to you, but it is not really new"; and that is not merely because they are trying to be both good psychologists "as well as" processors of purified epistemic information.

There is, then, a philosophically reflective "my-ownness" actually displayed in the *Meditations* that is occluded by later "reconstructions" merely of the line of reasoning that is reported in it. Moreover, this self-monitoring manner of thinking is not merely associated with Descartes' preparatory work against the influence of sense experience and the threat of skepticism, so that it disappears later when real thinking commences. About certainty, for example, Descartes refuses even to make any positive pronouncements at all until the beginning of Meditation III, and even then he is only willing to proceed by relating at the same time how he discovered what it is like to have it. By this time, the hyperbolic skepticism of Meditation I has failed to dislodge the insight that I must *be* a thinker while in the *act* of thinking; and an analysis of this thinking in Meditation II has begun to clarify the mind's nature. Then and only then – on the basis of the clear and distinct perceptions won through the efforts of the first two Meditations, and not in terms of some formal analysis of what Rule One as stated in the *Discourse* must mean – is Descartes prepared to say something about certainty "in general." At this point, he says,

39 AT, VII, 22; cf. 47–48.

> I will cast around more carefully to see whether there may be other things within me which I have not yet noticed. I am certain that I am a thinking thing. Do I not therefore also know what is required for my being certain about anything? ... So I *now* seem to be able to lay it down as a *general rule* that whatever I perceive very clearly and distinctly is true.[40]

Hence, even Descartes' conception of what the rules of method themselves involve is continually being enriched as he employs them. Recognizing precisely when and how this enrichment happens is an essential part of the meditative process – that is, it concerns the question of the self-discovery of what it is to see with certainty.

Rather than refer to Descartes' "theory of knowledge" or even his "rules of method," then, it would be better to speak of his *procedure for becoming knowledgeable*. Small wonder that he should find "synthetic," or syllogistic (Comte would say dogmatical, or just plain "logical"), reasoning unsuitable to his needs. The trouble with such reasoning, he explains, is that it tends to preoccupy the mind with formal rules of inference; and rules of this sort can seem to make

> conclusions follow with such irresistible necessity that if our reason relies on them, even though it takes, as it were, a rest from considering a particular inference clearly and attentively, it can nevertheless draw a conclusion which is certain simply in virtue of the form.[41]

We must "guard against our reason's taking [such] a holiday while we are investigating the truth," he says, because while "resting" so, we cannot learn anything. Conversely, even the most skilled thinkers cannot formulate a valid syllogism with a true conclusion unless they are also recognizing the very truth whose deduction is thus formally displayed. Descartes concludes that since no increase in the understanding of truth can come from studying the formal rules of reasoning, that kind of study should be "transferred from philosophy to rhetoric."[42]

(c) Descartes' meditation, finally, is no more autobiographical than it is tainted by the psychological. As first-personlike as his descriptions of it clearly are, they are simultaneously and just as clearly intersubjective in their intent, as the consistent use of the plural address in these discussions already suggests. Descartes is concerned with the discovery of something not just personally possible for me but ontologically possible for everyone, namely, learning what it is like to demand and obtain certainty in thinking. For this reason, he expects (not just invites) from his readers precisely what he demands of himself. After all, he explains,

---

40 AT, VII, 35 (my emphasis).
41 *Rules*, AT, X, 405–406; also *Meditations, Second Replies*, AT, VII, 155–56. Cf. L. J. Beck, *The Method of Descartes: A Study of the 'Regulae'* (Oxford: Clarendon Press, 1952), 102–10; and E. M. Curley, "Analysis in the *Meditations*: The Quest for Clear and Distinct Ideas," in A. O. Rorty, ed., *Essays on Descartes' 'Meditations,'* 153–76.
42 *Rules*, AT, X, 406. Actually, Descartes finds a number of objections to syllogistic/formal reasoning. John A. Passmore finds four, and emphasizes the one I cite here, in "Descartes, the British Empiricists, and Formal Logic," *Philosophical Review* 62 (1953), 546–50.

I wrote "Meditations" rather than "Disputations," as the [scholastic] philosophers have done, or "Theorems and Problems," as the geometers would have done. In so doing I wanted to make it clear that I would have nothing to do with anyone who was not willing to join me in meditating and giving the subject attentive consideration.[43]

The proper response to Descartes' meditation is therefore co-meditation, namely, the effort to experience the intuitive force of each of his discoveries until we, too, apprehend it. As Descartes says in the famous passage in his "Readers' Preface" to the *Meditations*, those who cannot or will not make this effort are urged not to read the work at all.[44] There is, then, a wonderful irony in the story recounted by Beck about the *Rules*. Rumors apparently circulated widely after Descartes' death that he had left an unfinished treatise on logic, but all that was found was the manuscript of the *Rules* (n.b., "for the *direction* of the mind in the *search* for truth"), which, in the unintentionally revealing words of his first biographer, Adrien Baillet, could not itself "be looked upon as a Logic, . . . [but] upon which a most excellent Logic may be modelled."[45] Comte would have approved that Descartes himself never wrote such an excellent Logic.

Calls for co-meditation are, however, difficult to heed when the discoveries we are asked to experience now seem highly questionable on their face. Nothing makes an allegedly philosophical method more quickly suspect than the claim that it will produce an experience of something that from the outset seems radically improbable. And indeed, what contemporary reader is optimistic about experiencing Descartes' certainties concerning Mind, God, and Nature? Perhaps it is such doubts as these that have always guaranteed that Descartes' fortunes would vary in accordance with reactions to his doctrines more than to his method. Compared with, say, Kantian criticism or Hegelian dialectic, relatively few have ever proselytized for Cartesian meditation.[46] At any rate, in the case of Comte at least, it is this sort of opposition to the substantive results of meditation, rather than conclusions drawn from a careful analysis of meditation itself, that animates his broadside against interior observation. The doctrines about Mind allegedly arrived at by meditation, like the apparently similarly derived theories of Cousin, are so distasteful to Comte's positivist sensibilities that the operation itself, let alone Descartes' call to co-meditation, seems unworthy of serious attention.

---

43 *Second Replies*, AT, VII, 157.
44 AT, VII, 9. Some might argue that both Descartes' limiting his reforms to "my" thoughts and his inviting consent only from co-meditators have a political motive, insofar as it would have been dangerous for him to demand universal reforms of his sort in a Christian world. I do not believe this paranoid line; but even if it were true, it is irrelevant here. The fact is that Descartes *does* make philosophical reflectiveness nonformal and co-meditative, and it is this model I wish to rethink.
45 Quoted in Beck, *Method*, 1.
46 Consider in this light, e.g., R. Rorty's discussion of A. O. Lovejoy's theory of "revolts against [Cartesian] dualism," in "Contemporary Philosophy of Mind," *Synthese* 53 (1982), 328–32.

6. Comte's ahistorical reflexivity

Yet as I have argued, if, because of his anti-reflective commitment, Comte has little to say in any direct fashion about monitoring one's own experience of becoming knowledgeable, he remains in his way very much concerned with philosophical self-understanding. In principle at least, he takes the question of the *emergence* of one's philosophical thinking just as seriously as does Descartes himself. Recall Descartes' joint conception, at the beginning of Meditation I, of the "whole doubtful edifice of beliefs" in which he finds himself initially entangled and of the methodological "demolition" he plans for it. Now notice that Comte has a historicized variation of the same two themes. In his hands, the initial "edifice" is widened and deepened to become the whole inherited human past; and his three-stage law replaces Descartes' four rules. I did not invent this parallel; it is Comte's own. He repeatedly refers to his positivism as "first philosophy"; he often describes the "positive method" as the means for realizing Descartes' ideal of intellectual liberation; and he even characterizes one of the *Cours'* concluding lessons as his contemporary equivalent of the *Discourse on Method*.[47]

Let me, however, be more careful about this comparison than Comte. There are fundamental differences, both in principle and in practice, between Descartes' and Comte's ideas of what it means for philosophical thinking to "emerge" from its intellectual preconditions; and spelling these differences out can tell us a good deal about how to understand Comte's failure to carry through on his historico-critical commitments.

As regards principle, we know of course that Descartes' is an objectivist ideal. He intends to use his method to "set aside" his mind's intellectual preconditions in order to gain certainty. In Part I, however, we saw that in contrast to this Cartesian vision of philosophy's becoming *free from* its past, Comte wants to use his method to *free up* an understanding precisely *of* those preconditions in order to discover what is scientifically and socially called for next. Comte's historico-critical positivist would therefore never aspire to be a self-possessed Cartesian "I"; for positive thought is always "relative" to current conditions and findings; and an "absolutist" quest for more is "immature." In other words, Descartes' announced obstacle is Comte's chosen topic. The very thing a good Cartesian must do battle with and try to overcome – namely, the initially contextualized condition of one's thinking – a good Comtean wants to clarify and cultivate instead.

In the two thinkers' writings, however, matters are often strangely turned around. The Descartes whose inquiry we actually follow in the *Meditations* will never be the Objective Thinker that is announced as the ideal. Conversely, the

---

47 The lesson's title is "Final Appreciation of the Positive Method as a Whole," CPP6(58), 784–85. More generally, Comte actually thinks of himself as finishing Descartes' work – by replacing the mathematical method (which is too narrow and puts mistaken emphasis on "precision" in knowledge); by extending the reach of method-guided thinking to all classes of phenomena (recall what Descartes leaves out); and by recognizing the philosophical importance (denied by Descartes) of historical knowledge. See Lévy-Bruhl, *History of Modern Philosophy in France*, 394–95, 477–82; and Pierre Ducassé, "Méthode positive et méthode cartesienne," *Revue de Synthèse* 14/1 (1937), 51–66.

Comte who speaks as Educator in the *Cours* and High Priest in the *Système* frequently seems to assume, ahistorically, that he already is that Thinker. How can this be? How could it happen that the unsurpassably determinate character of the reflective practice Descartes actually displays in the *Meditations* is ignored not just by Cartesians but even by someone like Comte, whose own historico-critical intentions would be so much better served by Descartes' image of reflective practice than by the ideally objective (Comte, in these moods, says "scientific" or "positive") alternative he often silently adopts?

The answer in the case of the Cartesians, and even with respect to Descartes himself, seems obvious enough. Given what the rules are supposed to accomplish, the specter of a forever resistant and incurably contextualized rationality is a philosophical embarrassment. But what about Comte? How could he fail to recognize that his own historico-critical line of reasoning is already prefigured in Descartes' actual meditative process? I am not, of course, pressing an empirical thesis here. I do not care, and it makes no difference to my point, whether Comte pored over the *Meditations* but in the end remained insufficiently moved by its historico-critical intimations. I am trying to show that there is something about his positivism – something Cartesian – that his bias against inward turns encourages him to miss and that ultimately makes Comte insensitive to his own tendency to cut the historico-critical ground out from under his dogmatical pronouncements.

Consider first what the historico-critical Comte *might* have seen in the *Meditations*. Recall the profoundly antiformalist conception of method implicit in its actual use. For Descartes the meditator, no moment occurs when his rules receive their full explication and he becomes their entirely competent instrument. What the rules mean and what it is to live up to them are uncovered jointly and within the ongoing meditative process itself; and as insightful as those rules promise to make him (and we are indeed struck today by how much allegedly becomes certain under their auspices), to some extent they invariably operate also as a humbling device – taken to heart, so to speak, in the many reminders of why we are never instantiations of Reason itself. Hence, we find caveats everywhere – for example, that old habits are never completely extinguished and that clarity slips away when attention weakens; that one can have "some understanding" but not full "comprehension" of God; that nature in its concreteness is too full of possibilities for reason alone to know it; that adventitious ideas are never more than "generally" reliable; and so on. Are these not elements congenial to the Comte who proudly rejects the whole idea of systematizing the positive method, who emphasizes the "feebleness" of the human mind that prevents it from effecting an "objective synthesis" of phenomenal knowledge, and who thus thinks of unifying that knowledge instead by "subjective synthesis" guided by respect for the particularities of current research and sociopolitical need?[48]

---

48 DEP, 22–25/35–41. Sometimes, Comte says that even in the case of Descartes himself, "the impossibility of including higher phenomena in [an objective] synthesis induced him subsequently to attempt to reach intellectual unity by the subjective mode" instead (SPP1, 583/472; also SPP3, 567, 590/483, 504).

In fact, however, it is not the meditating Descartes but a totally liberated Cartesian thinker who often speaks in Comte's writings. In this voice, he is at best enacting a kind of *reflexive substitute* for meditation. It is, to be sure, at least a substitute. Even at his most tyrannical, Comte still regards the positive method and thinking "scientifically" as being to him what the mathematical method and thinking "clearly and distinctly" are to Descartes, namely, a practice always in the making. Yet in spite of the fact that he sometimes even goes so far as to warn that a dogmatical thinking that forgets its sociohistorical origins faces the specter of vicious circularity,[49] there are many occasions when Comte is just as obviously reflexive rather than meditatively reflective – by which I mean he speaks as someone so fully in possession of his basic principles as to have no need for a method that would only work in the manner of Descartes' "gradual" and forever incomplete intellectual reformation.

In short, Comte's praise of the mature mind's "constant tendency ... to substitute the dogmatical for the historical" often applies less harmlessly to his own positive philosophy than to positive science. Messy details and recalcitrant facts are the life's blood of the latter; they are therefore never a mere drag on the intellectual tendency of science, but instead are the very thing that makes any of its dogmatical products "relative." Positive philosophers, however, take intellectual tendencies themselves for their subject matter, which creates the constant danger that their "dogmatical recastings" will feel too easy and look too impressive unless – as Comte in his historico-critical moods insists – one remembers what makes every recasting "artificial." And so does it happen, at all those other times, when Comte appears to forget this warning. Then his self-descriptions become uncritical and authoritarian. More than occasionally, he appears to treat the "positive method" less like a guide than an afterthought, a kind of slogan that merely gestures in the direction of his millenarian projections and his highly (on occasion, even wildly) speculative use of scientific theories. Sometimes he even characterizes his utopian dream of the coming Religion of Humanity, with himself installed as High Priest, as a "prediction" – a move so glaringly the display of unscientific projection that it prompted Thomas Huxley to ridicule the whole Comtean system as "Catholicism minus God."[50]

Read exclusively from this angle, Comte has been easy to dismiss. Undoubtedly, there even has to be a purely biographical side to all this excess.[51] He must have been the kind of person who could assume such an imperious pose. Moreover, and especially with the passage of time, many of his High Priestly pronouncements have come to seem truly outrageous. Something like this line of

---

49 CPP1(2), 76/46.
50 See, e.g., Boas, *French Philosophies*, 292–93; and Eric Voegelin, *From Enlightenment to Revolution*, ed. John H. Hallowell (Durham, NC: Duke University Press, 1975), 161–66.
51 On Comte's difficult marriage to Caroline Massin, Pickering's account is now the most judicious (see esp. PIC, 371–95, 398–400, 473–75, 489–93, 542–47); on Comte's chaste affair with Clotilde de Vaux, see Henri Gouhier, *La vie d'Auguste Comte*, 2nd ed. (Paris: J. Vrin, 1965), for a thorough but also somewhat too reverent an account of Comte's side in the relation (esp. 182–203).

criticism is, we know, already present in Mill, according to whom Comte's kind of imperious, foundationalist dogmatism is characteristic not only of Comte himself but of Descartes and Leibniz as well. Taken together, says Mill, these three were,

> of all the great scientific thinkers, the most consistent, and for that reason often the most absurd, because they *shrank from no consequences, however contrary to common sense,* to which their premises appeared to lead.[52]

Note with special care the later positivist attitude that lies behind Mill's ostensible appeal to "common sense" here, as regards its being both an aid to his diagnosis and a prescription for cure. On the one hand, he claims that in all three philosophers the cause of their tendency toward speculative outrageousness can be traced to a penchant for trusting what they think can be discovered from philosophical self-monitoring – that is, either meditatively, apperceptively, or historico-critically, respectively – and he defends this claim by working backward from common sense. All three philosophers, he argues, are either pre- or insufficiently positivist thinkers who could not or at least did not acquire enough trust in the superiority of scientific rationality from what was going on around them. Hence, notwithstanding their professed respect for science, they each started instead from some deeply felt, allegedly intuited premises (Descartes, Leibniz) or "laws" (Comte); self-consciously defined their viewpoints in terms of these premises or laws, and then employed them deductively, thus arriving at conclusions that are at best right for the wrong reasons or at worst simply "absurd." On the other hand, true positivists, as Mill represents them, no longer need to turn inward for such rational assurances before attending outwardly to the empirically obvious. The age of science has already arrived – not because Right Reason has been brought under an intuited premise or appealing slogan, but because the evidence of successful researching and predicting lies all around us.

Like Carnap and Reichenbach long after him, Mill already treats this sociological "fact" of actual scientific accomplishment as the "common sense" of every perceptive contemporary mind; and in this moment, to borrow Habermas' phrase, Descartes' epistemology is "flattened out" into positivist methodology.[53] The "correct analysis" of the methods of scientific inference now becomes philosophy's "main problem" – as the full title of *A System of Logic, Ratiocinative* [of course] *and* [yet also] *Inductive* announces. And although, admittedly, no logic – not even a properly codified one – can actually prevent people from embracing

---

52 ACP, 367–68/200, my emphasis.
53 *Knowledge and Human Interests*, 67–69. Habermas himself makes Comte the primary culprit in this flattening-out process by reading later positivism back into him. So, e.g., he thinks Comte's basic concern is the epistemic one of finding "normative methodological rules" (73, 76); he assumes Comte equates observation with "sense certainty" (74–75); and he claims that Comte regards metaphysics as "meaningless" (79). Having thus worked up a portrait of Comte as a thoroughly postmetaphysical thinker, Habermas has no trouble turning Comte's historico-critical expositions into a "pseudo-scientific" public relations device for the "propagation of the cognitive monopoly of science" (71, 73).

absurdities, just as obviously, neither can "traditional reflection." Resisting absurdity, like seeing what philosophy has to do in the first place, is ultimately a matter of "common sense."

Comte, not surprisingly, conceives of common sense quite differently. He thinks of it as keeping positive *scientists* honest, not positive *philosophers*. According to one of his favorite images, the positive spirit is the "methodological extension" of that simple, universal "good sense" that is to some degree evident in the lives of even the most primitively prescientific thinker. Whether Comte's "good sense" means precisely the same thing as Mill's "common sense" need not detain us here. What matters is the difference in their treatments of these at least clearly similar phenomena in connection to philosophy. In a long passage in his *Discours*, Comte sums up what he sees as the fundamental relation between good sense and the positive spirit by saying that

> both have the same experiential point of departure, the same interest in making connections and achieving foresight [*le même but de lier et de prévoir*], the same unceasing preoccupation with reality, the same basic concern with usefulness. The only essential difference between them is that the positive spirit, seeking necessarily after abstraction, is systematic and general, while good sense, being always involved with the concrete, tends to particulars and is given to inconsistency [*à l'incohérente spécialité*].[54]

In subsequent dogmatical and historical elaborations, Comte makes good sense the source of positive theory's recognition of the unprofitability of abstract logic and the inefficaciousness of theologico-metaphysical speculation, respectively. Yet in addition to the contributions of good sense and positive theorizing described here, there is also, present in and presiding over the whole discussion, Comte's historico-critical orientation. At the end of his discussion, Comte describes the positive spirit – now called humanity's "theoretical sense" *(sagesse théoretique)* – as having been pointed in the right direction and gradually educated through the continuous prodding of good – now called "practical" – sense *(sagesse practique);* and he concludes that the only fitting way for the latter to be repaid for its historical service is

> by the production of *a complete theoretical systematization*, in its generality and logical coherence, of all that the practical sense knows only as real and concretely useful. For to tell the truth, all the positive knowledge obtained in the last two centuries is much more valuable as material for furthering *a new general philosophy* than for its straight empirical worth....[55]

I have italicized two phrases in order to draw attention to the fact that the voice that is "telling the truth" in this passage cannot be understood as either that of

---

54 DEP, 45/72.
55 DEP, 48–49/77, my emphasis.

practical "good sense" itself or as that of the "theoretical sense" that generates our speculations about the reality good sense cares about. It is, we now recognize, the voice of Comte's historico-critical thinker "about" science.

Our analysis thus has returned to the distinction drawn earlier between Mill's philosophy "of" science and Comte's philosophizing "about" science. It is now possible, however, to see this distinction from an angle that sheds light on the question before us – namely, if Comte's historico-critical orientation is in principle something different from and superior to both Cartesian "traditional reflection," on the one hand, and Millian reconstructivism (plus perhaps an auxiliary appeal to common sense), on the other, then why is he not more successful in *practicing* the context-sensitive, carefully circumscribed sort of philosophizing he is supposed to? Reading backward from Comte to Descartes with Mill's treatment of common sense in mind, one can see where the answer lies.

7. Imperious claims and Comte's legacy

Consider the philosophical task Mill implies one ought to assign to common sense. Is he right to give it the role he denies to traditional (Cartesian and Leibnizian) reflection? Suppose that we agree with him – as we are likely to do in any case – that meditation, reflective apperception, and Comtean reflexivity are today all ultimately unacceptable varieties of philosophical self-monitoring. Should we follow Mill's suggestion and make common sense their *replacement*?

It is, of course, understandable that Mill himself should take this position. He has, after all, situated philosophy entirely within a scientific age – an age, he thinks, in which the question of how to obtain knowledge is settled; stories about the rise of science are passé; and the one form of intellectual inward turn that remains legitimate is introspection, which is empirical and first-personal and thus valuable in science but certainly not philosophy. Under such assumptions, one might well conclude that common sense is traditional reflection's obvious replacement. For its anonymous and transpersonal character might make it seem the only remaining authority powerful enough to force us, as Mill says, to "shrink" from otherwise plausible "premises."

For all the obvious reasons, appeals to common sense have never found lasting philosophical favor. There appears, however, to be something especially inappropriate about elevating it to the rank of Mill's place holder for reflection. Think of the contemporary philosophical controversies it cannot handle. It cannot, for instance, mediate the conflicting "intuitions" that have cursed so much writing on ethics in recent decades. For once cases begin to be tested by, for example, "what we would say in such circumstances," the appeal to common sense is already used up. Nor can common sense provide guidance for asking how subjective views of the world might be related to objective ones. For in a scientific age, common sense is likely either to be already tainted by science or else to stand, question-beggingly, beside it.⁵⁶ Nor can common sense clarify what sort of transition might be made from Philosophy to what comes after Philosophy. For if Heidegger is right, our common sense is still "forgetfully" Philosophical; whereas if Rorty is right, common sense is the source of an ironic kind of pragmatism that already puts it past the need of making any transition.⁵⁷ Nor, to take one more example, is common sense the likely adjudicator among competing experimental, brain scientific, and introspective claims about mental life. For according to current received wisdom among philosophers of mind, introspective reports are actually "folk-psychological" accounts of our cognitive and appetitive activities, given in terms of culturally shared (i.e., commonsense) models of what such activities are presumed to be. Hence, on this view, common sense is already represented by one of the competing parties to the controversy and thus is in no position to adjudicate among them.⁵⁸

In short, if what philosophy has available to it is basically the two options of either engaging the "obviously" important work of "correct [epistemic] analysis" or indulging in wider, extraphilosophical appeals to common sense, then it is unlikely in principle that such controversies as those just mentioned can ever be properly addressed, let alone resolved. What is more to be expected is what did in fact occur: The epistemic outlook – self-confidently attentive to, but of course

---

56 Thus, e.g., even Thomas Nagel – who wrote "What Is It Like to Be a Bat?" in order to focus on "how it is" for subjects themselves to be conscious, and who reprints this paper in a book stressing that there are neglected topics that "must be attacked by a philosophical method that aims at *personal* as well as *theoretical* understanding, and seeks to *combine* the two . . . into the framework of self-knowledge" – concludes by calling for an "objective phenomenology" of all this in the hope that physicalism might yet be vindicated. *Mortal Questions* (Cambridge: Cambridge University Press, 1979), ix, 176–80, my emphasis; cf. also, Nagel's *The View from Nowhere* (New York: Oxford University Press, 1986), esp. 3–17. Perhaps Nagel did actually begin by imagining himself to be the "self-knowledgeable" and "combination"-seeking defender of the intuition that the "personal" viewpoint has prerogatives, too; but his conclusion shows that in fact his philosophical method remains defined in terms of the very "theoretical understanding" that was supposedly going to be "combined" with the personal, not employed to judge it. Nagel therefore deserves R. Rorty's rejoinder that if the usefulness of his intuition about the personal is ultimately going to be evaluated in light of physicalism, this is simply another way of demanding that it must be capable of integration with our best scientific theories; and since those theories now reject introspection, Nagel's intuition fails his own test ("Contemporary Philosophy of Mind," 342–43).

57 In Rorty's words, "there is no hidden power called Being. . . . Nobody whispered in the ears of the early Greeks. . . . There is no point in looking around for a hidden choreographer. To see that there is *just us* would be simultaneously to see ourselves – to see the West – as a contingency and to see that there is no refuge from contingency" ("Heidegger, Contingency, and Pragmatism," PP2, 36).

58 See, e.g., Lyons, *Introspection*, esp. 113–15, 125–28, 137–56. Lyons picks up the story of the fate of introspection after Mill (at least in the English-speaking world) and describes its gradual "disappearance" from serious discussion among philosophers and psychologists. His aim is not to lament its passing but to argue that none of its opponents has produced a satisfactory explanation of what introspection really is or is not. Lyons himself then proposes the "folk-psychological" sort of interpretation mentioned previously. It makes no difference to my point, however, whether this construal of introspection does it justice; for as we saw earlier, even if one follows Flanagan in expanding it into something less subjective, more "phenomenological," and thus a source of greater importance for mental science than is currently assumed (see *Consciousness*, esp. Ch. 8), it is still one source among three and no candidate for the job of reflectively coordinating them.

also reconstructively critical of its analysand – comes to claim for itself and for properly reconstructed science, the wider adjudicative authority as well. In these somewhat sketchy but nevertheless prescient lines from an early draft of his *Autobiography*, Mill saw the future:

> I already regarded the methods of the physical sciences as the proper models for the political; but one important point in the parallelism much insisted on by M. Comte, had not before occurred to me. In mathematics and physics what is called the liberty of conscience . . . is merely nominal: though in no way restrained by law, the liberty is not exercised. . . . [I]f any one rejected what has been proved by demonstration or experiment, he would be thought to be asserting no right but the right of being a fool: those who have not studied these sciences take their conclusions on trust from those who have, and the practical world goes on incessantly applying laws of nature and conclusions of reasoning which it receives on the faith . . . of the authority of the instructed. *Hitherto it had not occurred to me that the case would be the same in the moral, social, and political branches of speculation if they were equally advanced with the physical.* . . . From this time my hopes of ["mankind's"] improvement rested less on the reason of the multitude, than on the possibility of effecting such an improvement in the methods of political and social philosophy, as should enable all thinking and instructed persons who have no sinister interest to be so nearly of one mind on these subjects, as to carry the multitude with them by their united authority.[59]

The step from being an epistemic analyst for the truly "instructed" to seeing oneself as a supreme adjudicator for extra- and metascientific issues is not a long one. I am tempted to say that Comte's crime, in his imperious moods, seems largely to have been that he attempted this step too soon.

But does the reflective orientation I have been attributing to Comte in his more historico-critical moods promise to put philosophy in any better position? On the one hand and at least prima facie, it appears that it should. It marks out a way for philosophy itself to undermine the seemingly forced option of (increasingly appealing) "correct analysis" and (decreasingly authoritative) "common sense" by revealing how each tends to forget the contextual indebtednesses that give "correct" and "common" whatever normative force they have. In addition, varieties of historico-critical understanding are in fact being tried out by some contemporary Anglo-American philosophers in response to the very dilemmas mentioned (for example, MacIntyre on ethics, Putnam and Taylor on objectivism in epistemology, Rorty in defense of a post-positivist pragmatism).

I will have more to say about all this in subsequent chapters. In the meantime, however, I conclude this chapter with a vital and troublesome "on the other hand." There is, I have been suggesting, a powerful internal reason – one, moreover, that even now we cannot afford to ignore – why Comte himself, at the very

---

59 A, 615–16, my emphasis. In a still earlier draft, we get a picture of the two-tier educational system this future must have, in which "the more the intelligence of *the multitude* became improved, the more they would appreciate the greater knowledge and more exercised judgment of *the instructed* and the more disposed they would be to defer to their opinion" (615n., my emphasis).

moment when his historico-critical orientation might seem most promising, lapses into the kind of objectivist reflexivity just described. The secret, I think, is to recognize that neither Mill nor Comte correctly diagnoses what prompts a philosophy to assume the sort of position in which, in Mill's phrase, it "shrinks from no consequences" of some principle. The explanation, in one sentence, is that there is Cartesianism before there is positivism. Here is why both thinkers wind up speaking – Comte inconsistently and intermittently, Mill and later positivists much more as a matter of course – from essentially ahistorical viewpoints.

Reading backward today from Mill to Comte, one easily misses this point. By present lights, Comte's ultimate claims are likely to seem even more absurd than they did to Mill; and it is bound to seem at first as if Mill – whatever his own failings – did in fact at least avoid the Comtean absurdities, by linking Comte's extrascientific use of the three-stage law with traditional speculative use of other premises, and by confining his own philosophizing to the Logic of Science (and the "Art of Life" to be based on it).[60] Yet at second glance, and especially in today's post-positivist climate, Mill's own "premises" – especially his convictions about the primacy of organons of proof and the sociopolitical extension of scientific authority – though not absurd in the manner of Comte's, now loom before us as philosophical principles from whose consequences we already find ourselves shrinking.

The right conclusion to draw from all this is that when Comte and Mill understand – or, better, behave without comment as if they understand – their own thinking as radically decontextualized, this really has nothing directly to do with the incompleteness of the former's acceptance or the completeness of the latter's rejection of historico-critical expositions in philosophy. Rather, it has to do with the fact that both of them, even before the issues of historical exposition and antireflective common sense can arise, are already convinced of the epistemic primacy of scientific rationality. Or to speak more of the disease and less of its symptom, they are both wedded to the normative idea that its method, whatever it is and however ramified, is *applied to and is the measure of reasoning in a way that is not itself historically determinate.* What is important, therefore, is not so much the "positive" or the "scientific" nature of their ideas of correct method. Nor is it whether one philosopher emphasizes method exclusively and the other only loosely. Comte is perhaps prescient in arguing that if epistemology is reduced to reconstructivist proportions, methodological imperialism is the eventual result; and Mill is probably right that the more epistemologists try to turn themselves directly into utopian social planners, the more outrageous grow their resulting philosophical claims. What is fundamental, however, is that both Comte's idea of defending scientific knowledge and Mill's idea of correctly analyzing it come too

---

60 The latter falls outside the purposes of this study, but I mention in passing that the "analytic" spirit that inspired the *Logic* is carried over into Mill's conception of ethics as a philosophy of action to be coordinated with his philosophy of scientific method. See Robson, *The Improvement of Mankind,* 160–81; and Ryan, *The Philosophy of John Stuart Mill,* xiii, 187–96.

late to alter their ahistorical sense of what it is like to reflect upon, defend, or analyze right reasoning. *After Descartes,* the epistemological task already arrives pre-understood with an ahistorical imperative built in. Thus Comte may still claim, with some lingering historico-critical sensitivity, that the kind of reasoning science only "tends toward" is "dogmatical"; and Mill may go on to claim, with greater self-possession, that scientific investigation largely "is" a matter of induction. In either case, however, although the empirical conditions under which Comte's dogmatical or Mill's formalizing accounts develop may differ, a Cartesian inheritance already teaches them both that *what it is to be dogmatical/inductive and how it is for positive philosophy to defend/analyze this* are themselves to be understood as "objective," that is, decontextualized issues.

We need, therefore, to go back to this Cartesian inheritance that sabotages Comte and satisfies Mill. We must reconsider at their roots *both* that straightforwardly ahistorical kind of reconstructive analysis that in the meantime has come to seem so much less satisfying *and also* Comte's initially more promising but finally ineffectual kind of historico-critical alternative. For contrary to a common assumption among aspiring post-positivists, the current task is not simply a matter of *replacing* a context-free, third-person standpoint with a socio-historically contextualized, interpersonal one. Rather, it is a matter of recognizing first that "replacement" is itself the expression of an ahistorical impulse. For a philosophy that is to come genuinely "after" positivism can only be ushered in by those who understand themselves as already having been, by inheritance, determinately modern-scientific thinkers who now find that outlook intolerably constraining.

5

CARTESIAN AHISTORICISM AND LATER EPISTEMIC ANALYSIS

The following attenuated tale of Descartes' epistemological turn serves as place holder for what could be a much longer story. Yet for everyone from Comte and Mill to the Logical Empiricists and post-positivists, this is of course a familiar story; hence, anything more ambitious seems unnecessary here. At the same time, when a story has become very familiar, one tends to hear it all too easily and to focus all too selectively on its most obvious – though not necessarily its most telling – features. It is now widely held that this has become the case with Descartes' story; and I have fashioned my tale to show I agree.

To explain my purpose, however, I need to emphasize that the story of Descartes' epistemological turn is about activities whose consequences we still inherit. It is eventually, crucially, and now more than somewhat uncomfortably our story – which means that its overfamiliarity can pose for us the following problem. In the very act of distancing ourselves from some obvious features of Cartesian thinking and in trying to formulate our own thinking in post-Cartesian terms, we may simultaneously fail to recognize how, in other ways, our very opposition continues to involve us crucially and uncomfortably in something Cartesian. As a matter of fact, I think that not only Comte but even some of today's most outspoken post-positivists are in precisely this fix. "Everyone knows" how Descartes made epistemology primary, placed it under the guidance of a single universal method, concluded that this would guarantee certainty in knowledge, and produced a lot of now dated materialist physics and a metaphysics of two (counting God, three) substances. Yet it is possible to challenge all of these obvious features of Cartesian philosophy – and still assume *with Descartes* that the whole matter is to be thought about *from a fundamentally ahistorical point of view.* Showing how this could in fact continue to be the case is the purpose of my tale. The reason why it starts with a preface on Socrates will become clear in a moment.

1. Socrates' epistemological silence

Suppose that we ask, without thinking too much about the current conditions under which we do so, "What did Socrates know about his own philosophizing?" At first, using nothing more than the *Apology*, we might venture that he knew a lot. After all, judging from what he told the jury, it appears that he could give an account of what it is to love wisdom and how that differs from the pursuit of expertise. He could explain that philosophy involves dialogues, and he could describe what happens in them. And he had a clear sense of why, even with his "special wisdom," he could never expect philosophizing to make him Wise.

Yet for modern ears, it is difficult not to hear Socrates' account as strangely indirect and unsatisfactory. Not only in the *Apology* but in all his discussions of the nature of philosophical activity, he proceeds mainly by way of anecdote and metaphor. Moreover, it is apparently not just that Socrates refrains from being more forthcoming about how philosophy is done on the occasion of his trial and because he is addressing a hostile jury. Rather, he seems to believe that even if dialogue were made an explicit topic in the presence of receptive minds, it still could not be straightforwardly and decisively clarified.

The problem, as we have all learned to say in the meantime, is that Socrates is insufficiently concerned with philosophical method. Granted that he does seek universal truth and that he does employ rational argument. The fact remains that in his actual searches, he simply operates spontaneously out of the concrete circumstances that at that moment bring him and his interlocutor together. Worse still, he would deny that when he gains the upper hand, it is because of any superior knowledge of correct reasoning. Rather, he would say that it depends on his "special wisdom"; and when he describes this, it is in the same indirect and anecdotal way that he describes his dialogues themselves. Thus, for example, he tells us about what it has done to him to engage in a lot of dialogues; about the importance of going into them with a heightened awareness and genuine sense of not already knowing; about the way the course of a dialogue depends somewhat on the kind of person he talks with; and finally, about the fact that he measures success in terms of how well he can now continue to risk in further dialogue the determinate and ever inadequate understanding of things he has thus far come to possess. No one can read, for example, the *Crito* without seeing how deeply this determinate and contextualized sense of philosophical practice runs in Socrates. Indeed, how many persons can even imagine possessing his "special wisdom" to so great a degree that, even after being unjustly condemned to death, they could be expected to say, as Socrates did to Crito, "I am eager to examine together with you whether [that which on reflection seemed best to me before] will appear in any way different to me in my present circumstances"?[1] As he explains, not only his trial itself and the subsequent sentencing but his own conduct during the proceedings happened for him "as an Athenian" – as did also

---

1 *Crito*, 46d.

the whole career of previous philosophizing through which he "became what he was" and simultaneously made himself so unpopular.

All of which means that in modern times, one is forced to the seemingly regrettable conclusion that there could in principle never have been a Socratic equivalent of a "discourse on method" or an "organon of reason." Socrates would never have imagined that such productions might improve his or anyone else's capacity to "follow the conversation wherever it may lead." Only engaging in dialogues can do that. Of course, historians might still urge us to admire these spontaneous ways of Socrates, but philosophers are bound to stress how enormous the distance is between so context-bound and "psychologically" oriented a conception of rationality and our own.[2] From the modern standpoint, Socrates' dialogues display his sense of attachment both to tradition and to current circumstance that is personal, provincial, and epistemically unproblematic in a way that can never be true for us. Socrates, one observes, did not have to contend with 2,500 years of philosophical practice. In the meantime, the weight of tradition has forced us to become mindful of the sheer variety of philosophical options and at the same time wary of the lingering power of the past to contaminate present thinking as much as to inspire it.

2. Descartes' epistemic imperative and history's irrelevance

It is with Descartes, of course, that the epistemological-mindedness just depicted assumes its still recognizable form. Descartes insists that, as a matter of psychological fact, the mind – even the "educated mind" – is typically in no condition to seek knowledge. In contrast to Socrates, who thinks one's pre-given intellectual state is something to be continually improved *through* dialogical activity, Descartes regards this same state as something that *obstructs* the light of reason. Before there can even be any genuine thinking, he concludes, the mind must be methodologically prepared; and his "meditation" therefore defines right reason as a much more explicitly rule-governed, deliberate, and initially distrusting activity than Socratic elenchus. Indeed, strictly speaking, true thinking begins only when the mind has learned to follow an "order of reasons" by bracketing off all those preexisting and ill-acquired beliefs that together constitute its premeditative condition.

Yet here again, as in the case of a Cartesian reading of Socrates, although one can in later empiricist–positivist retrospect still readily appreciate Descartes' move toward epistemological self-consciousness, it is not without also recognizing the enormous distance between his interpretation of that move in the *Meditations* and the ultimately reconstructivist interpretations of more recent times. For in

---

2 I have tried elsewhere to buck this trend by expressing some philosophical admiration for instead of just historical acknowledgment of Socrates' epistemological silence, in "Socrates' Successful Inquiries," *Man and World* 19 (1986), 311–27.

twentieth-century retrospect, despite all his introductory fanfare about sticking to the conditions that guarantee certainty, when Descartes is judged in terms of his results (and not, as in the previous chapter, by the missed opportunity represented by his actual meditative process), what we have is a thoroughly problematic metaphysics and a lot of bad science. Descartes still stands for us today, just as we have seen he already did for Comte, as a pointed reminder that rigorous thinking cannot be guaranteed by well-intentioned self-analysis, using a few generalizations from the ideas of mathematical intuition and deduction.

Recounting as we are on this occasion the empiricist–positivist side of the modern story, we know that subsequent development is one of increasingly science-minded attempts to take Descartes' epistemological turn more seriously than Descartes did himself.[3] What is for me most important about the plot of this side of the story is the fact that empiricists and positivists understand there to be not one but two basic tenets of the Cartesian approach to epistemology. In a famous passage in the *Rules*, Descartes asserts that

> even if we have read all the arguments of [say] Plato and Aristotle, we shall never become philosophers if we ourselves are unable to make a sound judgment on whatever comes up for discussion; in this case what we would seem to have learned would not be *science* but *history*.[4]

That for which Descartes is famous lies, of course, in what he says positively here, namely, that he cares about "science" and, in particular, the conditions of its rationality. But more important for my present purposes is something that Descartes takes just as seriously but for which he is not so famous, namely, his negative insistence that this science is *not about "history."* The contrast between science and history runs throughout his writings. He raises the question of what it is to make "sound judgments"; but whatever the answer, he is convinced in advance that knowledge of tradition cannot help. He seeks to establish a science of right reasoning; but he pursues this goal by first setting the philosophical past aside. He even writes in French rather than Latin because – as his forced option depicts it – he expects better justice from those who use only "natural reason" than from those who rely on "the writings of the ancients."[5] In short, in empiricist–positivist readings, Descartes is characteristically understood to believe that genuine philosophizing has at once two guiding imperatives, namely, that it must take on a fundamentally *epistemological* task and that it must do so in a thoroughly *ahistorical* manner.

Empirically minded philosophers have, of course, always tended to embrace

---

3 For a start on the "other" story, told in the name of those contemporaries whose inheritance is more rationalist–idealist than empiricist–positivist, see, e.g., Herbert Schnädelbach, *Reflexion und Diskurs: Fragen einer Logik der Philosophie* (Frankfurt: Suhrkamp, 1977); and Rodolphe Gasché, *The Tain of the Mirror: Derrida and the Philosophy of Reflection* (Cambridge, MA: Harvard University Press, 1986), 13–105. Cf. also Hans-Georg Gadamer, "The Problem of Historical Consciousness," *Graduate Faculty Philosophy Journal* 5 (1975), 1–52.
4 AT, X, 367, my emphasis.
5 *Discourse*, AT, VI, 77.

Descartes' epistemological imperative in principle but reject in practice his rationalist construal of it in terms of inwardly validated certainty. From Locke on, the idea that the alternative to trusting tradition and one's teachers must be "to seek knowledge in myself," and further, the expectation that this knowledge will be of the same foolproof sort found in mathematics, is increasingly condemned as unscientific. Hence, after Descartes – but in a manner more uncompromisingly Cartesian than the merely reformist Descartes himself, who "set aside" religion, ethics, and public affairs before beginning his epistemic inquiry specifically for the sake of natural knowledge – the problems of what knowledge is and how to obtain it are submitted to increasingly science-minded analyses and are conceived in increasingly universalizing terms.

This, however, is the familiar aspect of the story. For my purposes, the second aspect of the story is of greater concern. As I suggested at the end of Chapter 4, the empiricist–positivist tradition of epistemological analysis has been thoroughly bound up with the conviction that not only the *method(s)* of knowing but also the *investigation* of those methods should be ahistorically understood.

Descartes prepares the ground for this second conviction by damning history with faint praise. The study of tradition, he says, is like travel. It is good to broaden one's horizons and counteract provincialism. Yet in the end, just as

> one who spends too much time traveling eventually becomes a stranger in one's own country, and one who is too curious about the practices of past ages usually remains quite ignorant about those of the present,

so a mind that really cares about the principles of good reasoning must not be distracted by what other people happen to have thought.[6] In retrospect, Descartes' simile appears to have been very persuasive indeed. After his *Meditations,* the belief in leaving tradition behind was made integral to empiricist–positivist conceptions of both (a) the topic of epistemology and (b) the standpoint of epistemological analysis itself. And this was so in practice, even when not in expressed principle and even, as we have seen, in a Comte who actually set out in opposition to that very idea.

Cartesian epistemology's topic

In retrospect, it is certainly understandable why everyone from Locke the underlaborer to Reichenbach the reconstructionist should have offered fundamentally ahistorical characterizations of the conditions of rationality. In part, the example of mathematics but, above all, the successes of the emergent empirical sciences appeared to confirm the correctness of Descartes' methodological ideal. For was it not indeed those who confined themselves to "natural reason" and to the study of the "great book of the world" who were reaching knowledge of everything

---

6 *Discourse,* AT, VI, 6. Cf. Letter to Cornelis van Hogelande (February 8, 1640), XII (supplement), 2–3.

that could both be agreed on and proved "useful in life"?[7] The ahistorical moral of the story must have seemed obvious and compelling: What is epistemologically essential to those successes is one thing; what may once have been assumed essential before those successes, quite another.

There is, however, this difference between the ahistorical character of earlier (roughly, classical empiricist) and later (positivist) epistemologies; and recalling both Comte's critique of interiority and the eventual fate of introspection helps to bring it into relief. To positivists, an epistemological analysis like Descartes' own is still hopelessly subjective. His real point seems to be that every cogito must follow the same rules to obtain truth and avoid falsity. But then, what really matters is the analysis of these rules, not the story of someone's experience of discovering and using them. As Descartes admits, this story – even in someone like himself, who has stopped traveling – is often the sorry tale of "habitual opinions" recapturing his mind and preventing it from judging truly. Given this admission, the "purely" philosophical implication seems obvious. It is not just human history and tradition in general that are irrelevant to epistemological inquiry; so, too, is any individual's personal-psychological history. Actual minds may in fact continue inevitably to be shaped and bewitched by inherited opinion; but the rules that constitute the test of any opinion are themselves quite independent of all such shaping and bewitching. Since the point of epistemology is to get clear about these rules, the less said about the struggle to acquire and use them, the better.

One can see the result of this line of reasoning in the fact that earlier modern epistemologies still tend to follow Descartes in focusing on the ideal *knower* (its faculties, power, and relation to an external world), whereas later ones ask instead about the ideal *conditions for knowledge* (both logical and linguistic). The shift of focus is clearly marked out by Mill when he contrasts his study of reasoning with those of his predecessors by explaining that his *Logic*

> has no concern with the nature of the act of judging or believing; the consideration of that act, as a phenomenon of mind, belongs to another science [i.e., psychology]. Philosophers, however, from Descartes downwards, and especially from the era of Leibniz and Locke, have by no means observed this distinction.... A proposition, they would have said, is but the expression in words of a judgment....
>
> Conformably to these views, almost all the writers on logic in the last two centuries, whether English, German, or French, have made their theory of propositions ... a theory of judgments. They considered a proposition, or a judgment, for

---

7 One should remember in this context that not finding such "useful" knowledge is what Descartes says disillusioned him in college (*Discourse*, AT, VI, 4). Recall also his advice to Frans Burman that he should not dwell too long on the *Meditations*' "introductory" metaphysical material because that can "draw the mind too far away from ... observable things, and make it unfit to study them" [*Descartes' Conversation with Burman*, trans. John Cottingham (Oxford: Clarendon Press, 1976), 30]. Taken together, the expression of these two sentiments certainly makes it understandable that half of his readers thought Descartes the catalyst for empiricism rather than rationalism.

they used the two words indiscriminately, to consist in affirming or denying one *idea* of another.[8]

The old notion that "the importance to the logician in a proposition is the relation between the two *ideas* corresponding to the subject and predicate," argues Mill, "is one of the most fatal errors ever introduced into the philosophy of logic"; and it explains why, during these same two centuries, it is that vast array of successful "discoverers in the *other* sciences" who have shed whatever new light on human reasoning there is, whereas traditional logic has provided these sciences "no assistance whatever."[9] So does Mill oppose – but still feel the need to reject – a "psychological dimension" of thinking that our century's logicians no longer even bother to mention.

Cartesian epistemology's outlook

It is not, however, only epistemology's *subject matter* that gets increasingly purified and decontextualized in later enactments of Descartes' ahistorical imperative. So, too, does the *philosophical orientation* for epistemological inquiry. The argument – more often implied than given (i.e., more often passed through to rather than taken up) by Descartes' progeny – is that the standpoint for the analysis of knowledge conditions must be as free from inheritance and habit as are those conditions themselves; and the primary evidence for this requirement, especially as construed in positivist retrospect, is Descartes himself, who seems hopelessly mired in various historically specific entanglements. Not only is the *Meditations* itself written from a psychologically tainted angle; in the *Discourse*, Descartes even admits that he is not going ask about epistemic conditions for *all* knowledge claims. Theology and ethics, for example, are specifically exempted from meditative scrutiny. In preparing for my impending task, he says, and "in order to live as happily as I could" while pursuing it, I provided myself with four provisional moral maxims and then,

> having *set them aside* together with the truths of faith, which have always been foremost among my beliefs, I judged that I could freely undertake to rid myself of *all the rest* of my opinions.[10]

Descartes goes on to say, in his now famous phrasing, that he assumed this move

---

8 SL, I, v, 1 (87). As R. F. McRae argues in his Introduction to the *Logic* (SL, xxxix–xliv), such passages as these put Mill's characterizations of logic as "grounded in psychology" in their proper light.
9 SL, I, v, 1 (89). For analysis of Mill's clear (but not unproblematic) shift from ideas to linguistic meanings, see Willem Remmelt de Jong, *The Semantics of John Stuart Mill*, trans. Herbert Donald Merton (Dordrecht: D. Reidel, 1982), esp. 165–74.
10 AT, VI, 22 and 28 (my emphasis). In the *Rules*, he says that settling for nothing less than certainty in knowledge "does not preclude our believing that what has been revealed by God is more certain than any knowledge, since faith . . . is an act of will rather than . . . understanding" (AT, X, 370). "Who" is saying this?

would effectively make him "a spectator rather than an actor" in the world's affairs. Yet in the eyes of everyone from Mill to Reichenbach, he failed in two ways. Not only did he remain entangled in epistemically irrelevant (especially psychological) matters within the sphere of inquiry he had mapped out for himself, but by setting faith and morals aside as if they were extraphilosophical areas of concern, he failed to make epistemic inquiry truly universal in scope.

In the same manner as I suggested in the case of Socrates, we might again imagine historians urging us to sympathize with Descartes by reminding us of the private and public forces working here to make him so circumspect. Admittedly also, it has taken a long time for others to do better. Yet in the end, as the positivists insisted, there seems to be this inescapable philosophical conclusion. In carrying out Descartes' epistemological imperative, one cannot be bashful about exposing sensitive "areas" to the conditions of rationality. And to ensure sufficient boldness, the philosophical *inquiry standpoint* from which these conditions are established must itself be as removed from and immune to the influences of historical and psychological circumstances as the analytic, reconstructive picture it produces.

3. Logical Empiricism: The turn completed

Along the way, the idea of an ahistorically purified inquiry standpoint has been variously understood as, for example, God-like, scientific, objective, logical, transcendental, reconstructive, and as if from nowhere – agreement about this has never been achieved. What has been assumed in each case, however, is basically the same. Just as with the prime philosophical *subject matter* – namely, knowledge (or finally, science, as the epistemic paradigm) and its truth conditions – so also in connection with the orientation of any *philosophical analysis* of that subject matter, neither past thinking nor its lingering psychological presence in particular minds can be permitted a determinative role.

Following out this observation is, of course, the long story. What is important here, however, is that the circumstance that makes all of this so easy for us to follow is the fact that both the fullest expression of and also the seemingly most radical sorts of opposition to the twin Cartesian imperatives occur in our century. I refer, of course, to the emergence of Logical Empiricism and its post-positivist aftermath.

To focus again specifically on the ahistorical imperative, it is pre-eminently Logical Empiricism that appears to succeed in separating epistemology from world and personal history. Moreover, its proponents' own characterizations of their results show that they understand success in precisely these terms. Thus, to take Reichenbach's exemplary phrasing again, in place of the "system of [scientific] knowledge as it has been built up by generations of thinkers," Logical Empiricism substitutes a rational reconstruction of the way thought processes *ought* to occur if they are to be ranged in a consistent system . . . [with] . . . justifiable sets of operations which can be intercalated between the starting point and the issue of thought-processes, *replacing* the real intermediate links.[11]

The imperious tone is of the essence. The project of reconstructive inquiry may indeed take its point of departure from the social-psychological "fact" of scientific success; and by virtue of the idealized account of rational justification conditions it comes to possess, it does indeed claim the right to criticize existing practices. Once he gets this reconstructive project underway, however, Reichenbach comes to understand it as basically neither descriptive nor critical. Rather it is, at bottom, "logical *analysis*" – the process whereby actual thinking is purified into the "system" of valid thinking that remains unaffected by any personal or social contingencies.

At this point, my attenuated tale comes to a close with a wonderfully fitting image. For according to Reichenbach, with the advent of Logical Empiricism, philosophy finally succeeds in constructing the "adequate scientific expression" of Socratic maieutics.[12] Descartes' epistemological turn has been completed. The imperfect and unfinished *Rules* and the intolerably cryptic *Discourse*, Part 2, have been transformed into a fully objective theory of meaning. Real knowledge is actually being found in inductive science; and Logical Empiricists, as historically uncommitted logicians of science, simply help science grown mindful of itself by explicating its rational conditions. Indeed, according to one line of interpretation, their explications were so successful – so representative of what happens within science itself when science is done right – that *as philosophers* they self-destructed.

> Logical empiricism was the first philosophical trend . . . perhaps in the whole history of philosophy, which gained such a high level of clarity and precision in thinking that effective self-criticism proved to be possible. In science, it is a normal phenomenon – but it is far from being normal in philosophy. Before logical empiricism, philosophers used to kill other philosophers' views; neopositivism committed an intellectual suicide. . . . [T]hat is, the criteria of acceptance of their views appeared to be stronger than the views themselves.[13]

What is left under these circumstances is the job of being a methodological mouthpiece for science, that is, *really* reducing philosophy to the job of underlaborer. In this way, but mostly without actually drawing the conclusion, Logical Empiricists fashioned the image of "analytic" philosophy in the now "classical sense" and became, as Reichenbach puts it, the rightful replacement for that old-fashioned sort of thinker who,

---

11 *Experience and Prediction*, 3–8 (citation, 5, my emphasis).
12 *Experience and Prediction*, 6.
13 Leszek Nowak, "Some Remarks on the Place of Logical Empiricism in 20th Century Philosophy," in *The Vienna Circle and the Lvov–Warsaw School*, ed. Klemens Szaniawski (Dordrecht: Kluwer, 1989), 387. Neven Sesardić traces this line of exposition to Gilbert Ryle in "The Heritage of the Vienna Circle," *Grazer Philosophische Studien* 9 (1979), 127.

trained in literature and history, . . . has never learned the precision methods of the mathematical sciences or experienced the happiness of demonstrating a law of nature by a verification of all its consequences.[14]

To restate the point in a retrospective form that Reichenbach would almost certainly not approve, his scientific philosopher is one who finally gets Descartes' two basic teachings right. For this philosopher has indeed, as Descartes describes it himself in his still excessively autobiographical way, "entirely abandoned the study of letters" and concentrated on rational methodology and the observation of nature instead.[15] Further, and most important in the present context, all of this has been accomplished by nothing more than a completely strict adherence to Descartes' ahistorical imperative in the conceptualization of both philosophy's primary topic and its proper standpoint. To put it in Comtean language, in their dogmatical reconstructions of scientific process, the Logical Empiricists have completely forgotten themselves.

So much for my attenuated version of an easily followed story; let us now consider the sense in which it is a story all too easily followed.

4. Epistemic analysis "after" positivism

Today, generally speaking, the conclusion has been reached that the era of positivism is over. If contemporary analytic philosophers raise the question of their relation to it at all, their usual response is to describe their own activities as linked to it negatively, that is, as engaged in a long-term effort of demonstrating, either directly or more likely by the example of practice, the impossibility of realizing the goals of, say, Russell, Carnap, and Frege. There is, in other words, something just obvious about the difference between rational reconstruction and its theory of meaning and *whatever* philosophers say now about conditions of rationality for *whatever* purpose.

Yet given the complex legacy of the Cartesian ahistorical imperative that I have been examining, it should by now seem advisable to exercise extreme caution in the face of any such presumptions of easy distancing from philosophy's recent past. In fact, in the remainder of this chapter, I want to make quick preliminary use of two recent and apparently post-positivist retrospectives – one by Putnam, the other by Rorty – in order to set up a more sustained challenge in Chapter 6 to the very idea that a "post-positivist" *standpoint* is even possible for one whose opposition to positivism remains focused on the problems with its

---

14 *The Rise of Scientific Philosophy* (Berkeley: University of California Press, 1951), 308. On the idea that Logical Empiricist analysis (in contrast to the post-positivist Cambridge and Oxford varieties) is "classical," see J. O. Urmson, "The History of Philosophical Analysis [and Discussion]," in *The Linguistic Turn: Recent Essays in Philosophical Method*, ed. Richard Rorty (Chicago: University of Chicago Press, 1967), 294–311.
15 *Discourse*, AT, VI, 9.

epistemic *program*. (The ultimate point of this challenge will be, of course, that Comte can help us do better.)

According to Putnam's (interestingly tensed) contemporary retrospect on the recent Anglo-American past, analytic philosophy has for some time been claiming to be free of the old "dream of an integrated view." He refers to this dream specifically as "characteristic of what people refer to as continental philosophy"; but, as we shall see, it is in the spirit of his account for us to add here, "and also characteristic of the classical positivism of the Comtean sort." In any case, this claim of entirely wakeful analytic modesty, he observes,

> was always somewhat of a pretense. The logical positivists had very much an integrated view, and Quine has very much an integrated view. The "motor" of analytic philosophy was logical positivism (and, earlier, logical atomism); not because all analytical philosophers were positivists, but because the arguments pro-and-con positivism were what kept analytic philosophy in motion.[16]

In the way Putnam describes the demise of positivism, then, it appears to have had (though he does not explicitly distinguish these) two fundamental consequences. First, in place of the old enthusiasm for something like Reichenbach's grand monological system of rationality, there is a new preference for genuine epistemic pluralism in current conceptions of what is left for analysts to do. Pluralism, of course, does not mean utter fragmentation. There still is and probably always will be, in Putnam's words, "a good deal of philosophical work to be done" in general and in generalizing terms on our problematic beliefs about such matters as truth, reference, desire, and belief itself; and since on any given topic all these beliefs do "cohere" in a sort of "informal system," the "overarching mentalistic theory" resulting from work done on them will have a kind of coherence, too. Yet at the same time, the very idea of coherence has "proved to be extremely topic relative"; and that is why, according to Putnam, analysts now reject as mere "ideology" the positivist dream of turning all our "piecemeal" work into a totalizing scientific epistemology "that would make the structure of reason evident to reason itself." Second, however, the demise of positivism taken together with this pluralization of the analytic task seems to have had the effect of giving current practice something of an identity problem. Unfortunately, Putnam concludes, "with the disappearance of a strong ideological current at its center . . . analytic philosophy has already begun to lose shape as a tendency."[17]

At first glance, Rorty's post-positivist retrospective may appear to be something like a reversal of Putnam's. In Putnam's account, there is "substantive" continuity between positivist and post-positivist analysis – that is, solidarity concerning *issues and problems* (truth, reference, belief, mentality, realism, etc.) – but "methodological" discontinuity – that is, these matters are now to be handled

---

16 "Beyond Historicism," RR, 303; see also "Why There Isn't a Ready-Made World" and "Why Reason Can't Be Naturalized" (RR, 205–28 and 229–47) for Putnam's account of typical metaphysical and epistemological failed dreams, respectively.
17 Phrases in this paragraph are all drawn from "Beyond Historicism," RR, 301–303.

variously instead of monologically. Putnam's uncertainty about the fate of analysis as a distinctive philosophical tendency is thus grounded in his sense of its loss of a unifying conception of inquiry. Rorty, however, predicts the demise of precisely Putnam's whole ensemble of issues and problems – what he sees as forming a positivistically shaped, Platonically inspired "representationalist problematic" – and stresses instead a continuity of *general approach* between even his radically pluralized idea of analysis and the classical kind. Rorty insists, in other words, that the classical "style" of analysis that dominated mainstream thinking in the 1950s and early 1960s still resonates with considerable power in today's radically descientized interpretations of it. To quote more fully here from the passage cited in my Introduction:

> Reichenbach *redivivus* would presumably be appalled by . . . the confusion of tongues, the proliferation of problems and programs, in contemporary American philosophy. But he would admire the style, the insistence on argument, the dialectical acuity. He would approve of the widespread distrust . . . of those who . . . "never learned the precision methods of the mathematical sciences." He would agree with a distinguished analytic philosopher who urged that "intellectual hygiene" requires one not to read the books of Derrida and Foucault.[18]

Rorty admits that between Logical Empiricism and everything Reichenbach would now find appalling there has occurred a virtual revolution in the conception of philosophy's topics and programs. Against the old ideal of rational reconstruction, legitimate forms both of analysis itself and of language have multiplied. Against the formal image of a "methodological" system, scientific practice has been recontextualized. Openings have been made toward Continental philosophy and Continental themes; and positivistic pictures of human thought and action have been submitted to every kind of epistemic and ontological criticism. Sometimes, while itemizing all this discontinuity, Rorty can appear to believe that at least philosophically speaking, it is the last word – as, for example, when he says that

> "analytic philosophy" has become, in fact, a sociological description which conveys no knowledge of the interests or motives or predilections of those who practice it. It merely denotes membership in a certain tradition – acquaintance with certain writings and lack of acquaintance with others.[19]

---

18 "Philosophy in America Today," COP, 223–24. I do not know who the "distinguished analytic philosopher" is; nor do I know whether either that philosopher or Rorty is aware of the Comtean precedent for this (as Mill calls it) "tyrannical" attitude. For an argument that Rorty belongs to an American tradition of "aesthetic pluralism" that runs from Edwards to Dewey, Whitehead, and McKeon, "and ultimately" to Quine, Sellars, Goodman, Rawls, and Davidson, see David L. Hall, *Richard Rorty: Prophet and Poet of the New Pragmatism* (Albany: State University of New York Press, 1994), esp. 65–80.
19 "Epistemological Behaviorism and the De-Transcendentalization of Analytic Philosophy," *Neue Hefte für Philosophie* 14 (1978), 117. Cf. his description of the pragmatism Rorty thinks comes "after" analytic philosophy as a "lonely provincialism" that abandons altogether the idea that any construal of reasonableness transcends its sociohistorical context ("Solidarity or Objectivity?" PP1, 30).

Yet for the most part, Rorty has continued to insist that, despite all the obvious discontinuity and pluralism, there does remain an elusive but nonetheless influential continuity of "style." In one place, for example, he describes both positivist and post-positivist forms of analysis as essentially concerned with "argumentation." The difference is that – now that analytic philosophy's "internal anti-positivist dialectic" has played itself out and all the Platonic, reconstructive, and systematic pretensions in positivism's image of argument have been removed – analysis is no longer best likened to what is accomplished by the one authentic type of reasoner, for example, an ideal scientist or imperious judge. Instead, in one of his ironic images, Rorty suggests that we now might better compare today's philosophical analyst to a good lawyer. For, just as much for the analyst as for the lawyer, "it is sufficient . . . that you be able to see at a glance the inferential relationships between all members of a bewilderingly large set of propositions."[20] And in a thin and probably unintended tribute to the memory of Comte's and Mill's utopian social vision, Rorty adds that

> a nation can count itself lucky to have several thousand relatively leisured and relatively unspecialized intellectuals who are exceptionally good at putting together arguments and pulling them apart. Such a group is a precious cultural resource.[21]

This minimalist – to stop short of saying sophistic – construal of analytic continuity will certainly not ease the worries of someone like Putnam, in whose eyes the analytic movement lost an outlook with the synthesizing power of a "secularized theology" when it lost its scientistic ideology. Nor, apparently, does the lawyer comparison seem to have ever entirely satisfied Rorty himself.[22] At the moment, however, the relative richness or poverty of the metaphor of lawyerly analysis is not important. What matters is Rorty's general interpretive strategy.

Contrary to first impressions, Rorty's construal of the continuity between pos-

---

20 "Philosophy in America Today," COP, 221. Rorty's use of irony is as pervasive as it is controversial. For my purposes, it is especially important to note that he insists that his irony is an "anti-traditional" response to the realization that there is no ultimate, "criteria-" governed reflexive standpoint from which one might work out a "final vocabulary" to "put all doubts to rest" or "satisfy our criteria of ultimacy, adequacy, or optimality" ("Private Irony and Liberal Hope," CIS, 75). For as I shall argue, this shows that Rorty's irony is still driven by the memory of Descartes' twin imperatives. Cf. Hall, who (I believe rightly, but without considering this implication) makes the idea that "irony emerges in our tradition as a *theoretical* effluence" a central point in his exposition of Rorty's view (*Rorty*, 132).
21 "Philosophy in America Today," COP, 220–21.
22 I leave open until Chapter 6 the question of the degree to which this dissatisfaction is accompanied by a genuine move "outside" the analytic tradition, as Rorty himself already thinks of it in *Philosophy and the Mirror of Nature*, when he describes his pragmatist deconstruction of analytic epistemology as accompanied by a turn toward hermeneutics (315–20) and later, likens pragmatist deconstruction more with Derrida than with Heidegger ("Deconstruction and Circumvention," PP2, 85–106). In any case, considerations of irony aside, the lawyer comparison in "Philosophy in America Today" (1981) hints of being something of a historian's device, used to characterize a movement for which the author by then had limited sympathies. At the end of the same paper, Rorty approvingly cites feminist objections to this "adversary paradigm" of analysis, calling these objections "evidence of a certain discomfort with the analytic philosopher's *way of life*, and perhaps the beginning of something new" (COP, 230n.3, my emphasis).

itivism and its aftermath is not the reverse of Putnam's at all, but something rather more like a supremely confident radicalization of it. Where Putnam seeks to recontextualize analytic *topics*, Rorty pluralizes analytic *styles* appropriate to multiple topics. Either way, however, the revisions can be made without abandoning, or even recognizing, one's continuation of the same fundamentally ahistorical attitude that sustained the older, antipluralistic, and overtly Cartesian epistemologies. In the case of Rorty especially, it is such an attitude that seems to sustain his ostensibly radical idea of a literally "post-"positivist philosophy, of an intellectual revolution in which the traditional problems of modern philosophy would be simply dropped. Observe, for example, how he promotes this idea with an "irony" that leaves him willing to strip his thinking "style" of any epistemic, ontological, or ideological commitments that might stand in the way of "edification" or of simply "finding interesting new problems to argue about" or discovering new ways to "reweave our networks of beliefs and desires."[23]

Displays of such "willful" antimodernism suggest that our story of Descartes' legacy is far from over. They offer strong evidence that there are affinities between post-positivism and positivism that involve not just explicit, twentieth-century accords about problem sets and argument styles, but also, and more importantly, a silent agreement to carry forward Descartes' original ahistorical imperative of "choosing" one's philosophical starting point and "resolving" to follow a (or however many) method(s).

What an apparently radical post-positivism like Rorty's illustrates, I will argue next, is that it remains entirely possible to oppose the scientific outlook and to embrace pluralistic modes of analysis that, topically and stylistically, would appall any Reichenbach – and yet to do all of this from a viewpoint that is as confidently in possession of itself as positivism's own.[24] "Rorty's tone," as one recent observer puts it, "bespeaks a curiously detached attitude towards the evolution of new philosophical ideas, as if it were a process that proceeded quite independently of him and of his writing."[25] Hylton is not being deliberately Comtean, of

---

23 For these cited, and often repeated, portrayals of post-positivist "style," see, respectively, PMN, Ch. 8, passim; "Philosophy in America," COP, 227; PP1, 93–110; and PP2, 12ff.

24 Another way to make this point is to say that whether one embraces some species of antifoundationalism or so modifies the traditional foundationalism of Descartes and Kant that even the issues of skepticism, certainty, and the relative priority of scientific over moral knowledge are all dropped, either option can still be "chosen" without questioning the ahistorical standpoint from which the rejected traditional issues were also addressed. I take off here from the *conclusion* of Drew Christie's "Contemporary 'Foundationalism' and the Death of Epistemology," *Metaphilosophy* 20 (1989), 124–25.

25 Peter Hylton, *Russell, Idealism, and the Emergence of Analytic Philosophy* (Oxford: Clarendon Press, 1990), 15n.16. Cf., e.g., Rorty's PMN, 393–94, and PP1, 12, for continuity of this tone over a decade; and cf. his "Introduction" to *The Linguistic Turn*, esp. 38–39, for his report on the preparatory historical labors that gave birth to it. His later conclusions are present only as hints in that report, but they become more obvious when reread in light of the additional comments Rorty makes about the book in 1977 and 1992 (see the second edition, 1992, 361–70 and 371–74). Hylton, incidentally, identifies his book as "an attempt to come to terms with the tradition, and with our own relation to it, by understanding it historically" (15). But "understanding" in his sense is not the same as Comte's historico-critical variety, as will become clear later.

course; but in the next chapter I shall be. For by rescuing Comte's idea of a historico-critical defense of scientific rationality, I have intended to prepare the ground for an effective challenge to this "curiously detached" attitude at precisely the appropriate level, namely, that of reflective philosophical self-understanding rather than merely the level at which particular topics or correlated styles of analysis are consciously clarified. In the meantime, it should be clear why I prefer to think of Rorty as an analytic revisionary stylist rather than as a post-positivist. As to the further question of whether Putnam's root questioning promises anything better, I leave that open until Chapter 7.

6

COMTE AND THE VERY IDEA OF POST-POSITIVIST PHILOSOPHY

The Comte I have been trying to present in these pages has a Janus face. In his dominant and better-known mood, he speaks about the positive method and the religion of humanity as if from the same sort of ahistorically self-possessed viewpoint that his successors do about their more narrowly defined, more exclusively and formally epistemic projects. Yet operating silently throughout his works, inaccessible to him and largely unrecognized thereafter, there is Comte's other historico-critical impulse – one that constitutes a direct challenge in principle to the very attitude of self-possession and imperiousness he otherwise so often displays in practice. My purpose has not been to hold this double-sidedness against Comte, nor do I now wish to conclude by choosing a side. Instead, I am interested in showing that there is contemporary profit to be had in recognizing the ambiguity of Comte's position – or, more precisely, in understanding that ambiguity insofar as it essentially involves the continual sabotaging of a (still promising) historico-critical impulse by a dominant (originally Cartesian) ahistoricism. For *this sort of ambiguity, in just this configuration, also appears to haunt the work of some of our own post-positivists*. Like Comte, they also frequently start out by attempting to, in Putnam's words, "step back to diagnose our situation" and then repeatedly revert to speaking as if from nowhere.

Adequate discussion of all the ways this ambiguity shows itself in the contemporary situation is obviously out of the question here. Yet it does seem possible to outline the central problem quite clearly by reviewing, with Comte's help, a few representative writings on one specific question of current interest among aspiring post-positivists – namely, the question of the relevance of philosophy's past to contemporary practice – the so-called "philosophy in history" (PIH) issue, to use the title of one especially well-known collection of essays. I begin by discussing briefly the kind of hostility toward philosophy's past that positivists typically display. I then turn to a comparison between the mildly revisionist reaction that this hostility now frequently evokes and Rorty's seemingly much more radical reaction. Supplementing this comparison with some consideration of Taylor's historical-minded efforts to "overcome Epistemology," I want to argue that the very idea of practicing philosophy "after" positivism is being frustrated by the continuing presence, even in the more radically disposed post-positivists, of a Comtean tension between their new historical sensitivity and an old Cartesian ahistoricism. In the last section, I consider in detail how my efforts to rescue the historico-critical Comte can help us look beneath and beyond this tension and toward a genuinely transformed philosophical orientation – one that, for reasons to be explained in my final chapter, remains at present more evident in what post-positivists *say* a stiff dose of history is going to do for them than in the attitude they actually *display* while trying to administer it.

1. The Positivist Thesis: Hostility to philosophy's past

In a standard if often unexpressed form, positivists after Comte draw on their inheritance of the twin Cartesian imperatives to assume something like the following position regarding philosophy's past. Philosophy has at last come of age. It has developed into an essentially neutral and objective activity that, thanks to its recent affiliation with logic and science, is capable of determining not only which of the supposedly perennial philosophical problems are still worth addressing but also what if any value there is in traditional treatments of them. We now know, or (stated in its deceptively more humble form) at least we are presently in the process of working out, what it is to be rational (certain, rigorous, clear, logical, etc.) in one's thinking; and what little "philosophical" significance remains in past philosophies consists in their anticipations of and interesting deviations from current practice.

There is in this familiar position something like, let me call it, a "Positivist Thesis" concerning philosophy's past; and it has two parts. It is, first, scientistic in its epistemology and, second, ahistorical in its general outlook. The two parts clearly mirror the essential aspects of our Cartesian inheritance, and I will return to this main point in a moment. Before I do so, however, let me note that the Positivist Thesis also has a corollary.

If, as is clearly assumed by everyone from Mill to Reichenbach, the alliance with scientific activity means that contemporary *philosophy* has earned the right to evaluate the remaining *rational worth* of traditional teachings, then it follows that *historical* study of those teachings must do something else with them. Most typically since the early twentieth-century, and with the naive complicity of some advocates of the *Geisteswissenschaften*, that "something else" has been construed as the *understanding (Verstehen)* of past theories and systems "in their own terms" – an activity which involves the job of considering those theories and systems in accordance with their authors' intentions and within their cultural contexts, and may even include the attempt to cultivate a kind of sympathetic sense for all of this. The corollary to the Positivist Thesis, then, is that one must recognize a clear division of labor between (real) philosophy and (mere) history. Historians have the quasi-respectable job of narrating, understanding, and preserving the intellectual past, but today's philosophers reserve to themselves the weightier task of analyzing and judging that past and of putting a proper distance between ourselves and what is obsolete. One sure sign of commitment to this corollary is a generalized tendency to treat all previous thinkers as if they were colleagues, already (but, of course, imperfectly) concerned with many of the same "problems" we now recognize to be genuinely philosophical.[1]

The dichotomy I have just "dogmatically" described between historical and philosophical treatments of philosophy's past undoubtedly fails to do justice to any real position. It is difficult to imagine anyone actually practicing the perfectly and purely "antiquarian" sort of history, concerned entirely with the past "in itself," which the corollary to the Positivist Thesis envisages. Conversely, no contemporary philosopher is ever quite as "anachronistic" in the treatment of tradition as my "romantically idealized," hyper-Reichenbachian idea of reconstructive history might have us fear. As the editors of the anthology from which I have been drawing put it, the historian and the philosopher envisaged by my corollary are

> two impossibly ideal types. Our [merely] intellectual historian who has no interest in how the story comes out and our [truly philosophical] historian of philosophy who knows perfectly well what philosophy is, and can tell a central philosophical problem from a peripheral one or from a non-philosophical one at a glance, are caricatures.[2]

The truth, say the editors, is that there is something "praiseworthy" about each of the tendencies reflected in these two caricatures, something that is therefore found, at least to some degree, in every history or philosophy. In the real world, they insist, even the most exclusively historical study must do at least a little evaluating of past claims and practices; and even the most rigorously philosophical assessment of these claims and practices cannot do without at least a little "accurate" history. Nevertheless, it seems to me that in their eagerness to display a new post-positivist sensitivity, the PIH editors unfortunately blunt the power of their caricatures to underscore a problem that is still more pressing. The idea that

---

1 Perhaps the best-known and longest-running textbook example of this commitment is John Hospers, *An Introduction to Philosophical Analysis*, three editions (Englewood Cliffs, NJ: Prentice-Hall, 1953, 1967, 1987). In each edition, the specific problems and the relative weight given to each of them are changed in recognition of current preferences, but the "perennial problems" and "everyone's a colleague" structure remains the same.

2 Editors' "Introduction," PIH, 9. Rorty, Schneewind, and Skinner are hereafter referred to as the "PIH editors."

present philosophy is the real thing and yesterday's philosophies (together with the study of them) are at best an interesting anticipatory other continues to exert a powerful influence. In the English-speaking philosophical mainstream, there are still many for whom it just seems obvious that regardless of what tradition may have held, it is entirely *our* job to determine what knowing the true and the reasonable actually involves; and it seems equally obvious that one learns how to do this job in a spirit and from a standpoint that takes its cue primarily from the current successes of logic, mathematics, and empirical science, and certainly not from looking backward at the flounderings of philosophy's past.

Not everyone, of course, is still convinced of these supposedly obvious things. The Positivist Thesis is intended as a restatement, specifically with reference to the problem of PIH, of the general sentiments of the double Cartesian imperative discussed in Chapter 5. As I emphasized there, this imperative still especially influences the current understanding of an authentically philosophical *standpoint* to a much greater degree than it does today's ideas about philosophy's proper topics or inquiry styles. It is to this difference of degree in current influence that I will now return. In what follows, I want to show how a new contextual sensitivity and anti-positivist pluralism about philosophy's issues and practices can go hand in hand – just as it often did in Comte – with a lingering hostility to the very idea that the advocacy of such contextualism and pluralism is itself also inescapably the articulation of a historically contextualized outlook.

2. Revisionist reaction to the Positivist Thesis

The PIH editors represent a growing number of analytic philosophers who, especially in the last 10 years or so, have been criticizing especially the a- and anti-historical implications of that cluster of operative presumptions I am calling the Positivist Thesis.[3] They complain, among other things, that it has produced narrow, naive, and "sententiously" defended conceptions of philosophy; they point out that, correlatively, it tends to occlude "a desirable form of self-consciousness"; and perhaps most urgently, they explain that it seems to have fostered ignorance of what makes philosophical "problems" problematic in the first place.[4] In general, they argue that hostility (or even simple indifference) to philosophy's past promotes vanity in contemporary minds. It tempts them to "treat 'history' and 'philosophy' as names of natural kinds," and this kind of essentialism leads, in turn, to a lot of

> red-faced snortings about how a given book 'isn't what I call history' or 'doesn't

---

3 See, e.g., especially the papers (and self-citations) of Taylor, MacIntyre, Ian Hacking, Rorty, and Hylton in PIH; also David M. Rosenthal, "Philosophy and Its History," IOP, 141–76, and the literature cited there; and *Doing Philosophy Historically*, ed. Peter H. Hare (Buffalo, NY: Prometheus Books, 1988), esp. the editor's "Introduction," 11–24.

4 On the last point, see also, e.g., Hacking, *Why Does Language Matter to Philosophy?* (Cambridge: Cambridge University Press, 1975), 10–12, 157–87; MacIntyre, *After Virtue*, 264–72; and Hylton, *Russell, Idealism, and the Emergence of Analytic Philosophy*, 2–7, 13–17.

count as philosophy' . . . [all encouraged by the assumption] that there is a well-known part of the world – the past – which is the domain of history, and another well-known part, usually thought of as a set of 'timeless problems,' which is the domain of [today's] philosophy.[5]

This critique of positivist ahistoricism advocated by the PIH editors, who are perhaps mindful of their role as editors, is a carefully measured one – reflecting, I would estimate, the preference of the majority of analytic philosophers interested in the PIH question. It is my contention, however, that one should not mistake this sort of critique for opposition to the Positivist Thesis as such. In fact, it is so moderate as to be driven almost exclusively by the urge to displace scientistic epistemology. At best, it constitutes a merely indirect – and as I am about to argue – essentially ineffectual challenge to ahistoricism itself.

At bottom, critics like the PIH editors want to pry analytic philosophy loose from its hostile opinions about historical study simply because they are eager to enlist history's help against a dated self-image. They note the persistence among their colleagues of pinched visions of philosophy's job and chronic denseness about what makes philosophical problems problematic. They interpret these behaviors as evidence that here, alas, positivism is still alive in contemporary thought; and they determine that cultivating a renewed respect for historical sensitivity promises the solution. For such a renewal would permit everyone to see positivism, even in its last and most sophisticated Logical Empiricist form, for what it really is, namely, just one more time-bound and now outmoded intellectual position that failed to become the definitive philosophy its adherents (for "understandable" reasons) once believed it would be. In short, the PIH editors seek to undermine whatever still expresses positivism's imperious position by *relativizing* it. To mention three examples, they chastise some colleagues for remaining "pre-Kuhnian" in their continuing assumption that philosophical problems never change, only solutions; they dismiss as mere inherited prejudice a still all too common tendency to deem scientists "the only fitting conversational partners for philosophers"; and they argue that this latter prejudice tends to be accompanied by inflated nineteenth-century ideas about intellectual "progress."[6]

For moderate critics like the PIH editors, philosophy's past does have present philosophical relevance; but it is a carefully circumscribed relevance. In their view, today's analytic philosophers need some history to show them that positivism's exaggerated regard for science still affects a lot of current work. They hope that recognition of this uncomfortable inheritance will stimulate "a sense of historical contingency, a sense that 'philosophy' has meant many quite different things." For them, and for perhaps the majority of the authors in their collection, the desired outcome of this new sensitivity is pluralistic repudiation of the single-

---

5 PIH, 8. Here as often elsewhere, the language of the "Introduction" seems to bear the especially heavy stamp of Rorty; but I take the editors at their word that "the general ideas expressed [in it] are the work of all three of us" (ix).
6 PIH, 12–13.

model and science-topical form of analysis promoted by Logical Empiricism. A few of the authors in Part I (e.g., Rorty himself, Taylor, MacIntyre) go further and link such a repudiation with the beginnings of some sort of rapprochement with Continental philosophy. More typical, however, are the authors in Part II (e.g., Burnyeat, Frede, Hylton), who are satisfied simply to see analytic philosophy enriched from within by the demonstration, in terms of either analytic practice itself or the conception of its topics, that its legacy of resources has always been more various and its possibilities richer than certain Viennese zealots for a time made it appear.[7]

What makes the PIH editors seem persuasive to their colleagues, then, has little to do with any revived sense of the intrinsic attractiveness of historical self-consciousness in a philosopher. Their argument works because analytic philosophers no longer want to be thought of as unreconstructed Logical Empiricists. Or to put the point more precisely, their argument works *as soon as* this consequence becomes evident – and that is *too soon* to allow the various reformist responses to escape the influence of the Positivist Thesis entirely. Evidence of its remaining influence is to be found in the fact that most moderate critics emphatically do not think that their newfound historical sensitivity need have any effect on their own ideas about philosophy's *future*. In their eyes, history can help reformers of analytic philosophy free their *present* reflections from inherited positivist dogma – in a manner not unlike Descartes' rules supposedly did for him in relation to medieval dogma in the first two Meditations. But again in the manner of Descartes, when it comes to the task of working out what the actual reforms are going to be, the moderate critics make the question of what philosophy *once was* essentially irrelevant, now, for us, until and unless – as Descartes puts it in Meditation Four – "I decide" (from what viewpoint?) in some previously legitimated fashion to make it relevant.

I invoke the name of Descartes here deliberately. Moderate critics still silently reserve to themselves the position of an objectively constituted "intellect" (i.e., the analytic point of view), which is subject only to whatever is demanded by its chosen "rules" (i.e., whatever are today's, probably pluralistic, replacement for clarity and distinctness).[8] What is more, it seems clear that adopting some such standards is analytic philosophy's protection against "historicism." The point of using history, after all, was to relativize positivism, so goes the silent understanding; the strategy would appear to be unwarranted unless anti-positivism were already understood to be in some larger sense ... Right.

---

7 Another conclusion, not represented in PIH, is that historical study should lead to a reconceiving of "analytic philosophy" itself, for the purpose of making clear that "the metaphysical and logical form it had prior to its development in logical atomism is similar ... to the form it presently has in a framework that has ... superseded ordinary language philosophy" [Nino B. Cocchiarella, *Logical Studies in Early Analytic Philosophy* (Columbus: Ohio State University Press, 1987), 5].

8 "So what is the source of my mistakes? ... the scope of the will [*voluntas*] is wider than that of the intellect [*intellectus*]; but instead of restricting it, ... I extend its use to matters which I do not understand. ... If, however, I simply refrain from making a judgment [i.e., do not exercise my will]

The critical position taken by the PIH editors is thus a moderate one indeed. By advocating a preliminary and therapeutic use of history, they can challenge the falsely ahistorical presumptions of positivism – specifically, about method and topic – without ever noticing how this leaves them free to assume that they are still pursuing their own post-positivist interests in the same basically ahistorical way. In fact, a closer look at their arguments against scientism suggests that what they really believe is that Logical Empiricism was not ahistorical enough. To explain this, I consider further Rorty's own attempts to radicalize this moderate position.

3. Rorty's apparent radicalism

Compared to most English-speaking critics, Rorty's position appears to be antipositivist in the extreme. He rejects, of course, all the usual attempts to model analysis exclusively on logical or empirical scientific procedures. For him, the once "revolutionary [positivist] image" of the philosophers – the one that pictures them as sharing an "intellectual virtue" with mathematicians and physicists and working hard on their own special set of "problems" – has been completely "dismantled" by Wittgenstein, Quine, Sellars, Kuhn, and others. Rorty draws his example of this old revolutionary image from Reichenbach's famously "anachronistic" *Rise of Scientific Philosophy*, but the critique to which he subjects it is an unusually radical one.[9] To really put scientistic models of analytic philosophy behind us, he argues, we must realize that they do not simply derive from midcentury positivism; rather, all such models are in fact latter-day expressions of philosophy's oldest (essentially "Platonic") pretensions. Scientism is just one last attempt to portray philosophers, supposedly possessed of some special "method," as wiser or more comprehensive in vision than everyone else. But this claim, together with its companion notion that philosophers have a unique set of problems, is, asserts Rorty, patently "genealogical" rather than legitimating.

One feature of Rorty's position here that distinguishes it from that of more moderate post-positivists is that his use (though not, as far as I know, any self-description of this use) of history is twofold. Like them, of course, he has a *short-term* account that comes to the conclusion that in the last 40 years analytic philosophy has "moved by its own, internal anti-positivist dialectic" from a positivist to a post-positivist stage. In place of Reichenbach's grand scientistic scheme, Rorty sees the emergence of a more pedestrian, pluralist, nonrationalistically "argu-

where I do not perceive the truth with sufficient clarity and distinctness, then . . . I am . . . avoiding error" (AT, VII, 58–59).
9 (Berkeley: University of California Press, 1951), esp. 71–72, 121–22, discussed most fully in "Philosophy in America Today," COP, 211–16; see also "The Historiography of Philosophy: Four Genres," PIH, 56n.4, 66–67. In PMN, the prime dismantlers of positivism's revolutionary image are Quine and Sellars; in the 1980s, Davidson is added as a third (PP1, 1). Since the late 1970s, Rorty has held that the twentieth-century's three "most important" philosophers are Wittgenstein, Heidegger, and (ever more emphatically) Dewey (cf. PMN, 5, and PP1, 16–17).

mentative" alternative. Based on this short-term account alone, one might assume that even if Rorty did not write the PIH editors' Introduction, he could have; for this part of his historical account differs from that of most moderates primarily in the details, in his specific examples, and in the especially casual nature of his conception of how to understand analytic "style" after the death of rational reconstruction. To see what separates Rorty from the moderates, one must recognize that he also puts the analytic movement into *long-term* historical perspective. There is a reason, he argues, why positivists like Reichenbach failed to recognize where philosophy was really heading after the demise of traditional speculation. The reason is that they assumed that their "scientific" philosophizing was sufficiently post-traditional merely because it opposed theology and metaphysics; and given this assumption, they never saw their own complicity in philosophy's original master plan.

In retrospect, Rorty explains, we realize that the positivist defense of scientific procedure – like earlier defenses of, say, Kantian or Cartesian procedures – continues to express the old dream of finding "the" method for "the" set of philosophical problems. If we are to do any better, we must understand that the source of the positivists' mistake is not recent and specifically positivist; it is ancient and ultimately Platonic. An authentically post-positivist mind, argues Rorty, knows that there can never be a final, "canonical list" of philosophical methods or problems – which is why, if we view the demise of positivism without blinders, we must conclude that analytic philosophy is really left with no job more lofty than, in the pluralistically intended phrase cited earlier, "putting together arguments and pulling them apart."[10] In later writings, Rorty displays a growing personal disinterest even in such "relaxed" and post-Platonic analysis; but he does not put some other distinctively nonanalytical philosophy in its place. Instead, he cultivates a "privately ironic" and "politically liberal" stance of intellectual nonneutrality – an exemplary and persuasive turning, he hopes, toward the possibility of a "poeticized culture."[11]

Rorty's tendency toward hyperbole suggests that he wants us to be impressed above all by his radicalism; and indeed, in the essays just cited, we cannot fail to see how very different his "unspecialized intellectual" and "liberal ironist" both

---

10 "Philosophy in America Today," COP, 220–23. PMN, of course, constitutes Rorty's most famous version of the long-term story – this one offering "edifying [supposedly Gadamerian] conversations" as a nonanalytic alternative (357–72). For another version, see "Solidarity or Objectivity?" (PP1, 21–34), which confirms the impression one gets from PMN that the mediating figure between Rorty's long- and short-term histories is Kant – or, I think, better "Kant," so as to make it plain that this is not the full-blooded critical philosopher but rather a fiction one might create by reading the first *Critique*'s Transcendental Analytic with the intention of either being a positivist or engaging in polemics against it.

11 See esp., CIS, 54–55, 60–61, 68–69. That Rorty is now more likely to interpret everything that lies beyond analysis as partisan commitment – including, e.g., what others might want to call nonanalytic philosophy – is foreshadowed in his conclusion to "Philosophy in America Today" (1981), where he reduces the differences between analytic and Continental philosophy to "agendas" and makes them functions of a fundamentally "political split" between two "cultures" (COP, 229).

are from Reichenbach's scientific philosopher. For my purposes, however, it is more important to emphasize that all three of these contrasting images – precisely as images of recommended philosophical outlook – still have something important in common.

To take Rorty's earlier image of unspecialized intellectuals first, we recall that what "Reichenbach *redivivus*" would admire is their "style, the insistence on argument, the dialectical acuity." This emphasis on style makes Rorty more beholden to his positivist inheritance than he knows. Granted that, on the one hand, his insistence on the possibility of multiple legitimate styles does confirm his reformist desire – contra Reichenbach – to stretch and pluralize the ideas of "method" and "problem" until all the Platonism is forced out of them; and given the extent to which he is willing to push this epistemic liberalization, his position is certainly more extreme than that of most moderates. Yet on the other hand, Rorty's conception of *the source of the "legitimacy" of an analytic style* reveals the deep sense in which he still follows Reichenbach. Consider his remark that today there is

> little attempt to bring "analytic philosophy" to self-consciousness by explaining how to tell a successful from an unsuccessful analysis. The present lack of metaphilosophical reflection within the analytic movement is . . . symptomatic of the sociological fact that analytic philosophy is now, in several countries, the entrenched school of thought. Thus in these countries *anything* done by philosophers who employ a certain style, or mention certain topics, counts . . . as continuing the work begun by Russell and Carnap.[12]

At least, Rorty continues, pioneers like Russell and Carnap felt they had to give "metaphilosophical" accounts of themselves; but once their "radical movement" became dominant, there was simply "less need for methodological self-consciousness, self-criticism, or a sense of location in dialectical space or historical time." Given Rorty's own focus on the differences between positivist analysis in the 1930s and 1940s and post-positivist analyses today, however, let us note carefully the basic similarity he fails to discuss, namely, that from scientistic beginning to edifying end, whatever is acceptably "analytic" is understood as that which conforms to a *currently acknowledged* "stylistic paradigm." For positivists, it was today's science rather than yesterday's theology and metaphysics that provided "the" paradigm. For Rorty and moderate post-positivism, whatever may be our various replacements for mathematical calculation or empirical confirmation, all reference to previous philosophical inquiries that conformed, or almost conformed, or failed to conform to these new paradigms is "philosophically" beside the point – except, perhaps, to the extent that historical information about traditional inquiries might foster that more "desirable form of self-consciousness" that causes one to refrain from thinking of any present form of inquiry "as the culminating development of a natural kind of human activity."[13]

Rorty himself, of course, might well contest my portrait. After all, does he not

12 PMN. 172 (= "Epistemological Behaviorism . . . ," 123).
13 Cf. PIH, 13–14 (the editors) and 73–74 (Rorty himself).

reject the whole Cartesian–Kantian idea of "legitimating" paradigms, whether in the old form of metaphilosophical odes to science or the new sociological form of coded cultural reference? How can I say that his appeal to contemporary resources puts him in the same camp as both positivists before him and more moderate post-positivists today – as if he, too, understood a proper style of inquiry as deriving its "warrant" from these sources? In one respect, this objection has a point. It would be unfair to view Rorty's post-positivist outlook entirely in terms of his earlier work, where he still tends to speak approvingly and as a revisionist insider of stylistic and sociological unity among today's analytic philosophers. In more recent papers, he does in fact describe himself as breaking more radically with his analytic past. Instead of defending a pluralization of (in some loose and extended sense) legitimate inquiry styles, he now more clearly opposes the idea that any cultural activities – even scientific ones – ought to be seen as making conscious or unconscious use (and, by implication, as thus needing a philosophical explication) of some "method" at all. In line with his increasingly pragmatist self-descriptions, Rorty now tends to argue that the "rationality" of a cultural activity is best judged not epistemically and beforehand but by consensual outcome – that is, in terms of what he calls "solidarity." Most pointedly in the case of science, he insists that it is only its unusual degree of solidarity and not anything peculiar to its procedural style that makes it "exemplary." We may therefore

> think of the institutions and practices which make up various scientific communities as providing suggestions about the way ... the rest of culture might organize itself.... [But] if we say that sociology or literary criticism "is not a science," we shall mean merely that the amount of agreement among sociologists or literary critics ... is less than among, say, microbiologists.[14]

In the end, Rorty argues, "method of inquiry" goes together with a whole cluster of other traditional epistemological and metaphysical notions (e.g., subject–object, theory as representation, the "child–parent model of moral obligation") that post-positivism seeks to jettison.

None of these developments, however, speak to my basic point. I do not wish to decide whether Rorty retains some sympathy for prior, epistemic-like "legitimation" or ultimately switches to outcomes-based "consensus." Nor am I interested in simply taking note of the fact that all his "[quasi-]methods" (tests, standards, loosely criterialogical or culturally referential sources) for determining agreement or consensus are clearly contemporary, not traditional. I am concerned, rather, to show that whenever he seeks to contextualize analysis/inquiry and however he thinks current agreement/consensus is reached, Rorty's reforms – early or late, moderate or grand – are typically expressed in the same self-confident, post-traditional language of *choice*. For such choices – not of particular methods but of philosophical *standpoint* – are the sort of thing envisioned by "resolute" ahistorical minds, not by allegedly context-sensitive post-positivists.

14 "Science as Solidarity," PP1, 39–40; see also "Is Natural Science a Natural Kind?" PP1, 60–62.

Our proper aim, Rorty now typically says, is to become "pragmatists *without method*" – that is, to "throw away" the old epistemological and metaphysical notions that once shaped our understanding, so that intellectual life today can be

> pursued *without much reference to* the traditional distinctions between the cognitive and the noncognitive, between "truth" and "comfort," or between the propositional and the nonpropositional. In particular, . . . we could *get rid of* the notion that there was a special "wissenschaftlich" way of dealing with general "philosophical" ideas . . . [and] then we would have much less trouble thinking of the entire culture, from physics to poetry, as a single, continuous, seamless activity in which the divisions are merely institutional or pedagogical.[15]

Rorty's topic may now be "intellectual life" generally rather than cognitive inquiry specifically, but with full self-possession, he still identifies what we should simply "get rid of."

A careful reader will note that the Rorty who speaks here in his own voice depicts post-positivist philosophy as actually accomplishing what Rorty, as one of the PIH editors, condemns Logical Positivism for even imagining. The editors accuse positivism (and those colleagues who are still under its spell) of wanting to "have it both ways" – that is, of seeing itself, in emulating science, as both stepping beyond tradition and being its culmination – and they argue that

> this will not work. Analytic philosophers cannot both be the discoverers of what Descartes and Kant were really up to and be the culmination of a great tradition, participants in the final episode of a narrative of progress. They cannot construct such a narrative by leaving out, e.g., most thinkers between Ockham and Descartes, or between Kant and Frege. A gappy narrative of this sort will not explain "how philosophy became mature" but will merely show how, on various occasions, it narrowly failed to become mature.[16]

It is the latter half of this self-description, the part about maturation, that the editors insist is unacceptable. Their argument is that, strictly speaking, any philosopher who presumes to have surpassed tradition would have to say that "there is nothing which can properly be called 'the history of philosophy,' but only a history of almost-philosophy, only a pre-history of philosophy." Hence, if such philosophers – whether positivists in the 1940s or post-positivists today – went on to claim they had discovered, for example, "what Descartes or Kant [would now recognize he] was really up to," we can only understand this to mean that they are choosing an indirect way of praising their own present activities. What we must not do is to accept such claims as meaning that someone's philosophy represents the final chapter in a "narrative of progress" in which the founders of meditation and transcendental argument tried but failed to become like us.[17]

---

15 "Pragmatism without Method," PP1, 75–76, my emphasis.
16 PIH, 12.
17 PIH, 8–12. In his own essay, Rorty calls the maturation, or culmination, view an exercise in "doxography," and he urges its abolition ("Historiography of Philosophy," PIH, 63–66). For a

If we attend closely to what Rorty says in his own voice about a really post-positivist pragmatism, however, we see that he depicts it as in fact *succeeding* in having it both ways. For whatever the specific brand of "analysis" (or, later, "inquiry") on some specific occasion, he assures us that it will be *both* a "cultural activity" whose "style" is assessed by wholly present means and *also* the culmination of a historical process – in the double sense of being unspeculative ("post-Platonic") as well as "argumentative" (or, later, conducive to "solidarity").

It is no objection to this conclusion to reply that Rorty, like other moderate critics, will sometimes say that the *understanding* of a contemporary style requires reference to historical antecedents; for that is not where the issue lies. The point is that when it comes to the *choice* of a style, Rorty offers today's new pluralism as a reason to *deny* historical dependency. Given that it is always a *"current* consensus," together with what it tolerates by way of dissent, that defines an intellectual community, he argues that

> anybody can legitimize [sic] his use of the term "philosophical knowledge" simply by pointing to a self-conscious community of philosophers, admission to which requires agreement on some points (e.g., that there are, or are not, real essences, or inalienable human rights, or God).... [S]uch communities should be at liberty to seek out their own intellectual ancestors, without reference to a previously established canon of great dead philosophers. *They should also be free to claim to have no ancestors at all.* They should feel free to pick out whatever bits of the past they like . . . or *ignore the past entirely.*[18]

It is hard to imagine how better to encourage a real version of the sort of "anachronistic" history that the PIH editors assure us now exists only in conceptual caricature.

In short, there is a doublethink in Rorty's writings that prevents his reform of analytic philosophy from being as radical as it aspires to be. Of course, on the one hand, there is everything he says that puts him in agreement with the moderate criticism of the other PIH editors. Extending to historical studies a preliminary philosophical relevance, he recontextualizes "scientific thinking" so that it appears in its true light as just the idealization of one style of argumentation. Using the example of positivism's own scientific vanity, he unmasks all maturation narratives (that is, "doxographical" histories) as incurably selective, or "gappy." With these preliminaries settled, he presents a reconceptualization of analytic philosophy that promotes both sensitivity to the idea of multiple forms of inquiry and cultural modesty about any chosen form.

On the other hand, there is also this undeniable fact about Rorty's revisionism. The post-positivist outlook he *recommends* is in a significant respect at odds

---

glaring example of doxography, recall Ayer's claim that "the majority of those who are commonly supposed to have been great philosophers were primarily not metaphysicians but analysts" (*Language, Truth, and Logic,* 52).

18 "Historiography of Philosophy," PIH, 67, my emphasis.

with the outlook he *displays* in his efforts to recommend it. He may be loose and pluralistic about post-positivist style or consensus, but there is nothing modest about his defense of post-positivism itself. Much has been written recently about the allegedly political implications of this immodesty.[19] But here it is enough to note that this defense was epistemic before it was political and, more important, enough to see that in either case, Rorty's *rejection* of the scientistic part of the Positivist Thesis goes hand in hand with his remaining, in his own way, firmly *wedded* to its ahistorical part. Consider his picture: The moderate therapy of historical study is effected. Philosophical analysis gets reformed. The future belongs to argumentation (or consensus), now pluralistically (or even culturally) defined. And all of this together constitutes a fundamentally "progressive" break with our Platonic past. Now analytic philosophy is *really* mature. It no longer needs the services of either long- or short-term memory. It can forget itself in the consensus tests of its community. For not only has it followed positivism in freeing itself from the older theologico-metaphysical tradition; it has now also "gotten rid" of positivism as well.

It does not take much effort to see that such allegedly post-traditional maturity is in fact nothing of the kind. Suppose that, as sociology, Rorty's pluralized and diluted revision of Reichenbach's old epistemic imperialism is correct. Suppose that post-positivist analytic *philosophers* do, in fact, prefer any reasoning that is at least somewhat more appreciative of "scientific" rigor than of "historical-literary" sensitivity. Suppose, too, that liberal irony is indeed *no longer such philosophy* but rather "political commitment." If all of this is the case, then far from having surpassed tradition, both analytic and ironist "communities," along with anyone who does their "reflecting" for them, are taking sides – or, better, they are silently inheriting precisely the same two sides already envisaged as "choices" by their positivist forebears – in a very old, very stylized, and anything but settled dispute about philosophy's purposes.[20] In short, there appears to be something manifestly familiar about this clearly revisionist but nevertheless still ahistorical map of preferences. What kind of ahistoricism is this?

---

19 Rorty's fullest development of the political side of his post-positivism is *Contingency, Irony, and Solidarity*. Yet in 1984, he was already arguing *both* pluralistically, that (a) "what counts as rational or as fanatical is relative to the group to which we . . . justify ourselves" and (b) "for the purposes of liberal social theory, one . . . can get along with common sense and social science" and *also*, as if at last it can be said, that the act of rejecting "the idea that a single moral vocabulary . . . and set of moral beliefs are appropriate for every human community" is of a piece with seeing that "historical developments may lead us to simply drop questions and the vocabulary in which those questions are posed" ("The Priority of Democracy to Philosophy," PP1, 177, 192, 190).

20 Taylor makes a similar criticism of Rorty's unacknowledged traditionalism, focusing on its metaphilosophical operation behind the scenes in his polemical *anti*realism. Taylor does not, however, mention the way this hidden traditionalism continues to operate in Rorty's extra-analytical activities as liberal ironist; nor, apparently, does he see how both operations are actively reinforced by Rorty's explicit views on PIH. See "Rorty in the Epistemological Tradition," in *Reading Rorty: Critical Responses to "Philosophy and the Mirror of Nature" (and Beyond)*, ed. Alan R. Malachowski (Oxford: Basil Blackwell, 1990), 263–71.

4. Post-positivist ahistoricism

Certainly there are grounds for suspecting more moderate revisionists of taking pleasure in an unadmitted philosophical preference for argument over poetry; but Rorty himself has not been altogether insensitive to this objection. For a time, he had a tendency to psychologize it away. In "Philosophy in America Today," for example, he admits that what "Continentals" are doing may be something non-analytic. Yet when he tries to describe the "analytic–Continental Split" this leaves us with, he does so in terms of academic turf battles, humanistic versus positivistic intellectual agendas, and rival politics; and at no time does he connect these empirically depicted disputes with any deeper philosophical tensions that might cast doubt on the "maturity" of his own meta-analytic assessment of the two sides.[21] In more recent writings, however, and especially in those where historical therapy recedes in favor of discussion of the new pragmatism he thinks he makes possible by means of it, Rorty's orientation at least gives the appearance of being less analytically slanted. He has taken to dividing his whole post-positivist project into a "public" and a "private" question, and on the latter – that is, on "what should I do with my aloneness? . . . and [with] my obligation to, in Nietzsche's words, become who you are" – he offers a number of essays that are almost entirely on Continental material.[22]

Nevertheless, such gestures across the Split are typically made in passing and never pursued; and it is anyway not at all clear that Rorty's interest in Continental topics really has much to do with Nietzsche's project. A fair question, then, is, what has gone wrong? Why does Rorty's revisionism, so much more radical in some ways than that of the PIH moderates, continue to display so strong a streak of the old imperious conviction that there is, on the one hand, analytic philosophy, however pluralized, and on the other, what lies, of course, outside of philosophy (e.g., agendas, political commitments, cultural poetics, whatever it is that Continentals do)? Of more moderate critics, one probably should not expect any serious consideration of the idea that philosophical analysis – even pluralized to the Rortyean point of transforming questions of method into questions of consensual outcome – still has genuinely nonanalytic rivals. From the perspective of the PIH editors, after all, displacing scientism by pluralistic reforms simply *is* the project. Yet Rorty himself has clearly thought about this problem. He admits that, in the wrong philosophical hands, even his pragmatism might come to be just as overconfidently promoted as scientism was by any positivist. And like Putnam, he acknowledges that this sort of issue pushed him into exploring Continental sources.

> Analytic philosophers are not much interested in either defining or defending the presuppositions of their work. Indeed, the gap between "analytic" and "non-ana-

---

21 COP, 224–26, 228, 229.
22 PP1, 13; cf. Rorty's "Introduction" to PP2, 1–6; and his discussion of "the present situation" in "Philosophy as Science, as Metaphor, and as Politics," PP2, 21–26.

lytic" philosophy nowadays coincides pretty closely with the division between philosophers who are not interested in historico-metaphilosophical reflections on their own activity and philosophers who are.[23]

Rorty unquestionably *is* "interested." He thinks his own pragmatism is, at least in part, the result of his cultivating Continental sources to distance himself from analytic unreflectiveness; and whatever else this entails, it certainly means that he would now never think of himself as a pluralized, latter-day Reichenbach. His writings are full of denials that he either does or even wants to speak from an "objective" viewpoint; in fact, he repeatedly denies that there is one. Why, then, can he not stop sounding as if there is? I believe my previous chapters make an explanation possible.

Summarily stated, the problem that neither Rorty nor the moderates face squarely is that the positivist spirit they all feel uncomfortable about runs deeper as an inheritance than the epistemic scientism they all oppose. This spirit harbors, in my terms, a Positivist Thesis carrying with it the originally Cartesian and *doubly* ahistorical message that "the" conditions of rationality can "now at last" be set down. Everyone, certainly, is clear about the inappropriateness of the first part of the message; but neither the moderates nor Rorty are reflective enough to catch the way an ahistoricism about philosophical standpoints piggybacks on the monologicism about method.

On the one hand, when aspiring post-positivists follow the lead of the PIH editors and concentrate on opposing their forebears' mistakenly scientistic epistemological claims, they tend to reinforce in themselves – *precisely in making that oppositional move* – the old Cartesian self-confidence that "today" (instead of in, say, 1641, 1843, or 1937) philosophy has finally "broken free" of tradition. Moreover, once the oppositional stance is set up, no amount of renewed attention to tradition is likely to alter this self-confidence. For in moderate post-positivism, the value of historical study is defined at the outset in relation to the epistemic surpassing of scientism. Any attempt to extend the reach of such study from its job of facilitating epistemic pluralization to the "meta-epistemic" issue of self-understanding can be expected to result at best in platitudes about being intellectually modest, or perhaps more likely in resistance driven by fear of historicism, but in either case in responses articulated from the same, already established outlook of epistemic self-confidence that "today" seems so clearly and rightly to have liberated itself from traditional constraints.

On the other hand, what my comparison between the PIH editors and Rorty shows is that even Rorty's radicalization of their epistemic move does not provide fertile ground for exploration of the piggyback effect of the Positivist Thesis. What Rorty's writings exemplify so well is that even a brutally honest attempt to *enact* an intellectually modest philosophizing of the sort talked about by the PIH editors will likely remain self-sabotaging if it continues to be accompanied by a

---

23 "Philosophy as Science, as Metaphor, and as Politics," PP2, 21; cf. "Twenty-Five Years After" in the second edition of *The Linguistic Turn*, 374 n.9.

fundamentally Cartesian understanding of what philosophers must be doing when they "reflect" on their own standpoint. That Rorty retains such an understanding, both in relation to others and to himself, is easily demonstrated.

That the specter of Descartes' *Meditations* is fresh in Rorty's mind when he replies to criticism is evident from the way he depicts anyone put off by the alleged "relativism" of his pragmatic turn. Such persons, he says, have simply never stopped yearning for a philosophical "self-justification" – that is, the old idea that real thinking is foundationalist thinking that starts with a clean mental slate and possession of the right method. It makes no difference, Rorty argues, whether the magic method is an idealization of scientific research, as it once was, or a basic set of logico-linguistic conditions or a mature construal of tradition, as it more recently came to be. In each case, the supposition of self-justification remains. Accordingly, even self-regarding appeals to "history" (e.g., Hegel and Heidegger) must be seen as Continental equivalents of the old empirical–positivist appeal to the sociological "fact" of science (e.g., Carnap and Reichenbach); hence

> honesty here consists in keeping in mind the possibility that our *self-justifying* conversation is with creatures of our own phantasy rather than historical personages, even ideally re-educated historical personages. . . . In particular, when a professor of philosophy sets out on such a self-justificatory project he usually does so *only after decades of giving courses* on various great dead philosophers. . . . [24]

And what is true for the professor who tries to justify a current self-image on the basis of previous course work, Rorty continues, is true generally for anyone who tries to legitimate current intellectual convictions by an appeal to anything else that functions like the professor's tradition. Such foundationalist appeals are all (though Rorty usually says "Kantian" rather than "Cartesian") efforts to find an "intuitive natural starting point" for philosophy; and that is precisely what the post-positivist pragmatist promises to reject. The issue today, says Rorty, is therefore

> whether philosophy should try to find natural starting points which are distinct from cultural traditions, or whether all philosophy should do is compare and contrast cultural traditions. . . . The pragmatist does not think there is anything like [the first option]. . . . But he does think that in the process of playing vocabularies and cultures off against each other, we produce new and better ways of talking and acting . . . that come to *seem* clearly better than their predecessors.[25]

What is evident from passages such as these last two is that Rorty thinks of those who attempt to place themselves intuitively *outside* "the process of playing vocabularies and cultures off against each other" as latter-day Cartesians, but that he thinks of himself as having instead a pragmatist conception of the consequences of giving up such attempts. What is not likely to be so evident, however, is that

---

24 "Historiography of Philosophy," PIH, 71, my emphasis.
25 COP, xxxvii, author's emphasis altered.

Descartes still also haunts the tone of this pragmatist's own voice. For in spite of his clear lack of sympathy for the self-justifying moves of others and a sincere conviction that he avoids their foundationalism by refusing to wrap his own thoughts in a "metanarrative," both Rorty's presentation of the pragmatist and nonpragmatist outlooks and his way of granting preference to the former are themselves essentially Cartesian.

Compare, for example, what Rorty says earlier about foundationalism with what he says elsewhere about the "genres of historiography" that are useful in considering this issue. In both cases, everything is a matter of making fundamentally free and self-regarding "choices" regarding entirely "current" needs. Hence,

> rational reconstructions are necessary to help us present-day philosophers think through our problems. Historical reconstructions are needed to remind us that these problems are historical products . . . that were invisible to our ancestors. *Geistesgeschichte* is needed to justify our beliefs that we are better off than those ancestors by virtue of having become aware of those problems.[26]

"Who" is doing the talking here? Pronouncements are being made like Cartesian affirmations of intuition, resolutely chosen by a self-possessed and collectively authoritative contemporary mind that knows what it is doing *now that it has put its past behind it* – that is, just what Descartes' thinker can do, after the *Discourse* and the first two Meditations, when it has "set aside" religious/moral beliefs and "demolished" the rest. On the matter of philosophical orientation, there are for Rorty clear options – traditional *or* post-traditional styles, intuitive grounding *or* pluralistic play, self-justification *or* endless consideration of interesting options. In each case, there is a choice to be made between what historically has been the case and what is now, instead, possible. On the matter of historical study, once the present day has been chosen over yesterday, the three genres of history Rorty sanctions are all today's children. (a) Historical reconstructions "do not change us," except to temper present enthusiasms; (b) rational reconstructions are basically "our judgments" concerning previous thinkers; and (c) *Geistesgeschichten* "take responsibility" for placing into a context those practices that the other genres have together helped us see we already "need" to be engaged in. The credo of Descartes' ahistorical imperative echoes strongly here: Present philosophical inquiry is one thing; historical study – except to make one a little more broadminded – is altogether something else; and the pragmatist (like the cogito) "knows" to chose the former.

In short, Rorty's post-positivist "philosophers who leave Philosophy behind" are no more able to bring historical study to bear reflectively on their *own* philosophizing than anyone else from Mill to Reichenbach – because the issue of how they are situated is only permitted to arise for them in their capacity of already self-assured opponents of scientism. They are therefore barred by this leftover ef-

---

26 "Historiography of Philosophy," PIH, 67–68. The "fourth genre" is "doxography," which should be "allowed to wither away."

fect of Descartes' double imperative from asking, in relation to their own thinking, the question they use to embarrass the positivists, namely, have they in fact found a way to understand themselves so thoroughly that a belief in their full philosophical maturity is appropriate? At the same time, unlike all those philosophers from Mill to Reichenbach who see no need to countenance historical study at all, what these Rortyean anti-positivists can do – that is, if they are as serious about recontextualization as Rorty is himself – is to get wonderfully trapped between the historical-minded sense that any philosophical viewpoint, even one's own, must somehow already *be* contextualized and an anti-positivist intention to *re*contextualize a polemical viewpoint that has already been conceived ahistorically to be something chosen.

It is precisely when one brings this dilemma into focus that Comte begins to seem of current interest. Like both moderate post-positivists (at least in their criticisms of everyone else) and the more strongly revisionist Rortyean ones (in what they at least would like to claim about themselves as well), Comte believes that the Cartesian idea of an utterly mature and ahistorical philosophical outlook cannot be right. But unlike post-positivists of either sort, who begin by thinking in opposition to a movement Comte does not yet even know, he is at least sometimes still able to resist their negative application of the old idea of philosophical self-possession. Instead of trying to "make" tradition relevant again to a contemporary outlook that is suppressing it, he gives instead a historico-critical exposition of how, at any given moment, the past has always already made itself relevant *in* our thinking without our having to "choose" anything.

5. Comte and philosophy in history

In recent Anglo-American writings on the PIH issue, three basic (though not necessarily formulated) questions appear to drive most of the discussion. For what *purpose* is the issue raised? From what *standpoint* is it most appropriately raised? And what is expected to *result* from raising it? On all three questions, our Janus-faced Comte has contributions of contemporary significance to make.

PIH: Why raise the issue?

From the foregoing analysis of post-positivist treatments of the PIH issue, it should be clear that there is often a largely unacknowledged ambiguity in their accounts of why it is being raised. Initially, the targeted problem seems to have been that of putting positivistic epistemology (plus all the ontological and even axiological commitments implied by it) thoroughly behind us. The use of history was designed to help cut positivism down to size by exposing its socioculturally determinate, scientific underpinnings. Once this determinacy had been revealed and the legitimacy of its overblown and supposedly objective epistemic claims thereby undermined, however, post-positivists began to see themselves as really raising an additional question, namely, what would it take for today's analytic philosophers to be entirely rid of this now fully remembered scientific inheritance? In turn, consideration of this additional question ultimately raised (or better, is now beginning to raise) the still deeper issue of what sort of philosophical orientation would enable one to answer this additional question. In other words, what does (or would) it mean to actually think "*post*-positivistically"?

Root questioning. One crucial feature of this matter of (let us call it) "questioning at the roots" of philosophical analysis, however, is that at first it can easily appear as if, with the demise of positivism as a movement, the issue of what would constitute post-positivism has been effectively rendered moot. To see why this could appear to be so, one need only compare how various sorts of revisionist and radical root questioners (e.g., the PIH editors, Rorty, and here I shall add Taylor) might respond to a business-as-usual textbook recapitulation of up-to-date analytic philosophy.

Consider first Charlton's recent (1991) recapitulation – fairly typical in its confident assumption that positivism is dead, epistemic reform is being accomplished, and root questioning is therefore unnecessary. Given this background orientation, he begins with a resolutely contemporary outlook and posits a division between analytic and Continental philosophy that

> hardly goes back beyond the beginning of the present century. [For] English-speaking and Continental philosophers still acknowledge the same authorities down at least to Kant, and in the nineteenth century post-Kantian German philosophers were taken seriously in English-speaking universities: there was a British version of German Idealism. But then Russell and Moore . . . gave British philosophy a new orientation. *Since their methods caught on,* English-speaking and Continental philosophers have pursued their interests with very little regard for one another.[27]

Characteristically, the analytic–Continental split is portrayed as recent, mainly geographical, and differentiated in terms of the *procedures* by which the two types of philosophy are "conducted," not according to any substantive *claims* that they might "defend." Hence, in explaining further what analytic philosophy does, Charlton assures us that there is "no need" to refer to recent Continental developments, since analysis

> does not define itself in opposition to Continental philosophy any more than in opposition to Christian mysticism. . . . In fact it hardly defines itself at all. As there is *no set of doctrines* analytical philosophers hold in opposition to Continental philosophers so there is no set they hold in unison. . . . [But] they have a consensus about what is and what is not a satisfactory *treatment* of a topic . . . [and] some agreement about what *topics* are fit for philosophical treatment.[28]

---

27 William Charlton, *The Analytic Ambition: An Introduction to Philosophy* (Oxford: Basil Blackwell, 1991), 3, my emphasis. The story is quickly completed with an assurance to the effect that since then, it has clearly been a case of our Germans and Austrians being better than theirs because ours emigrated and "shared Russell's taste for empiricism and formal logic," whereas some of their most important ones either compromised with or were relied on by the Nazis.
28 *The Analytic Ambition,* 3–4, my emphasis. Charlton goes on to offer a case for the untapped promise of "their methods" and refers the reader to Hospers (see fn. 1) for a summary of differing arguments over agreed upon "topics."

What permeates this whole description is, of course, a supreme self-assurance concerning both its studiously incurious conception of extra-analytic activity and its conviction that the analytic "orientation" is fundamentally methodological, possessed of a loosely consensual list of "fit" topics, and certainly never "doctrinal." What is equally clear is that neither moderate root questioners like the PIH editors nor more ambitious revisionists like Rorty can accept this description. Most important here, however, is the difference we can expect to see in the kinds of objections they might raise to it. Moderates, as we have seen, are most likely to focus on the costs incurred by Charlton's historical naiveté; but for Rorty, this naiveté is merely a surface problem.

To more moderate root questioners, accepting an exposition of analytic philosophy like Charlton's puts contemporary practitioners at risk in several ways. It threatens to narrow their vision and produce insularity [e.g., analysts "hold no doctrines"? decide by internal consensus what topics are "fit for (no adjective) philosophical treatment"?]. It promotes denseness about what makes today's philosophical problems problematic [e.g., everyone "accepted the same authorities down to Kant (in the same spirit)"?]. And it encourages intellectual immodesty [e.g., is there really "no need" for extra-analytical comparisons?]. Against all of these dangers, a bit of historical study would appear to offer protection – by reinforcing existing efforts to deconstruct positivism and by broadening and humbling the contemporary analytic philosopher's attitude.

Rorty, however, would argue that there is a glaring weakness in this moderate historical prescription. For it fails to identify specifically the lingering positivism both in Charlton's description and in its own understanding of how to respond to him. Indeed, one can imagine recommending the same sort of historical cure for cases of intellectual insularity and immodesty in virtually any group of thinkers – for example, Continentals and Christian mystics. And that, for Rorty and for all of the more radical root questioners, is precisely the point. To them, the modest approach is too blunt-edged and pedagogical to identify the deeper and still specifically positivist bias that haunts even a methodologically pluralized analytic philosophy.

Reconsider, for example, how Charlton contextualizes philosophical analysis in the previous passages. Is it true that the split with Continental philosophy is largely a twentieth-century phenomenon – so that it makes no real difference that analysis has empiricist–positivist rather than rationalist–idealist roots? Is there nothing problematic about judging philosophies according to a forced option between "doctrine" and "method" (let alone to speak flatly of Russell and Moore offering a "new" form of the latter)? Is it correct to say that contemporary philosophical analysis is really not, in any important sense, "defined" in terms of "opposition" to what are presumed to fall outside of "English-speaking interests"? I have had occasion to mention questions like this before, of course, in previous chapters. The point here is that less moderate root questioners think these matters can no longer be silently avoided. Hence, from them one hears of the need, for example, to acquire an interest in "historico-metaphilosophical reflection" (Rorty), or to engage in "historical retrieval and redescription" for "recovering our own origins" (Taylor), or to find a new way to "step back and diagnose" the current situation (Putnam) – or, in general, to take seriously the idea that the demise of positivism ultimately implies that much of what still passes for philosophical analysis today is going to be "ending," too, and that one therefore needs to ask what it could be to philosophize "after" this has occurred.[29] A more radical root questioning, moreover, is typically accompanied by some milder or bolder suggestion that these circumstances make "interests" relevant that have heretofore been dismissed as better left to Continentals.

Regarding the purpose for which the PIH issue is raised, then, in part one must notice that once the effort to recontextualize questions of method is substantially underway (even Charlton speaks of "consensus" here), the further possibility of using historical studies for philosophical self-understanding tends increasingly to press forward and be taken seriously. Yet this is not a sufficient description. There are several ways in which self-understanding might now seem a desirable thing. Hylton, for example, describes his book as

> an attempt to suggest, by example, that [Hegel's heretofore questionable] idea can be profitably be applied to analytic philosophy: we can write a history of our own philosophical tradition, and thereby attain a kind of self-knowledge.[30]

Here self-understanding appears primarily to be something that might enrich business as usual, whatever this is turning out to be. Yet as Hylton himself points out one page earlier, the very possibility of self-understanding started to be taken seriously by analytic philosophers only in "reaction" to their failure to find the method that was finally going to "set philosophy on the sure path of a science." Thus to put it somewhat unfairly, on the question "Is the purpose of using history for philosophical self-understanding primarily to *clarify* or instead to *critically transform* one's contemporary practice?" Hylton appears to answer yes.

The case of Taylor. Initially, there might seem to be a similar ambiguity in Taylor. To be sure, his picture of the historical context for analytic philosophy's self-understanding is more broadly conceived than Hylton's; like Rorty's, it includes reference to both older and more diverse sources.[31] Yet as with Hylton, his defense of "historical redescription [retrieval]" in the PIH volume at least at first

---

29 In addition to *The Institution of Philosophy* and *After Philosophy*, see *Post-Analytic Philosophy*, ed. John Rajchman and Cornell West (New York: Columbia University Press, 1985).
30 *Russell, Idealism, and the Emergence of Analytical Philosophy*, 16; see also PIH, 392–96, where Hylton says (394n.22) that his thinking about the relation between philosophy and its history has received "recurrent inspiration and instruction" from the "Forward" to Stanley Cavell's *Must We Mean What We Say?* (New York: Scribners, 1969).
31 See, e.g., the "Introduction" to his *Philosophical Papers* [2 vols. (Cambridge: Cambridge University Press, 1985)], in which he explains how his polemic against "the ambition to model the study of man on the natural sciences" led him to the general critique of an inherited naturalism shaped by seventeenth-century science, in which he draws heavily on both traditional and contemporary

gives the impression that Taylor, too, is primarily interested in enriching whatever self-understanding we already have of our current doings. After registering his own root-questioning opposition to the still widespread "habit of treating philosophy as an exercise which could be carried on in entirely contemporary terms," he goes on to argue that philosophy is "inherently historical" and, moreover, that "this fact . . . is a manifestation of a more general truth about human life and society."[32] How frequently in life, Taylor notes, do we have recourse to history to clarify current practices. Sometimes, of course, we may be "driven . . . by the need to escape from a given social form, . . . [or by the need to] recover or restore one which is under pressure and in danger of being lost"; but on many if not most occasions, we have no especially emancipatory or restorational concerns. The point, says Taylor, is to recognize that

> what is common to all these enterprises is *the need to articulate the unsaid in present practices*. In all these cases, we are driven back to . . . the last . . . perspicuous formulation of the good or purpose embedded in the practice . . . and sometimes . . . even earlier, to the outlook against which this formulation was defined.[33]

The "articulation of the unsaid," however, is for Taylor not a primarily descriptive and merely informative device. Especially in his final three pages, when he turns from his defense of historical retrieval generally to an explanation of its usefulness in undermining analytical philosophy's lingering captivation by Descartes' "epistemological model," Taylor reveals a historico-*critical* conception of philosophical self-understanding that not only differs from Hylton's but is, I think, also more successfully radical that Rorty's.

Taylor's attack on the Cartesian epistemic imperative is in general the familiar post-positivist one. No one will ever become that mythical "disengaged" meta-understander whose capital "E" Epistemology achieves "total reflexive clarity" about the "correct representation of an independent reality."[34] We now experience everywhere the philosophical dead ends that come from thinking as if this Epistemology were still possible, says Taylor, and historical redescription of the

---

Continental sources (1–12, both vols.); also "Hegel Today" in *Hegel* (Cambridge: Cambridge University Press, 1975), 537–71; and his "Conclusion: Conflicts of Modernity," in *Sources of the Self: The Making of the Modern Identity* (Cambridge, MA: Harvard University Press, 1989), 495–521.

32 PH, 17.

33 PH, 27–28, my emphasis. I will return in the next section to the fact that Taylor's treatment of philosophy, like Rorty's construal of pragmatism, is already somewhat atypical in at least one respect, viz., that philosophy is for him, from its very inception, just one more "inherently historical" human "practice" – and thus always incorrectly conceived as a kind of superior metapractice for other practices. Though perhaps merely a faint echo from the robust old idea of philosophy as queen of the sciences, see contra, e.g., Charlton's assertion that "analytical philosophers do not study ordinary language in order to verify 'common sense beliefs': they aim at uncovering beliefs and ways of thinking which we do not know we have but which, they hope, are revealed by ordinary habits of speech. Do we think that time flows or passes? Common sense says, 'Ask a philosopher'; nonphilosophers are happy to confess that they do not know what they think" (*The Analytic Ambition*, 17).

34 PH, 28–30; phrasing cited from OE, 466–69. See also *Sources of the Self*, Ch. 8. For a good summa-

original formulation of this ideal is needed to enable us to see that there are productive alternatives – with respect to reason, moral practice, nonnatural human sciences, and much else. Against the anticipated objection that such historical redescription threatens the concept of enduring truth because it always emphasizes "alternatives" and thus inevitably leads to some species of relativism or "nonrealism" (the threat of emulating Rorty is mentioned), Taylor protests that this radically misinterprets the intent of historical redescription. My intent, he argues, is existential – that is, whatever the issue, I understand it to "arise within culture and history, within a set of practices, as [experientially] between rival formulations of these practices."[35] Anyone who thinks of such episodes of historical retrieval as if, at some point, both the now dominant formulation and a redescriptively revealed alternative might be placed before the mind and lie open for simple choice – anyone, that is, who treats such episodes "as though having understood both sides one could [then] be genuinely agnostic between them" – is relying on precisely that mythic "epistemological model" of understanding that is Taylor's prime example of a current formulation we are "driven by the need" to get free of.

Given this position, Taylor is especially concerned to emphasize the distance between his use of historical redescription and Rorty's. Both of us agree, he argues, that we need to "climb out" of the old Cartesian orientation; and both of us know that this is impossible without historical redescription [retrieval, narrative]. But

> Rorty believes that one can jettison the old epistemological view without espousing another one. One just leaves these old questions behind, like: what is the nature of knowledge? or self-understanding? of scientific truth? and moves forward into a post-philosophical world.... [Whereas I believe, on the contrary, that] this move is far from being a liberation. Just trying to walk away from the old epistemology, without *working out* an alternative conception, seems paradoxically a formula for remaining trapped in it to some degree.[36]

As we shall see in the next section, Taylor has much to say about this process of actually "working out" an alternative conception and how it differs from attempting to simply choose – that is, to "walk away" from or "move forward" to – another option. In the meantime, it should at least be clear that his concern for philosophical self-understanding is not captured either by Hylton's passing description of analytic philosophers as "reacting" to the failure of scientism or by Hylton's own preferred idea of making present practice more self-conscious.

On the one hand, then, it only seems at first as if Taylor is interested, just in general, in various ways of articulating the unsaid and "undoing the forgetting"

ry of Taylor's view of both the Epistemological standpoint and his proposal for displacing it, see his "The Dialogical Self" in *The Interpretive Turn: Philosophy, Science, Culture*, ed. David R. Hiley, James F. Bohman, and Richard Shusterman (Ithaca, NY: Cornell University Press, 1991), 304–14.
35 PH, 30.
36 "Rorty in the Epistemological Tradition," 273, my emphasis.

that tends to occur in any present practice. Actually, Taylor wants to explain what historical redescription can accomplish in one particular sort of situation – namely, when one is driven by the *experience of dissatisfaction* with a presently operative articulation of practice or, still more precisely, when a now unsatisfactory articulation remains "embedded" in our practices in such a way that it both eludes explicitation and continues to operate in our thinking in such a way that it makes alternatives seem "inconceivable." For example: In "Overcoming Epistemology," the unsatisfactory articulation considered is the classical foundationalist model of epistemology. In "Philosophy and Its History," it is this classical model specifically as he thinks it still haunts the work of Quine. In *Sources of the Self,* it is the modern ideal of a disengaged, autonomous agent. In many of the essays in his *Philosophical Papers,* it is naturalistic conceptions of the human sciences. And in *Multiculturalism,* it is the traditional idea of legal and political identity.[37] In each case, instead of simply marching forward toward a new articulation (regarding, respectively, rationality, semantic theory, agency, human science, and recognition/cultural identity), Taylor begins, Putnam-like, by "stepping backward" toward the sources of the relevant unsatisfactory articulation; and he then proceeds toward something more satisfying precisely by spelling out in detail how current experience renders the old articulation unsatisfactory.

On the other hand, finally, if one understands Taylor's real concern in each of these cases, it is easy to see that he intends to be critical of present practice without, like Rorty, being "reactive." In other words, I believe I can, more easily than with Rorty, relate Taylor's idea of historical retrieval both to Comte and with my rethinking of him. For in Comte's analyses of metaphysics – specifically, in his argument that this "method of philosophizing" is still hanging over the emergent scientific era like a blanket of distortion about what knowledge is – he is treating this old method as functioning precisely like an earlier version of Taylor's epistemological model: To some extent, it still somewhat stunts the growth even of the natural sciences; it still dominates the study of humanity and sociopolitical affairs; and it promises "total reflexive clarity" about the "independent reality" (beyond phenomena) through an entirely adequate "correct representation" (in an abstract, rational system).[38] Driven by his experiences with the natural and biological sciences, the historico-critical Comte seeks to free current practices from this metaphysical model of knowledge by "historical redescription" of earlier formulations of metaphysics whose less perspicuous versions are still being forgetfully recapitulated.

Yet Comte, as we know, could also be more like later positivists. As himself in certain ways the forgetful inheritor of the metaphysical model, there is also the

---

37 *Multiculturalism: Examining the Politics of Recognition,* 2nd ed. (Princeton, NJ: Princeton University Press, 1994), 26–36.
38 I am thinking here of the especially suggestive parallels/contrasts between Comte's arguments on behalf of natural science against late metaphysics and Taylor's account of how natural scientism now stands in the way of the development of interpretive human sciences – e.g., in "Interpretation and the Sciences of Man," *Review of Metaphysics* 25 (1971), 3–51 (reprinted in *Philosophical Papers,* Vol. 2, 15–57).

tyrannical Comte who passes on, with the same old Cartesian reflexive conviction of total clarity, the claims – for example, that positivity is the final state, that research will always be unified in his hierarchical fashion, that social reorganization means founding his Religion of Humanity, and so on.

In Taylor's terms, then, Comte is at once both "creative redescriber" and "disengaged subject," at once both "liberator" and "prisoner" of Cartesian epistemology. Hence, I am entirely in sympathy with Taylor's effort to develop a "contemporary" (we have been saying post-positivist) self-understanding that,

> instead of searching for an impossible foundational justification of knowledge or hoping to achieve total reflexive clarity about the bases of our beliefs, . . . [would cultivate an] . . . awareness of the limits and conditions of our knowledge, an awareness that would help us overcome the illusions of disengagement and atomic individuality that are constantly being generated by [our] civilization. . . . [39]

Yet if this comparison of Taylor with Hylton and Rorty helps to sharpen our focus on the *purpose* of philosophical self-understanding envisioned by our radical root questioners, it leaves in a somewhat unsatisfactory condition our conception of the *standpoint* from which it is understood that this purpose is to be pursued. Here again, some discussion of Taylor can be helpful.

From what standpoint?

In "Overcoming Epistemology," Taylor attempts to formulate his new conception of philosophical self-understanding by contrasting it with two conflicting strains of postmodern critique, each of which follows a line of thinking he finds only partially acceptable. I believe a close reading of this attempt reveals the degree to which Taylor is – and is not – able to follow his own good advice that a genuinely post-positivist (that is, "contemporary") standpoint would be one that is no longer either Epistemological or anti-Epistemologically reactive.

In general, Taylor depicts the desirable standpoint as one aiming at "continuity-through-transformation in the tradition of self-critical reason" – by which he means that it will have to involve a "radical break" with the old epistemology yet also "carry further [the traditional] demand for self-clarity about our nature as knowing [and acting] agents."[40] In searching for a proper discourse in which to spell out this continuity-through-transformation, however, Taylor reports that he finds himself torn between two insightful but deeply flawed postmodern critiques. On the one hand, there is the neo-Nietzscheans' "refusal" of modernity, which is full of telling insights about the impossibility of achieving the decontextualized outlook of Cartesian rationality. It rightly stresses that when it comes to

> settling the matter of truth between construals, . . . no construal is quite innocent, something is always suppressed; and what is more, some interlocutors are always advantaged relative to others, for any language. . . . [41]

---

39 OE, 479–80.
40 OE, 479, 483.
41 OE, 484–85, word order altered. In *Sources of the Self*, Taylor argues that this excess reflects only

Yet unfortunately, according to Taylor, neo-Nietzscheans also promote the undesirably excessive notion that "there can be no talk of epistemic gain in passing from one construal to another." In this fashion, they display a streak of irrationalism that threatens not just knowledge but human interaction generally. And just here, says Taylor, there are on the other hand, critics such as Habermas who, "against the neo-Nietzscheans . . . wants strongly to defend the tradition of critical reason." Indeed, he even wants

> to hold on to a formal understanding of reason . . . [albeit one that is] purged of the monological errors of earlier variants . . . [because he] fears for the fate of a truly universal and critical ethic should one go all the way with [a neo-Nietzschean] critique.[42]

Taylor shares Habermas' ethical concern, and he thinks the neo-Nietzschean "arguments for not taking argument seriously are uniformly bad." Yet he also believes that Habermas has failed to formulate a position that responds adequately to the Nietzschean recognition of the always less than "innocent" (that is, neutral, objective, autonomous) condition of reason.[43]

In summing up his reactions to these two forms of critique, Taylor concludes that their dispute is not quite a draw. "Whoever is ultimately right," he says, "the dispute has to be fought out on the terrain" of the Habermassian defenders of critical reason. For the neo-Nietzscheans have simply failed to establish that there can be no legitimate talk about "epistemic gain" or loss "between" one construal of truth and another. The "main weight" of their case, it seems, is

> carried by an utterly caricatural view of [critical rationality] as involving a belief in a kind of total self-transparent clarity which would make even Hegel blush. The rhetoric deployed around this has the effect of obscuring the possibility [of] a third alternative. . . .[44]

Taylor is convinced of such a third possibility, because the two options offered by the neo-Nietzscheans – that is, "naive, angelic" total clarity or uncompromising "Derridian" refusal to argue – both seem "rather dotty."

For my purposes, what is crucial here is that when Taylor characterizes the issue of an authentically post-positivist standpoint as involving a battle with Nietzsche and Habermas "over the corpse of epistemology," where the central issue is

---

one "strain" in Nietzsche's own writing that is given prominence by recent French writers like Foucault (487–88, 518–19).

42 OE, 483.

43 In *Sources of the Self,* this failure is traced to Habermas' "conception of modernity, which is partially inspired by Weber . . . [and] allows that there was a premodern sense that humans were part of a larger order, but sees the development of modern rationality precisely as showing the incoherence of this view" (510). This conception of modernity, Taylor argues, leaves Habermas without a way of recognizing – as one would have to in order to deal with the neo-Nietzscheans' point – that we all possess a nonobjectifiable, "personal, and hence, subjectively resonant . . . order in which we are set as a locus of moral sources."

44 OE, 484.

what "arguments" should go in the space "between" one knowledge construal and another, he appears to have forgotten his own advice. In other discussions, Taylor insists that the kind of reflection that is basic for a postmodern outlook – that is, the self-understanding that is able to monitor *the process of getting from one construal to another* – cannot be comprehended third person. As he puts it in the Rorty critique, what this self-understanding knows is that in actually "working out" an alternative to some constraining articulation, there is never any interval "between" articulations – and therefore never any separated inquiry products that need comparative "evaluation" via some sort of Habermassian criteria of critical reason.

To take this self-understanding seriously, however, is to see that Taylor's shift from its preferred discourse of process, articulation, and creative redescription to the more familiar discourse, at the end of "Overcoming Epistemology," about truth construals, arguments, and questions of cognitive continuity – this very shift betrays a partial reversion to precisely the outlook he himself admits is the old modern rival to post-positivism. The preferred discourse, the language of life's self-understanding, follows *from within* the articulation process itself. The all too familiar discourse, the language of knowing subjects armed with the rules of right reason, surveys *from without* the "terrain" of rational critique and "epistemic" gains and losses. And the latter discourse simply remains too disengaged from historical life to ever become genuinely post-positivist. As Taylor puts it in the Rorty critique, even if it is true to say that

> we are partly constituted by our self-understandings, we can't construe them as an independent object, in the way our descriptions of things are. When I move [e.g.,] from seeing myself as being disinterestedly benevolent to understanding how much I get out of my role as benefactor; when I get beyond a view of myself as a cool loner, and understand how much I'm involved in this relationship . . . I'm altering myself with my new self-descriptions . . . *and the terms in which to characterize [what now appears as a] distortion are only available to me now that I have climbed out of it.*[45]

Taylor's point is that these "characterizing terms" for (if one must put it so) evaluating a previous versus present self-description *emerge along with the present self-description* as part of the process of rearticulation, and not as products of any epistemic battle over "knowledge conditions" waged from a vantage point external to both the descriptions themselves and the process of developing them.

To take one more example of Taylor's conception of what it is to think from within a postmodern standpoint of self-understanding, in "Philosophy and Its History" he insists that in human life generally,

> we have a gamut of articulateness. At the bottom, there is the case where no descriptive words are used at all. We live our machismo, say, entirely in the way we stand, walk, address women and each other. . . . Or we have a language in which the fairs and fouls have names, but still it is not further formulated what makes

---

[45] "Rorty in the Epistemological Tradition," 271–72, my emphasis.

them fairs and fouls. At the upper end, we have practices where the point of the activity, the underlying goods, or embedded purposes, are fully worked out, and an elaborate justification of them made in philosophical terms. . . .[46]

The "Hegelian" idea that philosophy belongs at the "upper end" of articulateness is, of course, thoroughly modern. Consider, however, the epistemic implications of Taylor's account as a whole. Suppose that it is true, as he goes on to say, that

> the inarticulate end of this gamut is *somehow primary*. That is, we are introduced to the goods, and inducted into the purposes of our society much more and earlier through its inarticulate practices than through formulations.

If this is indeed, "ontogenetically speaking," clear to self-understanding, then it is fundamentally unhelpful for Taylor to continue thinking of the "struggle over the corpse of epistemology" as being fought out on Habermassian turf. For in Habermas' defense of critical reason – as in the influence it has on Taylor's account of "carrying forward the demand for self-clarity" – the process of "giving a defensible notion of what self-clarity is" starts with articulations. It is still envisaged as being conducted at least sufficiently apart from our lived and semi-articulated operative reasonings that it makes sense to say there can be a difference "between" two articulations that only an appeal to argument conditions can adjudicate. But where is this "between"? Does anybody *live* there? Taylor is certainly right that various neo-Nietzscheans have made these questions too easily rhetorical by giving Cartesian burlesques of all conceptions of argument standards. Nevertheless, there is still an alternative standpoint – not contemplated in either neo-Nietzschean "refusals" or Habermassian critique – that makes these questions seem to have a crucial point.[47] This alternative is the standpoint of life, whose self-understanding Taylor characterizes as that of a "we" that already has a "gamut" of articulateness, never faces an intervaled "succession of formulations" of anything. From this standpoint, there is simply that cluster of practices, languages, and existing articulations *within which* we are able to think and to engage in attempts to retrieve and transform whatever articulations, construals, or formulations – of the conditions of intentionality, or male chauvinist behavior, or whatever – we are currently coming to experience as unsatisfactory.

What I want to suggest is that Taylor's self-understood, already contextualized living experience is precisely "where" Comte, too, understands himself as being when he remains the historico-critical monitor of his experience of transition from metaphysics to science. This is the Comte who, in the first Lesson of his

---

46 PH, 23. Elsewhere, Taylor calls the standpoint of life described here "engaged agency" [e.g., "Engaged Agency and Background in Heidegger" in *The Cambridge Companion to Heidegger*, ed. Charles B. Guignon (Cambridge: Cambridge University Press, 1993), 317–36]. This notion figures centrally in *Sources of the the Self*, where Taylor tries to show that precisely this standpoint of living engagement is what modern philosophy moves to suppress.

47 I once tried (with Heidegger's help) to give this alternative standpoint to Nietzsche himself in "Nietzsche and the 'Use' of History," *Man and World* 7 (1974), 67–77.

Cours, rejects both organon making and the search for "ultimate" scientific laws as merely attempts to rescue something from a prescientific corpse. As I see him, in other words, this is a Comte who would have regarded Taylor's sympathy for some appropriately watered down "critical theory" as still basically a failure to "work through" completely an inherited theologico-metaphysical articulation of "Logic" as "intellectual system."

From this perspective, the trouble with Taylor's Nietzschean–Habermassian idea of an existentially deconstructive/critically reconstructive revision is not that it remains too Epistemological after starting off in the right direction. Rather, it is wrongly – that is, Epistemologically – inspired from the beginning. Or again, in Comte's terms, it constitutes a "dogmatical" departure from our lived situation that tries to make us forget our roots.[48] Granted, critical reconstruction and existential deconstruction each grab hold of a half truth. Habermassians see that it is indeed always possible to identify a "characteristic" intellectual approach in every articulation process; and neo-Nietzscheans know that every actual articulation emerges from and points back to what is still deeply contextualized and as yet unthought. But neither of these observations justifies our first generating and then philosophically favoring the dogmatical abstractions "rational method" and "nonrational data," and finally either choosing between them or being satisfied to say them rapidly together.

It is in the spirit of this last remark that Comte sets out to articulate his ideas "in terms of their history." As always, there are already received articulations of what ("one says") constitutes good reasoning; but Comte understands himself to be thinking at a time when these articulations are under the duress of an intellectual (and ultimately also sociopolitical) sea change. On the basis of what he is already experiencing of the promise of the emerging sort of intellectual activity, he tries to further its possibilities by understanding how it is already transforming the metaphysical mode of knowing. And his attempt, as we have seen, does indeed take the form of, in Taylor's words, a "historical retrieval and creative redescription" of metaphysics – one that emphasizes the way positive reasoning is able to fulfill experienced "needs" rather than the way it fails to stick to traditional methods. This effort prefigures, in my view, a genuine alternative to the two "continuities-through-transformation" that Taylor – understandably, given the mixture of his own vision of life's gamut of articulations with his slightly Habermassian leanings – cannot decide between.

The thinking-within character of Comte's alternative can be further clarified by reconsidering the temporal structure he gives to it. Mill, we remember, sees Comte's interest in historical retrieval and sociopolitical prevision as unfortunate distractions from what *he* knows to be today's real philosophical business of for-

---

48 Cf. Taylor himself: "It has been the persistent vice of the epistemological tradition to try to assimilate [our lived] pre-understanding to the representations it frames, as though it could be exhaustively accounted for in terms of *information about* the subject and his world. The latest example of this is to be found in contemporary simulations of Artificial Intelligence" ("Rorty in the Epistemological Tradition," 270).

mulating an organon of proof. In this criticism, Mill implicitly relies on what Comte calls time's "chronological order," namely, past–present–future; and his argument for an organon envisages a kind of paring down of this chronological order to focus on strictly "present" concerns. In Mill's eyes, Comte's dwelling on past and future matters costs him the chance to "choose" positive philosophy's main business. For this choice, as Mill conceives it, involves what we might call an implicit double favoring of the present – both in the sense of its being the focal moment when good philosophers free their minds from the mere precedent of what people "have been" thinking in order to get on with "today's" epistemic task, and also in the sense of there being a sort of timeless and ideal Now in which every successful thinker always has, does, and will think if (in this case) Mill's projected organon is wholly followed. We have, of course, seen this double favoring of the present before. It is, one might say, the condition of the possibility of every Cartesian epistemology, for each favoring reinforces the idea that history is irrelevant to epistemic success and that everyone who follows the rules of Right Reason at any (present) time thinks the same Correct Thoughts.

Comte himself, however, suggests a quite different ordering of the temporal phases and thus points philosophy in another direction. In 1822, at the very beginning of his career, he expresses the conviction that when it comes to the question of the intellectual past,

> the chronological order of epochs is not at all their philosophical order. Instead of saying the past, the present, and the future, we should say the past, the future, and the present. Indeed, it is only when we have conceived the future by means of the past that we can profitably return to the present so as to grasp its true character.[49]

Comte's description is wonderfully ambiguous. On the one hand, to write of temporally ordering the epochs one way rather than another is to contemplate a choice from that disengaged Cartesian vantage point that is exterior to any order, where "the" rules (here, what a dogmatically construed three-stage law tells us about how the future must look) already tell us which order is superior.

Yet on the other hand, the writer of this passage "conceives the future by means of the past" for the sake of a *return to the present*. This is someone for whom a retrieval of the past and a previsioning of the future are, from the outset, responses to an unsatisfactorily experienced present. When Comte starts writing about how to articulate the temporal order, he is already, as Taylor says, "driven by need" – in this case, the need to transform (sc., alter in a scientific direction) the manner in which "we" have tended to construe what knowledge is.

For the historico-critical Comte, current practice is therefore both first and last. It is, initially, "already" our field of need for transformed articulations; and *with this understood*, one may also say that it is "not yet" the place where, after his-

---

49 SPP4a, 100/563. Cf., e.g., Peirce's deliberately temporalized dictum that "the object of reasoning is to find out, from the consideration of what we know, something else which we do not know," where the whole point of this is to "produce beliefs" establishing modes of action that *will* "satisfy our desires" (*Collected Papers*, Vol. 5, pars. 365, 375, 397, 400).

tory has given current inquiry back its memory, philosophy can proceed with its "critical and educational task." Against Mill, this Comte understands "grasping the true character" of the presently emerging scientific times as *necessarily* involving historical research. What gets illuminated is not "the" past (springing up again, irrelevantly "now" as an object), but rather a lingering of inherited ways in current experience – especially, for Comte, a general lack of fit between emergent empirical research and the received, and still largely metaphysical, articulations (which, among other things, distort the existing natural sciences and block possible "sociological" ones).[50] For today's post-positivists, of course, the emergent practices and received articulations are different – one thinks, for example, of the struggle for methodological pluralization, both in and out of science, of debates over the denaturalizing of human (and perhaps even physical) science, and of still unsatisfactory "analytic" conceptions of method as well as knowledge. Yet the times certainly seem to be just as historico-critically needy.

With what (preliminary) result?

In raising the PIH question, then, some post-positivists have moved toward a more historically minded self-understanding and thus have helped to produce a crisis concerning how to characterize an authentically philosophical standpoint. It is not simply that this question is in fact currently raised, whereas in the heyday of Logical Empiricism it was suppressed for seeming too subjective and traditionalist. Rather, there now seems to be genuine and widespread uncertainty concerning how a philosophical orientation should be structured. What should the "analytic ambition" *be* if a scientistic or Epistemological standpoint is unacceptable, and if, we might now add, the Habermassian and neo-Nietzschean alternatives described by Taylor are, respectively, too conservative and too dotty?

Clearly, the outlook Taylor wants is not the sort from which one might employ historical studies "after the fact" – for example, as a means of either humbling (like a PIH moderate) or justifying (like Rorty's doxographers) a standpoint already self-confidently embraced. He sees too clearly the remaining arrogance in these epigonic variations on the old Epistemological theme; and he shares some of Nietzsche's contempt for the delusion of a pure and neutral rationality. Taylor says, moreover, that he has learned too much from Continentals like Heidegger and Merleau-Ponty about the "irrecusably" engaged/contextualized character of all human practice to simply *follow* Habermas, thereby somehow "holding on to a formal understanding of reason." Similarly, he is unwilling to copy Rorty and employ the "gambit" of historical study to tell "*re*contextualizing" narratives about the "contingency of the final vocabulary we choose."[51]

What Taylor appears to want is a philosophical self-understanding of Comte's

---

50 See CPP1(1), 31–56 [F, 18–33]; and SPP1, 1–6 *("Préface")*, 2–3/ix–xiii, 1–3.
51 See, e.g., Rorty's "Inquiry as Recontextualization: An Anti-Dualist Account of Interpretation," PP1, 93–110, esp. 95–101; "Heidegger, Contingency, and Pragmatism," PP2, 27–49, esp. 48; and Hall, *Rorty*, 213–21. For Taylor, see esp. "Rorty in the Epistemological Tradition," 267–73; "Engaged Agency and Background in Heidegger," 325–33; and OE, 475–79.

historico-critical sort. Such a self-understanding would enable us to monitor the process of "living our transition" from Epistemology to post-positivism, just as Comte tried to "climb out of the old error" of metaphysics for the sake of positive philosophy. More than Rorty, as it seems to me, and certainly more than Habermas,[52] Taylor tries to consider life's self-understanding "from within." He depicts it as a reflective accompaniment to the actual experience of being constrained by articulations that repeatedly sabotage our efforts to transform them; yet he also clearly recognizes that these received articulations, whatever they are, express the way we always already *are* contextualized. Hence, at least part of the time, he sees that it would be a betrayal, both of this reflectiveness and of the lived transitions it tries to monitor, if one were to "choose" to regard these articulations initially as something that has not yet engaged us and therefore as open to Rorty's "interesting" and "imaginative" *re*contextualizations or to Habermas' "transcendental-pragmatic" schematization.[53]

Taylor's conception of historico-critical self-understanding thus appears to promise a more thoroughly root-questioning, post-positivist standpoint than those offered by either the PIH moderates or Rorty. Yet his arguments suffer, I think, from this fundamental limitation. Most of his descriptions of self-understanding focus on its functions in ordinary human practice – and this means, typically, that the point of these descriptions is *not specifically integrated into his own philosophizing*. Here, perhaps, is the reason why the author of all the passages I have cited with praise – for their post-positivist spirit and for their critical bite against Rorty, the neo-Nietzscheans, and undiluted Habermas – can also be the author who finishes "Overcoming Epistemology" by informing us that he is planting himself on Habermassian "terrain." As I will argue in Chapter 7, on this question of what a genuinely post-positivist self-understanding *in philosophy* entails, Putnam's writings offer a bit more help.

For the moment, however, I offer this preliminary conclusion. The most illuminating way to read those post-positivists who move the PIH question from epistemic reform to root questioning is the same way I have suggested reading

---

52 " ... [I]n the communicative practice of everyday life," says Habermas, "in which cognitive explanations, moral expectations, expressions and evaluations interpenetrate, [their] unity is in a certain way *always already established*" ["A Reply to My Critics" in *Habermas: Critical Debates*, ed. John B. Thompson and David Held (Cambridge, MA: MIT Press, 1982), 250, author's emphasis]. Yet it is just such "formal pragmatic" *assertions* that Taylor, following Heidegger and Merleau-Ponty, wants to question first. Should we be satisfied, e.g., with this "transcendental pragmatic" procedure of first arranging human practice by type of "attitude" and correlated "domain of reality" – and in a way that *first* confidently carries forward the traditional classification of human phenomena into matters of cognition, will, and feeling and *then* raises the issue of the "unity of reason" that seems forced on us by this very schema (243–50)? On precisely the issue of whether transcendental reflection might be from the beginning (in Habermas' terms) "interest-laden" and thus itself something (in Taylor's terms) in need of prior self-understanding, Habermas replied that he will some day "have to come back to that question" (233).

53 Taylor thus has similar objections to a whole range of ethical positions that simply "begin" with the acceptance of everything from common, or intuitive, "evaluation terms" to Rawlsian "thin theories of the good" – views he calls "the ethics of inarticulacy" (*Sources of the Self*, 53–90).

Comte. Instead of reconstructing their "positions" from the outside (and thus precisely in accord with the epistemological model) and then tabulating what is discontinuous and continuous with tradition in their statements, it would be better to ask from what standpoint they are "already" trying to speak when they themselves express their "lived transition" from an inherited and constraining positivism to an analytic philosophy that has "climbed out of this error." Especially from their own efforts at self-understanding, when they try to deal with the tensions they sense in their own writings, we may learn how to consider the often unarticulated issues discussed previously. Think, for example, of Rorty's struggles to portray his pragmatism as neither self-justifying nor merely a choice: It is the right outlook for us, he says, because of the things that *"really matter,* relative to my community"; but he has never managed to gain much clarity about the italicized phrase. Think, also, of Taylor's response to this, especially his analysis of what is wrong with the various contemporary efforts to say something from "between" the old epistemic and a new anticipated (sometimes called by him, "hermeneutical") articulation of philosophy's proper outlook. Strictly speaking, however, neither Rorty (to a greater extent) nor Taylor (to a lesser one) is finally able to *be* where he wants to be; and that is because both of them, to some extent, still think with an epistemological imagery that in the end only permits them to *contemplate* reinstalling themselves in that circle of practices where they somehow *understand* they already are.

As opposed to Taylor's neo-Nietzscheans, the real Nietzsche, with his apparently strange grammar, may have had it right. Let us suppose that the purpose of philosophical self-understanding is, as he says, to *"Become who you are."*[54] It would be worse than useless to criticize his "statement" because "Logic" warns us that it confuses two tenses. To really hear what "Become what you are" says, we would have to listen from within a self-understanding that recognizes that, in Nietzsche's words, "existence is a fundamentally imperfect tense than can never become a perfect one."[55] Were we able to hear this, our resulting post-positivist credo might run: Having *already been* Cartesians, we struggle to *become* what we experience that inheritance as *currently* forbidding us to *be.* Thus, *past, future, present –* in just the right Comtean, "philosophical" and not "chronological," order.

---

54 See, e.g., Alexander Nehamas, *Nietzsche: Life as Literature* (Cambridge, MA: Harvard University Press, 1985), esp. Ch. 6, which is entitled "How One Becomes What One Is," 170–99.
55 Friedrich Nietzsche, "The Uses and Disadvantages of History for Life," *Untimely Meditations,* trans. R. J. Hollingdale (Cambridge: Cambridge University Press, 1983), 61. It is no accident that all the post-positivists who get this far have sooner or later gotten around to focusing upon "existential" matters – i.e., sociopolitical rather than (or rather than just) epistemic-ontological or logico-linguistic ones. We are now rightly suspicious of Comte's assumption that intellectual reform comes "before" sociopolitical; yet his insistence that the two are inseparable – all the more so when one thinks they are not – is surely right. In this study, I have tried to further the discussion of post-positivism by rethinking Comte on epistemic themes. Perhaps another study could do the same for sociopolitical themes, but I confess to not believing that Comte is in this regard worth the trouble.

7

COMTE FOR TOMORROW?

What kind of help, then, can Comte offer those post-positivists who have pursued the PIH question far enough to challenge not only the received conceptions of epistemic issues and their ontological implications but also the old understanding of the orientation from which these issues and implications should be "analyzed"? How can the historico-critical Comte help post-positivists work out a specifically *philosophical* stepping back to avoid further oscillation between the boring alternatives of positivism and historicism that Putnam sees as otherwise threatening to remain our lot? The answer, I think, depends on abandoning altogether the idea that such a historically minded stepping back would involve primarily either *opposing* or *avoiding* those old alternatives. For like both positivism and historicism, a post-positivism that contemplates philosophy literally "after" these two options is bound to get just as unreflectively caught up in an ahistorical orientation, and therefore to be just as unable to profit from rethinking Comte, as those options themselves.

1. Opposing positivism and historicism

To stop thinking of oneself as an opponent of positivism, however, is not easy. Even those who have taken the PIH question most seriously are rarely as eloquent about what ought to be the "next stage" in philosophy as they are about what it must not be. Rorty's pragmatism, for example, is much more clearly defined in its "antirepresentationalism" than it is as a vehicle for (re)new(ed) questioning of "what sort of human being you want to become." Indeed, even when he enlists the aid of Continental sources to articulate this latter question, he typically focuses upon what these sources, too, have *against* the modern philosophical outlook.[1] Similarly, Taylor's antinaturalist arguments and his criticisms of the Epistemological standpoint are strikingly less elusive than his vision of the new philosophical outlook to be ushered in by a transformed "tradition of self-critical reason."[2]

Yet what other possibilities are there in these transitional philosophical times? If we now see that there is something fundamentally unsatisfactory about being a positivist, representationalist, naturalist – or, in general, about continuing to follow out the Cartesian epistemological imperative – should we think with envy about, say, the situation of Socrates and try to recreate his *pre*-epistemological mood? Should we try to recapture an orientation in which, like Socrates, we would experience no *need* to be epistemological? Inheriting what we inherit now, should we use his example to fulfill the dream of simply *getting over* that need in ourselves? Perhaps it is only because we have been looking back at Socrates through several centuries of obsession with fixing the conditions of reason in advance that his dialogical naturalness has seemed somewhat unstructured and naive. If so, might we not purchase our new lease on philosophical life, and avail ourselves again of something like the Socratic outlook, by simply ridding the contemporary scene of the epistemological imperative that presently still distorts that outlook and stands in our way?

But none of this will do. There is serious, though perhaps not obvious, presentism in these questions. It is true that Socrates does "not yet" speak out of an understanding of himself as a third person detached from his own activities. He does not yet distrust the prephilosophical conditions of his thinking the way Descartes has taught us to do; and he certainly would have rejected the idea that he could improve his practice by reconstructing the procedural rules or the conditions of possibility for dialogical inquiry. Yet it is one thing to acknowledge all this – that is, to notice that for Socrates there never is a logico-linguistically conceptualized Method "plus" a socio-historically describable Context in which it would be employed. It would be quite another thing to romanticize his premodern situation into something like a philosophical Eden of unaffected, spontaneous conversations.

Observed with today's discontentedly epistemological eye, Socratic elenchus

---

1 One partial exception is Rorty's attempt to use the first half of Heidegger's *Being and Time* to sketch a pragmatist strategy for resolving or dissolving large chunks of analytic philosophy's traditional problem set. I have argued elsewhere, however, that this strategy is still largely conceived from the same philosophically detached and ahistorical viewpoint that is supposedly being surpassed. See "Rorty and Analytic Heideggerian Epistemology – and Heidegger," *Man and World* 25 (1992), 483–504.

2 For another example of clear anti-positivism and problematic post-positivism, cf. Hacking's concluding (n.b., not opening) self-description of his "anarcho-rationalism" as a "tolerance for other people [and their "styles of reasoning"] combined with the discipline of one's own standards of truth and reason" ("Styles of Scientific Reasoning," in *Post-Analytic Philosophy*, 164). Such tolerance does not appear to stimulate in Hacking the historico-critical reflectiveness about "one's own" standpoint that it does in Comte; hence, among the questions not asked are "Who is doing the combining?", "How is that process to be understood?", and "From what (synthesizing but not "imperial") vantage point?"

can indeed look like a wonderfully pure practice. Yet from this romanticized angle, we get at best a picture of Socratic practice as something that *is not thought* in terms of method and outcome. This picture utterly fails to illuminate what this practice actually *is*, which is not to be thought epistemologically and which nevertheless can somehow lead an inquirer to understand better how to live. It is a picture, that is, that utterly fails to make Socratic inquiry real and really available to us. To accomplish that, our picture would have to "historically redescribe" how his practice *is thinkable* by a lover of wisdom. During his trial, Socrates depicts the results of all his inquiries as having been cumulative. At this point, he thinks of them as enabling him now to "give an account" – that is, a philosophical (though not methodologically guided) self-description – of the difference between engaging in dialogical and sophistical inquiry. In other words, this cumulative result comprises for him a current, determinate condition of "what he has come to understand" of everything important in life. It is, at this time, his philosophical "having been." At the same time, however, Socrates insists that this understanding is always a "human" one – that is, that its forever incomplete and incompletely articulated character necessitates a willingness, at any given moment, to put it all to the test again in light of yet another interlocutor's claims and questions. In short, Socrates reports actually *doing* philosophy from within an orientation that, as Taylor says, takes "the inarticulate [and unsatisfactorily articulated] as somehow primary." And redescribing something like *that*, I think, might move us toward a genuinely post-positivist – and not merely anti-epistemological – orientation.

Twenty years ago, it would have been pointless to make this suggestion in Anglo-American circles. Such a redescription of Socratic practice would still have been mostly condemned as unsatisfactory in one of two directions. Either it would have seemed to represent an abdication of the philosopher's primary job: Where, in my account, is there any analysis of what Socrates "means" by dialogue and of "the sort of thing" he is really doing?[3] Or it would have seemed a mere capitulation to sheer historicism (relativism): After all, is it not obvious that recounting Socratic inquiry in narrative/contextualizing rather than analytic/epistemic terms simply obscures whatever logico-linguistic importance the practice might still have by reducing it to its "merely" sociohistorical particulars?

In this concluding chapter, I decline the chance to say anything further about

---

3 See, e.g., Gerasimos Xenophon Santas, *Socrates: Philosophy in Plato's Early Dialogues* (London: Routledge and Kegan Paul, 1979). Santas "concentrate[s] on the topics in which . . . I could make some progress, using contemporary techniques of analysis and scholarship" (xi–xii) and spends nearly half of the book analyzing the logico-linguistic structure of Socrates' "arguments" and "definitions." He expresses amazement that Socrates himself "did not seem to realize that none of his presuppositions" deserved to be "taken for granted" (96), and although he can find only nine trivial "examples of the sorts of definitions he wants" and "correct definitions he uses as premises" (98), Santas insists that the presence of these nine definitions "corrects" the otherwise "not unreasonable impression" that "it is impossible to give a definition that will satisfy Socrates" (100). His book is in "The Arguments of the Philosophers" series, whose editor promises emphasis on "the contentions and doctrines of the philosopher in question."

the first sort of objection. I trust that I have already made the portrait of a Socrates who was, alas, epistemologically silent seem anachronistic enough and that, at this point, one is either willing to reconsider him in light of post-positivist root questioning or not. As regards the second response, however, something further needs to be said. It is certainly true that the label "historicism" no longer functions today to enforce a majority's tyranny. Contextualizing accounts of philosophical inquiry may be controversial, but one can assume that they will get a hearing. Yet my redescription of Socrates has a special point. I want to show that there is profit in seeing *why* – even if we harbor the most radically post-positivistic intentions – we should not look on his pre-epistemological condition with envy or think of ourselves as weighted down by our epistemological past in a way Socrates happily was not. Radical post-positivism cannot move itself past Epistemology by trying to become Socrates' contemporary. To clarify this suggestion, I want to say a bit more – this time with some references to Putnam – concerning the way our skittishness about historicism might still undo our post-positivist intentions just as easily as any continuing resistance to root questioning.

2. Avoiding positivism and historicism (Putnam)

For my purposes, Putnam's treatment of analytic philosophy's present situation is especially suggestive in two ways. First, he takes the issues of historicism and positivism with *equal* seriousness. Too often, he argues, the specter of the former has been raised so quickly that it has kept us not only from seeing any truth in relativism but also from facing squarely some still influential aspects of positivism. Second, Putnam looks on historicism and positivism primarily as a twin *inheritance*, not as positions to analyze.[4] Calling them "boring" alternatives already hints at this. Of course, says Putnam, we can treat them simply as alternative "theories"; but if that were all they are, then given so many famous cognitive difficulties, one supposes that they would by now have been refuted. The reason they have not, he argues, is that historicism and positivism are also alternative "ideologies." By this he means that they also operate (or purport to operate) as

---

4 In what follows, I ignore the question of whether Putnam's retrospective portrait of positivism vs. historicism as it figures *in* contemporary philosophical deliberations could also serve as a narrative of the implicit context of understanding of this tension *before* the rise of analytic philosophy. Michael Rosen, I think, makes a good case that it could not, that after Hegel and before Frege and Russell's turn toward "concerns in logic and mathematics seen more narrowly," the tension was seen less linguistically and more metaphysically. Thus today, in our "world of 'language games' and 'radical translation' historicist questions have come to be transformed; they are now questions about the arbitrariness (or otherwise) of linguistic practice and interpretation rather than about the matrix through which the mind encounters the world" ["Modernism and the Two Traditions in Philosophy," in *Wissenschaft und Subjektivität: Der Wiener Kreis und die Philosophie des 20. Jahrhunderts/Science and Subjectivity: The Vienna Circle and 20th Century Philosophy*, eds. David Bell and Wilhelm Vossenkuhl (Berlin: Akademie, 1992), 279–81]. Rosen notes also that some analytic philosophers (e.g., John McDowell) would argue that Putnam's account exaggerates the degree to which a heightened twentieth-century concern for logic and language removes us from the older battles between "direct realism" and some form of Kantianism (281n.41).

"integrated views," that is, very deeply held, always somewhat implicit, more or less global understandings of the real and the rational – what Putnam sometimes follows Wittgenstein in calling "pictures."[5] Pictures in this sense are "at the root of all one's thinking" – "lived" pictures, we might label them – so that one should say that

> what is wrong is not that pictures are bad, but that certain pictures are bad – that there are pictures that should not "grip" one ... because they are not the sort of pictures which could be at the *root* of all one's thinking.[6]

According to Putnam, the ideologies of positivism and historicism are thus to be understood as actually being bad pictures, that is, "heroic attempts to do the impossible" – deeply influential modernist dreams of "reducing epistemic notions to non-epistemic ones" by explaining rationality either "syntactically" (in positivism) or "anthropologically" (in historicism).

Given this understanding of ideologies as inheritances, Putnam emphatically does not recommend confronting them polemically by arguing anti-relativist or anti-positivist theories.[7] For even if one agrees intellectually that historicism and positivism are over as modernist dreams, this is not to say that there is not *something* to each of them – and thus something deeply held that will not yield to a polemical thesis, no matter how well argued. In philosophy's (post-positivist) "next stage," therefore, the proper approach to historicism and positivism will have to be both appropriative and critical. On the one hand, we must learn to "accept" that "a certain duality in our ideology" is bound to remain – by finding new ways to acknowledge that both the "scientific" and the "historical" are genuinely "weighty" matters, in Wittgenstein's sense. On the other hand, "instead of continuing to breathe life into [two] failed intellectual positions," we must find less "grandiose" ways to accept their genuine insights.[8]

---

5 In Putnam's recent work, he even asks that he no longer be thought of as offering or criticizing "theories," "models," or "positions" at all in order to avoid the impression that he still thinks according to the old analytic model of philosophy-by-thesis/counterthesis. The request figures prominently in the collection of essays mostly written since 1990, *Words and Life* (Cambridge, MA: Harvard University Press, 1994), which appeared only after the present study was finished; but much of his work from the 1980s (especially when the topic is James, Wittgenstein, or Cavell) already conveys this idea – as, e.g., when he concludes that Bernard Williams' "*Ethics and the Limits of Philosophy* is...not a serious argument for ethical 'non-objectivism,' but rather the expression of a mood" (RP, 107); or when he says that "relativism and skepticism are all too easily refutable when they are stated as positions; but they never die, because the attitude of alienation from the world and from the community is not just a theory, and cannot be overcome by purely intellectual argument" (RP, 178).
6 "Wittgenstein on Religious Belief," RP, 156–57, author's emphasis; cf. "Wittgenstein on Reference and Relativism," where Putnam registers his agreement that ultimately, "our language game rests not on proof or on Reason but *trust*" (RP, 177).
7 Margolis is thus wrong to represent Putnam as never getting further than the attempt to *avoid* historicism (*The Flux of History*, 194–96).
8 "Beyond Historicism," RR, 290. In what follows, I rely especially on the way Putnam develops this point in "Beyond Historicism." Most of his other discussions of this twin inheritance either contrast positivism with "relativism" (see fn. 12) or offer critiques of pairs of contemporaries he thinks are still to some extent victims of this inheritance (e.g., Bernard Williams vs. Derrida in "Irrealism and Deconstruction," RP, esp. 108, 123). Readers should also be aware at the outset (I say more about

Certainly Putnam's recommendation puts him squarely in the root-questioning post-positivist camp: Rejecting positivism and historicism as inherited ideologies, he says, involves salvaging something from them as a joint legacy. It is only our lingering modernism, says Putnam, that "finds this thought hard to bear."[9] The problem, I want to suggest, is that in spite of his own best intentions, the deconstructive and constructive portions of Putnam's strategy often do not fit well together. Perhaps most significantly, it is precisely to the extent that he frames his critique of positivism and historicism in terms of *avoiding (bad) ideologies* that he tends in fact to subvert his efforts to transform what is left. I discuss the nature of this subversion in the next section; but first, we must see how Putnam understands avoidance.

Regarding the notion of ideology itself, as I have already noted, Putnam employs it in arguments against the widespread belief that positivism and historicism are basically "positions" that have been defended, criticized, and are now largely "refuted." Yet he does not think this belief is just stupid. Crucial aspects of both positivism and historicism are so easily interpreted as self-refuting theses that this alone can seem to render their pictures bad.

Regarding positivism, there are the Logical Empiricists' notorious problems with the verifiability theory; and in the (perfectly understandable) line of reasoning analytic philosophers have taken against the theory, it has been assumed that in dealing with this issue, they were also dealing with positivism as such. First, it became too obvious to be denied that the theory is open neither to empirical test nor to mathematical demonstration. Yet it was eventually agreed that rather than merely refuting a principle, this insight had shown that the criterion of verifiability is "actually a *proposal*" rather than a theory, and so is in no need of being either true or false. Finally, however, with the apparent heart of the positivist position thus explicated and loosened into a proposal, this general proposal itself came to seem, by contemporary lights, too narrow and scientistic for the whole of epistemology; hence, a kind of satisfied consensus grew that, philosophically speaking, positivism had now been simply "turned aside."[10]

Regarding historicism, says Putnam, it seems possible to be briefer because what is allegedly wrong with it is easier to state. The general tendency has been to think that because one can quickly show an obvious logical incoherence in any "assertion" of total relativism, this alone already makes the worthlessness of every variation on the same theme – and thus the worthlessness of the theme itself – obvious. Putnam likes to illustrate this line of reasoning by citing the witti-

---

this later) that I am putting Putnam's discussion to a use he himself does not emphasize and, in the end, might very well resist.

9 "Beyond Historicism," RR, 290; and "Wittgenstein on Reference and Relativism," RP, 177–78. On the idea that, in general, "the phenomenon called 'analytical philosophy' is best understood as part of the larger phenomenon of modernism," see "Convention: A Theme in Philosophy," RR, 179–83.

10 For Putnam's interpretation of Logical Empiricism as both a bad ideology and an enduring legacy, one should now consult the four essays in *Words and Life*, 85–148.

cism about the relativist who says, "I know where you're coming from, but, you know, Relativism isn't *true-for-me*."[11]

Yet it is just here, Putnam argues, that one should recognize the deeper problem. Neither a quick conclusion about the incoherence of total relativism nor an ultimate consensus about the epistemic narrowness of the positivist proposal can explain why the obvious correctness of these claims has not made positivism and historicism go away. To accomplish this greater purpose, he says, we must show that in addition to their containing the materials for formulating self-refuting "theories," positivism and historicism are themselves – and in an importantly different, deeper, and therefore less easily spotted sense – both self-refuting "ideologies."[12] So long as we remain satisfied with surface polemics against one or the other of their refutable theories, their ideological presence in and destructive effect on our thinking will fail to be appreciated, and we will continue to find ourselves stumbling over positivist and historicist themes in our analytic practice in spite of our conclusion that the positions themselves have "clearly" become dead letters.

The details of Putnam's arguments that each ideology is self-refuting need not detain us here. In general, the problem is that both receive their inspiration from something seemingly obvious in human life but then proceed to use it to construct an ideal picture of everything real and rational. Thus, positivists try to work out a syntactically formulated global defense of reason's "objectivity" modeled on the success of predictive (natural) scientific theorizing. Similarly, historicists try to debunk the very idea of objectivity by radically amplifying the observation that all concepts of rationality vary historically (as well as culturally, socially, and psychologically). What is generally missed, Putnam argues, is precisely that both of these globalizing moves are really attempts at philosophical "reduction"; and in the end, for him, the most revealing symptom of their twin impossibility is that if one places their efforts against the background of our sense of "total human flourishing" and *then* tries to follow positivism's effort to "explain" objectivity, the result is always "nonsense." And again, similarly, if one tries to emulate historicism's equally ambitious "denials" of objectivity, the result is always "self-defeating irrationalism."[13] Slightly rephrased, we might say that positivism and historicism as ideologies both tend to undermine in reductive *principle* the otherwise evident, but also always imperfect, reasonableness found in *life*.[14]

In "Beyond Historicism," Putnam devotes much less space to the reductive legacy of historicism and much more to that of positivism. There is, for example, a long discussion of how so-called ontological alternatives to syntactical reduc-

---

11 The saying is attributed to Alan Garfinkel and appears in both RR, 288, and RP, 89.
12 "Beyond Historicism," RR, 288–90; and the fuller discussion of relativism and "ideology" in relation to Foucault, RTH, 155–66.
13 "Beyond Historicism," RR, 290, 301.
14 Cf., "Why Is a Philosopher?" IOP, 61–63 [RHF, 105–107]. One should read the title of Putnam's *Words and Life* in this spirit.

tion proposed by some naturalists are just as self-defeating, but there is no criticism of historicism beyond the point already mentioned about its having one big obvious problem. Yet one should not be misled by this uneven treatment. It is not a sign that Putnam really believes that positivism is philosophically more significant. In part, of course, because his essay represents the effort of a contemporary thinker in the analytic tradition to come terms with a primarily empiricist–positivist inheritance, one can expect greater detail concerning issues with which his ties are most intimate. Moreover, Putnam thinks that for his tradition, it is primarily as a specter and not as a set of substantive issues that historicism seems the greatest threat; and he mentions in passing that he is thus of necessity "fascinated by the *different* ways in which relativism is incoherent or self-contradictory" and thereby poses a variety of threats in association with different analytic controversies.[15]

Perhaps the clearest evidence that Putnam means to take positivism and historicism equally seriously, however, is shown by what he tries to make of their post-positivist significance after unmasking their self-refuting structures as ideologies. In the last few pages of "Beyond Historicism," he reconsiders both ideologies, with a display of Taylor-like redescriptive sensitivity, regarding the matter of continuity-through-transformation. On the one hand and more to be expected, Putnam argues that for any "successful science of epistemology" of the future, it will still make sense to admit that there is *something* to the old idea of a grand "epistemological synthesis." Paralleling Taylor's reluctantly Habermassian nod in favor of continuing the talk about "conditions" of self-clarity, Putnam gives cautious permission to continue the quasi-positivist idea that there are at least "*informally* systematic" things to say about truth, reference, belief, desire, and so on.[16] Yet on the other hand and less to be expected, Putnam also displays redescriptive sensitivity toward historicism. For all his lingering sympathy regarding informal systematics, it is finally no greater than his insistence that "if there is anything we *have* learned from historicism, it is that there is no external place, no Archimedean point, from which we can do" successful epistemology or anything else philosophical.[17]

What is of primary interest about this for my purposes is that the historicism Putnam thus continues by transformation, he attributes as much to Comte as to Hegel.[18] This association, which he simply takes for granted, is my cue, first (in the remainder of this section), to link up the historico-critical Comte with Put-

---

15 RR, 288. The fascination is cashed out in, e.g., "Materialism and Relativism," RP, 67–79; RTH, 119–24 and 151–62; "Why Reason Can't Be Naturalized," RR, 234–38; "Realism with a Human Face," RHF, 18–29; and in numerous discussions in *Words and Life*.
16 "Beyond Historicism," RR, 301–302. In "Philosophers and Human Understanding," one finds Putnam "suggesting [as] a good title for a philosophy book: 'An essay concerning human understanding.' Seriously, human understanding *is* the problem, and philosophers *should* try to produce essays and not scientific theories" (RR, 199).
17 "Beyond Historicism," RR, 302.
18 Thus, he calls historicism a "Hegelian idea" for chronological reasons; Comte comes slightly later than Hegel but "seems to have arrived at his ideas alone" (287). In his 1993 August Comte Lec-

nam's post-positivist arguments against Archimedean points and, second (in the next section), to suggest how Putnam fails to take these arguments sufficiently to heart.

As the example of Charlton's 1991 textbook suggests, in the hands of someone who has no taste for root questioning, a methodologically pluralistic and "doctrinally" tolerant idea of analytic philosophy can still easily be the vehicle for recasting the same old imperial spirit in a new and temporarily more satisfying form.[19] Concerning the hollowness of this sort of satisfaction, there would be *in general* no disagreement between the historico-critical Comte and Rorty, Taylor, and Putnam. All would agree that the loudest proclamations of the impossibility of achieving Cartesian self-possession in philosophy can be issued by someone who still speaks as if from precisely the sort of standpoint that is being proclaimed unreachable. Comte himself, of course, often failed to live up to the anti-imperialist ideal his critical history implicitly promotes. Similarly, even root-questioning post-positivists are often haunted by unobvious versions of the Archimedean illusion – as, for example, when Rorty suggests the lawyer as the "most appropriate model" for the post-positivist philosopher and Taylor feels constrained to "choose" between neo-Nietzschean and Habermassian orientations, as if they exhausted the possibilities. In their more reflective and historically sensitive moments, however, they all see such models of philosophy-above-the-fray for what they are, namely, ideal projections of a supposedly ahistorical orientation that are always anything but ahistorical.

If one wants to consider the *differences* among these (at their best) historico-critical thinkers, however, a good question to ask is how they would have philosophy avoid the Archimedean illusion. At one point, the PIH editors remark that the appearance of a dichotomy between mere history and real philosophy is one "*created* by the attempt to be sententious about 'the nature of history' or 'the nature of philosophy' or both, treating 'history' and 'philosophy' as names of natural kinds." But is this really so? Is today's lingering hostility to philosophy's past really a product of (reducible to?) something so easily isolated as sententiousness about or excessive allegiance to the idea of natural kinds? If this were so, then Putnam's suggestion, in "Why Is a Philosopher?" – namely, that we simply "*declare* a moratorium on Epistemology and Ontology" – should by itself be enough

---

ture at the London School of Economics, Putnam begins with a quick, approving (and, I think, accurate) summary of Comte's approach to science, his fundamentally sociopolitical aims, and his anticipation of Rorty's pragmatist understanding of why such controversies as "*metaphysical* realism/idealism" should be put behind us ("The Question of Realism," *Words and Life*, 295–97); but he also says that, like Rorty, Comte would tend to base his case for this last point "on a mere induction from the history of philosophy" (296). That, I think, is precisely what my historico-critical Comte would not do – because inductions are performed by observers of life, not by someone engaged in self-understanding.

19 My favorite earlier version of imperial analytic detachment is G. J. Warnock's loving portrait of the real philosopher as one whose "eye is characteristically cold and his pen...employed as an instrument of deflation" [*English Philosophy since 1900* (London: Oxford University Press, 1958), 173].

to stop the hostility and undo the caricatures. For after all, the many efforts to establish "the One Method by which all beliefs can be appraised," like the many companion efforts "to describe the Furniture of the Universe and to tell us what is Really There and what is Only a Human Projection," have clearly all been miserable failures.[20] If these efforts really did rest on nothing deeper than a mistaken confidence in some objectivist or ahistorical "strategy," and if that strategy is now a widely recognized "disaster," one might expect that by this time both objectivism itself and its attendant strategies would have simply been repudiated and any lingering expressions of pigheadedness about all of this would have become a source of embarrassment.

How clearly Putnam himself sees this issue is, as I will argue in the next section, open to question. His actual analyses of reductive ideologies, however, offer especially incisive, root-questioning reminders that "Epistemology" and "Ontology" are precisely not just twentieth-century idiosyncrasies but are expressive of twin modern traditions that still live in us in ways that declaring moratoria against them cannot change. As a post-positivist himself, Putnam may already be convinced that Epistemology and Ontology attempt to go "beyond the bounds of any notion of explanation that we have." For everyone from Mill to Reichenbach, however, there is this obvious reply: "*Of course* our project goes beyond such bounds; it is philosophy's job to do better than actual reasoners; and that is precisely why we rationally reconstruct." The problem is, no one will agree to declare a moratorium on Epistemologizing and Ontologizing because of past failures so long as these activities are still understood to be "the kind of thing philosophers do." Putnam is therefore much closer to the mark when he emphasizes not past failures themselves but the fact that these are somehow connected with a growing sense that *"the time has come"* to stop pursuing that old goal. This phrase points away from the surface observation of the failures to the root question of *how we could know now* to take the past failures of Epistemologically and Ontologically inspired "philosophical analysis" as a signal to stop rather than as an incentive to try harder. What is it about the urge to *be* sententious, to *be* more drawn to logic and physics than to poetry and history, that now seems to necessitate the "rearticulation" of analysis itself? Why is it that a particular sort of "caricaturing" – for example, of philosophy/history and argument/narrative – now seems especially problematic, and yet especially elusive, whenever our sense of its unsatisfactoriness becomes impossible to ignore or suppress?

Putnam gets closer to this issue than most, then, because his root questioning begins with the realization that Logical Empiricism and radical historicism are

---

20 RHF, 118 [IOP, 73]. Thus, for Putnam, the thaw in attitudes concerning metaphysics that has come with the decline of Logical Empiricism is not an encouraging development. "As Dewey pointed out," he says, "the metaphysics of previous epochs had a *vital connection to the culture* of those epochs....[but] contemporary analytic metaphysics has *no connections with anything but the 'intuitions'* of a handful of philosophers. It lacks what Wittgenstein called 'weight'" ("A Reconstruction of Deweyan Democracy," RP, 197, my emphasis).

simply very late expressions of the empiricist–positivist and rationalist–idealist strains of our Cartesian legacy that, *as paired traditions,* have continued to shadow each other. Given his empiricist–positivist roots, he is understandably more concerned to grapple in detail with his inheritance of the tradition that predominates for him – that is, the one that has fostered the "great rejection of everything 'traditional.'"[21] What is crucial, however, is that he not only avoids the assumption that this dominant legacy is his only one, he explicitly denies that this is so. Indeed, he reports thinking that *both* positivism and historicism are "beginning to look very tired," and he does so *from within the current analytic situation.* Historicism, in contrast to the dominant positivism, may seem at first to be merely the "other" tradition, the one "they" have on the Continent. Yet Putnam insists on acknowledging its presence *as an analytic legacy,* and precisely in the condition of nondominant other. As a result, he portrays himself as being caught in a "boring" oscillation *between* the two; and it is this self-understanding that makes his "diagnosis of the situation" more promising that most.

Where others are still tempted to see analytic philosophy as only post-*positivist* – because historicism seems as if it has always been too obviously self-refuting for "us" to have ever taken it seriously – Putnam insists that nothing less than the effort to abandon an inherited *pair* of Grand Synthesizing ideologies will stop the Anglo-American tendency to meet every failed analytic strategy with the assumption that some Really Objective analysis lies just ahead. Here, I think, is the post-positivistically crucial feature of Putnam's argument. Rather than simply urging us to continue the search for positivist or historicist beliefs, theses, or assumptions still lingering in analytic practice, he insists that what makes the old inheritance so powerful is our retention of its general "picture" of philosophical practice as *everywhere required* to think about whatever matters as if it did not matter to it. Until we understand *how we still live ("trust") this Objective picture,* the "specter" of philosophy ever daring to settle for less will always seem (unhappily for some, "ironically" for others) a betrayal of its mission.

Viewed from Putnam's angle, then, the reason the caricatures of avoiding-mere-history/doing-real-philosophy continue to be *our* caricatures is not sententiousness or fondness for natural kinds. It is rather that so far, analytic philosophers have mostly tried to avoid this forced option by cycles of "piecemeal" revision. Summarily put, a cycle is pictured as follows. (a) Some new strategy is introduced that is touted as the one that is at last going to make analysis, at least of *this* problem area, objective, neutral, unbiased, or in general, logico-linguistically satisfactory. (b) In its satisfactoriness, the new strategy seems at first somehow immune to the sort of historicist-relativist attack that, although always obviously self-defeating, nevertheless tends to haunt any strategy whose objectivity, neutrality, lack of bias, and so on, come under question. (c) Yet gradually, the new strategy begins to seem a little less than completely satisfactory, its immunity to

---

21 "Beyond Historicism," RR, 303. See also "Why Reason Can't Be Naturalized," RR, 234–38.

historicist attack thus a little less secure, and variations on the strategy are tried. For each variation, the cycle of (a)–(c) is repeated; with each cycle, the stakes get higher; sententiousness about the strategy gets displayed and becomes stronger, until finally, the original strategy seems too full of liabilities to save. At this point, it is subjected to transformation or replacement, and the whole cycle begins again for a new strategy.

Putnam says that by 1981, he realized that it is *this whole cyclical process* that is endless and endlessly boring – and not because the right strategies remain to be found but because each cycle of "strategic revision/rising suspicions about its promised objectivity/further revision" in fact repeats the same tired pattern of reconstructive "explanation" followed by relativist "denial" of rationality that, *as a pattern*, he had already rejected "in principle" for being the mere oscillation between two mutually reinforcing ideologies of Grand Synthesis. For Putnam, then, if Anglo-American philosophy is going to move to its "next stage," post-positivist discomfort over business as usual will have to be rearticulated as a recognition that all the multiply and serially revisionist analyses sanctioned by someone like Hospers or Charlton or even Rorty (when he speaks of analysts being like lawyers, kibitzers, or private ironists) are in the end just microcosmic repetitions of the one inherited modern macrocosm of "explanatory nonsense" versus "irrationalist denial."

Here, as one might put it, is Putnam's globalization of Wittgenstein's idea of philosophical therapy. We must *understand,* Putnam says, "what makes *us* want to distance ourselves from *our own* language game." The choice of terms is telling. It is not a question of justifying this tendency "reflexively" or "metalinguistically" – that is, *from the same Cartesian standpoint* that operates in the phases of each cycle themselves. Rather, it is a matter of discovering the roots of this repeating positivist/historicist cycling *in ourselves,* so that the spell can be broken. The whole current situation will come to be understood, Putnam explains,

> if we see relativism [historicism, skepticism] not as a cure or a relief from the malady of 'lacking a metaphysical foundation,' but rather see relativism *and the desire for a metaphysical foundation* as manifestations of the same disease.[22]

Putnam argues here for a bit of Taylor-like self-understanding. Once this philosophical "disease" has been diagnosed as one from which we ourselves suffer, the twin ideologies of positivism and historicism that now hang like a threatening black cloud over every new strategic-analytic suggestion can be de-absolutized (i.e., continued through transformation). From each of them, in Putnam's view, something heretofore considered only in an oppressively exaggerated form may now be rearticulated as advice worth taking. It will, for example, seem appropriate to say both "informally systematic" and "topic relative" things about truth, reference, desire, and so on without feeling threatened by the idea that the for-

---

22 "Wittgenstein on Reference and Relativism," RP, 177, emphasis altered.

mer phrase is insufficiently synthetic or the latter already too relativist – because neither systematization nor contextualization will any longer be assumed to express the mutually exclusive global imperatives of Logical Synthesis and Total Relativism.

3. Transforming positivism and historicism

All of this is not to say, however, that once we move from the merely moderately historical PIH editors to the post-ideological Putnam, we obtain the picture of a thoroughly unproblematic and "transformed" post-positivist philosophy. For when Putnam tries to tell us what the transformations of positivism and historicism might yet be useful *for* instead of just what they enable us to *preserve*, his decisive equalization of the "weightiness" of positivism and historicism – the very feature of his self-description that makes his outlook seem so much less narrowly Anglo-American and Epistemological than, say, Charlton's textbook or even Rorty's in "Philosophy in America" – sometimes begins to weaken. Thus, to take "Beyond Historicism" again, after capping off his ideology critique with a few transformative suggestions, Putnam finishes by asking what will keep the "piecemeal" practices of analysis together in the future if it can no longer be an ideology. I return here to the full passage cited only partially in Chapter 5, in which Putnam confesses that everything he has said about positivism and historicism as positions, as ideologies, and even as transformable legacies seems to him "not enough" to get philosophical analysis past its experience of boring oscillation. "The problem" with our present circumstance, he laments,

> is this. Analytic philosophy claimed to be a piece-meal philosophy. It gave up, or said it gave up, the dream of an integrated view, which is so characteristic of what people refer to as continental philosophy. This *was always* somewhat of a pretense. The logical positivists had very much an integrated view, and Quine has very much an integrated view. The "motor" of analytic philosophy was logical positivism . . . not because all analytic philosophers were positivists, but because the arguments pro-and-con positivism were what kept analytic philosophy in motion. Analytic philosophy has already begun to lose shape as a tendency with *the disappearance of a strong ideological current at its center*. The desire for integration is so central to philosophy, I think, than no philosophical tendency will long endure without it. On the other hand, every attempt at integration which has been too grand has collapsed. The incoherence of the attempts to turn the world views of either physics or history into secular theologies . . . is, I hope, well underway. As philosophers, we seem *caught between our desire for integration and our recognition of the difficulty*. I don't know what the solution to this tension will look like. . . . [23]

For my purposes, the crucial feature to notice in reading these concluding remarks is the way they appear to manifest a gradual alteration of "mood" in Putnam's own sense. One may see him, I think, as passing through three philosophi-

---

23 "Beyond Historicism," RR, 303, my emphasis. Cf. "Convention: A Theme in Philosophy," RR, 179–83; and "After Empiricism," RHF, 51–53.

cal attitudes (see the italicized phrases) as he moves away from the topic of *past* ideologizing, through his recognition of analytic philosophy's *present* uncomfortable situation, toward his final consideration of its post-ideological *future*. And with every alteration, he becomes less radically post-positivist.

First, and so long as he is still concerned with carrying forward the basic theme of his essay, Putnam's mood seems fundamentally retrospective, redescriptive, and sensitive to the two traditions in our legacy, and there is not yet any sign of the "problem" he will raise in another few lines. His opening topic is simply current practices in relation to old rationales; and he seems to see the continuities among these practices, even with the removal of traditional epistemic imagery, as still somehow guaranteed by the very structure of the previous discussion. Thus "ideological" continuity, Putnam says, "was always . . . a pretense"; yet even with this pretense unmasked, a legitimate continuity remains. For as he has just finished suggesting, the themes of total system and "the" cultural context – already ours by inheritance but up to now extravagantly misunderstood and reductively employed – may be more sensibly redescribed and passed through to analytic practice in the transformed and domesticated form of informal systematization and topic relativity.

By the time of the second italicized phrase, however, Putnam speaks as if he is starting to forget the very "truth" he has just insisted must be retained from historicism. Recall that the lesson of Hegel and Comte is not that, alas, there has never *been* an Archimedean starting point but rather that, in principle, there can never *be* one. Hence, to view analytic philosophy as having had a "shape" and as now "losing" it – that is, to imagine that, once upon a time, its practices actually got whatever "integrity" they had from a positivist ideology, so that with the "disappearance" of this ideology the whole analytic movement now threatens to fly into disparate fragments – is itself to succumb to ideological thinking. (One recalls the panic of an earlier day that "the foundations of mathematics are crumbling.") This is the kind of thinking Putnam himself has elsewhere exposed as typical of a mind that confuses objectivity (or universality, or warrant, or whatever) with Objectivity (or Universality, or Warrant, or Whatever) – so that finding (or prescribing) these characteristics in any area and on any topic is always necessarily a matter of finding (or prescribing) the Same Thing. This mistake, as Putnam puts it three years later, is a function of an inherited penchant for construing any interest in, say, objectivity as really being

> not a craving for objectivity but a craving for absolutes . . . and a [relativist] tendency which is inseparable from that craving, [viz.,] the tendency to think that if the absolute is unobtainable, then "anything goes." But . . . [a] craving for absolutes leads to monism, and monism is a bad outlook in every area of human life.[24]

---

24 "The Craving for Objectivity," RHF, 131. The philosopher Putnam frequently thinks of in this connection is Bernard Williams (130). See his discussion of Williams' *Ethics and the Limits of Philosophy* (Cambridge: Cambridge University Press, 1985) in "Bernard Williams and the Absolute Conception of the World," RP, 80–107; and in "Objectivity and the Science/Ethics Distinction," RHF, 163–78.

Speaking now as an ideology critic about what should stop, Putnam shifts away from what he recognizes in most of "Beyond Historicism" and what he still recognized a few lines before, namely, that today's analytic philosophers should be "brought back" directly and without grand-synthetic worries to the "areas of human life" themselves.

In the final lines of "Beyond Historicism," this forgetfulness about Hegel and Comte's lesson (that there simply *is* no Objective viewpoint) leads to still more serious backsliding. The teaching of the essay as a whole has been that to understand the "truths" of transformed positivism and historicism is to know that grand syntheses are delusions but that a postideological "desire for ["informal" sorts of] integration" is nevertheless legitimate. After Putnam's focus narrows back down in midpassage to one of interring bad ideologies, however, these truths begin to look again like "positions" locked in a conflict he cannot "solve." Perhaps it is true, he says as his original transformational mood fails him, that positivism was just one more abortive "secular theology" – specifically, a "subjective preference for certain language forms (scientific ones) or certain goals (prediction)."[25] Yet if all secular theologies are dead or dying, he wonders, what is going to hold today's piece-meal philosophical activities together? In this closing mood, Putnam "doesn't know what the solution will look like," but he is sure that there must be one.

Let me be clear about the point of these remarks. I do not think there are (or have at various times been) three Putnams; and it would constitute a misunderstanding to object that I should have tried harder to integrate Putnam's statements – to see them as involving various emphases in one mood rather than as expressing three different moods. I am interested in the fact that with Putnam, as with Comte, there is a certain tension *in his writings* between a genuinely historico-critical impulse and a lingering Cartesian inheritance. Whatever self-description Putnam might give of it, this tension (and even its specific forms) is in fact widely shared by those contemporary analytic philosophers expressing reformist views. I think, however, that "Beyond Historicism" – for *most* but not *all* of its way – is especially suggestive of a historico-critical standpoint from which a kind of post-positivism can be developed that would actually put the old boring alternatives behind it. It is in this spirit that I present the author of this essay – my "first Putnam," Putnam at his best – as someone who, unlike many others proclaiming post-positivist sympathies, knows better than to be *anti*-ideological (as is the "second" Putnam) because that can only lead to more cycles in the same familiar game – but now with the additional worry (as with my "third" Putnam) about what will hold analytic philosophy together after the ideologies are gone. Putnam

---

25 "Beyond Historicism," RR, 288. In his "Preface" to *Renewing Philosophy* (1992), he reaffirms his sense that this preference still describes "the present situation in [analytic] philosophy as a whole" (ix). In this context, recall Comte's claim that his positivists might still pursue the old idea of grand synthesis, but only with the understanding that their efforts are "subjective," never "objective," and always "humanly," never "theologico-metaphysically," significant (e.g., CPP6, 645–50; DEP, 24–25 [37–41]; SPP1, 443–50 [359–65]).

at his best, however, appears to understand that when ideological positivism and historicism have really been displaced by a (Taylor-like) recognition that there is (only) "some truth" to our old ideas about the "need for integration" and the fact of rational and cosmological "disunity," there is simply nothing left for a Grand Synthesis to protect against Total Disunity.[26]

By contrast, most post-positivism appears to remain fundamentally anti-ideological – in the way exemplified by moderates like the PIH editors, by my second Putnam, and also even by Rorty to a perhaps greater degree than he knows. The problem is that "disengaging" from ideology, *if* it were possible at all, could only be accomplished from the same imperial standpoint as its "defense." Put more precisely, an anti-ideological thought, just as much as an ideological one, "assumes that one can stand *within* one's language and *outside* it at the same time."[27] Putnam's phrasing here is just right. However "opponents" of positivism describe themselves, they will tend to think and develop their views as if they were *former insiders* – that is, those who were once on intimate terms with positivist, historicist, representationalist, metaphysical, or analytic positions, schools, or movements, but who now *know* (from where?) that all of this deserves to be "over." For such ex-insiders, reasoning proceeds along the following lines – and backslides toward "worries" such as those represented by my third Putnam. First, if positivism is basically an outgrown ideology (subjective theology, grand theory, totalizing metanarrative), that is, something like a very complex but dated "background knowledge," then our task obviously is to identify, explicate, and remove it. This decision, however, involves an unsettling consequence. If the "pieces" of analytic practice have so far been held together ("pro-and-con") by this ideology, then precisely the idea of being a *post*-positivist philosopher creates a dilemma about the "integration" of these pieces. For not only does a decision to abandon positivism deprive them of their "unifying ideology," but the very act of "deciding" to abandon it simultaneously discloses the futility of accepting any *other* "position" with the old Epistemological/Ontological seriousness; for whatever this position might be, it too would of course be just another "choice."

The Putnam who wrote the bulk of "Beyond Historicism," however, has in principle no such dilemma. For he understands positivism as he understands its supposed opposite – that is, not as cognitive positions available as options to pure minds that may embrace or refute them, but as recent articulations of a larger and longer modern inheritance that is already inescapably being "lived" by us

---

26 In a complimentary (though not wholly uncritical) essay on "James' Theory of Perception," Putnam joins him in the thought that "there are ways of looking at the world in which it is a unity and [others]...in which it is a disunity; but...the pragmatist temperament favors, stresses, sees as of primary importance the disunities, the pluralities" (RHF, 234).

27 "Realism with a Human Face," RHF, 23. In a vein that (as we will see later) foreshadows his critique of Rorty, Putnam goes on to say that with ideologies (e.g., here, specifically, metaphysical realism), this paradox can go unnoticed for a while, "since the whole content of [e.g.,] Realism lies in the claim that it makes sense to think of a God's-Eye View (or, better, of a 'View from Nowhere')," whereas in the case of relativistic anti-ideologies, the assumption "constitutes a self-refutation."

more fully that it can be objectively thought. He is uninterested, then, in rejecting or replacing positivism; instead, as he puts it elsewhere, he simply wants to "bring us back" from this misguided battle over positions to our ordinary world where, he says, "claims of reasonableness and unreasonableness" are actually being made and where positivist "misrepresentations" are still operating. Occasionally, Putnam characterizes the standpoint for this post-positivist inquiry as having "a less distanced attitude from the lifeworld" – that is, the attitude that might remain for analytic philosophy after all attempts to "divide mundane reality, the reality of the Lebenswelt, into Real Reality and [Human] Projection" have "collapsed."[28] From this orientation, life appears as a "manifest image" – neither possessing nor awaiting the discovery of any Objective (monistic, transcendental, absolute-conceptual) Unity; hence even if the old "bad outlook" were to disappear completely, this would be no more a threat to the "piecemeal analysis" of life than it is to the "areas" of life analyzed. To the objection that this kind of attitude toward the "mundane" always makes philosophy too enamored of subjective difference and too little impressed by objective uniformity, Putnam replies that "it is only the weird notions of 'subjectivity' and 'objectivity' that we have acquired from Ontology and Epistemology that make us unfit to dwell in the common."[29]

According to some of Putnam's own descriptions, post-positivists with this attitude would be *neither* forced to choose between the ideologies of positivism and historicism *nor* worried about their replacement. In fact, they would not feel called on to make any global "choices" at all. Instead, says Putnam, they would see today a "third possibility," namely, a self-understanding of analytic philosophy's present situation that allows them

> to accept the position we are fated to occupy in any case, the position of beings who cannot have a view of the world that does not reflect our interests and values, but who are, for all that, committed to regarding some views of the world . . . as better than others. This may mean giving up a certain metaphysical picture of objectivity, but it does not mean giving up the idea that there are . . . objective resolutions to problems which are *situated* in a place, at a time, as opposed to an "absolute" answer to "perspective-independent" questions.[30]

And this, says the Putnam who is not anti-ideologically sliding back toward What Happens to Piecemeal Analysis When Ideology Is Gone? and who is therefore still speaking as a historically "situated" thinker, is "objectivity enough."

---

28 Combined quotation from "After Empiricism" and "Is the Causal Structure of the Physical Itself Something Physical?" RHF, 52–53 and 90. The English term, "lifeworld," is in this instance actually quoted with approval from Stanley Cavell; but in works of the 1980s – which emphasize "conceptual relativity" instead of "model-theoretic arguments against metaphysical realism" (RHF, x–xi) – Husserl's term, *"Lebenswelt,"* is employed untranslated in several places where Putnam wants to say what it is that philosophy starts with (e.g., RHF, 50, 118).
29 "Why Is a Philosopher?" 118 [IOP, 73].
30 "Objectivity and the Science/Ethics Distinction," RHF, 178, author's emphasis. Since the late 1980s, Putnam has increasingly identified the post-positivism that would know how to speak *from* this "situated" place/time as a species of (non-Rortyean) pragmatism. See, e.g., the four essays in Part III of *Words and Life*, 151–241; and his *Pragmatism: An Open Question* (Oxford: Basil Blackwell, 1995).

To put my point another way, it is this historically situated Putnam who can find both images of post-positivism offered in *Philosophy and the Mirror of Nature* equally unacceptable. There Rorty presents us with a forced option between (a) the sort of analytic practice that is really only a series of creative reinterpretations of epistemology that, "after Quine and Sellars," tries somehow to preserve philosophy's traditional role of "cultural overseer," and (b) Rorty's own brand of "hermeneutics."[31] Rorty himself must rule out (a) because, as we know, he thinks the post-positivist moral of the modern story is that epistemology and its whole cluster of representationalist topics and problems should just be dropped. The alternative, he argues here, is to see that "the conversation of the West," far from requiring an epistemological ground, is itself the only possible "foundation" (if one must still call it that) for knowledge. In *Philosophy and the Mirror of Nature*, post-positivists must both be antifoundationalist and be content to engage in "unspecialized" intellectual analysis – a "hermeneutic" practice characterized here as that of "the informed dilettante, the polypragmatic, Socratic intermediary between various discourses."[32]

Putnam acknowledges that Rorty's idea of Western culture as philosophy's foundationless foundation, when read together with Putnam's own allegation that other alleged post-positivists have remained closet Epistemologists, has led to his work's being compared with Rorty's. Yet what is missed, says Putnam, is that my reasons for declaring a moratorium on the further pursuit of the God's-Eye View, far from bringing me closer to Rorty, actually increase the distance between us. In a nutshell, Putnam thinks that Rorty's option (b) is just as much conceived from a fundamentally ahistorical standpoint as any species of option (a). In one recent (1988) essay, Putnam depicts this implicit ahistoricism as leading Rorty indirectly to foster a conception of philosophy that makes it *both* intellectually more ambitious *and* culturally less responsible than it should be.[33] A summary of Putnam's arguments on these two points can both clarify further his idea of

---

31 PMN, 315–56. As many have observed, Rorty promotes here a thoroughly Anglicized version of the Continental practice. See, e.g., John D. Caputo, "The Thought of Being and the Conversation of Mankind: The Case of Heidegger and Rorty," *Review of Metaphysics* 36 (1983), 661–85; Jeff Mitscherling, "Resuming the Dialogue," in *Anti-Foundationalism and Practical Reasoning: Conversations between Hermeneutics and Analysis*, ed. Evan Simpson (Edmonton, Alberta: Academic Printing and Publishing, 1987), esp. 125–30; and Fred R. Dallmayr, "Conversation, Discourse, and Politics," in *Polis and Praxis: Exercises in Contemporary Political Theory* (Cambridge, MA: MIT Press, 1984), 192–223.

32 PMN, 315–18. Cf. his critique of Cavell's *The Claim of Reason* (Oxford: Oxford University Press, 1979) as being two books – one (Parts I and II) that, alas, tries to explain how important "epistemology" has been and the other (Parts III and IV) that, happily, drops this old project in favor of transporting us from this dying project to questions of our mortality and of the experience of the contingency of everything. To Rorty, both the trouble with and the interesting thing about Cavell is that whereas usually "Anglo-Americans try to deromanticize the Continental tradition by showing that it has some good arguments...[he] tries to romanticize our own tradition by showing that it does not" ("Cavell on Skepticism," COP, 183). One should note carefully the relatively greater impatience Rorty displays here with historico-critical discussion in accusing Cavell of having wasted his time getting to what "we" can still find interesting.

33 "Realism with a Human Face (1988)," RHF, 20–25. Cf. "Why Reason Can't Be Naturalized (1981)," RR, 235–38. One difference between this second essay and the first one is that even

a "situated" post-positivism and shed some light on his own lingering difficulties with Epistemology. On the basis of this summary, too, I will be able to make some final comments concerning how Putnam, Taylor, and my redescribed Comte might help us to actually *become* the historico-critically situated post-positivists that our boredom with positivist and historicist alternatives tells us we already "inarticulately" *are*.

4. Becoming the "situated" post-positivists . . .

On the first objection, that Rorty appears to have excessive intellectual ambitions, Putnam argues that when Rorty says the end of the Epistemological search for foundations is just as important to the general culture as it is to professional analysts, this is strong evidence of Rorty's wanting to retain for himself a "gigantic seriousness" about being a philosopher that is just as excessive as that of any of his villainous Cartesian/Kantian "overseers."[34] For in presuming to speak not only against classical analysis but for the sake of ordinary life, Rorty appears to accept the old picture of philosophy according to which it "was not a reflection *on* culture, a reflection some of whose ambitious projects failed, but a *basis* . . . on which the culture rested." In other words, it is as if, now that he is equipped with a new and properly critical version of that model, Rorty still "hopes to be a doctor to the modern soul." In another place, Putnam puts this point somewhat differently and speculatively, accusing Rorty of being implicitly committed to, as one might phrase it, a gigantic kind of "local" seriousness:

> It is true that Rorty rejects the idea of an "absolute conception of the world" – but if it were made clear to Rorty that the conception in question is "absolute" *only from our local perspective*, would he still feel it necessary to reject it? Could it be that, even if they do not recognize it, Rorty and Williams are in complete agreement in metaphysics?[35]

In other words, Rorty appears to exemplify the possibility that post-positivism might end by producing pluralized, culturally isolated versions of Epistemology/Ontology.

On Putnam's second point, concerning the real cultural importance of philos-

---

where the criticisms are substantially the same, Putnam's tone is more tentative. He mentions in passing how "fruitful" it is to play his ideas off against Rorty's (RHF, 19), how he would like to "provoke" him into indicating where they agree (RHF, 21), and how he only "thinks" he is right about the picture of Rorty's relativism that he "risks" putting forward (RHF, 24). The later paper is not, however, indicative of any permanent shift in tone toward Rorty's reasoning. Cf. Putnam's discussion in "Materialism and Relativism," RP, 67–71; and "The Question of Realism" in *Words and Life*, 297–312. Since my interest in what follows is to sharpen my picture of Putnam's own post-positivism, I ignore these refinements and treat simply as arguments what he calls his "risks" in 1988.

34 With the exception of the passage cited at in fn. 33, all quotations in this paragraph and the next one are from "Realism with a Human Face," RHF, 20.
35 "Bernard Williams and the Absolute Conception of the World," RP, 104, author's emphasis.

ophy, he argues that Rorty's tendency to speak of an outright rejection of Epistemology, though in one respect at least giving the appearance of expressing a gigantic philosophical seriousness, actually has the effect of leaving today's philosophers with less of the sort of responsibility they genuinely can have. To simply "abandon," for example, the realist–antirealist and cognitivist–emotivist controversies once they are seen as cognitively "futile" is to ignore the fact that these "rival pictures" still carry enormous "practical and spiritual weight." As Putnam puts it, when Rorty speaks in scornful, "Carnapian" tones about these controversies – when he says with such finality, "That's a pseudo-issue" – he encourages contemporary philosophy to be satisfied with a purely conceptual overcoming of these rival pictures and thus to ignore the possibility that "philosophical reflection may be of some real cultural value" in exposing the way these pictures continue to "misrepresent the lives we live with our concepts."

To Putnam, then, whatever are Rorty's intentions, his allegedly radical post-positivist attitude seems actually to be a particularly "aggressive form of the metaphysical disease itself." In his dismissive treatment of what everyone should get over, Rorty sounds the same militantly (if now negatively) Epistemological note as the positivists themselves. Yet this is, of course, precisely the attitude Rorty has "decided" to leave behind; hence there appears to be something deeply paradoxical about Rorty's neo-pragmatism.[36] He seems torn between actively taking a stand Epistemologically against the old analytic problem set and insisting that he is too thoroughly Post-Epistemological to "advocate" any such thing. Actually, says Putnam, I suspect that

> most of the time anyway, Rorty really thinks that [say] metaphysical realism is *wrong*. . . . but this, of course, is something he cannot admit he really thinks. I think, in short, that the attempt to say that *from a God's-Eye View there is no God's-Eye View* is still there, under all that [pragmatist] wrapping.[37]

At present, I am less concerned with the fairness of this criticism than with Putnam's own solution to the problem it raises. *If* we were to find our own post-positivism afflicted by this paradox, how should we proceed? Putnam's answer – at least the answer that, in my view, the first Putnam is committed to giving – is that

---

36 In "What Is at Stake Between Putnam and Rorty?" [*Philosophy and Phenomenological Research* 52 (1992), 585–603], Paul D. Forster carefully recounts the central elements in Rorty's neo-pragmatism and argues that Putnam's objection (that this pragmatism boils down to a self-refuting irrationalism) is unfairly based on the idea that Rorty is offering "theories" or "criteria" that can then be shown he mistakenly affirms or denies (599–602). In what follows, I assume, on the contrary, that Putnam's interpretation is intended to identify an outlook that, in spite of all his affirmations, denials, and deferrals [e.g., "I refuse to be either an Epistemologist or a Relativist because these are flip sides of the old Cartesian coin"], Rorty is finally unable to avoid – viz., a Cartesian understanding of his philosophizing that prompts him to veer continually in an unwanted direction. For reasons already given in my tale of the three Putnams, I do not feel obliged to consider whether my interpretation is too generous.

37 "Realism with a Human Face," RHF, 25. "Rorty's present 'position' is not so much a position as the illusion or mirage of a position" (ix).

one must cultivate *in oneself* that sense of being historically (and presently also unhappily) contextualized that Rorty succeeds in demanding only *of others*. I admit that this historico-critical self-understanding, even when present in Putnam's writings, is more often spoken from than about; yet it involves, I think, this clearly promising idea for us to pursue: We must understand – and without irony – that the very distinction between "philosophical analysis" and our ordinary "knowing, doing, and desiring according to norms and standards" is *part of life*. It is, in other words, not a distinction between some sort of detached reflection *and* ordinary practices but a distinction between the reflective and operative dimensions *of* those practices themselves – a distinction that always occurs *within* a socioculturally determinate "situation" and that is therefore *always equally possessed of their "historicity."*[38]

This view is not, as I will explain in a moment, as Relativistic as it sounds; but first, let us note that it does in fact figure crucially in Putnam's reading of Rorty. For it is precisely because he thinks of the philosophical process of "adjusting and reforming" norms and standards (here called "reconstructive reflection") as itself part of life that he claims that neither of Rorty's options in *Philosophy and the Mirror of Nature* (and their later variations) make any genuinely post-positivist sense. Both "epistemology reconstituted after Quine" and Rorty's alternative of "just switching" to hermeneutics (or unspecialized analysis, kibitzing, neo-pragmatism, or whatever), Putnam argues, are laid out as options in that same self-assured tone as the old utopian dream of a "total and unique Reconstruction." Rorty is clearly right that advocates of epistemology after Quine never get Hegel's and Comte's message; but according to Putnam, it is just as obvious that Rorty's neo-pragmatists only appear to do so. It may seem perfectly harmless for Rorty to speak of the continuation of philosophical analysis "as a philosophical tendency" in terms of a weakly Reichenbachian concept of lawyerly method/style, or to perpetuate the idea of cultural consensus in the name of hermeneutics, pragmatic facilitation, or ironic liberalism. Yet in Putnam's eyes, these ideas in fact repeat, in initially hard to detect new forms, the old ideological alternatives. As we have already noted, for example, Putnam worries that the notion of cultural consensus, *when recommended with Rorty's attitude*, encourages "local absolutism." To take just one more example, he also thinks that Rorty's notion of "style" tends to cycle (pro-and-con) between an understanding of "philosophical analysis" so strong that it echoes the old prejudice of physics-over-poetry/argument-over-narrative and a redescription of "thinking" so weak that it makes every style equally welcome and thus, if it tries to be more than equal, equally "silly."[39]

---

38 I follow here especially Putnam's discussion of his "third and fifth principles concerning warranted belief and assertion" (not to be taken metaphysically) in "Realism with a Human Face," RHF, 23–27, which I ultimately quote later (fn. 40); but cf. RP, 177–79, 197–200. As I will explain in the next section, however, this explication is also somewhat *more* than he says.

39 "Why Reason Can't Be Naturalized," RR, 235–36; and, RTH, 216.

In the end, Putnam sees Rorty as, in spite of himself, "advocating" post-positivism in a kind of negative version of the old Epistemological attitude; and since this tends to make him uncompromisingly *against* positions, it repeatedly pushes him in the direction of "self-refutation." Yet Putnam is aware, too, that if Rorty is actually reduced to someone with self-refuting theses, this opens the door to what we might call a "neo-Epistemological backlash." By this, I mean that it sets conditions for a reaction in which the figure of "Rorty" is employed to justify Anglo-American business as usual – a "revised" business as usual, of course, with up-to-date opposition to positivism and broad-minded tolerance of the PIH question (though only for the purpose of epistemic revision), but a business still pursued with the same old self-assurance that if "analysis" is sufficiently pluralized, no other sort of philosophy is worth exploring. In Putnam's own best view, therefore, post-positivism really only begins once the God's-Eye View is neither accepted, rejected, nor silently reenacted in modified form, but is instead understood as *always having been an illusion*.

It is because Putnam so often speaks as if he understands matters this way that I want to credit him with also understanding what it implies about our "philosophical situation," namely, that the historicity of our efforts to reform our norms and standards is just as much "a fact of life" as the historicity of those norms and standards themselves. This, as far as I know, he never asserts in so many words; but what he does claim presupposes it. According to Putnam, there is only one way to face without Epistemologico-Relativistic fanfare *both* that "we *do* change our norms and standards" *and* that "doing so is often an *improvement*" – and that is to understand why, when we ask, "An improvement judged from where?" the right reply is, "From within *our* picture of the world, of course."[40] As we have seen, if one makes this reply while still thinking as if from Nowhere, it simply leads back to self-refutation:

ASSERTION: I know there are many cultures. Each has its norms. So does the one I to which I belong. And I (we) claim . . .
RESPONSE: But according to this assertion, all your claims are by definition both merely cultural and supposedly transcendental; hence, your assertion is self-refuting.

Putnam's point is that this boring pro-and-con exchange will continue to recycle until philosophy "returns" to common life without it. For only then will it be possible to understand nonideologically, that is,

> from within [our] picture itself, [that] *we* say that "better" isn't the same as "*we* think it's better." And if my "cultural peers" don't agree with me, sometimes I *still* say "better (or "worse"). There are times when . . . I "rest on myself as my own foundation."[41]

---

40 "Realism with a Human Face," RHF, 26.
41 RHF, 26. Putnam's quotation in the last line is from Cavell's *The Claim of Reason*, 125.

In short, we must understand that to "reconstructively reflect" is simply to join, "from within," our ongoing process of "normative readjustment and reform" – and understand, moreover, that this is enough. Of course, says Putnam, we post-positivists will continue to achieve what we can – namely, "to have insights and to construct distinctions and follow out arguments and all the rest" – but we will do these things without imagining we must also settle, now and forever, "what there is left for philosophy to do."[42]

Pronouncements such as these, appearing frequently in Putnam's recent writings, actually do seem to express the sort of "broad [post-ideological] attitude" he says must be assumed if the specific issues in current analytic philosophy are going to get handled in nonboring ways. Moreover, with every successive rethinking of these issues, he engages in historico-critical self-revisions so extensive that he is sometimes accused of trying to keep himself a moving target who is impossible to hit squarely. There is thus good reason to suppose, I think, that Putnam has to some extent found a way to practice "continuity through transformation" in his own work.[43]

Yet there is one potentially important result that his adoption of this broad, self-critical attitude in numerous *particular cases* has not produced. It has not led Putnam to self-criticism of his tendency to backslide toward God's-Eye View language when he speaks *in general* about analytic philosophy's current situation. Thus, one often finds Putnam explaining why he has abandoned this or that position – or, more recently, why he has given up positions for pictures – but on the general question of what it is to think post-positivistically, backsliding self-descriptions continue to appear and remain uncriticized. As we have seen, "Beyond Historicism" still ends with the specter of our whole inherited ensemble of analytic topics and problems, once "integrated" by a subjective or ideological "preference," now threatened by its "disappearance." And to name three more examples: (a) In "Why Is a Philosopher?" Putnam recommends "perhaps not putting away the grand projects of Metaphysics and Epistemology for good ... but *only for now*" – -even though the very idea of bringing them back can make no sense to a "situated" thinker. (b) In the "Preface" to *Realism with a Human Face*, he distinguishes a form of "verificationism" he rejects from one he still accepts on the grounds that the former expresses science worship and the latter James' generous and open-minded pragmatism.[44] In several articles, he considers examples of

---

42 "Why Is a Philosopher?" RHF, 118 [IOF, 73].
43 Asked recently by Josh Harlan about his work habits, Putnam replied that for him the benefit of self-criticism derives from the fact that "I am *always* dissatisfied with something or other about what I have previously written, and locating that something, and trying to think why I am dissatisfied and what to do about it, often sets the agenda for my next piece of work" ["Hilary Putnam: On Mind, Meaning, and Reality," *Harvard Review of Philosophy* 2 (1992), 24]. His remark is not, I am inclined to believe, as pedestrian as it may seem. How many other post-positivists would describe their own self-criticism so thoroughly from *within* – i.e., in terms of "locating and thinking out" something presently "dissatisfying" for them about their previous writing – and pass up completely the chance to mention how this writing now measures up when "one" applies some "norms and standards" *to* it?
44 RHF, viii–ix; see also *Pragmatism*, 10–12, 68–74.

James at work and explains what James means by verification; but he never discusses the issue of how *being Jamesian permits him to understand,* for example, the crucial difference between an acceptable and an unacceptable form of verification. (c) In "Realism with a Human Face," in the same place where Putnam argues that situated philosophizing is not a chosen replacement for the God's-Eye view but simply what is left to us when we "return" to the lifeworld that is ours in any case, he also speaks of having "my foundation" for philosophical judgments. Yet how could "my" situatedness ever be converted (from where? by whom?) into something I could wield "foundationally" in "disagreements" with "cultural peers" – as if there were a place from which some outlook so well formed and explicitly comprehensible as "our cultural picture" or "image of the world" might actually be identified by "me"?

None of these examples, of course, lead to knock-down arguments. All of them stress one, backsliding strain of reasoning at the expense of a more progressive strain. Each of them, however, raises an obvious issue for the Putnam who claims to be, respectively, post-ideological, over Epistemologico-Metaphysical delusions, neo-pragmatist (but not in Reichenbach's or Rorty's sense), and beyond cultural relativism. In one recent effort to stress the distance between his post-positivism and the old alternatives, Putnam concludes that

> at its best, philosophical reflection can give us an unexpectedly honest and clear look at our own situation, not a "view from nowhere" but a view through the eyes of one or another wise, flawed, deeply individual human being.[45]

This remark fairly bristles with ideas warranting reflective reconstruction. What makes reflection [only?] sometimes seem "unexpectedly" honest? [Is this like Nietzsche's writing "untimely" essays?] What sort of "wisdom" is this [Socratic?], and how does one acquire it [if not dialogically]? And are those who have remained modernists "unwise"?

How are we to understand Putnam's silence both concerning post-positivist "wisdom" and about those of his self-descriptions which seem clearly to perpetuate "unwise" notions held over from our "disastrous" traditional adventure? More important, how might philosophical "continuity-through-transformation" be done better? How, in other words, might one promote the idea of *becoming* a historically situated post-positivist by clarifying further why we already *are* bored with the old alternatives? Here, I think, is where my redescribed Comte can be of some contemporary help.

5. ... we ("inarticulately") already are

To state my conclusion at once, I think what Putnam calls the orientation "from within our culture" that "we are fated to occupy in any case" is not only the outlook toward which root-questioning post-positivists are slowly working; it is also

---

[45] "Wittgenstein on Reference and Relativism," RP, 178.

the outlook often historico-critically defended in principle but imperially betrayed in fact by Comte. In Comte's case, I have argued that his double-sidedness shows him to be *not yet* unhistorical enough as a positivist to abandon the idea of an encultured standpoint but *already* too Cartesian to avoid continually falling away from that idea. The contemporary relevance of this point is that, regarding the same two factors of historico-critical reflection and Cartesianism, Putnam since the early 1980s seems to have worked himself into a position where he has something like Comte's problem with the chronology reversed. For he is *already* historico-critical enough to insist that analytic practice should start from "within" our situation, but also apparently *not yet* post-Cartesian enough to be completely "situated" there himself.

To see the point another way, contrast Putnam with Taylor. On the one hand, to a somewhat greater extent than Taylor, Putnam appears to *have* enough self-understanding of "lifeworld truth" so that in his philosophical practice, he addresses numerous particular issues about norms and standards without initiating yet another boring cycle of strategic revision/relativist denial. On the other hand, to a discernibly lesser extent than Taylor, Putnam seems reluctant to capitalize on this self-understanding to *explicitly consider* the more general question of the character of the philosophical "attitude" that makes his practice possible.[46] Indeed, sometimes he even gives the impression of believing that one must avoid thinking very much in this generalizing direction at all. Hence, on numerous occasions, in many specific contexts, he uncovers yet another instance where the ideal of the God's-Eye View, or the dream of an Archimedean vantage point, or "the metaphysical picture of objectivity" still secretly reigns. Each time he argues that these tired old images should be exorcised from current analytic practices; and each time he explains why removing these Cartesian ghosts does not condemn the remaining practice to relativism.[47] Yet when Putnam steps back from

---

46 I have obviously neglected here at least one other figure who clearly belongs in the company of Taylor and Putnam, viz., MacIntyre. In part, this is because the primarily ethical–sociopolitical focus of MacIntyre's writings dating from *After Virtue* – which are exactly the works I would want to include in a discussion of root questioning among post-positivists – makes him a difficult fit in relation to the more epistemologically focused writings of those I have been treating. [But see, e.g., his discussion of "Adam Gifford's Project" in *Three Rival Versions of Moral Inquiry: Encyclopedia, Genealogy, and Tradition* (Notre Dame, IN: University of Notre Dame Press, 1990), 9–31; and "Epistemological Crises, Dramatic Narrative, and the Philosophy of Science," *Monist* 60 (1977), 453–72.] In addition, however, I see a more troublesome difference. To put the matter briefly and unfairly, it seems to me that MacIntyre experiences contemporary analytic philosophy's basic problem as one of everywhere confronting "incommensurable frameworks," one of which is his own, whereas Rorty, Taylor, and Putnam see themselves instead as starting from an experience of being entangled in a dying Epistemologico–Metaphysical outlook that is broadly enough conceived to encompass all of MacIntyre's "frameworks." There is, I think, no question that both experiences move philosophy in the direction of genuinely post-positivist and root-questioning inquiry; indeed, I agree with Borradori's "new cartography," which depicts many strands in the "post-analytical recomposition" of mainstream Anglo-American philosophy (*The American Philosopher*, 1–25; see also fn. 48). Given the differences I have identified, however, a separate case for MacIntyre's inclusion would first have to be made, and this is an additional burden I did not want to assign to the present study.

these episodes of criticism to tell us something about the philosophical standpoint he takes while engaged in them – that is, as soon as he starts *to reflect on the sort of post-positivist he has become* – he tends to grow curiously self-conscious and reticent, and even seems worried that he might just be responding to a discredited traditional expectation. I am aware, he says, that when I do not really offer a general explanation for my views,

> my failure to give any metaphysical story at all, or to explain even the possibility of [especially nonscientific] reference, truth, warrant, value, and the rest, often evokes the question: "But then, why aren't you a relativist too?" I can sympathize with the question . . . because I can sympathize with the urge to *know*, to *have* a totalistic explanation which includes the thinker in the act of discovering the totalistic explanation in the totality of what it explains. I am not saying this urge is "optional," or that it is the product of events in the sixteenth century, or that it rests on a false presupposition because there aren't really such things as truth, warrant, or value. But I am saying that the project of providing such an explanation has failed.[48]

But this is a completely unsatisfactory gloss – one, in fact, that cannot be squared with Putnam's own statements elsewhere. Why must all treatments of the question "What is it to give explanations of reference, truth, warrant, value, and the rest?" be defined in advance as "metaphysical," just because Epistemological answers to that question have in fact taken this form? Why not apply Putnam's "companions in guilt argument" *reflectively* here? Post-positivists understand that users of both images – that is, both the notion of an "urge" to construct a totalizing defense against relativism and the counter-notion of "sympathetic" resistance to making *any* such defense – play together in the same "metaphysical" field. Why, then, should either image dominate our general effort to monitor our post-positivist practice, since metaphysics is (to use Putnam's phrase for its scientific version) a "we-know-not-what"?

Actually, the materials for self-criticism can be found in Putnam's own writings. In many places, he is uncompromisingly deflationary in his treatment of the metaphysical urge – repeatedly dismissing it as just the basically Cartesian wish for a "totalistic explanation which [would somehow] include the thinker." Yet in other places, for example, in "Why Is a Philosopher?" he speaks in conciliatory tones. The metaphysical urge, he says, is not merely an "option," and it does not

---

47 Beginning in RTH, one of Putnam's favorite strategies is what he refers to as the "companions in guilt" argument ("Why Is a Philosopher?" RHF, 116–17). Stated quickly, the strategy is to disqualify any accusation of relativism against those defending nonscientific (or, more generally, less than ahistorical) construals of, e.g., justification, reasonableness, or value – if it can be shown that the accusation is lodged from the safety of some species of the (now discredited) Epistemological standpoint. Cf. Rorty's ironical version of this strategy in *Contingency, Irony, and Solidarity*, viz., to "make the vocabulary in which [anti-relativist] objections are phrased look bad, thereby changing the subject, rather than granting the objector his choice of weapons and terrain by meeting his criticisms head-on" (44). Putnam, of course, would object to the "Carnapian" aloofness of Rorty's suggestion that we attack "vocabularies" as if that could settle the existential matters they reflect.

48 "Why Is a Philosopher?" RHF, 117, author's emphasis.

just originate in sixteenth-century epistemology. "What human pressure could be more worthy of respect than the pressure to [totally] *know*?" How can he take both tacks? If the metaphysical urge really were a sort of Ur-tendency in our drive to "know" rather than something Cartesian, datable, and finally "illegitimate," then it would be pointless to take "Beyond Historicism" seriously. For there, Putnam tells us that giving in to this urge can lead *only* to nonsense or irrationalism, and he tries to undermine whatever respectability it might still have by making it the source of a disastrous "ideological" inheritance from which we may at most salvage the very untotalizing idea of "informal system," so long as we also jettison the rest as delusion.

In short, whenever Putnam responds to questions about his own philosophical outlook by refusing to tell a "metaphysical story," this is a clear case of empiricist–positivist backsliding. The old urge to think "against" his inheritance prevents him from speaking "as" a post-positivist, and he tends to revert to the standpoint of an Epistemologically cautious "subject." It is, to be sure, a negatively Cartesian subject, that is, one that resolves *not to be ahistorical;* but it is nonetheless a mind that thinks so much like its positive counterpart that it is unable to consider *being historically situated* in any other way but as a feature of an "object" (thesis, position, principle) that it must refuse to "explain."

I do not mean, of course, that when Putnam gets preoccupied in this way, he slides all the way back into the company of those moderate post-positivists who, like the PIH editors, are satisfied to recommend epistemic pluralism plus a little humility about programmatic "choices." For one thing, though he refuses to give a metaphysical story about his outlook, he does give self-critical accounts of his development, of his "influences," and of theories/positions/pictures he has retained or abandoned. He has, moreover, written numerous pieces explaining what seems admirable to him in the philosophizing of others (e.g., Wittgenstein and James). Yet there is a problem here, and it runs deeper than his occasionally falling for Epistemologically loaded images.

As noted earlier, Putnam has (at least so far) given no sustained attention to the question of what genuinely post-positivist philosophers – that is, ones who really *are* past caring about the old boring options – understand about their present situation.[49] His treatment of James and Wittgenstein typically focuses on what they do better than others, not on how he is like them. His self-criticisms are primarily about the specifics of what he has discarded or presently accepts, not

---

49 Cryptic remarks continue to appear, however – as, e.g., in "The Question of Realism," where Putnam makes "reflection on just what it is that makes thinkers like Rorty doubt the very idea of representing the world...[a] *part of understanding ourselves*, and not just part of understanding certain sophisticated and influential thinkers" (*Words and Life*, 309; my emphasis). In the same passage, Putnam also claims that both Rorty and Comte would regard such reflection as "pointless," but argues that by "understanding the temptations and seductions that Rorty and Comte share [viz., in taking, respectively, "playful" and "stern" anti-metaphysical stances toward there being even a "kernel of truth" in realism]...we can *live with* those temptations and seductions without succumbing to them...[or] pretending that the world is either just a playpen or *just* a scientific laboratory"

about the outlook he needed to acquire in order to make these moves. And none of the suggestive remarks about post-positivist self-understanding I cited in the previous section have been followed up: What sort of maneuver *is* historically "stepping back" for the sake of a better diagnosis of our present philosophical situation? What follows from recognizing the "historicity" of all our reflections? How does/will philosophy change when it "returns to the lifeword" without its old dream of a totalizing epistemology? What are unexpected philosophical "honesty" and "wisdom" like? All of these suggestive phrasings are clearly intended to depict features of Putnam's own philosophical attitude, and to do so in a quite explicitly "unmetaphysical" way. For a while in the 1980s, they seemed to be associated with some cryptic remarks (e.g., in the "Introduction" to *Realism and Reason*) in which Putnam linked a newly heightened concern for "being more sensitive to my philosophical position" to a planned consideration of "questions thought to be more the province of 'continental philosophy.'" But he has never removed the scare quotes from this tradition, and to date his only sustained forays into its province (sc., on Foucault and Derrida) are really just vehicles for showing that Rorty is not the only figure we should associate with Relativism.

Not surprisingly, then, without a sustained effort to, as Taylor says, "articulate by creative redescription" how genuine post-positivists understand their philosophical task, Putnam's self-descriptions (together with his idea of what it means to give one) often just recapitulate the old vocabulary in a negative form, focus on what philosophers can't do and will never know, and depict this condition as if it were timeless and had no resolution. In one recent (1992) version, for example, he characterizes the whole history of Western philosophy as if variations on our boring modern alternatives had occurred throughout its course. "People have always been torn," he says,

> between knowledge and skepticism . . . between regarding their mental powers as continuous with nature and regarding them as above nature . . . between regarding the claims of morality as objective . . . and conventional; and since the rise of science . . . between expecting science to answer all questions, and a wide variety of alternative attitudes. . . . [Now] it may well be that these conflicts, and the questions to which they give rise, need to be "radically recast," not by [(a)] ignoring them and turning to one or another "scientific" project instead, but by [(b)] seeing what the temptation to give them "metaphysical" answers finally comes to, and by [(c)] learning to . . . *live with both the temptation to give them such answers and the refusal to give in to that temptation.*[50]

Regarding the first two philosophical possibilities we know that for Putnam, (a) produced the so-called scientific philosophy of Logical Positivism, which developed into totalizing "nonsense"; and (b) comes from historical redescriptions that

---

(310, my emphasis). I am arguing here, of course, that at least with regard to Comte, the second italicized phrase misrepresents him and the first one promises us less than does his historico-critical reflection.

50 "Replies [to Burton Dreben]," *Philosophical Topics* (1992) 20, 398, emphasis altered.

show us how positivism (and its historicist–relativist shadow) got that way. (a) and (b) together provide the story of disappearing ideologies. But (c), which Putnam clearly intends as a philosophical self-description, is actually less promising, more tradition-bound and anti-ideological, than the idea of post-ideological continuity-by-transformation he describes in "Beyond Historicism." "Learning to live with" the tension between metaphysical temptation and ever-vigilant refusal might be a slogan for a humbled moderate, if taken "soberly," or for one of Taylor's neo-Nietzscheans (or Rorty?), if taken playfully (or ironically); but it is not yet post-positivism as both Putnam and Taylor say they want to practice it.

The problem here is nicely framed by Putnam's confession, in "Realism with a Human Face," that

> there is a part of all of us . . . which wants to see the God's-Eye View restored in all its splendor. The *struggle within ourselves,* the struggle to give up or to retain the old notions of metaphysical reality, objectivity, and impersonality, is *far from over.*[51]

But who is "us," and what "part" of us wants this splendid Restoration? The answer, I think, is one that Putnam sometimes appears to understand – but only when he is not self-consciously considering the question of his own standpoint. The "us" is precisely people like Rorty and Taylor and Putnam – that is, contemporary post-positivists who are already sufficiently engaged in root questioning to see that disentangling analytic philosophy from its modern legacy is above all a reflective task *for themselves.*[52] To take this task seriously, however, is to understand that all of Putnam's talk about holistic desires and totalizing urges is nothing but an exercise in nostalgia. The "part" of him that wants a splendid Restoration is not some irresistible metaphysical drive; it is the vestige of an inherited Cartesian imperative that glorifies the kind of all-knowing standpoint that Putnam's own "situated" reasoning already tells him to just stop worrying about because it is a disastrous fiction.

What, then, is the "next step" for radical post-positivists? Putnam is right, I think, that it cannot be liberal irony. Whatever Rorty's real aim, the attitude he actually describes under this title does not leave the God's-Eye View as far behind as he apparently intends. Nor, I think, can the next step be something like Taylor's mildly Habermassian hope of finding a formal understanding of reason that is not a formal understanding of reason. Indeed, Taylor himself appears to admit this when he replies quite differently to Rorty, by talking in terms of "the truth of [life's] self-understanding" – where truth in this sense is a very un-Habermassian matter of "living our transitions."

How might we follow up on Taylor's and Putnam's notion of a post-positivist

---

51 "Realism with a Human Face," RHF, 18, my emphasis.
52 On this topic, I think, the second half of the present study could be rewritten out of the experiences of a quite differently understood "us" that nevertheless also inherits the "same" modern legacy. See, e.g., Linda Alcoff and Elizabeth Potter, eds., *Feminist Epistemologies* (New York: Routledge, 1993); and Linda J. Nicholson, ed. *Feminism/Postmodernism* (New York: Routledge, 1990).

practice that really does think its way beyond the old boring alternatives? Moderates are likely to object that the very question exaggerates what changes are needed – that in fact "our philosophical community" has already grown as post-ideological, in Putnam's sense, as it needs to be. They might agree that, for a while, everyone needed to hear some stirring criticism of the bad old days of Objective Analysis. But now that we have all been properly humbled, so goes the argument, we are free to reconceive our philosophizing on the far side of all the grand debates over Objectivity and Relativism and see it simply as

> a form of critical discussion and reasoned questioning that results in plausibilistic evaluation of aporias and controversial issues where knowledge is insufficient to definitively solve the problem ... [so that] philosophy could still be a sober, restrained, controllable discipline, provided there are methods of informal logic to pin down the fallacies, errors of reasoning, biases, and other shortcomings of argumentation in such discussions.[53]

"Moderate," I think, is a very generous word indeed for this sort of post-positivism. Remove the modifier "informal" from "logic," and what Walton's (quite representative) description *says* is virtually indistinguishable from the self-descriptions of analytic philosophers 30 years ago.

Is my reading of this description regressive and perhaps unfair to its author? I welcome the objection; for it helps focus attention on the fact that if there is going to be any real difference between Walton's (or Rorty's, or Taylor's, or Putnam's or anyone else's) allegedly post-positivist practice and classical analysis, it will be because descriptions like Walton's are no longer taken *in the same old spirit*. And my question is, how different from Epistemological business as usual can we expect philosophy to be, whatever its author's hopes, when it rests on an attitude of "sober" methodological pluralism? How much less demanding of Objectivity can we expect its "critical discussions and reasoned questionings" to be if today's properly humbled analysts are still assuming that *all* the "conflicts of opinion that ... bother the ordinary person in everyday activities" are just so many opportunities for gauging "rational justification"? How much difference will it really make if one *says* that justification is now a matter of only "loose" rather than "tight disciplinary control"?[54] In other words, what is to prevent those who claim they accept Walton's modest proposal, especially if they have once *already been* less

---

53 Douglas Walton, "After Analytic Philosophy, What's Next?: An Analytic Philosopher's Perspective," *Journal of Speculative Philosophy* 6 (1992), 128–29. Walton admits that this may put him closer to the Sophists than to Plato (126), but he also thinks he can avoid Rorty's relativism by broadening analysis into a "dialectical logic of reasoned commitment" (136) rather than letting it degenerate into "telling stories" (134). The question, however, is why Walton would imagine that his "informal" version of "extracting...presumptions and subjecting them to argumentation" is any more likely to have "the personal (maieutic) function" of actually *affecting commitments* than the old formal variety of analysis (139–40). Socrates makes *this* question – and not a clear-headedness about the "logic of argumentation" it may involve – his primary concern. In my view, the most important implication of root-questioning post-positivism is that "the time has come" to ask how we can make this our primary concern again, too.

54 "After Analytic Philosophy," 123, 129, 136. In Walton's view, the problem with "anti-representa-

humble and more "rigorous," from continuing to think of the old Epistemological cycle (now "plausibilistically" watered down) as still the only game in town?

As I have explained in earlier chapters, I understand my questions here to be Comtean. Their point becomes clear once one recognizes the necessity of engaging *as a philosopher and for oneself* in historico-critical reflection – and no longer confuses this process with either Cousin-like interior observation, or Millian introspection, or the merely reflexive meta-analysis of, say, "critical discussion and reasoned questioning." Historico-critical reflection is neither the activity of a soul, nor a cogito's pursuit of an Objective order of reasons, nor a subjective monitoring of one's thinkings and feelings, nor the operation of meta-methodological self-consciousness. It is, rather, a vehicle for self-understanding – a *process* that, at least among the more radical post-positivists, has the twofold task, first, of disclosing the inherited orientation that comes most naturally to us and then, of considering the discomforting price its maintenance exacts from us under current circumstances.

Among moderate post-positivists, one does not find much reflectiveness of this sort. Their critiques of Epistemological arrogance tend to be short-term, third-person, sociological reports of what others in the twentieth century (or perhaps themselves in a bygone phase) have claimed; and as a result, their "sober" pledges to be less Epistemological are unconvincing. The lesson of both Putnam's analyses of our tendency to "picture" everything Epistemologically and Taylor's account of the Cartesianism that still dominates our "intentional stance" is that philosophical humility cannot be bought so cheaply. The roots of Rational Reconstruction run much deeper and go back much further than the twentieth century, and efforts to "choose" a more pluralistic, or playful, or ironic path only reproduce in some temporarily unrecognized form the supposedly rejected traditional outlook.

Of course, no Epistemological thinker – not Descartes or Hume or Kant, and not Mill or Carnap or Reichenbach – could entertain so *unmodern* (n.b., not antimodern) a notion. But Comte did. Like our root-questioning post-positivists, Comte, as philosopher, was not interested primarily in the genealogy of a constraining inherited (in his case, Theologico-Metaphysical rather than Epistemological) ideal. He did not, in other words, employ his three-stage law only sociologically to recount the factual history of an old ideal's presence in the "positions" of others. Rather, he stressed above all the need to consider that ideal's way of *continuing to operate "in himself."*

In this study, I have "creatively redescribed" Comte's historico-critical reflection because I see too little consideration of this issue in post-positivists. Opposition to Epistemology is everywhere. The desire to think *beyond* rather than just

tionalists," "deconstructivists," and hermeneuts is that they "make good reading for non-specialists, but may lack enough substance or underlying hard edges...to yield some critical basis for judging one argument as better than another" – which is what, in Walton's opinion, it would take to give them "lasting interest" (134).

against the old ideal is frequently expressed. But where are the sustained inquiries concerning what philosophical attitude or outlook it takes to fulfill this desire? A few persons, like Putnam and Taylor, at least speak of a present "struggle within ourselves" between metaphysical temptation and vigilant refusal. Yet for the most part, their self-descriptions get no further than the two terms of the conflict. Typically, they tell us that they are still forever resisting a tendency to be "worried" about total integration, or "sympathetic" to metaphysical urges, or Habermassian about rationality, or otherwise unhappy that we are so "very far away from that ultimate horizon from which the relative worth of different cultures might be evident."[55] Yet resisting these old worries, like the worrying itself, is only another expression of that boring cycle that post-positivists like Putnam and Taylor expect to put behind them.

Where, in short, are the reflective efforts that would make post-positivism *itself* the topic, analogous to Comte's self-descriptive struggle to explain how "mature" positivists carry forward their Theologico-Metaphysical inheritance while "adolescents" merely oppose it? Perhaps Taylor's accounts of *"mundane"* cases of how we "live our transitions" may yet be made to stimulate *philosophical* accounts of the same sort of experience, but he himself has not told us how.[56] And perhaps Putnam's topic-specific exercises in avoiding the old Epistemic cycle actually do amount to a post-positivist practice that outruns his general self-descriptions. Yet such exercises by themselves, though attractive to many, will only be properly understood by someone who *already has* post-positivist "wisdom." The obvious "next step," then, is to ask how we might acquire it. Post-positivists no longer need to fight to get a hearing. Self-critical interest in tradition is gradually expanding back beyond the twentieth-century. And everywhere we hear reports of philosophical experiences in which new paths of thought and action are still frustrated by inherited Epistemological habits. Suppose that, in this "present situation," we were to "step back" and ask: What is "understood" in these discomforting experiences? What is it that we have not yet *become* post-positivist enough to express properly but already *are* post-positivist enough to resist picturing in the same old Positivist (more generally, Cartesian) or Historicist (more generally, Relativistic) ways? Articulating the "truth" of this understanding would be the goal of a contemporary version of Comte's historico-critical reflection.

---

55 *Multiculturalism*, 73.
56 Nor, I think, does he fully trace out the implications of these accounts in his own practice – as, e.g., when he assumes that self-understanding is involved in founding the human but not the natural sciences [see Joseph Rouse, *Knowledge and Power: Towards a Political Philosophy of Science* (Ithaca, NY: Cornell University Press, 1987), 169–98].

BIBLIOGRAPHY

Achinstein, Peter, and Stephen F. Barker, eds. *The Legacy of Logical Positivism*. Baltimore: Johns Hopkins Press, 1969.
Acton, H. B. "Comte's Positivism and the Science of Society," *Philosophy* 26 (1951), 291–310.
Alcoff, Linda, and Elizabeth Potter, eds. *Feminist Epistemologies*. New York: Routledge, 1993.
Aliotta, Antonio. *The Idealistic Reaction against Science*, trans. Agnes McCaskill. London: Macmillan, 1914.
Anschutz, R. P. *The Philosophy of John Stuart Mill*. Oxford: Clarendon Press, 1953.
Arbousse-Bastide, Paul. *Auguste Comte*. Paris: Presses Universitaires de France, 1968.
  "Auguste Comte et la folie," in Roger Bastide, ed. *Les science de la folie*. Paris: Mouton, 1972, 47–72.
  La doctrine de l'éducation universelle dans la philosophie d'Auguste Comte: Principe d'unité systématique et fondement de l'organisation spirituelle du monde, 2 vols. Paris: Presses Universitaires de France, 1957.
Aron, Raymond. "Auguste Comte," in Raymond Aron. *Main Currents in Sociological Thought*, Vol. 1, trans. Richard Howard and Helen Weaver. Garden City, NY: Doubleday, 1968, 73–143.
Ayer, A. J. *Language, Truth, and Logic*, 2nd ed. New York: Dover, 1952.
  Philosophy in the Twentieth Century. New York: Random House, 1982.
  "The Vienna Circle," in Eugene T. Gadol, ed. *Rationality and Science: A Memorial Volume for Moritz Schlick in Celebration of the Centennial of His Birth*. Vienna: Springer, 1982, 36–54.
Ayer, A. J., ed. *Logical Positivism*. New York: Free Press, 1959.
Bailey, Samuel. "M. Comte on Psychology," in Samuel Bailey. *Letters on the Philosophy of the*

Human Mind, 3rd series. London: Longman, Green, Longman, Roberts, and Green, 1863, 1–13.
Bain, Alexander. *The Emotions and the Will.* London: Parker, 1859.
John Stuart Mill: A Criticism, with Personal Recollections. London: Longmans, Green, 1882 [reprinted Bristol: Thoemmes, 1993].
The Senses and the Intellect. London: Parker, 1855.
Baynes, Kenneth, James Bohman, and Thomas McCarthy, eds. *After Philosophy: End or Transformation?* Cambridge, MA: MIT Press, 1987.
Beck, L. J. *The Metaphysics of Descartes: A Study of the "Meditations."* Oxford: Clarendon Press, 1965.
The Method of Descartes: A Study of the "Regulae." Oxford: Clarendon Press, 1952.
Becker, Ernest. *The Structure of Evil: An Essay on the Unification of the Science of Man.* New York: Free Press, 1968.
Bell, David [A.], and Wilhelm Vossenkuhl, eds. *Wissenschaft und Subjektivität: Der Wiener Kreis und die Philosophie des 20. Jahrhunderts / Science and Subjectivity: The Vienna Circle and 20th Century Philosophy.* Berlin: Akademie, 1992.
Berlin, Isaiah. "Historical Inevitability," in Isaiah Berlin. *Four Essays on Liberty.* Oxford: Oxford University Press, 1969, 41–117.
Bernstein, Richard J. "Rorty's Liberal Utopia," in Richard J. Bernstein. *The New Constellation: The Ethical-Political Horizons of Modernity/Postmodernity.* Cambridge, MA: MIT Press, 1992, 258–92.
Blainville, Henri Marie Ducrotay de. *De l'organisation des animaux; ou, principes d'anatomie comparée.* Paris: Levrault, 1822.
Boas, George. *French Philosophies of the Romantic Period.* Baltimore, MD: Johns Hopkins Press, 1925.
Bonald, Louis [Gabriel Ambroise, vicomte de]. *Recherches philosophiques, sur les premiers objets des connaissances morales*, 2 vols. Paris: Adrien Le Clere, 1818.
Borradori, Giovanna. *The American Philosopher: Conversations with Quine, Davidson, Putnam, Nozick, Danto, Rorty, Cavell, MacIntyre, and Kuhn*, trans. Rosanna Crocitto. Chicago: University of Chicago Press, 1994.
Bouillier, Francisque. *Histoire de la philosophie cartésienne*, 2 vols., 3rd ed. Paris: Ch. Delagrave and Son, 1868.
Brentano, Franz. "Auguste Comte," in Franz Brentano. *Die vier Phasen der Philosophie.* Hamburg: Felix Meiner, 1926, 99–133.
Psychology from an Empirical Standpoint, trans. Antos C. Rancurello et al. New York: Humanities Press, 1973.
Bridges, J[ohn] H[enry]. "The Correspondence of Mill with Comte," *Positivist Review* 7 (1899), 89–94.
The Unity of Comte's Life and Thought: A Reply to the Strictures on Comte's Later Writings Addressed to J. S. Mill. London: Trübner, 1866.
Britton, Karl. *John Stuart Mill*, 2nd ed. New York: Dover, 1969.
Broussais, François Joseph Victor. *De l'irritation et de la folie, ouvrage dans lequel les rapports du physique et du moral sont établis sur les bases de la médecine physiologique.* Paris: Delaunay, 1828.
Buis, Gérard. "Le projet de réorganisation sociale dans les oeuvres de jeunesse d'Auguste Comte," in A. Amiot et al. *Régénération et reconstruction sociale entre 1780–1848.* Paris: J. Vrin, 1978, 133–48.

Caird, Edward. *The Social Philosophy and Religion of Comte.* Glasgow: James Maclehose and Sons, 1885.
Caputo, John D. "The Thought of Being and the Conversation of Mankind: The Case of Heidegger and Rorty," *Review of Metaphysics* 36 (1983), 661–85.
Cardaillac, Jean-Jacques Séverin de. *Études élémentaires de philosophie,* 2 vols. Paris: Firmin Didot, 1830.
Carnap, Rudolf. *The Logical Structure of the World / Pseudoproblems in Philosophy,* trans. Rolf A. George. Berkeley: University of California Press, 1969.
 "Psychology in Physical Language, " in A. J. Ayer, ed. *Logical Positivism,* 165–98.
 "Testability and Meaning," *Philosophy of Science* 3 (1936), 419–71; 4 (1937), 1–40.
Cassam, Quassim, ed. *Self-Knowledge.* Oxford: Oxford University Press, 1994.
Castañeda, Hector-Neri. "Philosophy as a Science and as a Worldview," in Cohen and Dascal, *The Institution of Philosophy,* 35–60.
Cavell, Stanley. *The Claim of Reason: Wittgenstein, Skepticism, Morality, and Tragedy.* Oxford: Oxford University Press, 1979.
 Must We Mean What We Say? New York: Scribners, 1969.
Centre international d'Études pédagogiques (Sèvres). *Victor Cousin: Les idéologues et les écossais.* Paris: Presses de l'École Normale Supérieure, 1985.
Chalmers, Alan. *Science and Its Fabrication.* Minneapolis: University of Minnesota Press, 1990.
Charlton, D. G. *Positivist Thought in France during the Second Empire, 1852–1870.* Oxford: Oxford University Press, 1959.
Charlton, William. *The Analytic Ambition: An Introduction to Philosophy.* Oxford: Basil Blackwell, 1991.
Christie, Drew. "Contemporary 'Foundationalism' and the Death of Epistemology," *Metaphilosophy* 20 (1989), 114–26.
Cocchiarella, Nino B. *Logical Studies in Early Analytic Philosophy.* Columbus: Ohio State University Press, 1987.
Cohen, Avner, and Marcelo Dascal, eds. *The Institution of Philosophy: A Discipline in Crisis?* La Salle, IL: Open Court, 1989.
Comte, Auguste. *Cours de philosophie positive,* 6 vols. Paris: Bachelier, 1830–42.
 Discours sur l'ensemble du positivisme. Paris: L. Mathias, 1848. [Became Part I of *Système de politique positive,* Vol. 1, 1–399.]
 Discours sur l'esprit positif. Paris: Carilian-Goeury and Victor Dalmont, 1844. [Also published as "Discours préliminaire" to *Traité philosophique d'astronomie populaire, ou exposition systématique de toutes les notions de philosophie astronomique, soit scientifiques, soit logiques, qui doivent devenir universellement familières.* Paris: Carilian-Goeury and Victor Dalmont, 1844.]
 Lettres d'Auguste Comte à M. Valat, 1815–1844. Paris: Dunod, 1870.
 Philosophie prémier: Cours de philosophie positive, leçons 1 à 45, ed. Michel Serres, François Dagonet, and Allal Sinaceur. Paris: Hermann, 1975 [reprint of *Cours de philosophie positive,* Vols. 1–3].
 Physique sociale: Cours de philosophie positive, leçons 46–60, ed. Jean-Paul Enthoven. Paris: Hermann, 1975 [reprint of *Cours de philosophie positive,* Vols. 4–6].
 Système de politique positive, ou traité de sociologie, instituant la religion de l'humanité, 4 vols. Paris: L. Mathias, 1851–54.
 Synthèse subjective, ou système universel des conceptions propres à l'état normal de l'humanité, Vol. 1:

Système de logique positive, traité de philosophie mathématique. Paris: Victor Dalmont, 1856.
Constant [de Rebecque, Henri] Benjamin. *De la religion, considérée dans sa source, ses formes, et ses développements,* 5 vols. Brussels: P. J. De Mat, 1824–34.
Cousin, Victor. *Fragmens* [sic] *philosophiques.* Paris: A. Sautelet, 1826.
"Sur le vrai sens du 'cogito, ergo sum,'" *Archives philosophiques, politiques et littéraires* 3 (1818), 316–25 [reprinted in *Fragmens philosophiques,* 312–22].
Curley, E. M. "Analysis in the *Meditations*: The Quest for Clear and Distinct Ideas," in A. O. Rorty, ed. *Essays on Descartes' "Meditations,"* 153–76.
Dallmayr, Fred R. "Conversation, Discourse, and Politics," in Fred R. Dallmayr. *Polis and Praxis: Exercises in Contemporary Political Theory.* Cambridge, MA: MIT Press, 1984, 192–223.
Dasenbrock, Reed Way, ed. *Redrawing the Lines: Analytic Philosophy, Deconstruction, and Literary Theory.* Minneapolis: University of Minnesota Press, 1989.
de Jong, Willem Remmelt. *The Semantics of John Stuart Mill,* trans. Herbert Donald Merton. Dordrecht: D. Reidel, 1982.
Descartes, René. *Descartes' Conversation with Burman,* trans. John Cottingham. Oxford: Clarendon Press, 1976.
Oeuvres de Descartes (new revised edition, 11 vols.), ed. Charles Adam and Paul Tannery. Paris: J. Vrin 1964–76.
Philosophical Writings of Descartes, 3 vols., trans. John Cottingham et al. Cambridge: Cambridge University Press, 1984–91.
Dewey, John. *The Quest for Certainty: A Study of the Relation of Knowledge and Action, Later Works, 1925–1953,* Vol. 4: *1929.* Carbondale, IL: Southern Illinois University Press, 1984.
Dilthey, Wilhelm. *Selected Works, Vol. 1: Introduction to the Human Sciences,* trans. Rudolf A. Makkreel and Frithjof Rodi. Princeton, NJ: Princeton University Press, 1989.
Dilworth, Craig. "Empiricism vs. Realism: High Points in the Debate during the Past 150 Years," *Studies in History and Philosophy of Science* 21 (1990), 431–62.
Ducassé, Pierre. *Essai sur les origines intuitives du positivisme.* Paris: Félix Alcan, 1939.
La méthode positive et l'intuition comtienne: Bibliographie. Paris: Félix Alcan, 1940.
"Méthode positive et méthode cartésienne," *Revue de Synthèse* 14/1 (1937), 51–66.
Dummet, Michael. *Origins of Analytic Philosophy.* Cambridge, MA: Harvard University Press, 1994.
Ebbinghaus, Hermann. "Über erklärende und beschreibende Psychologie," *Zeitschrift für Psychologie und Physiologie* 9 (1895), 161–205.
Eisen, Sydney. "H. Spencer and the Spectre of Comte," *Journal of British Studies* 7/1 (1967), 48–67.
Feigl, Herbert. "The Origin and Spirit of Logical Positivism," in Achinstein and Barker. *The Legacy of Logical Positivism,* 3–24.
Ficquelmont, Gérard Marie de, et al. *Auguste Comte: Qui êtes-vous?* Lyon: La manufacture, 1988.
Flanagan, Owen [J., Jr.] *Consciousness Reconsidered.* Cambridge, MA: MIT Press, 1992.
The Science of the Mind, 2nd ed. Cambridge, MA: MIT Press, 1991.
Flood, Emmet T. "Descartes' Comedy of Error," *MLN* 102/4 (1987), 847–66.
Forster, Paul. "What Is at Stake between Putnam and Rorty?" *Philosophy and Phenomenological Research* 52 (1992), 585–603.

Gadamer, Hans-Georg. "The Problem of Historical Consciousness," *Graduate Faculty Philosophy Journal* 5 (1975), 1–52.
Gasché, Rodolphe. *The Tain of the Mirror: Derrida and the Philosophy of Reflection.* Cambridge, MA: Harvard University Press, 1986.
Gouhier, Henri. "Blainville et Comte," in Henri Gouhier. *La philosophie d'Auguste Comte*, 165–78.
  La jeunesse d'Auguste Comte et la formation du positivisme, 3 vols. (vol. 3, 2nd ed.). Paris: J. Vrin, 1933, 1936, 1941 (1970).
  La philosophie d'Auguste Comte: Esquisses. Paris: J. Vrin, 1987.
  La vie d'Auguste Comte, 2nd ed. Paris: J. Vrin, 1965.
Gould, F. J. *Auguste Comte.* London: Watts, 1920.
Grene, Marjorie. "Idea and Judgment in the Third Meditation: An Approach to the Reading of Cartesian Texts," in Marjorie Grene. *Descartes.* Minneapolis: University of Minnesota Press, 1985, 3–22.
Grunicke, Lucia. *Der Begriff der Tatsache in der positivistischen Philosophie des 19. Jahrhunderts.* Halle (Saale): Max Niemeyer, 1930.
Gueroult, Martial. *Descartes' Philosophy Interpreted According to the Order of Reasons*, 2 vols., trans. Roger Ariew. Minneapolis: University of Minnesota Press, 1984.
Gusdorf, Georges. *Introduction aux sciences humaines: Essai critique sur leurs origines et leur développement.* Paris: Les Belles Lettres, 1960.
Habermas, Jürgen. *Knowledge and Human Interests*, trans. Jeremy J. Shapiro. Boston: Beacon Press, 1971.
  "A Reply to My Critics," in John B. Thompson and David Held, eds. *Habermas: Critical Debates.* Cambridge, MA: MIT Press, 1982, 219–83.
Hacking, Ian. "Styles of Scientific Reasoning," in Rajchman and West, eds. *Post-Analytic Philosophy*, 145–65.
  Why Does Language Matter to Philosophy? Cambridge: Cambridge University Press, 1975.
Hall, David L. *Richard Rorty: Prophet and Poet of the New Pragmatism.* Albany: State University of New York Press, 1994.
Haller, Rudolf. *Neopositivismus: Eine historische Einführung in die Philosophie des Wiener Kreises.* Darmstadt: Wissenschaftliche Buchgesellschaft, 1993.
  "Was Wittgenstein a Positivist?" in Rudolf Haller. *Questions on Wittgenstein.* Lincoln: University of Nebraska Press, 1988, 27–43.
Hamilton, William. *Lectures on Metaphysics and Logic*, 4 vols., ed. H. L. Mansel and J. Veitch. Edinburgh: Blackwood, 1859–60.
  [Review of Victor Cousin. *Cours de philosophie.* Paris: Ladrange, 1828], *Edinburgh Review* 50 (1829), 194–221.
Hare, Peter H., ed. *Doing Philosophy Historically.* Buffalo, NY: Prometheus Books, 1988.
Harlan, Josh [interviewer]. "Hilary Putnam: On Mind, Meaning, and Reality," *Harvard Review of Philosophy* 2 (1992), 20–24.
Hatfield, Gary. "The Senses and the Fleshless Eye: The *Meditations* as Cognitive Exercises," in A. O. Rorty, ed. *Essays on Descartes' "Meditations,"* 45–79.
Hawkins, M. J. "Reason and Sense Perception in Comte's Theory of Mind," *History of European Ideas* 5 (1984), 149–63.
Hawkins, Richmond Laurin. *Auguste Comte and the United States (1816–1853).* Cambridge, MA: Harvard University Press, 1936.

Positivism in the United States (1853–1861). Cambridge, MA: Harvard University Press, 1938.

Hayek, F. A. ed. *John Stuart Mill and Harriet Taylor: Their Correspondence and Subsequent Marriage*. Chicago: University of Chicago Press, 1951.

Head, Brian W. "The Origin of 'Idéologue' and 'Idéologie,'" *Studies on Voltaire and the Eighteenth Century* 183 (1980), 257–64.

Politics and Philosophy in the Thought of Destutt de Tracy. New York: Garland Publishing, 1987.

Herschel, John F. W. *A Preliminary Discourse on the Study of Natural Philosophy*. London: Longman, Rees, Orme, Brown, and Green, 1830.

Heyd, Thomas. "Mill and Comte on Psychology," *Journal of the History of the Behavioral Sciences* 25 (1989), 125–38.

Hospers, John. *An Introduction to Philosophical Analysis*, 3 eds. Englewood Cliffs, NJ: Prentice-Hall, 1953, 1967, 1987.

Hylton, Peter. *Russell, Idealism, and the Emergence of Analytic Philosophy*. Oxford: Clarendon Press, 1990.

Jacobs, Struan. "John Stuart Mill on Induction and Hypotheses," *Journal of the History of Philosophy* 29 (1991), 69–83.

James, William. *The Principles of Psychology* [1890], 3 vols. Cambridge, MA: Harvard University Press, 1981.

Kant, Immanuel. *Idea of a Universal History from a Cosmopolitan Point of View*, trans. Lewis White Beck, in L. W. Beck, ed. *Kant on History*. Indianapolis, IN: Bobbs-Merrill, 1963, 11–26.

Kennedy, R[obert]. Emmet. *A Philosophe in the Age of Revolution: Destutt de Tracy and the Origins of "Ideology."* Philadelphia: American Philosophical Society, 1978.

Kolakowski, Leszek. *The Alienation of Reason: A History of Positivist Thought*, trans. Norbert Guterman. Garden City, NY: Doubleday, 1968.

Kosman, L. Aryeh. "The Naive Narrator: Meditation in Descartes' *Meditations*," in A. O. Rorty, ed. *Essays on Descartes' "Meditations,"* 21–43.

Kraft, Victor. *The Vienna Circle: The Origin of Neo-Positivism*, trans. Arthur Pap. New York: Philosophical Library, 1953.

Kremer-Marietti, Angèle. *Le Concept de science positive. Ses tenants et ses aboutissants dans les structures anthropologiques du positivisme*. Paris: Klincksieck, 1983.

Entre le signe et l'histoire: l'anthropologie positiviste d'Auguste Comte. Paris: Klincksieck, 1982.

Kubitz, Oskar Alfred. *The Development of John Stuart Mill's System of Logic*. Urbana: University of Illinois Press, 1932.

Laudan, Larry. "Peirce and the Trivialization of the Self-Corrective Thesis," in Larry Laudan. *Science and Hypothesis*, 226–51.

Science and Hypothesis: Historical Essays on Scientific Methodology. Dordrecht: D. Reidel, 1981.

"Towards a Reassessment of Comte's 'Méthode Positive,'" in Larry Laudan. *Science and Hypothesis*, 141–62.

"Why Was the Logic of Discovery Abandoned?" in Larry Laudan, *Science and Hypothesis*, 181–91.

Lavine, Thelma Z., and Vincent Tejera, eds. *History and Anti-History in Philosophy*. Dordrecht: Kluwer, 1989.

Lepenies, Wolf. *Between Literature and Science: The Rise of Sociology*, trans. R. J. Hollingdale. Cambridge: Cambridge University Press, 1988.
Lévy-Bruhl, Lucien. *History of Modern Philosophy in France*, trans. G. Coblence and W. H. Carruth. London: Kegan Paul, Trench, Trübner, 1899.
  The Philosophy of Auguste Comte, trans. Kathleen de Beaumont-Klein. London: Swan Sonnenschein; New York: G. P. Putnam's Sons, 1903.
Lévy-Bruhl, Lucien, ed. *Lettres inédites de John Stuart Mill à Auguste Comte avec réponses de Comte*. Paris: Félix Alcan, 1899. [*The Correspondence of John Stuart Mill and Auguste Comte*, trans. Oscar A. Haac. New Brunswick, NJ: Transaction Publishers, 1994.]
Lewes, G[eorge]. H[enry]. *The Biographical History of Philosophy: From Its Origins in Greece Down to the Present Day*, rev. ed. New York: D. Appleton, 1875.
  "Comte and Mill," *Fortnightly Review* 6 (1866), 385–406.
  Comte's Philosophy of the Sciences: Being an Exposition of the Principles of the "Cours de philosophie positive" of Auguste Comte. London: Henry G. Bohn, 1853.
Lewisohn, David. "Mill and Comte on the Methods of Social Science," *Journal of the History of Ideas* 33 (1972), 315–24.
Littré, Émile. "M. Auguste Comte et M. J. Stuart Mill," *Revue des Deux Mondes* 36 (1866), 829–66.
  De la philosophie positive. Paris: Ladrange, 1845 ["System of Positive Philosophy," trans. John Henry Young (from *Le National* article of November and December, 1844), *United States Magazine and Democratic Review* 20 (1844), 145–52, 254–63, 321–27, 440–48].
  Auguste Comte et la philosophie positive. Paris: L. Hachette, 1863.
Lloyd, Walter. "J. S. Mill's Letters to A. Comte," *Westminster Review* 153 (1900), 421–26.
Lyons, William. *The Disappearance of Introspection*. Cambridge, MA: MIT Press, 1986.
Macherey, Pierre. *Comte. La philosophie et les sciences*. Paris: Presses Universitaires de France, 1989.
MacIntyre, Alasdair. *After Virtue: A Study in Moral Theory*, 2nd ed. Notre Dame, IN: University of Notre Dame Press, 1984.
  "Epistemological Crises, Dramatic Narrative, and the Philosophy of Science," *Monist* 60 (1977), 453–72.
  "The Relation of Philosophy to Its Past," in R. Rorty et al., *Philosophy in History*, 31–48.
  Three Rival Versions of Moral Inquiry: Encyclopedia, Genealogy, and Tradition. Notre Dame, IN: University of Notre Dame Press, 1990.
Mandelbaum, Maurice. *History, Man, and Reason: A Study in Nineteenth-Century Thought*. Baltimore: Johns Hopkins Press, 1971.
Mandt, A. J. "The Inevitability of Pluralism: Philosophical Practice and Philosophical Excellence," in Cohen and Dascal, *The Institution of Philosophy*, 77–101.
Manicas, Peter T. *A History and Philosophy of the Social Sciences*. Oxford: Basil Blackwell, 1987.
Manuel, Frank. *The New World of Henri Saint-Simon*. Cambridge, MA: Harvard University Press, 1956.
  The Prophets of Paris: Turgot, Condorcet, Saint-Simon, Fourier, and Comte. Cambridge, MA: Harvard University Press, 1962.
Margolis, Joseph. *The Flux of History and the Flux of Science*. Berkeley: University of California Press, 1994.

Markie, Peter J. *Descartes' Gambit*. Ithaca, NY: Cornell University Press, 1986.
Maudsley, Henry. "Recent Metaphysics [Review of J. S. Mill's *An Examination of Sir William Hamilton's Philosophy*]," *Journal of Mental Science*, 11 (1866), 533–56.
Mazlish, Bruce. "Auguste Comte," in Paul Edwards, ed. *Encyclopedia of Philosophy*, 8 vols. New York: Macmillan, 1967, II, 173–77.
Merz, John Thomas. *A History of European Thought in the Nineteenth Century*, 4 vols. Edinburgh: William Blackwood and Sons, 1904–12 [reprinted Glouster, MA: Peter Smith, 1976].
Mill, James. *Analysis of the Phenomena of the Human Mind*, 2 vols., 2nd ed. London: Baldwin and Cradock, 1869.
Mill, John Stuart. *The Collected Works of John Stuart Mill*, 33 vols. Toronto: University of Toronto Press, 1963–91.
Mitscherling, Jeff. "Resuming the Dialogue," in Evan Simpson, ed. *Anti-Foundationalism and Practical Reasoning: Conversations between Hermeneutics and Analysis*. Edmonton, Alberta: Academic Printing and Publishing, 1987, 121–34.
Mueller, Iris W. *John Stuart Mill and French Thought*. Urbana: University of Illinois Press, 1956.
Münch, Dieter. "Brentano and Comte," *Grazer Philosophische Studien* 35 (1989), 33–54.
Myers, Gerald E. "Introspection and Self-Knowledge," *American Philosophical Quarterly* 23 (1986), 199–207.
Nagel, Thomas. *Mortal Questions*. Cambridge: Cambridge University Press, 1979.
The View from Nowhere. New York: Oxford University Press, 1986.
Nehamas, Alexander. *Nietzsche: Life as Literature*. Cambridge, MA: Harvard University Press, 1985.
Nersessian, Nancy, ed. *The Process of Science: Contemporary Philosophical Approaches to Understanding Scientific Practice*. Dordrecht: Martinus Nijhoff, 1987.
Neurath, Otto. "The Orchestration of the Sciences by the Encyclopedism of Logical Empiricism [and "Annotations"]," *Philosophy and Phenomenological Research* 6 (1945), 496–508, 526–28.
"Unified Science and Psychology," trans. Hans Kaal, in Brian McGuinness, ed. *Unified Science: The Vienna Circle Monograph Series*. Dordrecht: D. Reidel, 1987, 1–23.
Nicholson, Linda J., ed. *Feminism/Postmodernism*. New York: Routledge, 1990.
Nickles, Thomas. "Discovery," in R. C. Olby, G. N. Cantor, J. R. R. Christie, and M. J. S. Hodge, eds. *Companion to the History of Modern Science*. London: Routledge and Kegan Paul, 1990, 148–65.
"Discovery Logics," *Philosophica* 45 (1990), 7–32.
"Scientific Discovery and the Future of Philosophy of Science," in Thomas Nickles, ed. *Scientific Discovery, Logic, and Rationality*. Dordrecht: D. Reidel, 1980, 1–59.
Nielsen, Kai. *After the Demise of the Tradition: Rorty, Critical Theory, and the Fate of Philosophy*. Boulder, CO: Westview Press, 1991.
Nietzsche, Friedrich. "The Uses and Disadvantages of History for Life," in Friedrich Nietzsche. *Untimely Meditations*, trans. R. J. Hollingdale. Cambridge: Cambridge University Press, 1983.
Nowak, Leszek. "Some Remarks on the Place of Logical Empiricism in 20th Century Philosophy," in Klemens Szaniawski, ed. *The Vienna Circle and the Lvov–Warsaw School*, 375–89.

Packe, Michael St. John. *The Life of John Stuart Mill.* London: Secker and Warburg; New York: Macmillan, 1954.
Passmore, John A. "Descartes, the British Empiricists, and Formal Logic," *Philosophical Review* 62 (1953), 545–53.
Peirce, Charles Sanders. ["Critique of Positivism,"] in *Writings of Charles Sanders Peirce: A Chronological Edition,* Vol. 2. Bloomington: Indiana University Press, 1984.
Pickering, Mary. *Auguste Comte: An Intellectual Biography,* Vol. 1. Cambridge: Cambridge University Press, 1993.
"Auguste Comte and the Saint-Simonians," *French Historical Studies* 18 (1993), 211–37.
"New Evidence of the Link between Comte and German Philosophy," *Journal of the History of Ideas* 50 (1989), 443–63.
Popper, Karl. *The Poverty of Historicism.* Boston: Beacon, 1957.
Puntel, Lorenz B. "The History of Philosophy in Contemporary Philosophy: The View from Germany," *Topoi* 10 (1991), 147–53.
Putnam, Hilary. "After Empiricism," in *Realism with a Human Face,* 43–53.
"Beyond Historicism," in *Realism and Reason,* 287–303.
"Convention: A Theme in Philosophy," in *Realism and Reason,* 170–83.
"The Craving for Objectivity," in *Realism with a Human Face,* 120–31.
"Is the Causal Structure of the Physical Itself Something Physical? in *Realism with a Human Face,* 80–95.
The Many Faces of Realism. La Salle, IL: Open Court, 1987.
"Objectivity and the Science/Ethics Distinction," in *Realism with a Human Face,* 161–78.
Philosophical Papers [Mathematics, Matter, and Method; Mind, Language, and Reality; Realism and Reason], 3 vols. Cambridge: Cambridge University Press, 1975–83.
Pragmatism: An Open Question. Oxford: Basil Blackwell, 1995.
"The Question of Realism," in *Words and Life,* 295–312.
"Realism with a Human Face," in *Realism with a Human Face,* 3–29.
Realism with a Human Face, ed. James Conant. Cambridge, MA: Harvard University Press, 1990.
Reason, Truth, and History. Cambridge: Cambridge University Press, 1981.
Renewing Philosophy. Cambridge, MA: Harvard University Press, 1992.
"Replies [to 11 papers in a special issue on "The Philosophy of Hilary Putnam," ed. Christopher S. Hill]," *Philosophical Topics* 20/1 (1992), 347–408.
Representation and Reality. Cambridge, MA: MIT Press, 1988.
Words and Life, ed. James Conant. Cambridge, MA: Harvard University Press, 1994.
"Why Is a Philosopher?" in Cohen and Dascal. *The Institution of Philosophy,* 61–75 [reprinted in *Realism with a Human Face,* 105–19].
"Why Reason Can't Be Naturalized," in *Realism and Reason,* 229–47.
"Why There Isn't a Ready-Made World," in *Realism and Reason,* 205–28.
Rabb, J. Douglas. *John Locke on Reflection: A Phenomenology Lost.* Lanham, MD: University Press of America, 1985.
Rajchman, John, and Cornel West, eds. *Post-Analytic Philosophy.* New York: Columbia University Press, 1985.
Reichenbach, Hans. *Experience and Prediction: An Analysis of the Foundations and Structure of Knowledge.* Chicago: University of Chicago Press, 1938.

The Rise of Scientific Philosophy. Berkeley: University of California Press, 1951.
Rescher, Nicholas. "American Philosophy Today," *Review of Metaphysics* 46 (1993), 717–45.
Ribot, Théodule [Armand]. *La psychologie anglaise contemporaine.* Paris: Ladrange, 1870.
Robson, John M. *The Improvement of Mankind: The Social and Political Thought of John Stuart Mill.* London: Routledge and Kegan Paul; Toronto: University of Toronto Press, 1968.
Rorty, Amélie Oksenberg. "The Structure of Descartes' Meditations," in A. O. Rorty, ed. *Essays on Descartes' "Meditations,"* 1–20.
Rorty, Amélie Oksenberg, ed. *Essays on Descartes' "Meditations."* Berkeley: University of California Press, 1986.
Rorty, Richard. "Cavell on Skepticism," in *Consequences of Pragmatism,* 211–30.
   Consequences of Pragmatism: Essays, 1972–1980. Minneapolis: University of Minnesota Press, 1982.
   "Contemporary Philosophy of Mind," *Synthese* 53 (1982), 323–48.
   Contingency, Irony, and Solidarity. Cambridge: Cambridge University Press, 1989.
   "Epistemological Behaviorism and the De-Transcendentalization of Analytic Philosophy," *Neue Hefte für Philosophie* 14 (1978), 115–42.
   "Heidegger, Contingency, and Pragmatism," in *Philosophical Papers,* Vol. 2, 27–49.
   "The Historiography of Philosophy: Four Genres," in R. Rorty et al., eds. *Philosophy in History,* 49–75.
   "Overcoming the Tradition: Heidegger and Dewey," in *Consequences of Pragmatism,* 37–59.
   Philosophical Papers [Objectivity, Relativism, and Truth; Essays on Heidegger and Others], 2 vols. Cambridge: Cambridge University Press, 1990–91.
   Philosophy and the Mirror of Nature. Princeton, NJ: Princeton University Press, 1979.
   "Philosophy in America Today," in *Consequences of Pragmatism,* 211–30.
   "A Reply to Six Critics," *Analyse und Kritik* 6 (1984), 78–98.
Rorty, Richard, ed. *The Linguistic Turn: Recent Essays in Philosophical Method,* 2 eds. Chicago: University of Chicago Press, 1967, 1992.
Rorty, Richard, J. B. Schneewind, and Quentin Skinner, eds. *Philosophy in History: Essays on the Historiography of Philosophy.* Cambridge: Cambridge University Press, 1984.
Rosen, Michael. "Modernism and the Two Traditions in Philosophy," in David Bell and Wilhelm Vossenkuhl, eds. *Wissenschaft und Subjektivität,* 258–81.
Rouse, Joseph. *Knowledge and Power: Towards a Political Philosophy of Science.* Ithaca, NY: Cornell University Press, 1987.
   "Philosophy of Science and the Persistent Narratives of Modernity," *Studies in History and Philosophy of Science* 22 (1991), 141–62.
Ryan, Alan. *John Stuart Mill,* 2nd ed. Atlantic Highlands, NJ: Humanities Press, 1990.
Samuelson, Franz. "History, Origin Myth, and Ideology: Comte's 'Discovery' of Social Psychology," *Journal of the Theory of Social Behavior* 4 (1974), 217–231.
Santas, Gerasimos Xenophon. *Socrates: Philosophy in Plato's Early Dialogues.* London: Routledge and Kegan Paul, 1979.
Scarre, Geoffrey. *Logic and Reality in the Philosophy of John Stuart Mill.* Dordrecht: Kluwer, 1989.
Scharff, Robert C. "Habermas on Heidegger's *Being and Time,*" *International Philosophical Quarterly* 31 (1991), 189–201.

"Nietzsche and the 'Use' of History," *Man and World* 7 (1974), 67–77.
"Rorty and Analytic Heideggerian Epistemology – and Heidegger," *Man and World* 25 (1992), 483–504.
Schlick, Moritz. "The Turning Point in Philosophy," in A. J. Ayer, ed. *Logical Positivism*, 53–59 ["Die Wende der Philosophie," trans. David Rynin from *Erkenntnis* 1/*Annalen der Philosophie* 9 (1930), 4–11].
Schmaus, Warren. "A Reappraisal of Comte's Three-State Law," *History and Theory* 21 (1982), 248–66.
Schnädelbach, Herbert. *Reflexion und Diskurs: Fragen einer Logik der Philosophie*. Frankfurt: Suhrkamp, 1977.
Schouls, Peter A. *Descartes and the Enlightenment*. Kingston and Montreal: McGill-Queens University Press; Edinburgh: Edinburgh University Press, 1989.
Sellars, Roy Wood. "Positivism in Contemporary Philosophic Thought," *American Sociological Review* 4 (1939), 26–42.
Sesardić, Neven. "The Heritage of the Vienna Circle," *Grazer Philosophische Studien* 9 (1979), 121–29.
Simon, W. M. *European Positivism in the Nineteenth Century*. Ithaca, NY: Cornell University Press, 1963.
"The 'Two Cultures' in Nineteenth-Century France: Victor Cousin and Auguste Comte," *Journal of the History of Ideas* 26 (1965), 45–58.
Skarga, Barbara. "Le Coeur et la raison, ou Les Antinomies du système de Comte," *Les Études philosophiques* 3 (1974), 383–90.
Skorupski, John. *English-Language Philosophy, 1750 to 1945*. Oxford: Oxford University Press, 1993.
Smith, Barry. "Austrian Origins of Logical Positivism," in Barry Gower, ed. *Logical Positivism in Perspective: Essays on "Language, Truth, and Logic."* London: Croom Helm, 1987, 35–68 [reprinted in Klemens Szaniawski, ed. *The Vienna Circle and the Lvov–Warsaw School*, 19–53].
Sorrell, Tom. *Scientism: Philosophy and the Infatuation with Science*. London: Routledge, 1991.
Spencer, Herbert. *The Principles of Psychology*. London: Longman, Green, and Longmans, 1855.
Reasons for Dissenting from the Philosophy of M. Comte and Other Essays. Berkeley, CA: Glendessary Press, 1968.
Standley, Arline Reilein. *Auguste Comte*. Boston: Twayne, 1981.
Szaniawski, Klemens, ed. *The Vienna Circle and the Lvov–Warsaw School*. Dordrecht: Kluwer, 1989.
Tannery, Paul. "Auguste Comte et l'histoire des sciences," *Revue générale des sciences ces pures et appliqués* 16/9 (1905), 410–17.
Taylor, Charles. "The Dialogical Self," in David R. Hiley, James F. Bohman, and Richard Shusterman, eds. *The Interpretive Turn: Philosophy, Science, Culture*. Ithaca, NY: Cornell University Press, 1991, 304–14.
"Engaged Agency and Background in Heidegger," in Charles B. Guignon, ed. *The Cambridge Companion to Heidegger*. Cambridge: Cambridge University Press, 1993, 317–36.
Hegel. Cambridge: Cambridge University Press, 1975.
"Interpretation and the Sciences of Man," *Review of Metaphysics* 25 (1971), 3–51 [reprinted in *Philosophical Papers*, Vol. 2, 15–57].

Multiculturalism: Examining the Politics of Recognition, 2nd ed. Princeton, NJ: Princeton University Press, 1994.
"Overcoming Epistemology," in Kenneth Baynes et al. *After Philosophy,* 464–88. [Reprinted in *Philosophical Arguments* (Cambridge, MA: Harvard University Press, 1995), 1–19.]
Philosophical Papers, 2 vols. Cambridge: Cambridge University Press, 1985.
"Philosophy and Its History," in R. Rorty et al. *Philosophy in History,* 17–30.
"Rorty in the Epistemological Tradition," in Alan R. Malachowski, ed. *Reading Rorty: Critical Responses to "Philosophy and the Mirror of Nature" (and Beyond).* Oxford: Basil Blackwell, 1990, 257–75.
Sources of the Self: The Making of the Modern Identity. Cambridge, MA: Harvard University Press, 1989.
Tugendhat, Ernst. *Traditional and Analytical Philosophy: Lectures on the Philosophy of Language,* trans. P. A. Gorner. Cambridge: Cambridge University Press, 1982.
Tuschling, Burkhard, and Marie Rischmüller. *Kritik des Logischen Empirismus.* Berlin: Duncker and Humblot, 1983.
Urmson, J. O. "The History of Philosophical Analysis [and Discussion]," in R. Rorty, ed. *The Linguistic Turn,* 294–311.
Vernon, Richard. "Auguste Comte and 'Development': A Note," *History and Theory* 21 (1978), 323–26.
Voegelin, Eric. *From Enlightenment to Revolution,* ed. John H. Hallowell. Durham, NC: Duke University Press, 1975.
von Kempski, Jürgen. "Zum Selbstverständnis des Positivismus," in Jürgen Blühdorn and Joachim Ritter, eds. *Positivismus im 19. Jahrhundert: Beiträge zur seiner geschichtlichen und systematischen Bedeutung.* Frankfurt a.M. : Vittorio Klostermann, 1971, 15–26 ["Diskussion," 27–37].
von Wright, Georg Henrik. *The Logical Problem of Induction,* 2nd ed. Oxford: Basil Blackwell, 1957.
Walton, Douglas. "After Analytic Philosophy, What's Next?: An Analytic Philosopher's Perspective," *Journal of Speculative Philosophy* 6 (1992), 123–42.
Warnock, G. J. *English Philosophy since 1900.* London: Oxford University Press, 1958.
Watson, John. *Comte, Mill, and Spencer: An Outline of Philosophy.* Glasgow: James Maclehose and Sons, 1895.
Whewell, William. "Comte and Positivism," *Macmillan's Magazine* 13 (1866), 353–62.
History of the Inductive Sciences, from the Earliest to the Present Times, 3 vols. London: John W. Parker, 1837.
Novum Organon Renovatum: Being the Second Part of the Philosophy of the Inductive Sciences, 3rd ed. London: John W. Parker and Son, 1858.
Of Induction, with Especial Reference to Mr. J. Stuart Mill's System of Logic. London: John W. Parker, 1849.
On the Philosophy of Discovery. London: Parker and Son, 1860.
Whittaker, Thomas. *Comte and Mill.* London: A. Constable, 1908.
Wick, Warner A. "The 'Political' Philosophy of Logical Empiricism," *Philosophical Studies* 2/4 (1951), 49–57.
Williams, Bernard. *Descartes: The Project of Pure Inquiry.* Atlantic Highlands, NJ: Humanities Press, 1978.
Ethics and the Limits of Philosophy. Cambridge, MA: Harvard University Press, 1985.

Wilson, Fred. "Mill and Comte on the Method of Introspection," *Journal of the History of the Behavioral Sciences* 27 (1991), 107–29.
Psychological Analysis and the Philosophy of John Stuart Mill. Toronto: University of Toronto Press, 1990.
Wilson, Margaret D. "History of Philosophy in Philosophy Today; and the Case of the Sensible Qualities," *Philosophical Review* 101 (1992), 191–243.
Wright, T. R. *The Religion of Humanity: The Impact of Comtean Positivism on Victorian Britain*. Cambridge: Cambridge University Press, 1986.

INDEX

ahistorical imperative in philosophy. *See also* epistemology, Cartesian (modern)
   evidence of, in post-positivism, 155–60, 190–92, 198–99, 205–7
   in Descartes, 131–32, 141, 148, 157–59
   in Logical Empiricism, 135–37, 144–46
   as a problem for current analytic philosophy, 145–46, 174, 176–79, 184–85, 199–207
anachronistic history of philosophy. *See* presentism
analytic philosophy, 137, 137–38, 145n, 161–63, 179n, 184n, 190–92, 205–6. *See also* post-positivist analytic philosophy
   Putnam on, 179–84, 186–88, 190n, 198–99
   Rorty on, 139–40, 156–57, 162–63, 193n
Anschutz, R. P., 52n
Arbousse-Bastide, Paul, 85n
Aristotle, 83, 131
Ayer, A. J., 97n, 153n

Bacon, Francis, 23, 24, 88, 103, 106n
Bailey, Samuel, 37
Baillet, Adrien, 117
Bain, Alexander, 40, 43n, 59n
Beck, L. J., 112n
Beesly, Edward Spencer, 99n
Berlin, Isaiah, 109n
Blainville, Henri Marie Ducrotay de, 26n
Bonald, Louis de, 29n
Borradori, Giovanna, xiii, 200n
Brentano, Franz, 19, 35, 36n
Broussais, François, 22n, 29, 35, 44

Brown, Thomas, 40n
Buis, Gérard, 76n
Burman, Frans, 134n
Burnyeat, M. F., 148

Cardaillac, Jean-Jacques Séverin de, 37n
Carlyle, Thomas, 62n
Carnap, Rudolf, 4, 7, 60n, 69n, 107n, 108, 121, 137, 151, 158, 195, 201n, 206
Cartesianism, 20n, 126
Cavell, Stanley, 163n, 180n, 192n, 193n
Charlton, D. G., 97n
Charlton, William, 161–63, 164n, 184, 187
Comte, Auguste
   and behaviorism, 26
   causal law(s), his rejection of, 63–67, 99–100
   on Cousin, 22–24
   defense of positivism by, 6–9, 87–89, 121–23, 166n
   on Descartes, 20–22, 36–40, 88, 106n, 109–11, 118–20
   on the "dogmatical method," 100–102
   on fetishism (animism), 77–78
   and the French Enlightenment, 20n
   hierarchical classification of the sciences by, 25–26, 26n, 54–55, 61–62, 74n, 76n, 104–5
   on the "historical method," 31, 98–100
   historical vs. dogmatical accounts of the sciences in, 98–105, 120
   interior observation, his critique of, 11, 24–30, 33, 43–44. *See also* interior observation

Comte, Auguste (*cont.*)
  Mill's misreading of, 11–12, 36–38, 43
  on the law of three stages. *See* law of three stages (Comte's)
  mental breakdown, 38n
  on monotheism, 79–81
  mysticism and empiricism, his rejection of, 31–32, 61–62, 99–100
  on observation, the four modes of, 30–34, 82
  organon of proof, his opposition to, 61–63, 106n, 170–71
  on the "philosophical order" of time's three phases, 172–73, 175
  on philosophy's relation to science, 45–46, 67–71, 96–98, 106, 118–20
  on polytheism, 78–79
  positivism, dogmatical tendencies in his, 109–11, 119–20
  positivism of, vs. later, 75–76, 83–85, 89–91, 96–97, 108, 125–27, 190n
  pragmatism in, 105–8
  on social progress, 75n, 86–87, 89, 97n, 174n
  on women, 41–42, 97n
Condillac, Etienne Bonnot de, 22n, 32
Condorcet, Marie-Jean Antoine-Nicolas Caritat de, 75n
Constant, Benjamin, 77n
Continental philosophy, 139, 150n, 156, 158, 161–62, 176, 193n, 205–6n
Cousin, Victor, 11, 20, 23, 28, 117

Davidson, Donald, 149n
Derrida, Jacques, 139, 141n, 180n, 203
Descartes, René, 19, 20, 27, 206
  the ahistorical imperative in, 131–32, 148, 157–59
  epistemology after, 126–27, 130–31, 142n, 153
  formal reasoning, his objections to, 116–17
  as reflective ("meditative") thinker, 111–17, 133
Destutt de Tracy, Antoine-Louis Claude de, 22n
Dewey, John, 32n, 149n, 185n
Dilthey, Wilhelm, 35n
dogmatical method, Comte on the, 100–102
Dummet, Michael, 8n

Ebbinghaus, Hermann, 35n
Eclecticism, 22, 24
Eichthal, Gustave d', 54n
epistemology
  Cartesian (modern), 132–35, 177
    earlier (empiricist) vs. later (positivist) versions of, 133–34
    Putnam's critique of, 137–38, 182, 186–87
    Rorty's critique of, 138–42, 150–52, 157–59
    Taylor's critique of, 164–66
  feminist, 204n

fetishism (animism), 77–78, 80n
Feyerabend, Paul, 2, 4
Flanagan, Owen, 112–14, 124n
Forster, Paul, 195n
Foucault, Michel, 2, 4, 139, 168n, 182n, 203
foundationalism. *See* epistemology, Cartesian (modern)
Frede, Michael, 148
Frege, Gottlob, 137, 153, 179n

Gadamer, Hans-Georg, 150n
Galileo, 66, 88
Gall, Franz Joseph, 38n, 40, 44
Garfinkel, Alan, 182n
Gasché, Rodolphe, 132n
Gouhier, Henri, 35, 120n

Habermans, Jürgen, 108n, 121, 167–71, 173, 174, 183, 207
Hacking, Ian, 177n
Hall, David L., 140n, 141n
Harlan, Josh, 198n
Hartley, David, 40n, 51
Hawkins, M. J., 31n
Hegel, Georg Wilhelm Friedrich, 158, 163, 170, 179n, 183, 189, 196
Heidegger, Martin, 2, 124, 141n, 149n, 158, 170n, 173, 177n
Herschel, John, 50n, 58n
Heyd, Thomas, 25n, 26n, 29n
historical method
  Comte on the, 31, 98–100
  Mill on the, 99n
historicism (historical relativism), 2–4, 15–16, 148, 157, 178–79, 181, 183n, 186–87, 200–201
historico-critical self-understanding, Comtean, 8–10, 89–91, 119–20, 125–27, 170–73, 184–85, 187–88, 199–200, 205–7
Hospers, John, 145n, 161n, 187
Hume, David, 50n, 63–64n, 65n, 66, 111, 206
Husserl, Edmund, 192n
Huxley, Thomas, 120
Hylton, Peter, 141, 148, 163–164

ideology. *See* Putnam, Hilary
interior observation, 20, 35–36
  Comte's critique of, 11, 24–30, 33, 43–44
  Lewes' opinion of Comte on, 26–27n
  Mill's misreading of Comte on, 11–12, 36–38
  recent misreadings of Comte on, 25n, 26n, 28–29
introspection, 35–36, 111–12, 124. *See also* Mill,

John Stuart
   Flanagan on, 112–13
   irony. *See* Rorty, Richard

Jacobs, Struan, 50n
James, William, 36, 180n, 191n, 199, 202
Jouffroy, Theodore, 22, 35

Kant, Immanuel, 32, 33, 51, 54n, 77n, 83, 111, 142n, 150n, 153, 161, 162, 179n, 206
Kepler, Johannes, 49, 65, 66
Kolakowski, Leszek, 109n
Kuhn, Thomas, 4, 147, 149

Laudan, Larry, 59n, 66n, 71–72n, 99n, 101n
law of three stages (Comte's)
   basic character of, 55–57, 74–76, 104n, 206–7
   Constant's possible influence on, 77n
   as a developmental law, 76, 103–4
   Kant's influence on, 54n
   metaphysical stage, 81–87
   Mill on, 55–56, 81–82, 108
   as the principle of philosophical self-understanding, 8–10, 170–73, 184–85, 206–7
   positive (scientific) stage, 87–91
   theological stage, 77–81
Leibniz, Wilhelm Gottfried, 121, 133
Lepenies, Wolf, 42n
Lévy-Bruhl, Lucien, 70
Lewes, George
   Henry, 26–27n, 63n
Littré, Émile, 6, 97
Locke, John, 51, 111, 132, 133
Logical Atomism, 148n
Logical Empiricism, 2, 68, 69n, 71, 76n, 106–8, 135–37, 138, 139, 147, 153, 181, 185n, 206–7
Logical Positivism. *See* Logical Empiricism
Lyons, Williams, 13n, 19n, 124n

Macha, Ernst, 35n
Macherey, Pierre, 29n
MacIntyre, Alasdair, 3n, 125, 148, 200n
Mandelbaum, Maurice, 46n, 68
Manicas, Peter, 42n
Margolis, Joseph, 3n, 180n
Massin, Caroline, 120n
Maudsley, Henry, 38n
McDowell, John, 179n
McRae, R. F., 135n
Merleau-Ponty, Maurice, 173
Mill, James, 40, 44
Mill, John Stuart
   causal law(s), his defense of, 63–67, 99n
   Comte's philosophy of science, his critique of, 52–63, 120–22

on Comte's positivism, 6–7, 171–72
on induction, 63–64n
on introspection, 36–40
inverse deductive method, defined by, 31n
on an organon of proof, 58–62
philosophy of science of, 48–52, 67–71, 108, 121, 206
   temporal structure of the, 52–57, 172
on psychology, 43–44, 133–34
on Samuel Bailey, 37n
on social progress, 53n, 124–25, 126
on Whewell, 49–51, 59, 70–71
on women, 42–43
monotheism, 79–81
Moore, G. E., 161, 162
Mysticism, 31–32, 61–62, 99–100

Nagel, Thomas, 124n
Neurath, Otto, 60n, 69n
Newton, Isaac, 21, 39
Nichol, John, 57n
Neitzsche, Friedrich, 2, 4, 156, 168, 170n, 175, 199

observation. *See* Comte, Auguste
organon of proof
   Comte's opposition to, 61–63
   Mill on, 58–62
   vs. organon of discovery, 58–59

Passmore, John, 116n
Peirce, Charles Sanders, 102, 171n
philosophy's relation to history
   basic issues concerning, 160–63, 173–75, 200n, 204–7
   in Descartes, 132
   in Logical Empiricism, 144–46
   in moderate post-positivism, 147–49, 161–63, 184–85, 202, 204–6
   in Putnam, 200–204, 207
   in Rorty, 147n, 149–50, 153–54, 159–60
   in Taylor, 163–64, 167–71, 173–75, 203, 207
phrenology, 38n
Pickering, Mary, 38n, 66n, 83n, 86n, 120n
Plato, 131, 140, 149, 150
Polytheism, 78–79
Popper, Karl, 108n, 109n
positivism
   Comte's, vs. later, 75–76, 83–85, 89–91, 96–97, 108, 125–27, 190n
   dogmatical side of Comte's, 109–11, 119–20
   Mill on, 57–61
   systematic vs. critical, 45–46
post-positivist analytic philosophy
   ahistoricism in, 155–60

post-positivist analytic philosophy (*cont.*)
in moderate revisionists, 146–49, 157, 161–63, 177*n*
Putnam's, characterized, 140–41, 180–81, 186–88, 192*n*, 195–99, 200–204, 207
Rorty's, characterized, 157–60, 176–77, 193–97
Rorty's description of, 139–42, 150–55
Taylor's, characterized, 168–70, 200, 207
pragmatism. *See also* Rorty, Richard
in Comte, 105–8
Putnam's appeal to, 198–99
Reichenbach on, 106–8
Rorty's conception of, 152–53, 156, 158–59, 164*n*, 176–77, 195, 196–97
presentism
in the interpretation of Descartes, 111–12, 114–15
in Reichenbach's philosophy of science, 149
in Rorty's treatment of modern epistemology, 154
psychology
and contemporary philosophy of mind, 111–14
Lewes on, in Comte, 26–27*n*
Mill's conception of, 43–44, 133–34
Putnam, Hilary
"companions in guilt" argument of, 201
on Comte, 183–84, 189–90, 196, 202–3*n*
critique of objectivism in epistemology by, 125, 137–38, 182, 186–88, 191*n*, 197–98
on historicism and positivism as "boring" alternatives, 4–5, 179–84, 186–88, 200–201, 203–4
ideology, Putnam's conception of, 138, 179–82, 191, 202
philosophy's relation to history in, 200–204, 207
as a post-positivist, 140–41, 180–81, 186–88, 192*n*, 195–99, 200–204, 207
pragmatism, his appeal to, 192*n*
on Rorty, 4, 183–84*n*, 191*n*, 193–97, 201*n*, 202*n*
on "stepping back" to better diagnose the current philosophical situation, 4, 13, 166, 202–3
and Taylor, compared, 200–203
use of Continental sources by, 156–57, 192*n*, 203

Quine, W. V. O., 138, 149, 166, 188, 196

Rabb, J. Douglas, 112*n*
Rawls, John, 173*n*
Reichenbach, Hans, 3, 62, 69*n*, 85, 106–8, 121, 135–37, 139, 144, 149–51, 155, 158, 159, 185, 196, 199, 206
Reid, Thomas, 22*n*, 51
Rescher, Nicholas, 1*n*
Ribot, Théodule, 35
Rorty, Richard, 117*n*, 124*n*
critique of objectivism in epistemology by, 138–42, 150–52, 157–59
evidence of ahistoricism in, 154–60
hermeneutics, Rorty's conception of, 141*n*, 192
irony, in the post-positivism of, 141, 150, 155, 187, 201*n*, 204
philosophy's relation to history in, 147*n*, 149–50, 153–54, 159–60
as a post-positivist, 2, 124, 125, 148, 150–55, 157–60, 204
pragmatism, his conception of, 152–53, 156, 158–59, 164*n*, 176–77, 195, 196–97
Taylor on, 155*n*, 165–66
use of Continental sources by, 150*n*, 156–57, 176, 177*n*, 193*n*
Rosen, Michael, 179*n*
Royer-Collard, Pierre-Paul, 22
Russell, Bertrand, 137, 151, 161, 162, 179*n*
Ryan, Alan, 51*n*, 52*n*
Ryle, Gilbert, 137*n*

Santas, Gerasimos, 178*n*
Scarre, Geoffrey, 49*n*, 50*n*, 56*n*, 63–64*n*
Schlick, Moritz, 60*n*Schmaus, Warren, 97–98*n*
Schnädelbach, Herbert, 132*n*
Schneewind, J. B., 145*n*
Schouls, Peter, 20*n*
Sesardi'c, Neven, 137*n*
Sellars, Wilfred, 149
Sextus Empiricus, 50*n*
Simon, W. M., 35*n*
Skinner, Quentin, 145*n*
social progress
Comte on, 75*n*, 86–87, 89, 97*n*, 174*n*
Mill on, 53*n*, 124–25, 126
sociology ("social physics"), 26, 31, 103, 106
Socrates, 135, 136
epistemological silence of, 128–30, 177–78
Spencer, Herbert, 40, 105*n*
Spurzheim, Johann Gaspar, 38*n*

Taylor, Harriet, 42
Taylor, Charles
concept of "(historical) redescription" in, 164–67, 170–71
critique of objectivism in epistemology, by, 125, 164–66, 170*n*
on "neo-Neitzschean refusals" of modernity, 167–68, 173
philosophy's relation to history in, 163–64, 167–71, 173–75, 207

as a post-positivist, 2, 148, 168–70, 177, 200, 204, 207
and Putnam, compared, 200–203
qualified defense of Habermas by, 167–71, 173, 183
on the standpoint of "engaged agency," 169–70, 170n, 178
use of Continental sources by, 173

Vaihinger, Hans, 35n

Valat, Pierre, 22n, 29n, 70n
Vaux, Clotilde de, 36n, 42n, 120n

Walton, Douglas, 205–6
Warnock, G. J., 184n
Whewell, William, 49–50, 59, 70–71
Williams, Bernard, 112n, 180n, 189n
Wilson, Fred, 19n, 25n, 28n, 29n, 30n, 40n
Wittgenstein, Ludwig, 149, 180, 185n, 187, 202
Wundt, Wilhelm, 19, 20